Clerical Continenc
Century England and Byzantium

Why did the medieval West condemn clerical marriage as an abomination while the Byzantine Church affirmed its sanctifying nature? This book brings together ecclesiastical, legal, social, and cultural history in order to examine how Byzantine and Western medieval ecclesiastics made sense of their different rules of clerical continence. Western ecclesiastics condemned clerical marriage for three key reasons: married clerics could alienate ecclesiastical property for the sake of their families; they could secure positions in the Church for their sons, restricting ecclesiastical positions and lands to specific families; and they could pollute the sacred by officiating after having had sex with their wives. A comparative study shows that these offending risk factors were absent in Byzantium: clerics below the episcopate did not have enough access to ecclesiastical resources to put the Church at financial risk; clerical dynasties were understood within a wider frame of valued friendship networks; and sex within clerical marriage was never called impure, as there was no drive to use pollution discourses to separate clergy and laity. These facts are symptomatic of a much wider difference between West and East, impinging on ideas about social order, moral authority, and reform.

Maroula Perisanidi is a Leverhulme Early Career Fellow at the University of Leeds, UK, researching reform and clerical authority in the eleventh century. She has published articles on canon law and on the history of sexuality in several major journals.

Clerical Continence in Twelfth-Century England and Byzantium

Property, Family, and Purity

Maroula Perisanidi

First published 2019 by Routledge

2 Park Square, Milton Park, Abingdon, Oxfordshire OX14 4RN
52 Vanderbilt Avenue, New York, NY 10017

Routledge is an imprint of the Taylor & Francis Group, an informa business

First issued in paperback 2020

British Library Cataloguing-in-Publication Data
A catalogue record for this book is available from the British Library

Library of Congress Cataloging-in-Publication Data
A catalog record for this book has been requested

ISBN: 978-1-138-49513-5 (hbk)
ISBN: 978-0-367-58893-9 (pbk)

Typeset in Times New Roman
by Apex CoVantage, LLC

Printed in the United Kingdom
by Henry Ling Limited

To Oliver

Contents

Acknowledgements

This research was originally funded by a European Union Research Excellence Scholarship and the History Department at the University of Nottingham. More recently, an Early Career Fellowship sponsored by the Leverhulme Trust and the University of Leeds has helped me bring the work to completion. In between I had the benefit of a one-month research award at Dumbarton Oaks in summer 2016. I am grateful to all these institutions for their generosity.

I also need to thank a series of people who helped me in the writing of this book. First among these is Professor Julia Barrow, who not only supervised my PhD but also has been a continuous source of encouragement and is now my mentor in my current fellowship. My other supervisor, Dr Mary Cunningham, was invaluable in fostering my enthusiasm for the history of the Byzantine Church. She also introduced me to Dr Ruth Macrides, whose work on canon law was an inspiration for this book, and who has remained supportive since examining my thesis.

Professor Hugh Thomas reviewed the draft manuscript of the whole book and provided very useful comments which pushed me to think about the topic more broadly. A number of scholars have kindly given up their time to comment on individual chapters: Prof. Michael Angold, Prof. Anthony Kaldellis, Dr Charis Messis, Prof. Sara McDougall, Dr Claire Taylor, and in particular Prof. David D'Avray, whose advice on a draft of Chapter 7 led to a shift of emphasis and a major improvement.

Next, I would like to thank three friends. Gemma Evans and Siobhán Hearne shared my moments both of complaining and of excitement, proofread many drafts, and have learned more about the Middle Ages than they probably ever anticipated. The same goes for one of my most recent but most attentive readers, Steven Kaye: I was lucky to find a proofreader who could save me from errors not only in English but also in French, German, Turkish, Hungarian, Greek, and Latin.

Finally I have to turn to the person to whom I have dedicated this book, Oliver Thomas. Thank you for all your advice about my work, but also for giving meaning to my life beyond it.

Abbreviations

Councils & Synods	D. Whitelock, M. Brett and C.N.L. Brooke, *Councils & Synods: with other documents relating to the English Church, vol. I: 871–1066, vol. II: 1066–1204* (Oxford, 1981).
d.a.c.	*dictum ante canonem*; for Gratian's commentary preceding a canon
d.p.c.	*dictum post canonem*; for Gratian's commentary following a canon
DOP	*Dumbarton Oaks Papers*
EEA	*English Episcopal Acta*
Fasti	D.E. Greenway (I–VII and X), J.S. Barrow (VIII), M. Pearson (IX), C. Brooke, J. Denton, and D. Greenway (XI) (eds.), *Fasti Ecclesiae Anglicanae* (London, 1968–2011).
Gemma Ecclesiastica	J.J. Hagen (trans.), *The Jewel of the Church: a Translation of Gemma Ecclesiastica by Giraldus Cambrensis* (Leiden, 1979).
Gir. Camb. opera	J.S. Brewer, J.F. Dimock, and G.F. Warner (eds.), *Giraldi Cambrensis opera*, 8 vols., RS, 21 (London, 1861–91).
JGR	I. Zepos and P. Zepos, *Ius graecoromanum*, 6 vols. (Athens, 1931; repr. Aalen, 1962).
Leo VI	P. Noailles and A. Dain (eds.), *Les novelles de Léon VI le Sage* (Paris, 1944).
Les regestes de 715 à 1206	V. Grumel and J. Darrouzès (eds.), *Les regestes des actes du patriarcat de Constantinople, I: Les actes des patriarches, fasc.ii et iii: Les regestes de 715 à 1206* (Paris, 1989).
Magistri Honorii	R. Weigand, P. Landau, and W. Kozur (eds.), *Magistri Honorii Summa "De iure canonico tractaturus"*, 2 vols. (Vatican City, 2004, 2010).
Magister Rufinus	H. Singer (ed.), *Die Summa decretorum der Magister Rufinus* (Padeborn, 1902).

OCP	*Orientalia Christiana Periodica*
PG	J.-P. Migne (ed.), *Patrologiae cursus completus. Series graeco-latina*, 166 vols. (Paris, 1857–66).
PL	J.-P. Migne (ed.), *Patrologiae Latinae Cursus Completus*, 221 vols. (Paris, 1844–64).
REB	*Revue des études byzantines*
Summa des Stephanus	J.F. von Schulte (ed.), *Die Summa des Stephanus Tornacensis über das Decretum Gratiani* (Giessen, 1891).
Summa Lipsiensis	P. Landau et al. (eds.), *Summa 'omnis qui iuste iudicat' Sive Lipsiensis*, 3 vols. (Vatican City, 2007, 2012, 2014).
Summa Parisiensis	T. McLaughlin (ed.), *The "Summa Parisiensis" on the "Decretum Gratiani"* (Toronto, 1952).
Syntagma	*Σύνταγμα τῶν θείων καὶ ἱερῶν κανόνων*, 6 vols., G.A. Rhalles and M. Potles (eds.) (Athens, 1852–9).

1 Introduction

Defining the problem

The sexual life of clergymen and in particular their marital duties have long been an issue of controversy among historians and theologians.[1] Questions of scriptural interpretation, apostolic tradition, ritual purity, and pastoral responsibility have featured prominently in writings considering and contesting the acceptability of a sexually active priesthood. Today, the ban on clerical marriage is still debated within the ranks of the Catholic Church and celibacy remains a contentious issue across Christendom, dividing Catholics from Protestants and Orthodox Christians. Given the continuing importance of this topic for the different denominations, it is unsurprising that much of its historiography has focused on the origins of clerical celibacy.[2] The question is often posed in binary terms: was continence adopted by the apostles when they decided to follow Jesus, thus creating an apostolic tradition and model to be followed by future clerics, or was it rather a stricter policy advocated by fourth-century popes and accommodated to new historical circumstances? Answering one way or another means vindicating or undermining the current practice of thousands of clergymen around the world.

In addition to attempting to determine the origins of the rules of clerical continence, scholars have examined the motivations behind these rules in different periods when the Church has tried to enforce them. Two influential ideas concerning the earlier period revolve around Western requirements for ritual purity and asceticism. The purity argument was most notably put forward by Roger Gryson, who maintained that as clerics began to celebrate the Eucharist more frequently, and eventually daily, they came under more pressure to observe complete abstinence from sex as a preparation for their liturgical duties.[3] Others, such as Callam, have argued instead that the clergy were pressured to embrace continence because of the popularity of the ascetic ideal which exalted virginity over marriage.[4] A third possibility that combines the two has been suggested more recently by Hunter – namely, that both asceticism and ritual purity functioned as a means by which the male clergy in the later fourth-century West established their identity and defended their authority against the increased stature and visibility of ascetic women, and particularly consecrated virgins.[5]

For the later period of the eleventh century, interpretation of the motives behind the rules of clerical continence has been bound up with theories on the so-called

Gregorian reforms, which saw successive popes, with strong support from the higher echelons of much of the Western Church, fighting to end simony, lay investiture, and clerical marriage.[6] In this context, arguments about ritual purity remained prominent and were further linked to the threat of heresy, while a new array of issues came to the fore.[7] Notably, it has been recognised that the rules against clerical marriage acted as a means of limiting hereditary succession to ecclesiastical positions and the alienation of Church property for the sake of clerical wives and children.[8] More generally, historians have seen the reforms as an attack against ecclesiastical abuses and the worldliness of the Church, aiming to eradicate clerical participation in kin networks and to increase the divide between sacred and profane.[9] More recently, David D'Avray has argued that the eleventh-century reforms had their origins in the discrepancy that developed between law and practice. The former remained static and available, while the latter evolved between Late Antiquity and the High Middle Ages through social and economic developments, such as the creation of a system of rural parishes and the rise of the money economy. Once the gap had widened to such an extent that the discrepancy became obvious to any educated cleric, conflict and an attempt towards resolution were on the cards.[10]

My study focuses on the post-Gregorian era, and discusses many of these issues, while adopting a comparative perspective. At the heart of the comparison lies a basic difference: in the twelfth century, clerical marriage was decried as an abomination in the West, while in the East it maintained a sanctifying nature. What were the reasons that made such unions highly problematic in England but not in Byzantium? My central argument homes in on three of the aforementioned criticisms: concerns about property alienation; objections to hereditary succession; and fears of pollution of the sacred.

To do this, I use primarily legal sources, which provide the perspective of the higher echelons of the Church hierarchy. In the East, canon law was meant to apply to all Orthodox Christians across the Byzantine Empire, and, as a divinely inspired rule, was expected to have a lasting effect that extended across the centuries.[11] But as with any body of law, this was not the case in practice, and external circumstances, such as frontier warfare, could determine whether a rule was applied. So although I often refer to 'Byzantium' or the 'Byzantine Empire', my main focus is on Constantinople and the surrounding areas, where most of the authors examined in this study lived and wrote. Whenever possible and relevant, I also refer to other areas of the empire which exhibited distinctly different patterns. In the West, I concentrate primarily on England, making references to the Anglo-Norman realm as a whole when appropriate. Although again Rome's rules of clerical celibacy were meant to apply to all of the Western Church, the situation in practice differed substantially across Europe, depending on both geography and the initiatives of the local Churches. For example, England, lying at the periphery of Catholic Christendom, in some ways felt the impact of reform more slowly than more central areas, such as Milan.[12] But due to the initiatives of its Benedictine communities in the tenth century, who provided the clergy with a monastic model to follow, it experienced reform earlier than its neighbour Normandy.[13]

Comparisons of Byzantium with a different area, such as France or Italy, might have yielded different results, as no single region can be thought of as representative of Western Europe as a whole.[14] This, however, is exactly why such a detailed study is necessary. Focusing on only one area helps us avoid misleading generalisations. In this context, England is a good unit of comparison to choose because of its wealth of relevant sources. In the twelfth-century flourishing of canon law English ecclesiastics played an important role, with at least 359 decretals known to have been dispatched to them from the papal *curia*, many of them addressing the very issue of clerical marriage.[15] These canonical sources can be supplemented with episcopal charters and other administrative documents that reveal how the law worked on the ground locally. At the same time, the wider European perspective need not be entirely lost, as most of the canonists under consideration were educated in Paris or Bologna and their views were formed by Italian and French canonical works, some of which will form the wider background of this study.

Finally, the chronological end-point of my research has been influenced by important events in the two societies under consideration. In Byzantium it makes sense to stop before the Fourth Crusade (1204), which brought a radical disruption of normal ecclesiastical life, with Greek bishops being driven out of their churches and replaced by Latins.[16] In England I will continue up to Lateran IV (1215), which made important changes concerning the celebration of weddings. A chronological starting point is harder to define, since canonical legislation in the twelfth century forms an uninterrupted continuation of previous ecclesiastical councils. But the 1130s and 1140s could represent such a nominal beginning, as it was during this period that substantial canonical works started to be composed in both England and Byzantium. I will discuss these presently, after I lay out the advantages and challenges of taking a comparative approach.

Doing comparative history

Comparative history is still unusual and controversial; I will begin with two well-known areas of risk.[17] The availability of primary sources presents the first important challenge and to a large extent determines the focus and chronology of the study. Ideally both units of comparison should be rich in the same types of sources. For example, an absence of charters in one area would hardly recommend a comparative study of diplomatics. Sometimes, however, the same type of information can be provided by different genres and even the categorisation itself can be misleading. The present study is based primarily on legal sources. The fact that the twelfth century was a period of flourishing of canon law in both East and West was a driving force behind the chosen chronological framework. There are in this period canonical commentaries for both Byzantium and England, which systematically discuss ecclesiastical laws that were broadly shared and often treat the same topics. As such, they provide a good starting point for a comparative study. However, although in both cases we can talk of 'canonical commentaries', Byzantine authors tend to go into more detail than their Western counterparts. To remedy this imbalance, I have supplemented the Western canonical sources through the use of another closely related genre, the *summae confessorum*. This is not always possible and some difference in the level of information available for each area of comparison is to be expected, both due to the survival of sources and due to their editorial state. For example, much more information on the circumstances of the English clergy has become accessible in the last thirty years through publications such as the *English Episcopal Acta* and the *Fasti Ecclesiae Anglicanae 1066–1300*, which have no equivalent in Byzantium.[18] This inevitably makes it easier in the case of England to substantiate the evidence we get from the laws with examples of what happened in practice.

These difficulties with regard to the primary material are exacerbated by differences in focus of the secondary literature of each society under consideration. Often, a topic of great importance in one area has received little consideration in the literature of the other. This is certainly the case with many ecclesiastical topics and clerical marriage in particular. Byzantine historians have paid little attention to the history of the Church as an institution or to its relationship with society at large.[19] This signals an opportunity, where the comparative historian can test ideas and questions known to be illuminating for one society on another. However, this may lead to uncertain results if previous scholarship has not laid sufficient foundations for interpreting the evidence base appropriately.

So much for risks; comparisons also introduce great possibilities. They allow us to ask new questions. This has already been appreciated by historians of England, who have often studied English history in close comparison with that of the continent. The argument of Patrick Wormald regarding medieval England and France can easily be generalised:

> 'One of the advantages of considering early English history in the widest possible continental context is that one then sees not only what is (often surprisingly) similar, but also what is significantly different'. A continental perspective brings out precisely those English phenomena which cannot be passed off as manifestations of the *Zeitgeist* (always a temptation in this sort of exercise), and which cry the louder for explanation.[20]

The same can profitably be said in our case. The juxtaposition of Byzantine and English contexts through a comparison of their legal treatment of clerical continence allows for a clearer picture of these two societies' views on purity, sexuality, marriage, and ecclesiastical property. The rarity of contacts between them makes the difference even starker. England and Byzantium were selected not because of any mutual interactions but because they were similar enough for their particularities to warrant explanation. It is not a question of who influenced whom, but rather the comparison is here to help us view each of the two societies with new eyes, momentarily taking it out of its context, only to put it back with a clearer idea of its position.

There have of course been many studies of the Eastern and Western Churches. But most of these are not strictly speaking comparative, as they bring together the two Churches only to account for their eventual division, focusing not so much on the comparison *per se* but on the events that led to the 1054 schism.[21] Andrew Louth, in his *Greek East and Latin West*, has attempted a comparison for its own sake, but considers East and West to have become such distinct entities that he prefers to treat them in parallel, noting only the points at which their destinies coincided or conflicted.[22] I diverge from this approach by interrogating Byzantine and English sources on the same topics, asking the same questions, noting and explaining particular absences. In some respects, my study is more akin to the work of Clarence Gallagher, whose monograph *Church Law and Church Order in Rome and Byzantium* deals with ecclesiastical issues in a comparative perspective, analysing the similarities and differences in the views of important Eastern and Western canon lawyers.[23] Such parallel discussions of Eastern and Western topics can help to integrate Byzantine history into the wider field of medieval studies and will hopefully be of interest to scholars of both Eastern and Western medieval cultures.

Legal sources

In this study, I focus on legal sources and specifically on canon law. Foremost in my discussions is evidence from councils and synods, as well as commentaries from canonists who tried to harmonise and make sense of the often contradictory laws. There were seven ecumenical councils whose decisions were meant to be equally applicable in East and West: Nicaea I in 325; Constantinople I in 381; Ephesus in 431; Chalcedon in 451; Constantinople II in 553; Constantinople III in 680/1; and Nicaea II in 787. Two more synods were considered to be ecumenical in nature: the Council in Trullo of 691/2 and Constantinople V of 879–880.[24] These, along with the local synods of Carthage (255), Ancyra (314), Neocaesarea (314/19), Gangra (c. 340? 355?), Antioch (c. 328), Laodicea (before 380), Serdica (342), and Carthage (419), formed the basis of the twelfth-century canonical commentaries in Byzantium. The Council in Trullo, which to a great extent fixed the legislation on clerical marriage for the Byzantine Church, will feature particularly frequently.[25] In addition to ecclesiastical law, civil law will be considered when it is invoked in contrast to or in support of canonical sources. Of particular importance is the legal work of Emperors Justinian and Leo VI. Justinian's compilation, later known as the *Corpus iuris civilis*, consists of the Digest (533), the Institutes (533), the Codex (revised 534), and the Novels, which cover his decrees from 535 to 565.[26] Leo VI's legal collection contains 113 novels, about one third of which deal with ecclesiastical issues (888–889).[27] In addition to promulgating new laws, Leo revised the codified work of Emperor Basil I, republishing it in sixty books, known as the *Basilika*.[28] These ecclesiastical and secular sources of law will be explored primarily through the eyes of three twelfth-century canonists: Alexios Aristenos (d. after 1166), Ioannes Zonaras (d. after 1150), and Theodoros Balsamon (c. 1140–after 1195).[29]

Similarly for the West, I will focus on legal sources and in particular conciliar canons, decretals, canonical commentaries, and penitentials.[30] In terms of conciliar sources, I will concentrate on twelfth-century Anglo-Norman councils, keeping also in mind those Roman councils which included representatives of the English Church. In terms of Western canonical commentaries, I will make use of Gratian's *Decretum* and two of its Anglo-Norman glosses.[31] The nature of these glosses varies, ranging from simple explanations of words to much fuller discursive passages providing contemporary examples. This means that while for some passages we get much useful and original information, for others there is little more than a comment on vocabulary or grammar. This does not mean that the decretists did not consider important the point made in the *Decretum*; they might simply have thought that it was sufficiently clear. The interpretations we find in the Byzantine canonical commentaries are generally fuller. To counterbalance this, I will use a series of twelfth-century penitentials, whose authors were not decretists themselves but were aware of the *Decretum* and the new developments in law. These penitentials were meant to be used by parish clergy, so they can also help us examine the extent to which canon law had an impact on the English clergy on a more local level. More specifically, I will consider the penitentials of Bishop Bartholomew of Exeter (1161–1184), Robert of Flamborough (d. 1224), and Thomas of Chobham (d. c. 1236).[32]

Although the legal material for both East and West is plentiful, it is not without its challenges. For one, in England the canonical commentaries and much of the legislation in the form of councils or decretals come from the eleventh and twelfth centuries. In Byzantium, on the other hand, while the canonical commentaries were written in the twelfth century, almost all of the canons they commented upon were promulgated much earlier. While the status of clerical celibacy was still in flux in the West, it had long been crystallised in the East. This needs to be kept in mind in our interpretation of the canons. Furthermore, we must be cautious with any assumptions about the wider acceptance and enforcement of any given law. For one, in the case of Byzantium a tradition of applying the rules with *oikonomia* meant that in certain cases the letter of the law could be relaxed without setting a precedent for the future.[33] Although this was to some extent similar to the Western concept of dispensation, as we will see, these rulings were harder to obtain and often up to the discretion of the papal *curia*. For another, although legislation might reflect long-standing oral tradition and as such it can provide us with an accurate image of society, it can also be more aspirational, representing at the time of promulgation nothing more than discussions between lawyers. For example, Angold has noted that in Byzantium a gap existed between legal and literary representations in the case of secular marriage: Balsamon's legislation concerning the Church's involvement in the marital ceremony was far removed from the marital ethos witnessed in contemporary texts, such as the *Digenes Akrites*, with legal texts also taking a much harder line regarding betrothals and the prohibited degrees of affinity.[34] This argument, however, can also go the other way. These ideas, written down in the twelfth century, acquired a life of their own which extended well beyond that of their authors. Even when the laws did not reflect the exact situation on the ground at the time of writing, the ideas behind them could be enforced at a later date. Indeed, the works of canonists such as Balsamon or

Gratian had a long-lasting effect on the canonical tradition of their Churches. This adds an extra layer of importance to their study.

In the pages that follow, I will provide some prosopographical details for the main authors discussed in this book, focusing on their work as a whole and the motivations, dates, and context for their writing.

Byzantium

Alexios Aristenos (d. after 1166)

Aristenos wrote the earliest of the three twelfth-century canonical commentaries, initiating its composition at the behest of Emperor John Komnenos (r. 1118–1143) around 1130.[35] He pursued from the beginning an ecclesiastical career, first acquiring the rank of deacon and then ascending to a number of offices in the Hagia Sophia, including those of *nomophylax* and *protekdikos*, which would have enhanced his legal knowledge; those of *orphanotrophos* and *megas oikonomos*, which would have involved him with ecclesiastical finances; and the position of *hieromnemon*, which would have put him in charge of clerical ordinations.[36] He also received the office of *dikaiodotes*, another legal position, but he was forced to abandon it after the 1157 decree of Patriarch Luke Chrysoberges, which prohibited clerics from engaging in secular professions.[37] His comments are much shorter than those of Zonaras and Balsamon but do occasionally offer a different perspective.

Ioannes Zonaras (d. after 1150)

Zonaras began his career in a secular rather than an ecclesiastical setting.[38] He was president of the court of the hippodrome (*megas droungarios tes viglas*) and head of the imperial secretariat (*protasekretis*).[39] Only later did he become a monk and write his canonical commentaries as well as his more famous *Epitome of Histories*, a political history from the creation of the world to 1118.[40] Despite Zonaras' monastic status, in his writings he was often negative towards other monks whom he accused of ignorance and whom he considered unqualified to receive confessions.[41] It was the secular clergy that he considered the 'intercessors between God and humankind'.[42] We are not certain what Zonaras' motives were for writing his canonical commentaries. In his introduction to the canons of the Apostles, he stated that he did not undertake this work on his own initiative, but out of obedience towards those who requested it.[43] This could be merely a *topos* of modesty and in any case tells us little about the identity of the supposed instigators. There is also considerable debate about the date of composition of Zonaras' canonical commentaries. The main piece of evidence for his chronology is his comment on canon 7 of Neocaesarea, in which he claimed to have seen a patriarch and several metropolitans present at the second wedding of an emperor.[44] This is usually taken to refer to the second wedding of Emperor Manuel I Komnenos (r. 1143–1180).[45] If we accept this, the most likely reconstruction of Zonaras' life posits that he was born between c. 1080 and 1098; retired to a monastery in the 1120s or 1130s; and completed the *Epitome* between 1143 and c. 1150, and his canonical commentary in or after 1161.[46] In addition to these two major works, Zonaras wrote a variety of theological treatises on topics including the potential impurity of nocturnal emissions.

Theodoros Balsamon (c. 1140–after 1195)

Balsamon entered the church of the Hagia Sophia as a deacon when he was young. During his service there, he occupied several offices, including the positions of *nomophylax* and *chartophylax*.[47] As *chartophylax* he had juridical and administrative control over marriages – for example, he was in charge of gathering the documents necessary for the celebration of weddings.[48] He was also responsible for examining candidates to the priesthood. These tasks must have necessitated a high level of knowledge of matrimonial law in the case of both laymen and clerics. Balsamon has left us a variety of legal sources: canonical commentaries on the *Nomokanon of Fourteen Titles*, the canons of the Church Fathers, and the Church councils, as well as legal treatises and a set of canonical responses dealing *inter alia* with issues of purity and ecclesiastical property.

Balsamon's commentaries incorporated many details of twelfth-century life and as such reflect the preoccupations of his contemporaries.[49] At the same time, the personal views he expressed represent to a large extent the official views of the Orthodox Church. Indeed, his commentary on the *Nomokanon* enjoyed both imperial and ecclesiastical sanction, as it was commissioned by Emperor Manuel I Komnenos and Patriarch Michael III Anchialos (1170–1178).[50] Balsamon's initial task in writing this commentary was to ascertain which parts of the *Nomokanon* still remained in force and which parts had become obsolete.[51] He is thought to have written the entire commentary on the *Nomokanon* in 1177, before he continued with his comments on the rest of the canons. These would not be completed before the end of his life. They are believed to have attained a first stage of composition before the death of Emperor Manuel in 1180, but Balsamon continued making additions in the margins. The latest addition that can be dated was that of a novel by Emperor Isaak II, issued after April 1193.[52] Around 1195, and after he had become patriarch of Antioch, Balsamon also wrote a set of answers to a series of questions posed by his contemporary, Patriarch Mark of Alexandria (1180–1209).[53] These fit within the well-known genre of *questions and answers*, questions usually asked by a priest or bishop to the patriarch or the *chartophylax* of the Hagia Sophia.[54]

Despite his elevation to the patriarchate, Balsamon could not be installed in his see because of its occupation by the Latins. This could help explain the hostile stance which he adopted towards the Catholic Church, seen especially in his views on papal primacy.[55] He remained in Constantinople, residing at the monastery of the Virgin *Hodegetria*, which was the official property of the patriarch of Antioch in Constantinople.[56] But he probably spent the last years of his life in another patriarchal property, the monastery of Zipoi, in an unknown location near

Constantinople.[57] Balsamon is thought to have died after 1195.[58] His works had a great influence on later Orthodox canon lawyers, such as Matthew Blastares, the most prominent canonist of the fourteenth century.[59]

The canonical commentaries by Aristenos, Zonaras, and Balsamon are most widely read in the first four volumes of the Rhalles and Potles edition. This edition was based on an eighteenth-century copy of a manuscript produced in Trebizond in 1311.[60] Rhalles and Potles collated against this text all editions appearing up to 1852, including the one in the *Patrologia Graeca*.[61] Tiftixoglou, who has examined the manuscript tradition of Balsamon's commentaries, has found substantial differences between the various manuscripts.[62] Certain passages are omitted, displaced, marginal, or integral in different manuscripts. Tiftixoglou concluded that this was due to Balsamon's writing process: after he finished the first version of his commentaries, he added marginal notes to his own text in preparation for a second version. Copies were made of his text at each stage, and some later copyists integrated the marginalia, though they rarely added new ones. These complications mean that the Rhalles and Potles edition does not present the original redaction of Balsamon, but one containing secondary additions by the canonist, though not necessarily at the point he intended. Balsamon's and Zonaras' commentaries are sometimes found together in manuscripts, as we see them in the Rhalles and Potles edition.[63] However, Aristenos' comments never accompany them, but have their own significant manuscript tradition.[64]

England

Gratian 1 & 2

Gratian's *Decretum* was the single most important canonistic work of the Middle Ages, despite never being officially promulgated by Church authorities. It became the standard textbook for teachers of canon law, and officials in the papal chancery not only knew its contents but also assumed knowledge of it by people with whom they corresponded.[65] By producing a harmonising interpretation of contrasts between the canons, it set the basis for the development of Western canon law into 'a juridical self-supporting science', leading to the establishment of canonical schools and to the subsequent increase in the use of legislation as a reforming tool in the hands of the papacy.[66] It remained the foundation of canonical jurisprudence until the twentieth century.[67] From the twelfth century, there survive about 160 manuscripts of Gratian's *Decretum*.[68] Although it was composed in Bologna, extensive knowledge of Gratian can be seen in England through the flourishing of the Anglo-Norman school of canon law after 1180.[69] The oldest surviving English manuscript of Gratian is believed to be the unglossed codex MS 138 (B. 1. 4.) in Lincoln (1190–1199).[70]

Gratian was the most important canon lawyer of this period, yet practically nothing is known about his life. Until Noonan's 1979 article, he was thought by most scholars to have been a Camaldolese monk and a canon law teacher at the monastery of Saints Felix and Nabor in Bologna.[71] Some authors still believe him to have been a monk; others claim he was a bishop; others again believe him to have been a lawyer and not an academic teacher of law.[72] Gratian used a variety of ecclesiastical sources in the making of his *Decretum*. These included conciliar canons, papal decretals, and patristic writings, spanning the period from the early Church to the 1139 council of Pope Innocent II (1130–1143).[73] He tried to harmonise the canons, first presenting opposing points of view and then offering his own opinion in the so-called *dicta Gratiani*.

Winroth has shown that there are two recensions of the *Decretum*. In fact, the text usually referred to as Gratian's *Decretum* (Gratian 2, about 4,000 canons) was an expansion of an original text (Gratian 1, about 2,000 canons), which was more succinct and to the point.[74] Winroth further suggested that only the first of the two recensions was written by Gratian himself.[75] Both recensions were completed within the short timespan between 1139 and, at the very latest, 1158.[76] In this book it will be explicitly stated when a quotation exists in Gratian 2 but not Gratian 1. The distinction between the two 'Gratians' has also led to further speculation about the career of these two separate canonists. Gratian 1 seems to have been a theologian. The vast majority of biblical citations came from his recension, which was at the same time lacking in references to Roman law.[77] Gratian 2, on the other hand, seems to have been more learned in Roman law: it was he who introduced into the *Decretum* texts from the Justinianic corpus.[78] Gratian 2 is more likely to have been educated as a jurist.

Two Anglo-Norman decretists

From the commentaries on Gratian's *Decretum*, we will focus in particular on the Anglo-Norman school.[79] One of the most influential members of this school was the author of the *Summa 'Omnis qui iuste iudicat'* or *Summa Lipsiensis*. His work on the *Decretum* was composed around 1186 and it has been called the most elaborate commentary on Gratian before Huguccio.[80] Since the nineteenth century, when the manuscript was discovered by Friedrich von Schulte, the author of this *summa* has been unknown, but was thought to have been familiar with Paris. It was only recently that Peter Landau proposed a possible identification of the author with Rodoicus Modicipassus.[81] Landau believes that Rodoicus began his career in Lincoln, where he wrote the *Ordo 'Olim edebatur'* and where he might also have acquired his theological education. In that case he may have started his *summa* in Lincoln and completed it in Paris. In addition to England and France, Rodoicus might also have spent some time in Bologna as a student and/or as a teacher, but we know that he finished his life as precentor in the cathedral of Sens.[82]

Another member of the Anglo-Norman school about whom more is known is Master Honorius (d. c. 1213).[83] He was the author of two important legal works: the *Summa quaestionum decretalium* (1185x1188) and the *Summa de iure canonico tractaturus* (1188x1190).[84] The latter, which was a commentary on Gratian's *Decretum*, survives in only one manuscript, but the number of copies of Honorius' *Summa quaestionum* exceeds by far the number of extant manuscripts of any other work of the Anglo-Norman school. This highlights the reputation of

Honorius as a teacher. It is also the only work of the Anglo-Norman group whose author can be identified with certainty. Honorius' name can be found in two out of the seven extant manuscripts.[85]

We know little of Honorius' early life. An Honorius was recommended by Pope Lucius III in 1184 or 1185 to the abbot and monks of St Augustine's for the church of Willesborough in Kent, on account of his learning and his poor means. The mandate contains a clause of dispensation from which it appears that the beneficiary was a priest's son. Although the identification with our Master Honorius is proposed by Kuttner and Rathbone, the authors also question it. No irregularity regarding Honorius' birth was ever brought forward in the bitter three-sided dispute between Archbishop Geoffrey, the kings Richard I and John, and the dean and chapter of York regarding his appointment as archdeacon of Richmond. Such an allegation could have provided a weapon for his adversaries, who had not hesitated to accuse him of 'murder, sacrilege, arson, and other grave and enormous sins'.[86]

Honorius' scholarly career can be divided into two phases, one from 1185 to c. 1191 when he studied at the Parisian school of canon law, and another from 1191 or 1192 to 1195 when he taught and practised law in Oxford in the company of other English canonists, such as Simon of Sywell and John of Tynemouth. Following his return to England, Honorius developed strong links with both York and Canterbury. Already c. 1191 he had become a clerk of Archbishop Geoffrey Plantagenet of York and from 1195 he went on to become his chief judicial officer (*officialis*). He acted also for some time as the latter's vicar general (*procurator spiritualium*) and as administrator of his see during Geoffrey's absences between 1195 and 1198.[87] During his stay in Geoffrey's household, Honorius was one of the fifty *magistri* who made up almost one third of the total members of the archi-episcopal *familia*.[88] In the early thirteenth century, his allegiance changed from York to Canterbury.[89] From c. 1201 to 1205 he joined the household of Arch-bishop Hubert Walter (d. 1205).[90] There he could enjoy the company of other canonists, such as Ricardus Anglicus (d. 1242).[91]

Continental decretists

Apart from these two Anglo-Norman decretists, we will also consider some texts from the continental schools of Bologna and Paris. This will be useful for two reasons. First, it will give us a better idea of the works that clergy in England would have been familiar with, especially given the great mobility between the different canonistic schools.[92] Second, it will allow us to see some of the influences on the Anglo-Norman canonists as well as some of the points where their opinions diverged from those of their continental counterparts. Our analysis would ideally consider all surviving canonistic writings; however, a selection has been made to keep the project within manageable limits. In any case, given the hazards of manuscript preservation even an analysis that took into account all the known canonistic writings would not guarantee that we could recognise all the sources of influence on the Anglo-Norman decretists.

What is more, we should keep in mind that even when the canonists borrowed their comments verbatim from other sources, they chose to do so; as such their composition was no less their own because it was influenced by that of others. This does mean, however, that some of the comments they have copied might not reflect present or local circumstances. In order to gain a better idea of their contemporary significance, I will combine the study of their *summae* with the study of papal decretals to English bishops. Letters from the pope were written in response to local circumstances.[93] If a decretal exists from around the same period, treating the same topic as a canonist for the same region, the topic in question would have been an issue of actual importance and not just a remnant copied from one canonical commentary to another.

For our current purposes, I will consider Rufinus and Stephen of Tournai from the Bolognese school.[94] Both of these decretists were part of the mainstream of canon law and enjoyed wide circulation. From the Parisian school I will focus on the *Summa Parisiensis*, not because it was popular but precisely because it was not. Schulte noted with surprise that the author of the *Summa Lipsiensis* did not make use of the *Summa Parisiensis* although he could not have avoided being aware of it.[95] This way we will get an idea not only of the sources that might have influenced the canonists but also of the sources they chose to ignore. Fortunately, in terms of direct influences, we are provided with a great deal of information from the authors themselves, who often named their sources, but also from the excellent recent editions of the works which identify parallels to other canonical collections, both editions and manuscripts.

Rufinus' *Summa*, completed sometime around 1164, was the most influential commentary on the *Decretum* in Bologna during the 1160s and 1170s. His work was still cited at the end of the twelfth century and the beginning of the thirteenth by decretists such as Huguccio and Johannes Teutonicus. But there is little that we know for certain about Rufinus himself. He was born in central Italy; he may have been Gratian's student; he taught canon law in Bologna. He was long thought to have become bishop of Assisi, but this has been assumed on tenuous evidence.[96] Stephen of Tournai was Rufinus' student. For this reason he is included among the Bolognese canon lawyers, although he also had important links with the Parisian school. Stephen had begun his career as a regular canon at Saint-Euverte in Orléans (1155), becoming abbot of that house (1167) and also of Sainte-Geneviève in Paris (1176), before being made bishop of Tournai (1191–1203). He composed his *summa* around 1165–1167.[97]

Unlike the *summae* of Rufinus and Stephen of Tournai, the *Summa Parisiensis* was almost certainly not written as a commentary, but as notes from an oral lecture (a *reportatio*), which were recopied at least once before arriving at their present form.[98] Its author seems to have spent some time in Italy but was writing for those who were not familiar with the country.[99] He showed some familiarity with Lombard law and had special knowledge of the French Church in general and of French churches in particular.[100] Although not much is known about his identity, it is believed that he was not a monk.[101] The *Summa Parisiensis* was most probably written in the late 1160s and survives in one known manuscript.[102]

Penitential authors

Of the penitential authors we will be concerned with here, Bartholomew was the earliest.[103] He rose to the position of archdeacon in 1155 and then bishop of Exeter in 1161. He was heavily involved in legal affairs, acting as papal judge-delegate and being the addressee of many decretals.[104] Bartholomew had been trained in Paris in the early 1140s, when Gratian's *Decretum* had not yet overshadowed the older canonical collections. This is reflected in his penitential, where he used the older collections of Burchard of Worms (d. 1025) and Ivo of Chartres (d. 1115) alongside the new texts of Gratian, Peter Lombard (d. 1164), and possibly Rufinus.[105] For him they all remained equally authoritative, but were considered insufficient in themselves; a new compilation of them was deemed necessary. Bartholomew's penitential was aimed at priests and had an instructional purpose: it was meant to teach them the canons they should live by and preach.[106] His penitential enjoyed widespread popularity, with no fewer than twenty-two copies surviving.[107] It cannot have been written before 1150 and a more likely period of composition is the 1160s, after Bartholomew's episcopate had begun.[108]

Robert of Flamborough was born near Scarborough in Yorkshire, but spent most of his life in Paris within the cloister of Saint-Victor, where he was a canon and penitentiary.[109] It was at the request of a fellow Englishman, Richard Poore, then dean of Salisbury, that Robert composed his *Penitentiale* to serve as a practical manual for the administration of penance by parish priests in England. In his work, Robert employed papal decretals from Alexander III and Innocent III in the manner of a canonist. He was also influenced by the collections of Bartholomew of Exeter and Ivo of Chartres. Robert's *Penitentiale* can be dated between 1208 and 1213.[110]

Thomas of Chobham is believed to have been born between 1158 and 1168 at the village of Chobham in Surrey.[111] He studied in Paris during the 1180s, where he came under the influence of Peter the Chanter, the only contemporary master whose work he quotes regularly.[112] By 1190–1192 he was back in England, and had joined the household of Richard fitz Nigel, bishop of London, as a *magister*.[113] In 1198, after Bishop Richard died, Thomas took up service in the household of Herbert Poore, bishop of Salisbury.[114] In October 1206, he was appointed perpetual vicar of Sturminster, and not long thereafter he became subdean of Salisbury Cathedral. In 1213, he acted as a royal emissary abroad on behalf of King John. Shortly after, and probably due to royal influence, he received not only a substantial amount of money but also a canonry in Salisbury Cathedral along with the 'golden prebend' of Charminster in Dorset.[115] As such he would have been better endowed than most clerics. Between 1215 and 1217 he acted as Bishop Herbert Poore's chief judicial officer (*officialis*), but after the bishop's death in 1217 and the succession of his younger brother, Richard Poore, Thomas left Salisbury to return to Paris, where he taught theology between 1222 and 1228.

Thomas' comments on issues of clerical marriage and ecclesiastical property are particularly interesting in light of his familiarity with episcopal households as well as his own financial and personal circumstances. During his stay at the household of Richard fitz Nigel, between 1192 and 1198, he would have experienced first-hand the influence of clerical dynasties. Bishop Richard was the illegitimate son of Nigel (c. 1100–1169), Henry I's treasurer and bishop of Ely, who in turn was nephew of Roger, bishop of Salisbury (d. 1139). According to the *Liber Eliensis*, Richard's father had provided for his son's career as a treasurer by offering £400 to Henry II.[116] What is more, Thomas himself was illegitimate. When after 1228 he went back to England, he was considered as an episcopal candidate for the see of Salisbury, but was disqualified because the papal dispensation that he had received from Pope Gregory IX (1227–1241) for his illegitimate birth stipulated that a further dispensation would be required should he ever wish to become bishop. He remained subdean of Salisbury until his death. Our last record of Thomas dates to 19 October 1233. A new subdean of Salisbury is documented on 17 February 1236.

Thomas' *Summa confessorum*, composed around 1215, was hugely successful.[117] It survives in more than 160 manuscript copies. It is an important source for the study of the early thirteenth century, as in it are intermixed the doctrines of the canonists, the theology of Parisian masters, and civil and canonical legislation, as well as Thomas' personal comments on everyday life. According to Baldwin, Thomas' penitential was most probably composed in England because of the predominance of English cases cited and the author's concern for the needs of the English clergy.[118]

A final work of clerical instruction which I will be using in this book is Gerald of Wales' *Gemma Ecclesiastica*. The *Gemma* was written when Gerald was residing in Lincoln, sometime between 1196 and 1199, when he was in his fifties. It was the work of a man who had been educated in Paris; had acted as teacher of the trivium; had served as archdeacon of Brecon; had returned to Paris to pursue higher studies in civil and canon law, as well as theology; had lectured on Gratian's *Decretum*; and had served as royal clerk for twelve years. The *Gemma* was written to instruct the Welsh clergy, but was also presented to Pope Innocent III on the occasion of Gerald's visit to argue the cause of his election to the bishopric of St David's and to lobby for its independence from the see of Canterbury. As such, it was a text that Gerald could be proud of and whose outlooks he believed to have been agreeable to the papacy.[119]

Outline

Using these sources I will examine how Byzantine and English ecclesiastics viewed clerical continence and will ask why the marriage of clerics was allowed in one area and condemned in the other. I will explore three concerns which were put forward in the West as justifications for the requirement of sexual continence: the alienation of Church property; hereditary succession; and ritual pollution. First, I will discuss the finances of the clergy. I will explore in particular the link between a cleric's access to ecclesiastical resources, his familial status, and the laws that controlled clerical spending. I will address these issues by focusing both on bishops (Chapter 3) and on clerics below the episcopate (Chapter 4). Then I will look at the association between ecclesiastical dynasties and clerical marriage, examining laws which aimed to restrict hereditary succession to churches (Chapter 5). In the final part, I will deal with questions of purity and pollution. I will start by exploring wider issues of impurity associated with nocturnal emissions and the sacred, in order to establish whether the two societies used impurity discourse to control ritual participation in comparable ways (Chapter 6). Finally, I will ask whether marriage was deemed polluting in twelfth-century Byzantine and Western sources, before I explain why we see a great divergence of opinion on this topic (Chapter 7). However, before any of this, and in the anticipation that many readers will be relatively unfamiliar with either the Byzantine or the English Church in the twelfth century, I will begin by giving a brief overview of the two ecclesiastical hierarchies and their legal interactions, as well as their rules of clerical continence (Chapter 2).

Notes

1 See, for example, Roskovány's collection of authors from the first to the mid-nineteenth century discussing the topic of clerical celibacy, in A. Roskovány, *Coelibatus et breviarium: duo gravissima clericorum officia e monumentis omnium seculorum demonstrata, accessit completa literatura*, 4 vols. (Pestini, 1861).

2 Cochini gives an in-depth review of some twenty studies on the topic extending from the eleventh century to his own time. See C. Cochini, *Apostolic Origins of Priestly Celibacy*, trans. N. Marans (San Francisco, CA, 1990). See also E. Peters, 'History, Historians, and Clerical Celibacy', in *Medieval Purity and Piety: Essays on Medieval Clerical Celibacy and Religious Reform*, ed. M. Frassetto (London, 1998), 3–21; R. Cholij, *Clerical Celibacy in East and West* (Leominster, 1988); A.M. Stickler, *The Case for Clerical Celibacy: Its Historical Development and Theological Foundations* (San Francisco, CA, 1995); S. Heid, *Celibacy in the Early Church: The Beginnings of a Discipline of Obligatory Continence for Clerics in East and West* (San Francisco, CA, 2000).

3 R. Gryson, *Les origines du célibat ecclésiastique du premier au septième siècle* (Gembloux, 1970); R. Gryson, 'Dix ans de recherches sur les origines du célibat ecclésiastique', *Revue Théologique de Louvain*, 11 (1980), 157–85. Daily celebration of the Eucharist was one of the main early differences between East and West, dating from around the fifth century. See R. Kottje, 'Das Aufkommen der täglichen Eucharistiefeier in der Westkirche und die Zölibatsforderung', *Zeitschrift für Kirchengeschichte*, 82 (1971), 218–28.

4 D. Callam, 'Clerical Continence in the Fourth Century: Three Papal Decretals', *Theological Studies*, 41 (1980), 3–50.

5 D.G. Hunter, 'Clerical Celibacy and the Veiling of Virgins: New Boundaries in Late Ancient Christianity', in *The Limits of Ancient Christianity: Essays on Late Antique Thought and Culture in Honor of R.A. Markus*, eds. W.E. Klingshirn and M. Vessey (Ann Arbor, MI, 1999), 139–52.

6 On the Gregorian reforms, see K.F. Morrison, 'The Gregorian Reform', in *Christian Spirituality: Origins to the Twelfth Century*, eds. B. McGinn and J. Meyendorff (New York, NY, 1985), 177–92; U.-R. Blumenthal, *The Investiture Controversy: Church and Monarchy from the Ninth to the Twelfth Century* (Philadelphia, PA, 1988); G. Tellenbach, *The Church in Western Europe from the Tenth to the Early Twelfth Century*, trans. T. Reuter (Cambridge, 1993); I.S. Robinson, 'Reform and the Church, 1073–1122', in *The New Cambridge Medieval History VI*, eds. D. Luscombe and J. Riley-Smith (Cambridge, 2004), 268–334.

7 On ritual purity, see R.I. Moore, 'Family, Community and Cult on the Eve of the Gregorian Reform', *Transactions of the Royal Historical Society*, 30 (1980), 49–69; P. Beaudette, '"In the World but Not of It": Clerical Celibacy as a Symbol of the Medieval Church', in *Medieval Purity and Piety: Essays on Medieval Clerical Celibacy and Religious Reform*, ed. M. Frassetto (London, 1998), 23–46. For the heresy of 'nicolaitism', see G. Fornasari, *Celibato Sacerdotale e "Autoconoscienza" Ecclesiale: Per la storia della "Nicolaitica Haeresis" Nell'Occidente Medievale* (Udine, 1981).

8 Ecclesiastical property and poverty were the main themes at the council of Pavia in 1022. See, for example, U.-R. Blumenthal, 'Pope Gregory VII and the Prohibition of Nicolaitism', in *Medieval Purity and Piety: Essays on Medieval Clerical Celibacy and Religious Reform*, ed. M. Frassetto (New York, NY, 1998), 239–67, at 240–2. See also how clerical celibacy fits into Goody's historico-anthropological analysis of the Church as a corporate entity whose matrimonial strategies were meant to increase its financial standing, in J. Goody, *The Development of the Family and Marriage in Europe* (Cambridge, 1983), 79–81.

9 See, for example, M.C. Miller, 'Clerical Identity and Reform: Notarial Descriptions of the Secular Clergy in the Po Valley, 750–1200', in *Medieval Purity and Piety: Essays on Medieval Clerical Celibacy and Religious Reform*, ed. M. Frassetto (New York, NY, 1998), 305–35; J. Laudage, *Priesterbild und Reformpapsttum im 11. Jahrhundert* (Cologne, 1984), 207–50.

10 D. D'Avray, 'The Origins and Aftermath of the Eleventh-Century Reform in the Light of Niklas Luhmann's Systems Theory', in *"Vicarius Petri", "Vicarius Christi". La titolatura del Papa nell'XI secolo: Dibattiti e prospettive*, eds. F. Amerini and R. Saccenti (Pisa, 2017), 211–27.

11 An ecclesiastical law was not formally revoked even when it was found to be contradictory to other laws. See S. Perentidis, 'Un canon peut-il être périmé? Mentalités et autorité du texte canonique au XIIe siècle', in *Byzantium in the 12th Century: Canon Law, State and Society*, ed. N. Oikonomides (Athens, 1991), 141–7.

12 See, for example, C. Violante, *La pataria milanese e la riforma ecclesiastica* (Rome, 1955).

13 See, for example, R.R. Darlington, 'Ecclesiastical Reform in the Late Old English Period', *The English Historical Review*, 51:203 (1936), 385–428.

14 See also Brett's reasons for and against using England as a case study of Western law and his emphasis on the lack of a unified Western experience. M. Brett, 'The Bishop's Charter and the Law in Twelfth-Century England', in *Proceedings of the Thirteenth International Congress of Medieval Canon Law; Esztergom, 3–8 August 2008*, eds. P. Erdő and Sz.A. Szuromi (Vatican, 2010), 3–16, at 5: 'One may reasonably propose that the Western Church was entirely composed of exceptional cases, even that the very notion of a norm is a convenient delusion.'

15 C. Duggan, *Twelfth-Century Decretal Collections and their Importance in English History* (London, 1963), 7.

16 M. Angold, *Church and Society in Byzantium under the Comneni, 1081–1261* (Cambridge, 1995), 515.

17 The present comparative research fits within a wider category of studies which adopt a global historical perspective. See J. Belich, J. Darwin, and C. Wickham, 'Introduction', in *The Prospect of Global History*, eds. J. Belich, J. Darwin, M. Frenz, and C. Wickham (Oxford, 2016), 3–22. For what follows, see also C. Wickham, 'Problems in Doing Comparative History', in *Challenging the Boundaries of Medieval History: The Legacy of Timothy Reuter*, ed. P. Skinner (Turnhout, 2009), 5–28.

18 There are currently forty-four published volumes of the *English Episcopal Acta*. For the *Fasti* there are eleven volumes for the period from 1066 to 1300.

19 See also Angold, *Church and Society*, 1–4. It is telling that in a recent handbook of Byzantine History, 'political history' receives four different chapters divided chronologically, while ecclesiastical history is dealt with in two chapters, divided

into 'church' and 'monasticism'. See J. Harris (ed.), *Palgrave Advances in Byzantine History* (New York, NY, 2005).

20 P. Wormald, 'Æthelwold and His Continental Counterparts: Contact, Comparison, Contrast', in *Bishop Æthelwold: His Career and Influence*, ed. B. Yorke (Woodbridge, 1988), 13–42, at 14–15. Indeed, as Airlie noted, 'this is something that [Wormald] believed so fervently that he wrote it twice.' See S. Airlie, 'Patrick Wormald the Teacher', in *Early Medieval Studies in Memory of Patrick Wormald*, eds. S. Baxter, C.E. Karkov, J.L. Nelson, and D. Pelteret (Farnham, 2009), 29–35, at 31.

21 A. Louth, *Greek East and Latin West: The Church AD 681–1071* (Crestwood, NY, 2007), xv. For examples of other studies comparing East and West, see H. Chadwick, *East and West: The Making of a Rift in the Church: From Apostolic Times Until the Council of Florence* (Oxford, 2003); F. Dvornik, *Byzantium and the Roman Primacy* (New York, NY, 1966).

22 Louth, *Greek East and Latin West*, xv.

23 C. Gallagher, *Church Law and Church Order in Rome and Byzantium* (Aldershot, 2002). See also his articles C. Gallagher, 'Marriage in Eastern and Western Canon Law', *Law & Justice*, 157 (2006), 7–16; C. Gallagher, 'Gratian and Theodore Balsamon: Two Twelfth-Century Canonistic Methods Compared', in *Byzantium in the 12th Century: Canon Law, State and Society*, ed. N. Oikonomides (Athens, 1991), 61–89.

24 For an introduction to these councils and their context, see C. Gallagher, 'The Episcopal Councils in the East', in *The Oxford Handbook of Byzantine Studies*, eds. R. Cormack, J.F. Haldon, and E. Jeffreys (Oxford, 2008), 583–91, at 583–9. For the English texts of the conciliar canons quoted in the following chapters I have consulted P. Schaff (trans.), *The Seven Ecumenical Councils of the Undivided Church* (Grand Rapids, MI, 1979).

25 C. Pitsakis, 'Clergé marié et célibat dans la législation du Concile in Trullo: le point de vue oriental', in *The Council in Trullo Revisited*, eds. G. Nedungatt and M. Featherstone (Rome, 1995), 263–306.

26 S. Troianos, 'Byzantine Canon Law to 1100', in *History of Byzantine and Eastern Canon Law to 1500*, eds. W. Hartmann and K. Pennington (Washington, DC, 2012), 115–69, at 125–9.

27 P. Noailles and A. Dain (eds.), *Les novelles de Léon VI le Sage* (Paris, 1944).

28 For the *Basilika*, see H.J. Scheltema, N. van der Wal, and D. Holwerda (eds.), *Basilicorum libri LX, Text*, 8 vols. (Groningen, 1953–88).

29 For canon law in an earlier period, see also D. Wagschal, *Law and Legality in the Greek East: The Byzantine Canonical Tradition, 381–883* (Oxford, 2014).

30 Quotations from the *Liber Extra* found in this book are based on E. Friedberg (ed.), *Corpus Iuris Canonici, Pars secunda: Decretalium Collectiones* (Leipzig, 1881; repr. Graz, 1959). Similarly, for references to the Compilatio antiqua (prima-quinta), see E. Friedberg (ed.), *Quinque Compilationes Antiquae* (Leipzig, 1882).

31 Quotations from Gratian's *Decretum* found in this book are based on E. Friedberg (ed.), *Decretum Magistri Gratiani* (Leipzig, 1879). For a translation into English of the first twenty distinctions and their ordinary gloss, see A. Thompson (trans.), J. Gordley (trans.), and K. Christensen, *The Treatise on Laws (Decretum DD. 1–20) with the Ordinary Gloss* (Washington, DC, 1993).

32 A. Morey (ed.), *Bartholomew of Exeter: Bishop and Canonist. A Study in the Twelfth Century* (Cambridge, 1937); J.J.F. Firth (ed.), *Robert of Flamborough, Liber Poenitentialis* (Toronto, 1971); F. Broomfield, *Thomae de Chobham summa confessorum* (Paris, 1968).

33 W. Adam, *Legal Flexibility and the Mission of the Church: Dispensation and Economy in Ecclesiastical Law* (London, 2011).

34 Angold, *Church and Society*, 408–9.

35 S. Troianos, 'Byzantine Canon Law From the Twelfth to the Fifteenth Centuries', in *History of Byzantine and Eastern Canon Law to 1500*, eds. W. Hartmann and K. Pennington (Washington, DC, 2012), 170–214, at 179.

36 For the office of the *nomophylax*, see S. Troianos, 'Η νεαρά Κωνσταντίνου του Μονομάχου ἐπὶ τῇ ἀναδείξει καὶ προβολῇ τοῦ διδασκάλου τῶν νόμων', *Βυζαντινά Σύμμεικτα*, 22 (2012), 243–63, at 254–5. For the *protekdikos*, see R.J. Macrides, 'Killing, Asylum, and the Law in Byzantium', *Speculum*, 63 (1988), 509–38. For the *orphanotrophos*, see R. Guilland, 'Études sur l'histoire administrative de l'empire byzantin: L'Orphanotrophe', *REB*, 23 (1965), 205–21, at 206. For the *megas oikonomos*, see J. Darrouzès, *Recherches sur les offikia de l'Église byzantine* (Paris, 1970), 60–1. For the *hieromnemon*, see Darrouzès, *Offikia*, 65, 84.

37 Darrouzès, *Offikia*, 81–2; *Les regestes de 715 à 1206*, 505 n. 1048.

38 On Zonaras, see also P. Pieler, 'Zonaras als Kanonist', in *Byzantium in the 12th Century: Canon Law, State and Society*, ed. N. Oikonomides (Athens, 1991), 601–20.

39 Troianos, 'Twelfth to the Fifteenth Centuries', 177.

40 For Zonaras' family connections and the monastery, see C. Mango, 'Twelfth-Century Notices From cod. Christ Church Gr. 53', *Jahrbuch der Österreichischen Byzantinistik*, 42 (1992), 221–8.

41 *Syntagma* 4.598–9. See also H.-G. Beck, 'Zur byzantinischen Mönchschronik', in *Speculum historiale: Geschichte im Spiegel von Geschichtsschreibung und Gesichtsdeutung, Festschrift K. Adler*, eds. A. Bauer, L. Boehm, and M. Müller (Freiburg and Munich, 1965), 188–97, at 190–1.

42 Commentary on canon 3 of Carthage in *Syntagma* 3.301: 'Οὗτοι γάρ εἰσι μεσῖται Θεοῦ καὶ ἀνθρώπων, ἐξιλεούμενοι τὸ θεῖον τοῖς ἄλλοις, καὶ σωτηρίαν αἰτούμενοι τοῖς πιστοῖς, καὶ εἰρήνην τῷ κόσμῳ.'

43 *Syntagma* 2.2.

44 *Syntagma* 3.80.

45 Troianos, 'Twelfth to the Fifteenth Centuries', 177; R. Macrides, 'Perception of the Past in the Twelfth-century Canonists', in *Byzantium in the 12th Century: Canon Law, State and Society*, ed. N. Oikonomides (Athens, 1991), 589–99, at 591 n. 13; *Syntagma* 3.80.

46 See T. Kampianaki, *John Zonaras' Epitome of Histories: A Compendium of Jewish-Roman History and Its Readers* (DPhil, Oxford, 2018), xxiv. An alternative chronology has been suggested by Banchich, who took the 'second wedding' to refer to Nikephoros Botaneiates' (r. 1078–1081) union with Vevdene, which he placed in 1078 along with Botaneiates' coronation. In this reconstruction, Zonaras would have been in his twenties at the time of the wedding, would have retired to the monastery in his fifties c. 1112, finished his canonical commentary first, and completed the *Epitome* c. 1134. See T.M. Banchich, 'Introduction: The Epitome of Histories', in *The History of Zonaras. From Alexander Severus to the Death of Theodosius the Great*, ed. and trans. T.M. Banchich and trans. E.N. Lane (London, 2009), 1–19, at 7. However, Kampianaki has argued that Botaneiates' wedding to Vevdene is more likely to have taken place before his rise to the throne, on the grounds that had he been unmarried in 1078 he would have made a political marriage, choosing a match that would enhance his legitimacy to the throne, as he did later with Maria of Alania.

47 The prosopographical information presented here is largely from G.P. Stevens, *De Theodoro Balsamone: analysis operum ac mentis iuridicae* (Rome, 1969) and S. Troianos, 'Twelfth to the Fifteenth Centuries', 170–214. It has been argued that Balsamon was also *protos* of the Blachernai church, but Stevens has expressed doubt about this. See Stevens, *De Theodoro Balsamone*, 6–7 n. 11. For more details on these offices, see Darrouzès, *Offikia*, 82, 508–25; R. Macrides, 'Nomos and Kanon on Paper and in Court', in *Church and People in Byzantium*, ed. R. Morris (London, 1990), 61–85, at 69.

48 Darrouzès, *Offikia*, 338. For the *nomophylax*, see footnote 36.

49 See Angold, *Church and Society*, 101, 148; O. Lampsides, 'Πῶς εἰσάγουν εἰς τὰ κείμενά των οἱ ἐξηγηταὶ τῶν κανόνων τὰς εἰδήσεις διὰ τὸν σύγχρονόν των κόσμον', in *Byzantium in the 12th Century: Canon Law, State and Society*, ed. N. Oikonomides

(Athens, 1991), 211–27; R. Browning, 'Theodore Balsamon's Commentary on the Canons of the Council in Trullo as a Source on Everyday Life in Twelfth-Century Byzantium', in *Η καθημερινή ζωή στο Βυζάντιο*, ed. C. Angelidi (Athens, 1989), 421–7.

50 *Nomokanones* were legal compilations that combined secular laws (*nomoi*) and ecclesiastical laws (*kanones*). The original version of the *Nomokanon of Fourteen Titles* does not survive but is thought to have been completed by 641. Around 882/3, this version was expanded through the addition of canons issued in the intervening period. In 1089/90, Theodore Bestes made a third edition, which included passages from the *Basilika*, a late ninth-century collection of civil laws which had also been revised in the early eleventh century. Balsamon's commentary on the *Nomokanon* was based on Bestes' version. The best edition for the *Nomokanon of Fourteen Titles* is J.-B. Pitra (ed.), *Iuris ecclesiastici graecorum historia et monumenta*, vol. II (1868; repr. Rome, 1963), 433–640.

51 Troianos, 'Twelfth to the Fifteenth Centuries', 181; Troianos, 'Canon Law to 1100', 138–40.

52 A. Schminck, 'Zur Entwicklung des Eherechts in der Komnenenepoche', in *Byzantium in the 12th Century: Canon Law, State and Society*, ed. N. Oikonomides (Athens, 1991), 555–87, at 584 n. 171; Troianos, 'Twelfth to the Fifteenth Centuries', 181.

53 There is some debate regarding when Balsamon became patriarch of Antioch. Tiftixoglou argues that it was during the patriarchate of Theodosios Boradiotes (1179–1183). Troianos places the date within the reign of Isaak II Angelos (r. 1185–95). So do Stevens and Pitsakes. See Troianos, 'Twelfth to the Fifteenth Centuries', 180; V. Tiftixoglou, 'Zur Genese der Kommentare des Theodoros Balsamon. Mit einem Exkurs über die unbekannten Kommentare des Sinaiticus gr. 1117', in *Byzantium in the 12th Century: Canon Law, State and Society*, ed. N. Oikonomides (Athens, 1991), 483–532, at 489; Stevens, *De Theodoro Balsamone*, 8; C. Pitsakes, 'Ἡ ἔκταση τῆς ἐξουσίας ἑνὸς ὑπερόριου πατριάρχη: ὁ πατριάρχης Ἀντιοχείας στὴν Κωνσταντινούπολη τὸν 12ο αἰῶνα', in *Byzantium in the 12th Century: Canon Law, State and Society*, ed. N. Oikonomides (Athens, 1991), 91–139, at 97. See also Angold, *Church and Society*, 507.

54 Y. Papadoyannakis, 'Instruction by Question and Answer: the Case of Late Antique and Byzantine Erotapokriseis', in *Greek Literature in Late Antiquity: Dynamism, Didacticism, Classicism*, ed. S.E. Johnson (Aldershot, 2006), 91–105; A.-L. Rey, 'Les erotapokriseis dans le monde byzantin: tradition manuscrite des textes anciens et production de nouveaux textes', in *Erotapokriseis, Early Christian Question-and-Answer Literature in Context*, eds. A. Volgers and C. Zamagni (Leuven, 2004), 165–80. See also P. Magdalino, *The Empire of Manuel I Komnenos, 1143–1180* (Cambridge, 1994), 375.

55 Angold, *Church and Society*, 507.

56 Pitsakes, 'Ἡ ἔκταση τῆς ἐξουσίας ἑνὸς ὑπερόριου πατριάρχη', 117–23.

57 See Stevens, *De Theodoro Balsamone*, 9. Pitsakes refutes the suggestion that the monastery of the Virgin *Hodegetria* and the monastery of Zipoi were one and the same. He argues that the monastery of Zipoi was a personal donation from the emperor to Balsamon, who aimed to restore it but might not have had the time to do so. See Pitsakes, 'Ἡ ἔκταση τῆς ἐξουσίας ἑνὸς ὑπερόριου πατριάρχη', 133–9.

58 He might have been still alive in 1198. See Troianos, 'Twelfth to the Fifteenth Centuries', 180.

59 Troianos, 'Twelfth to the Fifteenth Centuries', 183, 185–7.

60 *Syntagma* 1.ι-ια. The fourteenth-century manuscript was considered lost, but has now been identified as Istanbul, Topkapı Sarayı Müzesi Kütüphanesi, 115. See S. Troianos, 'Ράλλης και Ποτλής', in *Byzantium in the 12th Century: Canon Law, State and Society*, ed. N. Oikonomides (Athens, 1991), 17–24, at 20–1.

61 The version found in the Patrologia Graeca (c. 1672) was based on the cod. Bodl. Barocc. gr. 205. See Tiftixoglou, 'Zur Genese der Kommentare des Theodoros

Balsamon', 520. See also H. Ohme, 'Greek Canon Law to 691/2', in *The History of Byzantine and Eastern Canon Law to 1500*, eds. W. Hartmann and K. Pennington (Washington, DC, 2012), 24–114, at 26–7.

62 For what follows, see Tiftixoglou, 'Zur Genese der Kommentare des Theodoros Balsamon', 483–95.

63 Troianos, 'Twelfth to the Fifteenth Centuries', 178.

64 Troianos, 'Twelfth to the Fifteenth Centuries', 179.

65 M.H. Hoeflich and J.M. Grabher, 'The Establishment of Normative Legal Texts: The Beginnings of the *Ius commune*', in *The History of Medieval Canon Law in the Classical Period, 1140–1234: From Gratian to the Decretals of Pope Gregory IX*, eds. W. Hartmann and K. Pennington (Washington, DC, 2008), 1–21, at 7. See also J.A. Brundage, 'The Teaching and Study of Canon Law in the Law Schools', in *The History of Medieval Canon Law in the Classical Period, 1140–1234: From Gratian to the Decretals of Pope Gregory IX*, eds. W. Hartmann and K. Pennington (Washington, DC, 2008), 98–120.

66 S. Kuttner, 'The Father of the Science of Canon Law', *The Jurist*, 1 (1941), 2–19, at 2.

67 P. Landau, 'Gratian and the *Decretum Gratiani*', in *The History of Medieval Canon Law in the Classical Period, 1140–1234: From Gratian to the Decretals of Pope Gregory IX*, eds. W. Hartmann and K. Pennington (Washington, DC, 2008), 22–54, at 23.

68 Landau, 'Gratian and the *Decretum Gratiani*', 48.

69 Brett has seen dramatic change in English ecclesiastical law already in the period between 1115 and 1175. A wide range of legal texts is to be found in manuscripts and a knowledge of law is displayed in the writings of many English ecclesiastics. This is accompanied by a change in the character of the surviving episcopal *acta*, which become much more frequent. After 1175 there is further change, with acts containing fuller accounts of arguments, more detail on procedure, and references to precise authorities, usually a conciliar canon or a papal decretal. See Brett, 'The Bishop's Charter and the Law in Twelfth-Century England', 8–11.

70 Among the oldest codices of Gratian in England are also Cambridge, Pembroke College 162 (from Italy) and Cambridge, Gonville and Caius 6 (from France). See Landau, 'Gratian and the *Decretum Gratiani*', 49; R.M. Thomson, *Catalogue of the Manuscripts of Lincoln Cathedral Chapter Library* (Woodbridge, 1989), 106–7.

71 J.T. Noonan, 'Gratian Slept Here: The Changing Identity of the Father of the Systematic Study of Canon Law', *Traditio*, 35 (1979), 145–72.

72 A. Winroth, *The Making of Gratian's Decretum* (Cambridge, 2004), 6. The theory that Gratian became bishop in Chiusi after he stopped teaching in Bologna has recently received further support. See A. Winroth, 'Where Gratian Slept: The Life and Death of the Father of Canon Law', *Zeitschrift der Savigny Stiftung für Rechtsgeschichte: Kanonistische Abteilung*, 99 (2013), 105–28.

73 Winroth, *Making of Gratian's Decretum*, 5.

74 Winroth, *Making of Gratian's Decretum*, 3.

75 Winroth, *Making of Gratian's Decretum*, 4.

76 Winroth, *Making of Gratian's Decretum*, 136–45. Although it has been further proposed by Carlos Larrainzar that there was a third version of Gratian's *Decretum*, found in MS Saint Gall, Stiftsbibliothek 673, which was even shorter and earlier than Gratian 1 (Gratian 0, about 1,000 canons), this suggestion has not met with the same acceptance as Winroth's two-layered construction of Gratian's text. See C. Larrainzar, 'El borrador del la "Concordia" de Graziano: Sankt Gallen, Stiftsbibliothek MS 673 (=Sg)', *Ius ecclesiae: Rivista internazionale di diritto canonico*, 9 (1999), 593–666. See also J. Werckmeister, *Décret de Gratien – Causes 27 à 36: Le Mariage* (Paris, 2011), 15–16; Winroth, 'Where Gratian Slept', 110.

77 Werckmeister, *Le Mariage*, 17.

78 Werckmeister, *Le Mariage*, 19.

79 For the spread of canon law in England, see C. Duggan, 'The Reception of Canon Law in England in the Later-Twelfth Century', in *Proceedings of the Second*

International Congress of Medieval Canon Law, Boston College, 12–16 August 1963, eds. S. Kuttner and J.J. Ryan (Vatican City, 1965), 359–90. For the sources of the decretists, see P. Landau, 'Vorgratianische Kanonessammlungen bei den Dekretisten und die frühen Dekretalensammlungen', in *Proceedings of the Eighth International Congress of Medieval Canon Law, San Diego, University of California at La Jolla, 21–27 August 1988*, ed. S. Chodorow (Vatican, 1992), 93–116.

80 S. Kuttner and E. Rathbone, 'Anglo-Norman Canonists of the Twelfth Century', *Traditio*, 7 (1949–51), 295–6; R. Weigand, 'The Transmontane Decretists', in *The History of Medieval Canon Law in the Classical Period, 1140–1234: From Gratian to the Decretals of Pope Gregory IX*, eds. W. Hartmann and K. Pennington (Washington, DC, 2008), 174–210, at 195–6.

81 P. Landau, 'X. Rodoicus Modicipassus – Verfasser der Summa Lipsiensis?', *Zeitschrift der Savigny-Stiftung für Rechtsgeschichte: Kanonistische Abteilung*, 92:1 (2006), 340–54.

82 Landau, 'Rodoicus Modicipassus', 352–4.

83 For what follows on Honorius, see Kuttner and Rathbone, 'Anglo-Norman Canonists', 279–358, 304–316; C. Duggan, 'Honorius, canonist', *Oxford Dictionary of National Biography*. www.oxforddnb.com/view/article/50350. Accessed 17/01/2017.

84 B. Grimm (ed.), *Die Ehelehre des Magister Honorius: ein Beitrag zur Ehelehre der anglo-normannischen Schule* (Rome, 1989), 9; R. Weigand, 'Bemerkungen über die Schriften und Lehren des Magister Honorius', in *Proceedings of the Fifth International Congress of Medieval Canon Law, Salamanca, 21–25 September 1976*, eds. S. Kuttner and K. Pennington (Vatican, 1980), 195–212, at 205.

85 Kuttner and Rathbone, 'Anglo-Norman Canonists', 304.

86 Kuttner and Rathbone, 'Anglo-Norman Canonists', 305.

87 Kuttner and Rathbone, 'Anglo-Norman Canonists', 305; Duggan, 'Honorius, canonist', *Oxford Dictionary of National Biography*.

88 See Lovatt's section on 'Archbishop Geoffrey's *familia* and chancery', in *EEA*, XXVII, xcvi–cxiv, at cvi–cvii, cxii.

89 *EEA*, XXVII, xcvii and cxii.

90 On Hubert Walter's household see also *EEA*, II, xxviii.

91 Duggan, 'Honorius, canonist', *Oxford Dictionary of National Biography*.

92 See also J. Peltzer, *Canon Law, Careers and Conquest: Episcopal Elections in Normandy and Greater Anjou c. 1140–c. 1230* (Cambridge, 2008), 12.

93 On decretals and their authority, see A.J. Duggan, 'Making Law or Not? The Function of Papal Decretals in the Twelfth Century', in *Proceedings of the Thirteenth International Congress of Medieval Canon Law*, eds. P. Erdő and Sz.A. Szuromi (Vatican City, 2010), 41–65.

94 K. Pennington and W.P. Müller, 'The Decretists: The Italian School', in *The History of Medieval Canon Law in the Classical Period, 1140–1234: From Gratian to the Decretals of Pope Gregory IX*, eds. W. Hartmann and K. Pennington (Washington, DC, 2008), 121–73. On Rufinus, see also R. Deutinger, 'The Decretist Rufinus – A Well-known Person?', *Bulletin of Medieval Canon Law, New Series*, 23 (1999), 10–15.

95 J.F. von Schulte, 'Die Summa Decreti Lipsiensis des Codex 986 der Leipziger Universitätsbibliothek', *Sitzungsberichte Vienna*, 68 (1871), 37–54, at 52.

96 Pennington and Müller, 'The Decretists: The Italian School', 135–7.

97 J.W. Baldwin, 'Masters at Paris from 1179 to 1215: A Social Perspective', in *Renaissance and Renewal in the Twelfth Century*, eds. R.L. Benson and G. Constable with C.D. Lanham (Toronto, 1991), 138–72, at 146; Pennington and Müller, 'The Decretists: The Italian School', 136.

98 *Summa Parisiensis*, viii–ix.

99 *Summa Parisiensis*, xvii.

100 *Summa Parisiensis*, xviii.

101 *Summa Parisiensis*, xx.

102 Staatsbibliothek of Bamberg, Can. 36. See Weigand, 'The Transmontane Decretists', 181–2.
103 For a recent re-evaluation of Bartholomew's work, see J. Taliadoros, 'Bartholomew of Exeter's Penitential: Some Observations on his Personal Dicta', in *Proceedings of the Thirteenth International Congress of Medieval Canon Law*, eds. P. Erdő and Sz.A. Szuromi (Vatican City, 2010), 457–73.
104 Morey, *Bartholomew of Exeter*, 130.
105 Weigand, 'The Transmontane Decretists', 175; Morey, *Bartholomew of Exeter*, 170, 173–4. For Burchard and Ivo, see also L. Kéry, *Canonical Collections of the Early Middle Ages (c. 400–1140): A Bibliographical Guide to the Manuscripts and Literature* (Washington, DC, 1999), 133–55, 250–60; C. Rolker, *Canon Law and the Letters of Ivo of Chartres* (Cambridge, 2009); P. Corbet, *Autour de Burchard de Worms* (Frankfurt am Main, 2001). For Ivo's manuscripts in England, see Brett, 'The Bishop's Charter and the Law in Twelfth-Century England', 8.
106 Morey, *Bartholomew of Exeter*, 175.
107 Taliadoros, 'Bartholomew of Exeter's Penitential', 458 n. 9.
108 Morey, *Bartholomew of Exeter*, 174.
109 J.W. Baldwin, *Masters, Princes, and Merchants: The Social Views of Peter the Chanter & His Circle*, vol. I (Princeton, NJ, 1970), 32–4.
110 Baldwin, *Peter the Chanter & His Circle*, 1.32.
111 Baldwin, *Peter the Chanter & His Circle*, 1.34. For what follows, see also J. Goering, 'Chobham, Thomas of (d. 1233x6)', *Oxford Dictionary of National Biography*. www.oxforddnb.com/view/article/5007. Accessed 09/06/2014.
112 Baldwin, *Peter the Chanter & His Circle*, 1.35.
113 Richard fitz Nigel is also known as Richard of Ely. For more on his household, see *EEA*, XXVI, xxxvii–xxxviii, xliv–xlv.
114 On the household of Herbert Poore, bishop of Salisbury, see *EEA*, XVIII, lxxv–lxxx.
115 Baldwin, *Peter the Chanter & His Circle*, 1.34–5. For a list of the prebendaries of Charminster, see *Fasti*, IV, 60–1.
116 J. Fairweather (trans.), *Liber Eliensis: A History of the Isle of Ely From the Seventh Century to the Twelfth* (Woodbridge, 2005), 461. This money might also have been part of the assessment laid on the clergy for the war in Toulouse. See E.U. Crosby, *The King's Bishops: The Politics of Propaganda in England and Normandy 1066–1216* (New York, NY, 2013), 134.
117 Baldwin, *Peter the Chanter & His Circle*, 1.35.
118 Baldwin, *Peter the Chanter & His Circle*, 1.36.
119 For a brief introduction to Gerald of Wales, see R. Bartlett, 'Gerald of Wales', *Oxford Dictionary of National Biography*. https://doi.org/10.1093/ref:odnb/10769. Accessed 19/12/2017. For a fuller account, see R. Bartlett, *Gerald of Wales, 1146–1223* (Oxford, 1982).

2 Overviews

The Byzantine Church in the twelfth century

Church organisation

Bishops

The highest ecclesiastical order in the Byzantine Church was that of the bishop.[1] By 'bishop' we mean any cleric who had received episcopal ordination, be it a 'suffragan', 'metropolitan', 'archbishop', or 'patriarch'. These titles indicated a hierarchy of honour, with the patriarch standing at the top. It was his duty to ensure that all the faithful, including the emperor, followed the biblical and canonical teachings. There were five patriarchates (Rome, Constantinople, Alexandria, Antioch, and Jerusalem), but in the twelfth century some of them had more than one patriarch owing to historical schisms within the Church.[2] Relations between them were often problematic, with Rome and Constantinople being in schism since 1054.[3] Nonetheless, the ideal of the pentarchy remained alive, and Balsamon defended the divine origin of the complete equality of the five patriarchal sees.[4] The patriarch of Constantinople was elected by the emperor based on three recommendations by the metropolitans.[5] He, in turn, crowned the emperor in the church of the Hagia Sophia.[6] Together, they were the twin pillars upholding Byzantine society.

After the patriarch came the metropolitans. These were bishops who resided in major cities and not only were responsible for their own territory but also had rights over their comprovincial bishoprics, their suffragan sees.[7] There were over ninety metropolitans in the twelfth century, at least thirty of whom were within the political frontiers of the Byzantine Empire.[8] Vacant seats were filled by a Constantinopolitan synod of other metropolitans and archbishops who were present in the capital at any given time. The patriarch was not meant to take part in the discussions, but made the final decision between three selected candidates.[9] During this period, most metropolitans began their careers in the patriarchal administration.[10]

Archbishops were similar to metropolitans and the two terms are often used interchangeably. In theory, archbishops were in charge of important sees which did not have suffragans and remained under patriarchal supervision.[11] But there were important exceptions. Notably, the archbishopric of Ohrid, created in 1018 after Basil II's annexation of Bulgaria and Macedonia, was allowed to keep its suffragan sees and was placed under the authority of the emperor.[12] In the twelfth century, there were over fifty archbishoprics in Byzantium.[13]

Suffragan bishops were responsible for their individual sees, ensuring the standards of clerics, monks, and laymen within them. Each diocese was usually quite small, often not much bigger than a village. There were more than 750 bishoprics in this period, with around 400 of them within the political frontiers of the empire.[14] Bishops were meant to reside within their episcopal see and absenteeism was decried by the canons. Visits to the capital were often necessary, but it was compulsory to obtain prior permission from the patriarch. Starting in the eleventh century, this rule was relaxed as bishops from Asia Minor and Syria found refuge in Constantinople after they were driven from their sees by Turkish raids.[15]

According to canon law, bishops were to be elected locally by their metropolitan based on recommendations of at least three of their comprovincials.[16] Already in the ninth century, however, episcopal elections were taking place at synods in Constantinople. In the mid-eleventh century, this uncanonical practice was criticised by Patriarch Michael Kerularios (1043–1059), before it was accepted in 1072 by John VIII Xiphilinos (1064–1075).[17] In terms of the candidates, typical paths for those who aspired to a bishopric in the twelfth century included a distinguished teaching career and service in the patriarchal administration. Many bishops came from ecclesiastical families, often with their uncles and other relatives also holding episcopal honours. Some bishops were drawn from monasteries, but these do not seem to have formed the majority.[18]

Priests, deacons, and subdeacons

The rank of priest was immediately below that of bishop. Because of the small size of bishoprics, priests were normally attached to a diocese. A system of parish churches similar to that in the West never developed in Byzantium. The bishop's cathedral church and its immediate dependencies were referred to as καθολικαὶ ἐκκλησίαι, 'catholic' or public churches. These were the principal churches of a diocese, where services were open to everyone, and were most commonly found in cities rather than the countryside.[19] Priests also served in private foundations, such as family chapels, where they could perform mass, baptisms, and weddings.[20] The minimum age of ordination to the priesthood was 30.[21]

Deacons were under the authority of bishops and priests, whom they assisted with the celebration of sacraments. Despite their subordinate position in the liturgy, they often came to exercise considerable authority, and could claim precedence over priests.[22] The minimum age of ordination to the diaconate was 25. Subdeacons occupied a liminal position between major and minor orders.[23] Their minimum age of ordination was 20.[24] This younger age reflects the lesser responsibilities that a subdeacon would have compared to a deacon or a priest. Nonetheless, for our purposes this was an important stage in a cleric's life: it was by this point that he had to decide between celibacy and marriage. If he decided to marry, he would need to observe temporary abstinence before his service at the altar. This was expected of all married subdeacons, deacons, and priests. The exact time of abstinence for those in sacred orders was not clearly defined. Based on the rules on nocturnal emissions and on marital intercourse between lay spouses, we can conjecture that they would have needed to abstain at least on the day of their service as well as on the night before it.[25] Balsamon further informs us that in big churches (αἱ μεγάλαι ἐκκλησίαι) the ministrations of those in sacred orders had been divided into weekly periods. In this way, they could abstain from their wives during the time of their service and assume their conjugal duties only on alternate weeks.[26]

Minor orders

The two most important minor orders were those of the reader and the singer.[27] Neither had access to the sanctuary (βῆμα) where the Eucharistic sacrifice was celebrated. Initially, the reader's role was to read the Epistles from the ambo, an elevated platform in the middle of the *naos*, where the lay congregation attended services.[28] In Zonaras' time, it was rare for readers to read; instead their main duty was to sing.[29] Singers could be located above and beneath the ambo, directly in front of the altar, or, increasingly in the twelfth century, on either side of the *naos* as choirs often worked antiphonally.[30] Both singers and readers had limited access to the sacred and both were allowed to marry and follow the same rules of abstinence as laymen.[31] Married singers, however, must have been unusual in the twelfth century, as many among them were eunuchs.[32] Eunuchs were forbidden to marry, but were allowed to adopt children.[33]

Offices

In addition to these ranks, there were ecclesiastical offices.[34] These were in principle clerical positions attached to certain responsibilities, but also financial benefits and honours. They represented a separate hierarchy and their ranking complicated the picture. The two most important offices of the Hagia Sophia were those of the *oikonomos*, who was responsible for the administration of revenues and properties, and the *skeuophylax*, who acted as treasurer.[35] The right of nomination to these offices was in itself an important privilege. By the eleventh century, it had become an imperial prerogative, but Emperor Isaac I Komnenos (r. 1057–1059) granted it back to Patriarch Kerularios as a reward for political support.[36]

The English Church in the twelfth century

Church organisation

Clerics formed a minority group, composing perhaps about 1 to 1.25 per cent of the adult male population towards the end of the twelfth century.[37] They played important roles in Anglo-Norman society and could be found in a variety of settings, acting as cathedral or parish clergy, chaplains, scribes, and teachers. As in Byzantium, they were divided into ecclesiastical grades.[38] In the Roman Church the clerical orders were fixed in the middle of the third century and consisted of the following ranks: doorkeeper, exorcist, reader, acolyte, subdeacon, deacon, priest, and bishop.[39] In England, the same list was stabilised by about the end of the eighth century. Priests and deacons were clearly part of the sacred orders; subdeacons occupied a liminal position; and clerics below the subdiaconate formed the minor orders. The grades of doorkeeper and exorcist had already become dead letters before the end of the eighth century, while the duties of readers were taken over by deacons and subdeacons. By the eleventh century references to readers had become extremely rare, and references to exorcists and doorkeepers non-existent except in ordination liturgies. The most important of the minor orders was that of the acolyte and many young trainee clerics were at that grade. Although acolytes could not perform mass or provide pastoral care, they could hold churches as long as they provided a priest who would undertake these services.[40]

Archbishops

At the head of the Church in England stood the archbishop of Canterbury.[41] He was responsible for the supervision of clergy and laity within his archdiocese as well as the management of the great estates attached to his position. He was one of the wealthiest landholders in England (with revenues in 1086 to the value of £1,750), and played an important role in the politics of the realm. His main competition within England came from the archbishop of York, with whom a long-running dispute regarding the primacy of Canterbury over York began in the autumn of 1070, causing disunity within the English Church and allowing for papal interventions. The position of the archbishops of York was that the two prelates were equal, while the archbishops of Canterbury demanded a profession of obedience.[42]

Bishops

In the mid-twelfth century, there were seventeen bishoprics in England, divided into ten with monastic cathedrals (Canterbury; Bath and Wells; Carlisle; Coventry; Durham; Ely; Norwich; Rochester; Winchester; Worcester) and seven with secular cathedrals (Chichester; Exeter; Hereford; Lincoln; London; Salisbury; York).[43] In territorial terms there were three very large bishoprics (Lincoln, York, and Coventry), several of middling size, and three very small ones (Canterbury, Rochester, and Ely).[44] The average size was about 3,000 square miles.[45] How easily this distance was traversed depended on the bishopric's shape. At one extreme we find Rochester, measuring no more than 35 miles at its widest, a distance that could be covered in two days; at the other, Lincoln, requiring eight days of riding to go from its cathedral to its southern tip near Reading, some 170 miles away.[46]

Bishops could come from a variety of backgrounds. Under the first three Norman kings, most bishops rose through the royal chancery or chapel. This changed during King Stephen's reign (r. 1135–1154), when almost all new bishops were either monks or clerics affiliated with episcopal households. During Henry II's reign (r. 1154–1189), there was a halt to new appointments between 1163 and 1173. When appointments resumed, many royal clerics were once again established to the episcopal bench. Clerics related to other ecclesiastics, however, also became a permanent fixture and even outnumbered royal favourites. Episcopal elections were meant to be free, with the body of canons or monks deciding on their next bishop, but the vote was normally held in the royal chapel and only a small, and therefore more pliable, part of the chapter was present.[47] As such, the king could have great influence over the decision. The reigns of Richard I (r. 1089–1099) and John (r. 1099–1216) also saw the rise of highly learned clerics, many of whom bore the title *Magister*, suggesting the growing importance of education in clerical recruitment.[48]

The cathedral chapter

Cathedral communities could consist of monks or canons.[49] Monastic cathedrals were a particularly English phenomenon, established by the Anglo-Saxons. The Normans approved of them and established new ones at Rochester, Durham, and elsewhere. Canons were divided into regular and secular. Regular canons were similar to monks in that they had to take vows of poverty, chastity, and obedience and agree to live under a Rule. Instead of St Benedict's Rule, regular canons followed the Rule attributed to St Augustine. The order of the Augustinians blossomed during the reign of Henry I (r. 1100–1135). Notably, in 1133 the new diocese of Carlisle housed a group of Augustinian canons, instead of monks.[50] Secular canons, on the other hand, did not have to follow a specific Rule, could own property, and were not required to lead a communal life.[51] More generally, they were expected to engage with the world, providing pastoral care for the laity.[52] Secular cathedrals in England were organised along the continental model of the chapter, in which three major officers, the precentor, the chancellor, and the treasurer, served under the presidency of the dean and had responsibility for liturgy, education, and financial administration. The cathedral's revenues were largely divided between the bishop and some of the chapter's canons, called prebendaries. In the English Church as a whole there were about 300 prebendaries attached to secular cathedrals (25 to 50 per cathedral) and many more attached to major collegiate churches – that is, non-monastic communities of clergy with no diocesan responsibilities.[53] A prebend was the canon's benefice with its material appurtenances, in lands, tithes, churches, and so forth.[54] Cathedral and collegiate clerics had wealth, learning, and authority: they had a solid financial foundation in their prebend, were well educated, and participated in both royal and ecclesiastical government.[55]

Parish clergy

In addition to canons, parish personnel composed the overwhelming majority of the secular clergy.[56] Parish churches in England were many and small. There was a great increase in their number from the late tenth to the mid-twelfth centuries, a phenomenon that was not paralleled elsewhere in northern Europe. To give just two examples, by the beginning of the thirteenth century, London had ninety-nine parish churches within its walls, and Winchester fifty-seven.[57] On average, in London there was one parish church per 3.5 acres.[58]

Parish churches were served by priests, who could provide liturgical and pastoral duties, but they were not necessarily held by them. Often a rector (or parson) would take the income provided through offerings, tithes, and the church's landed endowment, but another person, called a vicar, would be appointed in his stead to be resident at the parish. Successful rectors might be pluralists and hold many parishes. The rector's link with his parish could be of a purely financial nature.[59] From the time of the Conquest and especially during the first half of the twelfth century there was a decrease in lay profits from proprietary churches, and ownership was largely reduced to patronage and the right to nominate a priest who had to be found suitable by the bishop. The rapid flourishing of canon law helped shape public opinion against lay reception of tithes and spiritual offerings, leading to a tendency to grant parish churches to monasteries. This did not guarantee that parish churches would avoid financial exploitation, but in some cases simply changed the recipient of misappropriated revenues.[60]

Archdeacons

The great size of sees combined with the growing amount of ecclesiastical business meant that further territorial subdivision was necessary. The main ecclesiastical unit below the bishopric was the archdeaconry. Archdeacons acted as episcopal deputies and were in charge of supervising the parishes within their archdeaconries. This meant supervision of moral standards, including the prevention of clerical concubinage, and more practical issues, such as the availability of liturgical vessels. Archdeacons in this territorial sense were a new introduction into England in the 1070s.[61]

Mutual interactions

The primary purpose of this study is to compare the Anglo-Norman and Byzantine contexts as separate entities, yet it is worth giving an overview of the contact that did exist between these two societies, and especially their legal interactions, in order to establish the extent to which Eastern and Western canonical views were based on common foundations.[62] The focus will be on the twelfth century, but it is important to contextualise the study within significant developments in the eleventh century. First, there was the 1054 schism, which brought East and West into direct opposition, particularly on the topics of papal primacy, the use of unleavened Eucharistic bread, and clerical celibacy. This confrontation made Byzantine ecclesiastics reflect on their own customs and influenced their later relations with the papacy.[63] However, even after 1054, friendly relations continued and the importance of the schism should not be overstated. Tension between

Rome and Constantinople did not stop many Anglo-Saxons from seeking refuge in the Byzantine Empire after the Norman Conquest of 1066.[64] The Crusades, on the other hand, were to a great extent to blame for solidifying differences, by introducing hostile feelings at a popular level. A notable example is that of the capture of Antioch by the Norman crusader Bohemond I in 1098 and his subsequent appointment of a Latin patriarch, which caused an outcry in both Antioch and Constantinople.[65] Emperor Manuel Komnenos was keen on a reunion of the two Churches, but his attempts were unsuccessful. The culmination of the strong anti-Latin sentiment that had taken over Constantinople came with the 1182 massacre of the Latins.[66] Then, in 1204, the disastrous Fourth Crusade took place; it started as an attempt to recapture Jerusalem and ended as the sack of Constantinople – an event that is still remembered sorely by the Greek Church.[67]

Legal interactions

Ecclesiastical councils

One of the consequences of the 1054 schism was the separation of Eastern and Western conciliar traditions.[68] In Byzantium, the gap was filled by the patriarchal council of Constantinople, the so-called Endemousa Synodos. By this time, the Endemousa had become a more or less permanent assembly, presided over by the patriarch and composed of bishops, visiting or residing in the vicinity. It met often but not on a regular basis, and its decisions affected the religious and the laity within the Byzantine Empire, occasionally including those under the jurisdiction of other Eastern patriarchates.[69] The Roman Church also continued its own conciliar trajectory, with both local and Lateran councils (Lateran I in 1123; Lateran II in 1139; Lateran III in 1179; and Lateran IV in 1215). Local councils were important for the dissemination of papal ideas on the ground. This was especially the case during the eleventh century, when the papacy was trying to spread its reformist views against clerical marriage around Western Europe. In the twelfth century, there were still periods of intense conciliar activity, but the number of local councils went into decline.[70] Lateran councils had a more universal character, but were still meant to promulgate law primarily for the Churches under Rome's jurisdiction. Almost all of their participants came from the West, or in rare cases, from Eastern Churches in communion with Rome. One exception was Lateran III, to which Manuel Komnenos sent Nektarios, abbot of Casula, as an observer.[71] In Lateran IV another Byzantine featured in the conciliar list, Theodore of Negroponte, a bishop who had yielded to Latin control after the Fourth Crusade and was there to accompany Gervais, the Latin patriarch of Constantinople (1215–1219).[72]

Despite this divergence, East and West shared much of their conciliar tradition, especially when it came to the ecumenical councils. As we have seen, these formed the basis of the twelfth-century canonical commentaries in Byzantium. In the West too, they shaped the law both as authorities in support of newer conciliar decrees and through their inclusion in canonical collections, such as Ivo's

Decretum, the *Tripartita*, and the *Panormia*.[73] Importantly, Gratian's *Decretum* quoted almost 200 chapters from Eastern councils, ranging from Nicaea I (325) to Constantinople IV (869–870), and including eighteen references to the Council in Trullo (691/2). Although the latter was not generally accepted as ecumenical in the West, Gratian had no problem receiving the Trullan canons, ascribing them to Constantinople III (680–681).[74] Constantinople IV (869–870), the council that deposed Patriarch Photios, was accepted in Gratian (D.16 c.8) as an eighth ecumenical council.[75] The decretists made use of this material, following Gratian (D.15 c.2), and placed particular importance on the first four councils (Nicaea I; Constantinople I; Ephesus; Chalcedon), which already from the time of Gregory the Great had been compared to the four gospels.[76] Nonetheless, we should not assume that the decretists had a great knowledge of this material, as some seem confused about the numbering and even the exact list of ecumenical councils.[77]

What is more, even when East and West shared the text of the canons, there could occasionally exist drastically different interpretations of even their basic meaning. A case in point was canon 3 of Nicaea I (325), which forbade certain 'suspicious women' from cohabiting with clerics, without making an explicit reference to wives.[78] This absence allowed for a different interpretation: in the West, wives were included in the list of suspicious women, while in the East they were excluded. As such, it is not surprising that this canon, which was perfectly acceptable in Byzantium, was quoted by Lateran I (1123) in favour of clerical celibacy.[79] Other canons were understood *ex tempore* or *ex loco* – that is to say, they had been promulgated for a different time or place and no longer applied.[80] This is, for example, how the *Summa Lipsiensis* explained a letter of Pope Gregory the Great (591) which made allowances for married subdeacons who had not vowed continence upon ordination.[81] Finally, some canons were altogether rejected, although the council they belonged to was accepted.[82]

Church fathers

In addition to conciliar legislation, patristic canons formed an important part of Byzantine ecclesiastical law. The list of Fathers included in canonical collections was stabilised in the twelfth century, with many earlier manuscripts presenting variations in content and sequence.[83] The Fathers whose writings were ratified by canon 2 of Trullo were Cyprian of Carthage (d. 258); Dionysios of Alexandria (d. 264x265); Gregory Thaumaturgos (c. 210–c. 270); Peter of Alexandria (d. 311); Athanasios of Alexandria (c. 295–373); Basil the Great (330–379); Timotheos of Alexandria (d. 385); Gregory of Nazianzos (d. 390); Gregory of Nyssa (331/340–c. 395); Amphilochios of Iconium (340–345; 394–403); Theophilos of Alexandria (c. 345–412); Cyril of Alexandria (c. 380–444); and Gennadios of Constantinople (c. 400–471).[84] A notable absence is that of John Chrysostom, whose writings were of a literary rather than a disciplinary nature, and as such did not figure in Trullo's list. Nonetheless, they had great influence on the later commentaries of Zonaras and Balsamon.

In the West, the first collection containing texts from patristic literature was the Irish *Hibernensis*, composed in the early eighth century. In addition to Eastern, Gallic, and Irish councils, it included 479 quotations from Church Fathers. Jerome (168), Augustine (94), Isidore (65), and Gregory the Great (54) topped the list of patristic extracts, but a number of Greek Fathers also featured, including Origen (43), Gregory of Nazianzus (11), and Basil (3). In the following centuries references to the Eastern Church Fathers remained infrequent.[85] The early eleventh-century *Decretum* of Burchard of Worms contained around 14 per cent patristic texts, with Augustine (79 texts), Gregory the Great (77), Isidore (31), and Jerome (19) being the most represented, followed by three Eastern Fathers: Basil (11), Origen (7), and John Chrysostom (5).[86] The *Decretum* of Ivo of Chartres also contained 10 quotations by Chrysostom, but the number seems meagre compared to 456 quotations from Augustine. The latter's popularity in this period had much increased and many of the new quotations related to his views on marriage and sexuality.[87] In Gratian's *Decretum*, Augustine's passages represented 44 per cent, Jerome's 14 per cent, Ambrose 13 per cent, and Gregory the Great's 8 per cent, while the Greek Fathers, as a whole, constituted only 7 per cent.[88] In Gratian's section on marriage (Causae 27–36), the difference is again significant, with seventy-eight quotations from Augustine and two from Chrysostom.[89] After Gratian's *Decretum*, the influence of patristic sources in canon law began to decline and later canonical collections, such as the *Liber Extra*, focused instead on papal decretals.

If the Eastern Fathers had little influence in the West, how much impact did Western patristics have on Byzantine canon law? Of particular interest are Augustine and Gregory the Great, whose views shaped discussions about sexuality and marriage in Western canon law. Of the two, Augustine was far less influential, as it was only in the thirteenth century that substantial parts of his work were translated.[90] Nonetheless, as a Father, Augustine was held in high respect and his name was mentioned at the ecumenical councils of Ephesus (431), Constantinople III (680–681), and Nicaea II (787). Importantly, he was also quoted as an authority at a synod under Manuel Komnenos (1166), which examined the meaning of the biblical verse 'For my Father is greater than I' (John 14:28).[91] His expertise, however, was thought to lie in heresy, not marriage.

Gregory the Great formed an exception to the Byzantine indifference towards Latin authors in general.[92] What made him acceptable was his very affinity with Byzantine ascetic thought: his work was incorporated into the Eastern tradition because it corresponded with it in the first place. His most popular work, his *Dialogues*, was translated into Greek by Pope Zacharias (741–752).[93] Its influence is seen in the eleventh century in the *Synagoge* of Paul Evergetinos, a monastic florilegium of spiritual texts, put together for the monastery of Theotokos Evergetis.[94] The topics for which Gregory was used as an authority were primarily monastic in nature, or concerned with death, dreams, and the afterlife.[95] One of the passages from the *Dialogues* which was included in the *Synagoge* dealt with clerical marriage. It was the story of a cleric who, after being ordained to the priesthood, 'loved his wife as a brother loves his sister' and avoided her like an enemy. Even on his deathbed, he forbade her from approaching him, fearful of rekindling his passions. This priest was going above and beyond; he was not only abstaining from marital sex (which was unlawful to engage in according to the Western Church) but also avoiding his wife's domestic services (which would have been lawful to accept). This makes Gregory exclaim, 'It is characteristic of holy men always to keep their distance from what is unlawful, and in doing so they usually deny themselves even what is lawful.'[96] This story would have an obvious appeal for the Western Church where clerical celibacy was required, but at the same time was not problematic for the East. A Byzantine reader would have understood sexual intercourse as one of the lawful things that the priest in his pious zeal preferred to abstain from. As with the canons, so with patristic stories, interpretations could be found which justified, instead of challenging, existing custom.

Canons of the Apostles

The canons of the Apostles were a collection of eighty-five rulings included at the end of Book 8 of the Apostolic Constitutions, itself a pseudepigraphic compilation produced in Syria around 380. Only fifty of them were translated into Latin by Dionysius Exiguus (c. 500), who raised doubts about their apostolic origins. Later on Pope Hormisdas (514–523) decreed the compilation to be apocryphal, but part of it managed to enter the pseudo-Isidorian Decretals as well as Gratian's *Decretum*, which included seventeen of the fifty canons translated by Dionysius.[97] In the East, all eighty-five canons were considered authoritative. They were ratified by Justinian's legislation and canon 2 of the Council in Trullo placed them ahead of the canons of Nicaea I in its list of authorities.[98]

Papal decretals

Greater divergence between East and West came with the growing importance of papal letters. In England, their flow increased in the twelfth century when decline in royal power in the case of Henry II, and royal absence in the case of Richard, allowed for papal intervention. Although such decretals were meant to deal with specific problems, their inclusion in canonical collections guaranteed their continuing influence. Anne Duggan has looked at the three earliest surviving decretal collections, *Wigoriensis altera*, *Belverensis*, and *Cantuarensis*, which were compiled in episcopal households in England in the decade 1172/3–1184. She concludes that there was a lively exchange of material between episcopal and academic centres, which spread across the Latin Church and was not dependent on papal initiative.[99] These letters also played an important role in the formulation of English conciliar legislation: they were used, alongside the *Decretum*, to validate canonical decisions. For example, it has been shown that the opening canon of the 1175 Westminster council, which dealt with clerical marriage and hereditary succession, was based on a decretal known as *Inter cetera sollicitudinis* sent to Bishop Roger of Worcester in 1164. English ecclesiastics used decretals not only as inspiration for their councils but also as supplements when decisions could not be made based on existing authorities. Notably, following the same council,

Archbishop Richard of Canterbury (1173–1184) obtained from Pope Alexander III (1159–1181) nine additional decretals related to conciliar topics on which it had not been possible to reach a decision.[100] Such decretals had no validity in Byzantium and were probably not known to the canonists. Indeed, no concrete proof exists that even the latest of the three canonists, Theodore Balsamon, had read Gratian's *Decretum*, although the regular contact between the court of Manuel Komnenos and the West could have made it possible.[101]

Imperial legislation

Imperial legislation was very important for the twelfth-century Byzantine Church and had been so for many centuries, with a tradition of emperors legislating heavily on ecclesiastical matters.[102] The Byzantines even combined their ecclesiastical canons (*kanones*) with civil laws (*nomoi*), creating the so-called *nomokanones*, such as the *Nomokanon of Fourteen Titles*.[103] It is therefore not surprising that the twelfth-century canonists used civil laws in their commentaries.[104] Indeed, Balsamon notoriously quotes more imperial decrees than canons in his commentary to the *Nomokanon*.[105] These included Justinian's and Leo VI's legislative works, as well as newer imperial laws, with the last novel of certain chronology mentioned having been issued after April 1193 in the reign of Isaak II Angelos.[106] These civil and ecclesiastical laws could complement each other, but they could also clash. When that happened both Zonaras and Balsamon would support the power of the canon over that of a civil decree.[107]

In the West, there was a revival of Roman law in the eleventh and twelfth centuries triggered by the rediscovery of Justinian's *Digest*.[108] Gratian's first recension largely excluded Roman law and his compiler seems to have had a poor grasp of it.[109] Gratian 2, on the other hand, incorporated just short of fifty Justinianic texts from the *Digest*, the *Codex*, and the *Authenticae* (twelfth-century summaries of Latin texts of imperial laws collected after the publication of Justinian's Code and entered in the margins of its manuscripts).[110] It also included texts from other collections of imperial laws, such as the *Breviarium Alaricianum* (506), the *Codex Theodosianus* (438), and the *Constitutions of Sirmond*.[111] All newer imperial decrees, however, were excluded.

Overall, East and West shared a canonical tradition which included most ecumenical and some local councils of the pre-1054 period. Other canons, such as those of the Apostles and the Church Fathers, were also selectively shared, but the overlap was not great. Augustine, who came to dominate the West on questions of sexuality and marriage, was thoroughly ignored in Byzantium. Papal decretals did much to widen the divide, as did newer imperial decrees, with only some Late Antique civil laws, and especially Justinian, being common to both. To some extent, these differences must have shaped twelfth-century views on clerical marriage. Attitudes might have been different if John Chrysostom had been as frequently cited in the West as Augustine, or if Augustine had managed to gain a foothold in Byzantium. Nonetheless, the similarities must not be underestimated, as the two societies had their firmest common foundation in the Bible.

The rules of clerical abstinence

Clerical marriage in Byzantium

In the twelfth century, the main distinction in terms of clerical marriage in Byzantium was drawn along hierarchical lines: bishops were subject to different rules from priests, deacons, and subdeacons, and those in turn differed from the rules for readers and singers. Bishops were expected to observe complete abstinence after their ordination to the episcopate. If they happened to be married, they had to put their wife away in a monastery and no longer cohabit or have sexual intercourse with her. Priests, deacons, and subdeacons, if married, had to observe only temporary abstinence before their service at the altar. Readers and singers followed the same rules as laymen, meaning that they had to abstain mostly as a preparation for communion and during certain feast days; they could also choose to marry at any point. It was only after ordination to the subdiaconate that clerics no longer had the right to take a wife. Such prohibitions of marriage after ordination applied not only to first wives but also to subsequent ones in the cases of widowhood or divorce. These rules, however, were not fixed as such from the beginning, but changed over time, especially in relation to bishops and subdeacons.

Initially, subdeacons were not explicitly included in the list of clerics who needed to observe temporary abstinence or who were forbidden to marry.[112] In fact, even deacons were at first treated more leniently. Acknowledging the difficulty of deciding on celibacy at a young age, canon 10 of the council of Ancyra (314) allowed deacons to declare during their ordination their wish to marry at a later date.[113] This practice was prohibited in the sixth century by Emperor Justinian (r. 527–565), but seems to have continued.[114] We hear of a similar occurrence in the late ninth century, when Emperor Leo VI (r. 886–912) had to forbid the custom of priests marrying within two years of their ordination.[115] In theory, however, an implicit prohibition against marrying after the subdiaconate had already been included in the canons of the Apostles (c. 380). More specifically, it could be *inferred* from canon 26 that subdeacons were not allowed to take a wife, as they were not mentioned alongside readers and singers, who were given permission to do so.[116] This was already assumed in Justinian's civil legislation, but the Council in Trullo (691/2) was the first to incorporate it into canon law.[117] Balsamon in his commentary acknowledged the ambiguity and stated that Trullo was filling a gap.[118] He clearly considered subdeacons part of the major orders and expected them to follow the same rules as priests and deacons.[119]

The right of priests, deacons, and subdeacons to marry before their ordination to the subdiaconate and enjoy sexual intercourse with their wives was never seriously challenged in Byzantium. It came up as an issue of contention in the discussions surrounding the 1054 schism between Rome and Constantinople, when the Byzantines vigorously defended their position against Latin accusations of sexual pollution.[120] This was probably the closest that the Byzantine clergy came to being confronted with Western reformist ideas on the unsavoury nature of clerical sexuality.

Episcopal marriage, however, came to an end at least as early as the Council in Trullo, which was the first to promulgate an ecclesiastical law imposing celibacy upon bishops.[121] This applied to all clerics who had received episcopal ordination, including metropolitans, archbishops, and patriarchs. It stipulated that bishops who were married had to separate from their spouses by mutual consent.[122] Episcopal wives would live in monastic communities and, if necessary, would receive support from their ex-husbands, who were otherwise to keep their distance.[123] Previous canonical legislation required bishops to observe only temporary abstinence. There had, however, been civil laws, issued by Emperor Justinian (528), which prohibited not only wives but also any descendants.[124] Canon law never considered children an obstacle to ordination, and the discrepancy was finally resolved by Emperor Leo VI, who abolished Justinian's law.[125] The topic of episcopal marriage came up again briefly in 1186/7, when Isaac II Angelos decreed that episcopal wives had to agree not simply to live in a monastery but to fully embrace monastic life. The emperor also decried the fact that many bishops ignored previous legislation, refusing to put their spouses away and continuing to live with them after ordination.[126]

Clerical celibacy in England

The beginnings of the imposition of clerical celibacy in the Roman Church are hard to determine.[127] Already in the first two centuries some restrictions were in place, including the expectation that clergymen would be married only once and would not marry after ordination.[128] However, no universal policy seems to have been established. In the fourth century, with the expansion of Christianity under Emperor Constantine (r. 306–337) and the rise of monasticism, many attempts were made to police clerical sexuality.[129] Canons in favour of continence for priests and deacons continued to appear in Western legislation of the fifth and sixth centuries, but their enforcement varied greatly across Europe.[130] The expectation was that although a cleric in major orders could have a wife, he would stop having sexual intercourse with her after his ordination and would observe absolute continence.[131]

In England, clerical marriage was discussed in seventh- and eighth-century ecclesiastical sources, with evidence from Bede (c. 673–735), Theodore's penitential (c. 700), and the dialogues of Archbishop Ecgbert of York (after 735) suggesting that there were married priests and deacons and that they needed to abstain from sex.[132] In the ninth century, King Alfred's (r. 871–899) efforts to reduce clerical concubinage were praised by Fulk, archbishop of Rheims.[133] In the tenth century, King Edmund's code (941x946) put the question of clerical chastity first amidst a list of ecclesiastical issues that needed to be dealt with. Those who did not follow the rules would lose their property as well as forfeit the right to a consecrated burial.[134] But it was during King Edgar's reign (r. 959–975) that reforming efforts were particularly strong.[135] Edgar himself was actively involved, along with Bishops Dunstan, Oswald, and Æthelwold, who agitated for change, such as the replacement of married clerics with monks.[136] Rules about the celibacy of priests also appeared in canonical collections of the time, such as the 'Canons of Edgar' (1005x1108), drafted by Wulfstan, archbishop of York (1002–1023).[137] These emphasised the connection between the priest and the Church, which was presented as his wife. The expectation of absolute continence applied not only to parish priests but also to all cathedral canons, whose communal life of sharing food and property seemed incompatible with having a family.[138] One of the novelties in England was the preponderance of vernacular preaching, which helped promote the reforms in a language that could be easily understood by clergy and laity.[139] There was, however, regional variation and in some areas in the north clerical marriage seems to have been tolerated more than in the south.[140] Yet it is clear that efforts to establish a celibate priesthood had already begun in England on a local level before the Gregorian reforms of the eleventh century.

The eleventh and twelfth centuries saw increased interest in the mores of the English clergy.[141] In 1076, Archbishop Lanfranc decreed that any priest who already had a wife could continue living with her, but no priest or canon would be allowed to marry in the future; priests and deacons were to take a vow of chastity upon ordination.[142] In 1102, Archbishop Anselm adopted a stricter approach, including subdeacons in the list of clerics who needed to profess chastity, and expecting archdeacons, priests, deacons, and canons who had already taken a wife to abandon her.[143] A generation later, in 1129, another council gave archdeacons and priests two months to give up their wives, but this ultimatum was undermined by King Henry I's willingness to accept cash payments from those who preferred to keep their spouses.[144] In terms of papal legislation, a turning point was reached at Lateran II in 1139, which made ordination a diriment impediment to marriage and included subdeacons among the list of clergy who needed to be celibate.[145] Previously there would have been financial penalties for ordained clerics who chose to take a wife, but their marriage would still be considered valid.

Legislation against clerical marriage continued to be promulgated in the later twelfth century. In 1175, the Council of Westminster reminded priests who lived with 'harlots' (*fornicaria*) that they needed to disown them or lose their office and benefice.[146] Yet in 1208 clerics still had concubines whom King John could seize and use to extract a heavy ransom.[147] In 1215, Pope Innocent III at Lateran IV would reaffirm the Gregorian commitment to celibacy.[148] But in 1225, a further order of the archbishop of Canterbury and his suffragans was necessary, threatening clerical concubines that they would be denied church burial, the kiss of peace, and the reception of communion, unless they reformed their lives.[149] The large number of reiterations of the laws of clerical celibacy suggests that nothing much was changing. Yet, despite early and intense opposition, results were achieved.[150] In the thirteenth century, no English bishop is known to have been a husband or father.[151]

Notes

1 See also M. Cunningham, 'Clergy, Monks, and Laity', in *The Oxford Handbook of Byzantine Studies*, eds. R. Cormack, J.F. Haldon, and E. Jeffreys (Oxford, 2008),

527–35; K. Kotsis, 'The Greek Orthodox Church', in *Handbook of Medieval Culture: Fundamental Aspects and Conditions of the European Middle Ages*, ed. A. Classen (Berlin, 2015), 628–52.

2 J. Richard, 'The Eastern Churches', in *The New Cambridge Medieval History IV, c. 1024–c. 1198, Part I*, eds. D. Luscombe and J. Riley-Smith (Cambridge, 2004), 564–98; J. Binns, *An Introduction to the Christian Orthodox Churches* (Cambridge, 2002).

3 Louth, *Greek East and Latin West*, 305–18; B.E. Whalen, 'Rethinking the Schism of 1054: Authority, Heresy, and the Latin Rite', *Traditio*, 62 (2007), 1–24; J.R. Ryder, 'Changing Perspectives on 1054', *Byzantine and Modern Greek Studies*, 35:1 (2011), 20–37.

4 Gallagher, *Church Law and Church Order*, 164–74.

5 See also the case of Alexios the Studite (1025–1043), who was appointed without nominations by the metropolitans, in J.M. Hussey, *The Orthodox Church in the Byzantine Empire* (Oxford, 2010, 2nd edn.), 127–8, 312–14. For a twelfth-century example, see J. Darrouzès, 'L'éloge de Nicolas III par Nicolas Mouzalon', *REB*, 46 (1988), 5–53, at 40–4.

6 Although it was acclamation that made an emperor, it was believed that in the case of usurpations only coronation by the patriarch could remove the stigma. See Angold, *Church and Society*, 23.

7 For example, metropolitans could inflict ecclesiastical punishment on a suffragan bishop, but were not allowed to perform liturgical services in the latter's diocese without permission. E. Herman, 'The Secular Church', in *The Cambridge Medieval History, Vol. IV: The Byzantine Empire, Part II*, ed. J.M. Hussey (Cambridge, 1967), 104–33, at 111.

8 The hierarchy of bishoprics was recorded in the *Notitiae Episcopatuum*. Here see Notitia 12 in J. Darrouzès, *Notitiae Episcopatuum Ecclesiae Constantinopolitanae. Texte critique, introduction et notes* (Paris, 1981), 348–50. See also Angold, *Church and Society*, 141.

9 Hussey, *The Orthodox Church*, 320.

10 Angold, *Church and Society*, 146.

11 Hussey, *The Orthodox Church*, 325.

12 Before Ohrid turned into an archbishopric, it held the status of a patriarchate. See J.V.A. Fine, *The Early Medieval Balkans: A Critical Survey From the Sixth to the Late Twelfth Century* (Ann Arbor, MI, 1991, 2nd edn.), 199. See also Angold, *Church and Society*, 158–9.

13 Notitia 12 in Darrouzès, *Notitiae Episcopatuum*, 351–2.

14 Notitia 13 in Darrouzès, *Notitiae Episcopatuum*, 354–69. See also Angold, *Church and Society*, 141.

15 Herman, 'The Secular Church', 112.

16 Canon 4 of Nicaea I (325) decreed that a bishop was to be chosen by at least three of his future colleagues and the metropolitan was to ratify their decision. This was reiterated at Nicaea II (787), canon 3, and at Constantinople IV (869/870), canon 22. See B. Moulet, *Évêques, pouvoir et société à Byzance (VIIIe–XIe siècle)* (Paris, 2011), 246–7. See also *Syntagma* 2.122–4 and 2.564–6.

17 Hussey, *The Orthodox Church*, 326.

18 Angold has argued that the supposition that the majority of bishops were monks receives little support from episcopal seals, comparatively few of which bear the legend 'monk and bishop'. He therefore concludes that 'the monastic contribution was important, but must be kept in proportion.' See Angold, *Church and Society*, 146–7. See also M. Angold, 'The Imperial Administration and the Patriarchal Clergy in the Twelfth Century', *Byzantinische Forschungen*, 19 (1993), 17–24.

19 M. Angold and M. Whitby, 'III.11.1 Church Structures and Administration', in *The Oxford Handbook of Byzantine Studies*, eds. E. Jeffreys, J. Haldon, and R. Cormack

(Oxford, 2008), 571–82, at 578–9; J.P. Thomas, *Private Religious Foundations in the Byzantine Empire* (Washington, DC, 1987), 5.

20 Baptisms in private foundations had been officially allowed by Leo VI. In the twelfth century the main distinction between public and private churches was that the former usually housed saints' relics and had received an episcopal dedication. See more on Balsamon's view on the role of private religious foundations, in Thomas, *Private Religious Foundations*, 142, 228–38.

21 *Syntagma* 2.337.

22 This was particularly true of the deacons of the *Hagia Sophia*, who were singled out by the twelfth-century historian John Kinnamos as a distinct and powerful group. See Angold, *Church and Society*, 89.

23 See also H. Petzold, 'Das Verhältnis des Subdiakonats zum Weihesakrament in der alten Kirche und seine Stellung im klassisch-orthodoxen Kirchenrecht', *Österreichisches Archiv für Kirchenrecht*, 18 (1967), 394–455.

24 *Syntagma* 2.337–8.

25 We see, for example, in one of the spiritually beneficial tales of Paul, bishop of Monembasia, that a priest who had had sexual intercourse with his wife the night before could not perform the liturgy. See J. Wortley (trans.), *The Spiritually Beneficial Tales of Paul, Bishop of Monembasia and of Other Authors* (Kalamazoo, MI, 1996), 127–8.

26 *Syntagma* 3.483–4.

27 See also G. Dagron, 'Remarques sur le statut des clercs', *Jahrbuch der Österreichischen Byzantinistik*, 44 (1994), 33–48.

28 V. Marinis, *Architecture and Ritual in the Churches of Constantinople: Ninth to Fifteenth Centuries* (Cambridge, 2004), 54 and n. 27.

29 *Syntagma* 3.191.

30 Marinis, *Architecture and Ritual*, 54–5.

31 *Syntagma* 3.483.

32 Balsamon was surprised to find singers among the list of clerics who could be punished for having intercourse with a nun. See *Syntagma* 2.315–6. This statement is confirmed by depictions of beardless singers in manuscripts of the Middle Byzantine period. See N.K. Moran, *Singers in Late Byzantine and Slavonic Painting* (Leiden, 1986), 26; N. Moran, 'Byzantine Castrati', *Plainsong and Medieval Music*, 11:2 (2002), 99–112. See also the account of Odo of Deuil (d. 1162), the chaplain of Louis VII in the Second Crusade (1147–1149), who praises the sweet chanting of the Byzantine clerics sent to assist the Latin mass, in V.G. Berry (ed. and trans.), *Odo of Deuil: The Journey of Louis VII to the East* (New York, NY, 1965), 69.

33 *Leo VI*, 320–7, 100–5.

34 On ecclesiastical offices see B.A. Leontaritou, *Εκκλησιαστικά αξιώματα και υπηρεσίες στην πρώιμη και μέση βυζαντινή περίοδο* (Athens, 1996).

35 Two other offices, whose status was debated in the twelfth century, were those of the *protekdikos* and the *chartophylax*. See Angold, *Church and Society*, 127.

36 Darrouzès, *Offikia*, 52.

37 Neither the total number of clerics nor the general population can be securely known. This rough figure has been arrived at based on numbers of ordinands from the thirteenth century, the eleventh-century Domesday book, and fourteenth-century poll taxes. See H.M. Thomas, *The Secular Clergy in England, 1066*–1216 (Oxford, 2014), 219–20. The best short overview of the Church in England is C. Harper-Bill, 'The Anglo-Norman Church', in *A Companion to the Anglo-Norman World*, eds. C. Harper-Bill and E. van Houts (Woodbridge, 2003), 165–90. See also J. Barrow, *The Clergy in the Medieval World: Secular Clerics, Their Families and Careers in North-Western Europe c. 800 – c. 1200* (Cambridge, 2015), 27–70, 269–343; H. Mayr-Harting, *Religion, Politics and Society in Britain, 1066–1272* (Harlow, 2011), 22–44, 95–129,

183–204; R. Bartlett, *England under the Norman and Angevin Kings, 1075–1225* (Oxford, 2000), 377–441.

38 These grades were not, however, the same as the ones we find in the Byzantine Church, even when the same name is used. They could correspond to different duties that gave clerics more or less access to the sacred.

39 R.E. Reynolds, 'The De officiis vii graduum: Its Origins and Development', in his *Clerical Orders in the Early Middle Ages: Duties and Ordination* (Aldershot, 1999), 113–51.

40 J. Barrow, 'Grades of Ordination and Clerical Careers c. 900–c. 1200', in *Anglo-Norman Studies XXX: Proceedings of the Battle Conference 2007*, ed. C.P. Lewis (2007), 41–61, at 42, 47–8.

41 See also M. Brett, *The English Church Under Henry I* (Oxford, 1975), 63–100.

42 See 'The Primacy of Canterbury' in R.W. Southern, *St Anselm: A Portrait in a Landscape* (Cambridge, 1990), 330–64.

43 In 1066 the English episcopal church comprised fifteen bishoprics. During the eleventh century, some of the sees moved to new places for economic and safety reasons. The cathedral church at Ely abbey was founded in 1109 and the Augustinian priory of Carlisle in 1133. See E.U. Crosby, *Bishop and Chapter in Twelfth-Century England: A Study of the Mensa Episcopalis* (Cambridge, 2008), 32–35.

44 For a map, see Ordnance Survey, *Map of Monastic Britain: South Sheet* (Chessington, 1950).

45 Bartlett, *England Under the Norman and Angevin Kings*, 388.

46 This is if we calculate with a distance of about 20 miles a day for a bishop. See J. Barrow, 'Way-Stations on English Episcopal Itineraries, 700–1300', *English Historical Review*, CXXVII (2012), 549–65, at 554.

47 Harper-Bill, 'The Anglo-Norman Church', 175.

48 Thomas, *Secular Clergy*, 112. For the rising number of bishops who were *magistri* from 1180 to 1223, see Baldwin, 'Masters at Paris from 1179 to 1215', 154. For canons who were *magistri* in Wells, St Paul's, Hereford, Lincoln, and Salisbury, see J. Barrow, 'Education and the Recruitment of Cathedral Canons in England and Germany 1100–1225', *Viator*, 20 (1989), 117–37, at 134, 138.

49 See also Brett, *The English Church*, 186–98.

50 See also J.C. Dickinson, *The Origins of the Austin Canons and their Introduction into England* (London, 1950); J. Burton, 'Les chanoines réguliers en Grande-Bretagne', in *Les Chanoines réguliers: Émergence et expansion (XIe–XIIIe siècles)*, ed. M. Parisse (Saint-Étienne, 2009), 477–98.

51 On the term 'secular' cleric and its evolution, see A. Boureau, 'Hypothèses sur l'émergence lexicale et théorique de la catégorie de séculier au XIIe siècle', in *Le clerc séculier au Moyen Âge*, ed. F. Rapp (Paris, 1993), 35–43.

52 See also Thomas, *Secular Clergy*, 10–13.

53 Brett, *The English Church*, 198–9.

54 Initially the word 'prebend' referred to the distribution of food that was given to monks and canons as well as their servants and guests. Later on it was applied to the totality of the property which was especially used to guarantee this distribution of food to the members of a community. E. Lesne, 'Praebenda: Le sens primitive du terme prébende', in *Mélanges Paul Fournier* (Paris, 1929), 443–53.

55 For more, see chapter 9, 'Clergy of Cathedral and Collegiate Churches' in Barrow, *Clergy in the Medieval World*, 269–309.

56 See also Brett, *The English Church*, 216–33.

57 C. Brooke, 'The Central Middle Ages: 800–1270', in *City of London from Prehistoric Times to c. 1520*, ed. M.D. Lobel (Oxford, 1989), 30–41, at 34–5; M. Biddle (ed.), *Winchester in the Early Middle Ages: An Edition and Discussion of the Winton Domesday* (Oxford, 1974), 329–36. For more examples of parishes per town, see

J. Barrow, 'Churches, Education and Literacy in Towns 600–1300', in *The Cambridge Urban History of Britain*, ed. D.M. Palliser (Cambridge, 2000), 127–52, at 134–5.

58 Harper-Bill, 'The Anglo-Norman Church', 184–5.

59 Bartlett, *England Under the Norman and Angevin Kings*, 378–80.

60 Harper-Bill, 'The Anglo-Norman Church', 186–7.

61 See also Brett, *The English Church*, 199–211; Barrow, *Clergy in the Medieval World*, 304–7; C.N.L. Brooke, 'The Archdeacon and the Norman Conquest', in *Tradition and Change: Essays in Honour of Marjorie Chibnall*, eds. D. Greenway, C. Holdsworth, and J. Sayers (Cambridge, 1985), 1–19.

62 C. Gallagher, 'The Two Churches', in *The Oxford Handbook of Byzantine Studies*, eds. R. Cormack, J.F. Haldon, and E. Jeffreys (Oxford, 2008), 592–8.

63 See also T. Kolbaba, *The Byzantine Lists: Errors of the Latins* (Chicago, 2000); Chadwick, *East and West: The Making of a Rift*, 206–21, 233–7.

64 On the eleventh-century migrations, see K.N. Ciggaar, *Western Travellers to Constantinople: The West and Byzantium, 962–1204, Cultural and Political Relations* (Leiden, 1996), 129–60; K. Ciggaar, 'England and Byzantium on the Eve of the Norman Conquest', in *Anglo-Norman Studies V: Proceedings of the Battle Conference, 1982*, ed. R.A. Brown (Woodbridge, 1983), 78–96; J. Shepard, 'The English and Byzantium: A Study of their Role in the Byzantine Army in the Later Eleventh Century', *Traditio*, 29 (1973), 53–92.

65 S. Runciman, *A History of the Crusades*, vol. I (Cambridge, 1951), 321.

66 J.R. Melville-Jones (trans.), *Eustathios of Thessaloniki: The Capture of Thessaloniki* (Canberra, 1988), 33–5.

67 M. Angold, *The Fourth Crusade: Event and Context* (Harlow, NY, 2003).

68 For the role that the Council in Trullo played in sustaining Christian unity and legislation, see J. Herrin, 'The Quinisext Council (692) as a Continuation of Chalcedon', *Chalcedon in Context: Church Councils 400–700*, eds. R. Price and M. Whitby (Farnham, 2009), 148–68, at 156–64.

69 J. Hajjar, *Le synode permanent (σύνοδος ἐνδημοῦσα) dans l'Église byzantine des origines au XIe siècle* (Rome, 1962), 150–60. For a brief introduction to the synod and a selection of some important laws it promulgated in the tenth and eleventh centuries, see Troianos, 'Byzantine Canon Law to 1100', 163–8.

70 For example, in the three years between the disputed papal elections of 1159 and the end of 1162 there were no fewer than five papal councils, while in the twenty years between the 1139 Lateran council and the death of Hadrian IV in 1159 there seem to have been only two. See R. Somerville, *Pope Alexander III and the Council of Tours (1163)* (London, 1977), 6–7.

71 Nektarios proved to be quite hostile towards the Latins. See R. Foreville, *Latran I, II, III et Latran IV* (Paris, 1965), 150, 205.

72 Foreville, *Latran*, 256, 392.

73 Tanner has noticed similarities in style and content between the canons of Nicaea I and Lateran IV. He attributed the great respect for the ecumenical councils to the Western Church's hesitation about the status of its own medieval councils. While the early Eastern councils were certainly of a universal character, later Lateran councils were described at the time as 'general' and it is only later that they came to be ranked by the Catholic Church as 'ecumenical'. See N. Tanner, 'Eastern Influences Upon the West: Canonical Evidence From Ecumenical and General Councils, and Some Other Sources, During the Middle Ages', in *Proceedings of the Thirteenth International Congress of Medieval Canon Law*, eds. P. Erdő and Sz.A. Szuromi (Vatican, 2010), 661–8, at 661–2, 665. For the canonical collections, see Rolker, *Letters of Ivo of Chartres*, 100–51. These, although produced on the continent, were particularly important for England, with English copies dating from at least the mid-twelfth century. See P. Wormald, *The Making of English Law: King Alfred to the Twelfth Century* (Oxford, 1999), 471–2.

74 Landau, 'Gratian and the Decretum Gratiani', 26; P. Landau, 'Überlieferung und Bedeutung der Kanones des Trullanischen Konzils im westlichen kanonischen Recht', in *The Council in Trullo Revisited*, eds. G. Nedungatt and M. Featherstone (Rome, 1995), 215–27, at 216–7, 220–1.
75 See also Troianos, 'Canon Law to 1100', 149–50.
76 See *Summa Lipsiensis* 1.3.
77 The author of the *Summa Parisiensis* got the list right, but others were confused about the punctuation, not realising that the fifth and sixth ecumenical councils took place in Constantinople. See *Summa Parisiensis*, 16; *Magister Rufinus*, 38. Master Honorius misses out Chalcedon and expresses his confusion about which one the fifth ecumenical council was. See *Magistri Honorii* 1.47; 1.52.
78 *Syntagma* 2.120–2.
79 Canon 7 of Lateran I in N.P. Tanner (ed. and trans.), *Decrees of the Ecumenical Councils: Volume One Nicaea I to Lateran V* (London, 1990), 191.
80 *Summa Lipsiensis* 1.100.
81 *Summa Lipsiensis* 1.116.
82 See, for example, canon 28 of the Council of Chalcedon, which dealt with the primacy, in J. Werckmeister, 'The Reception of the Church Fathers in Canon Law', in *The Reception of the Church Fathers in the West: From the Carolingians to the Maurists*, ed. I. Backus, vol. 1 (Leiden, 1997), 51–81, at 58.
83 Ohme, 'Greek Canon Law to 691/2', 85–6. According to Joannou, most pre-twelfth-century manuscripts containing the canonical collections do not confirm the content and order found in the second canon of Trullo – with some Fathers not being represented at all and others not included in the list taking their place. See P.-P. Joannou, *Discipline générale antique: vol. 2. Les canons des pères grecs* (Rome, 1963), xiv–xxv, at xv–xvi, xix–xxi. In the eleventh century, Timotheos and Dionysios were two of the few Fathers to be mentioned as canonical authorities by Michael Psellos in his *Synopsis Legum*. See PG 122.921; G. Weiss, 'Die "Synopsis Legum" des Michael Psellos', *Fontes Minores*, 2 (1977), 147–214. See also the second letter of Nikephoros the *chartophylax*, who at the end of the eleventh century mentions the list of the council in Trullo as authoritative, in P. Gautier, 'Le chartophylax Nicéphore. Œuvre canonique et notice bibliographique', *REB*, 27 (1969), 159–95, at 176–7.
84 *Syntagma* 2.309.
85 Werckmeister, 'The Reception of the Church Fathers', 58–60. Canonical collections found in manuscripts from eleventh- and twelfth-century Southern Italy form an exception to this. See R.E. Reynolds, 'The Influence of the Eastern Patristic Fathers on the Canonical Collections of South Italy in the Eleventh and Early Twelfth Centuries', in *Proceedings of the Thirteenth International Congress of Medieval Canon Law*, eds. P. Erdő and Sz.A. Szuromi (Vatican City, 2010), 645–50, at 646.
86 C. Munier, *Les sources patristiques du droit de l'Église du VIIIe au XIIIe siècle* (Strasbourg, 1954), 35. In his preface, Burchard gave a list of the authorities he used in his *Decretum*. The order he chose is interesting: 'corpus of canons'; 'canons of the apostles'; councils; popes; Bible; patristic writers (Gregory, Jerome, Augustine, Ambrose, Benedict, Isidore, and Basil); penitentials. His *Decretum* includes a total of 1,785 canons. See G. Austin, *Shaping Church Law Around the Year 1000: The Decretum of Burchard of Worms* (Farnham, 2009), 128.
87 Munier, *Les sources patristiques*, 39.
88 Werckmeister, 'The Reception of the Church Fathers', 66–7.
89 The two quotations are from Chrysostom's Homily 4 of Matthew. In this section, there are also seven false attributions to Chrysostom. See Werckmeister, 'The Reception of the Church Fathers', 68–9. Overall in Gratian's *Decretum* there are 469 passages from Augustine and 14 from Chrysostom. See Munier, *Les sources patristiques*, 126.
90 Crostini notes that we should not exclude the possibility that in the Late Antique East Augustine's work was read in the original. See B. Crostini, 'Byzantine World (to

1453)', in *The Oxford Guide to the Historical Reception of Augustine*, vol. II (Oxford, 2013), 726–34. See also A. Nichols, 'The Reception of St. Augustine and his Work in the Byzantine – Slav Tradition', *Angelicum*, 64 (1987), 437–52, at 443–44; J. Lössl, 'Augustine in Byzantium', *Journal of Ecclesiastical History*, 51:2 (2000), 267–95.

91 A brief quotation by Augustine was included above John Damascene, in PG 140, 217. See also G.E. Demacopoulos and A. Papanikolaou, 'Augustine and the Orthodox: "The West" in the East', in *Orthodox Readings of Augustine*, ed. A. Papanikolaou (New York, NY, 2008), 11–40, at 13. On this council, see G. Thetford, 'The Christological Councils of 1166 and 1170 in Constantinople', *St. Vladimir's Theological Quarterly*, 31:2 (1987), 143–61.

92 Louth attributed this indifference to 'an inherited sense of cultural superiority' (p. 344). For what follows, see A. Louth, 'Gregory the Great in the Byzantine Tradition', in *A Companion to Gregory the Great*, eds. B. Neil and M. Dal Santo (Leiden, 2013), 343–58. On Gregory the Great and his relation with the East, see also P. Booth, 'Gregory and the Greek East', in *A Companion to Gregory the Great*, eds. B. Neil and M. Dal Santo (Leiden, 2013), 109–31.

93 Another one of Gregory's works, the *Regula pastoralis*, was translated into Greek during his lifetime (c. 602) by Anastasius, patriarch of Antioch. However, this translation was lost, and as such little can be said about its impact. See Louth, 'Gregory the Great in the Byzantine Tradition', 344. Michael Glykas also quotes a story by Gregory the Great in his *Questions and Answers* on the topic of lay marital abstinence during feast days. See S. Eustratiades (ed.), *Μιχαὴλ τοῦ Γλυκᾶ. Εἰς τὰς ἀπορίας τῆς Θείας Γραφῆς*, vol. II (Alexandria, 1912), 177.

94 Makarios of Corinth and N. Hagiorites (eds.), *Εὐεργετινὸς ἤτοι Συναγωγὴ τῶν θεοφθόγγων ῥημάτων καὶ διδασκαλιῶν τῶν θεοφόρων καὶ ἁγίων πατέρων* (Venice, 1783; 6th ed. in 4 vols., repr. Athens 1996–7). See also J. Wortley, 'The Genre and Sources of the Synagoge', in *The Theotokos Evergetis and Eleventh-century Monasticism*, eds. M. Mullett and A. Kirby (Belfast, 1994), 306–24. For a list of the passages of Gregory the Great included in the *Synagoge*, see G. Rigotti, 'Gregorio il Dialogo nel mondo Bizantino', *L'eredità spirituale di Gregorio Magno tra Occidente e Oriente*, ed. G.I. Gargano (Verona, 2005), 271–92, at 284–6.

95 There were also some references to liturgical music, providence, and the value of pilgrimage. See Louth, 'Gregory the Great', 350–2.

96 Dialogue 4.12 in *Εὐεργετινὸς ἤτοι Συναγωγὴ*, I, Z.

97 Landau, 'Gratian and Decretum Gratiani', 26.

98 Ohme, 'Greek Canon Law to 691/2', 28–33.

99 Duggan, 'Making Law or Not?', 48–56.

100 Duggan, 'Making Law or Not?', 43–6.

101 Gallagher, *Church Law and Church Order*, 166.

102 Werckmeister, 'The Reception of the Church Fathers', 55.

103 Macrides, 'Nomos and Kanon', 61–85.

104 See also B. Stolte, 'Civil Law in Canon Law: A Note on the Method of Interpreting the Canons in the Twelfth Century', in *Byzantium in the 12th Century: Canon Law, State and Society*, ed. N. Oikonomides (Athens, 1991), 543–54.

105 Gallagher, *Church Law and Church Order*, 160; Magdalino, *Empire of Manuel*, 294.

106 Troianos, 'Twelfth to the Fifteenth Centuries', 181.

107 B.H. Stolte, 'Balsamon and the Basilica', *Subseciva Groningana*, 3 (1989), 115–25, at 122–4.

108 Hoeflich and Grabher, 'The Establishment of Normative Legal Texts', 4–5. See also C.M. Radding and A. Ciaralli, *The Corpus Iuris Civilis in the Middle Ages* (Leiden, 2007).

109 Winroth, *Making of Gratian's Decretum*, 146–7.

110 A. Winroth, 'Roman Law in Gratian and the Panormia', in *Bishops, Texts and the Use of Canon Law around 1100: Essays in Honour of Martin Brett*, eds. B.C. Brasington and K.G. Cushing (Aldershot, 2008), 183–90.

111 Landau, 'Gratian and Decretum Gratiani', 29–30.
112 For example, canons 5, 17, and 18 of the Apostles referred to 'bishops, priests and deacons', or to 'bishops, priests, deacons, and any other of the sacerdotal list'. See *Syntagma* 2.7; 2.23; 2.25. Similarly, the Council of Carthage promulgated three canons on clerical abstinence and two of them omitted any mention of subdeacons. See canons 3, 25, and 79 of Carthage in *Syntagma* 2.301; 2.369; 2.482.
113 *Syntagma* 3.39–41.
114 Novel 123, c. 14 translated in Cochini, *Apostolic Origins*, 363–5.
115 Novel 3 in *Leo VI*, 18–21; *Syntagma* 3.41.
116 See *Syntagma* 2.33. An implicit prohibition against marrying after the subdiaconate can also be found in canon 14 of the council of Chalcedon (451). See *Syntagma* 2.251–4. See also Cochini, *Apostolic Origins*, 412–6.
117 Cochini, *Apostolic Origins*, 352–70. For Trullo, see canons 6 and 13 in *Syntagma* 2.318 and 2.333.
118 See *Syntagma* 2.318.
119 *Syntagma* 2.485. Balsamon mentioned the custom of deacons contracting marriages, but did not tell us whether it continued in his time. He told us only that it ought not to (οὐκ ὀφείλει κρατεῖν). See *Syntagma* 3.41.
120 C. Will, *Acta et scripta quae de controversiis ecclesiae Graecae et Latinae saeculo undecimo composita extant* (Leipzig, 1861), 133, 147.
121 See also L'Huillier, 'Episcopal Celibacy in the Orthodox Tradition', 271–300; D.J. Constantelos, 'Marriage and Celibacy of the Clergy in the Orthodox Church', *Concilium: Theology in the Age of Renewal*, 8 (1972), 30–8.
122 *Syntagma* 2.330–1.
123 *Syntagma* 2.419–23.
124 1.3.41 (2–3) in *The Codex of Justinian* 1.106–7.
125 Novel 2, in *Leo VI*, 16–19.
126 *Syntagma* 5.321–3; *JGR* 1.435–6; *Les regestes de 715 à 1206*, 585 n. 1171.
127 See also Chapter 7 'Clerical Marriage and Clerical Celibacy' in Thomas, *Secular Clergy*, 154–89; Chapter 4 'Clergy as Family Men' in Barrow, *Clergy in the Medieval World*, 115–57; D.G. Hunter, 'Married Clergy in Eastern and Western Christianity', in *A Companion to Priesthood and Holy Orders in the Middle Ages*, eds. G. Peters and C. Colt Anderson (Leiden, 2016), 96–139; chapters 2 and 3 of H. Parish, *Clerical Celibacy in the West: c. 1100–1700* (Farnham, 2010), 183–202.
128 See, for example, the *Refutation of All Heresies* of Hippolytus of Rome (170/75–235), in Cochini, *Apostolic Origins*, 152–4.
129 For an early attempt to police clerical sexuality, see the Spanish Council of Elvira in M. Meigne, 'Concile ou collection d'Elvire?', *Revue d'histoire ecclésiastique*, 70 (1975), 361–87; M.J. Lázaro Sánchez, 'L'état actuel de la recherche sur le concile d'Elvire', *Revue des sciences religieuses*, 82:4 (2008), 517–46.
130 For a list and description of the different canons on clerical continence in this period, see Cochini, *Apostolic Origins*, 323–51, 382–410.
131 See, for example, the letter of the mid-fifth century pope Leo I in PL 54. 1204: 'Vnde ut de carnali fiat spirituale conjugium, oportet eos nec dimittere uxores, et quasi habeant sic habere, quo et salva sit charitas connubiorum, et cessent opera nuptiarum'.
132 C. Cubitt, 'Images of St Peter: The Clergy and the Religious Life in Anglo-Saxon England', in *The Christian Tradition in Anglo-Saxon England: Approaches to Current Scholarship and Teaching*, ed. P. Cavill (Cambridge, 2004), 41–54, at 50–4.
133 *Councils & Synods* 1.12–3.
134 *Councils & Synods* 1.61–2.
135 Barrow, *Clergy in the Medieval World*, 92–5.
136 N. Ramsey, M. Sparks and T. Tatton-Brown (eds.), *St Dunstan: His Life, Times and Cult* (Woodbridge, 1992); B. Yorke (ed.), *Bishop Æthelwold: His Career and Influence* (Suffolk, 1988); N. Brooks and C. Cubitt (eds.), *St Oswald of Worcester* (London,

1996); D.G. Scragg (ed.), *Edgar, King of the English, 959–975: New Interpretations* (Woodbridge, 2008).

137 *Councils & Synods* 1.313–37.

138 See V Æthelred in *Councils & Synods* 1.338–73.

139 See, for example, the pastoral letters that Ælfric of Eynsham wrote for Wulfsige III, bishop of Sherborne (993xc. 995) in *Councils & Synods* 1.191–22.

140 More tolerant regulations can be found in *The Northumbrian Priests' Law* (cap. 35), promulgated not long before the Conquest in the mid-eleventh century, which stated, 'If a priest leaves a woman and takes another, let him be anathema!' See *Councils & Synods* 1.449–67.

141 For a comparison with Normandy, see J.D. Thibodeaux, *The Manly Priest: Clerical Celibacy, Masculinity, and Reform in England and Normandy 1066–1300* (Philadelphia, PA, 2015), 46–57.

142 *Councils & Synods* 2.616–20.

143 Anselm also sent letters to English bishops, such as Herbert Losinga, the bishop of Norwich, asking them to remove married priests from their churches. See *Councils & Synods* 2.668–88.

144 *Councils & Synods* 2.750–4.

145 Canon 7 of Lateran II in Tanner, *Decrees of the Ecumenical Councils*, 198. See also J.A. Brundage, *Law, Sex, and Christian Society in Medieval Europe* (London, 1987), 220. Legislation on clerical marriage promulgated in the first half of the eleventh century paved the way for the development of the subdiaconate into a sacred order. See R.E. Reynolds, 'The Subdiaconate as a Sacred and Superior Order', in his *Clerics in the Early Middle Ages* (Aldershot, 1999), IV 1–39. The status of subdeacons remained unclear until 1207, when Pope Innocent III (1198–1216) declared officially that the subdiaconate was a holy order. See J.E. Lynch, 'Marriage and Celibacy of the Clergy: The Discipline of the Western Church: An Historico-canonical Synopsis', *The Jurist*, 32 (1972), 189–212, at 14–38.

146 *Councils & Synods* 2.965–93.

147 J.A. Giles (trans.), *Roger of Wendover's Flowers of History*, vol. II (London, 1849), 247.

148 Canon 14 of Lateran IV in Tanner, *Decrees of the Ecumenical Councils*, 242. See also A.J. Duggan, 'Conciliar Law 1123–1215: The Legislation of the Four Lateran Councils', in *The History of Medieval Canon Law in the Classical Period, 1140–1234: From Gratian to the Decretals of Pope Gregory IX*, eds. W. Hartmann and K. Pennington (Washington, DC, 2008), 341–66.

149 Giles, *Roger of Wendover's Flowers of History*, 2.459.

150 L. Melve, 'The Public Debate on Clerical Marriage in the Late Eleventh Century', *Journal of Ecclesiastical History*, 61 (2010), 688–706.

151 Lynch, 'Marriage and Celibacy of the Clergy', 200.

3 Episcopal finances

In both England and Byzantium, canon law was used to safeguard the property of the Church against episcopal rapacity. As possible beneficiaries of ecclesiastical wealth, episcopal families could find themselves at the centre of polemical discussions. Accusations against them influenced, and were influenced by, current ideas on clerical marriage, especially in cases where wives and children were singled out. In this chapter, I discuss the development of laws that aimed to limit the personal and familial expenditure of bishops, and their relation to the rules of clerical celibacy. Then I consider the kinds of resources that were available to twelfth-century bishops in Byzantium and England, their potential for misappropriation, and the extent to which they could be used for the benefit of episcopal families. I argue that there were many similarities between English and Byzantine bishops: they had significant control over ecclesiastical property; they were limited by laws against misappropriations on behalf of their families; but they were also ultimately allowed to take care of their legitimate wives and children. This chapter on bishops and their families offers the closest parallels between English and Byzantine views on marriage and property, but also highlights some aspects of difference that will come up again and again throughout this book.

Misappropriations and the need for celibacy

Concerns about the bishop's potential mismanagement of Church resources were expressed early on in canonical and civil legislation.[1] Canon 25 of the Council of Antioch (341) raised the possibility that a bishop could redirect ecclesiastical funds to his own private uses, and instead of administering the revenues with the consent of the priests and deacons, he 'might give their control to his own men and relatives, or brothers, or sons, so that through this the accounts of the Church may secretly suffer'.[2] Similarly, canon 38 of the Apostles (c. 380) warned that a bishop should act as the overseer, not the owner of the property of God, and emphasised that he is not allowed to usurp ecclesiastical funds or 'to grant to his own relatives the things of God'. The bishop's relatives could be provided for, if they happened to be poor, 'but they should not become an excuse for him to sell what belongs to the Church.'[3]

These concerns were followed by further legislation which tried to limit the bishop's power to alienate ecclesiastical property for the sake of his family. Canon

40 of the Apostles asked for the private property of the bishop to be clearly distinguished from the property of the Church:

> so that, when he dies, the bishop may have power to bequeath his own property as he wishes and to whom he wishes, and so that the bishop's goods may not slip away under guise of ecclesiastical property; for he might have had a wife and children, or relatives or servants. For it is right, before God and men, that the Church should not suffer any loss through not knowing the bishop's property, nor the bishop or his relatives have their goods confiscated by reason of the Church, nor should his kin be involved even in lawsuits, nor should his death be surrounded by slander.[4]

This canon seems friendlier towards the episcopal family, as it aims to protect it at the same time as it protects the finances of the Church. Canon law allowed bishops to grant to their heirs the property they possessed before their accession to the episcopate. Later civil law, issued by Justinian I in 528, extended this right by allowing bishops to bequeath property which they had acquired after their election through certain familial bequests – namely, from their parents, uncles, or brothers.[5] Nonetheless, these attempts to delineate more closely what constituted the private property of the bishop and what belonged to the Church reflected fifth- and sixth-century fears about the alienation of ecclesiastical wealth in favour of the bishop's family and wider circle, which is indeed attested in surviving sources from the period.[6]

An even more direct link between ecclesiastical finances and the bishop's familial status was made by Justinian in 528:

> Therefore such men should be chosen and elected as bishop who have neither children nor grandchildren; for he who is preoccupied by the everyday cares that children give their parents cannot give all his attention and devotion to divine worship and ecclesiastical matters. For although some men resort to the most holy churches out of their hope in God and to save their own souls, and offer their possessions, leaving them behind to be spent on beggars and the poor and other such pious uses, it would be perverse if the bishops diverted this property to their own profit or spent it on their own children and relations.[7]

Justinian presented the episcopal family both as a distraction and as an unlawful beneficiary of ecclesiastical property.[8] His concerns about this issue continued, and episcopal wives and especially children appeared again in 535 and in 565 as an impediment to ordination to the episcopate.[9] We see, then, that the link between control of ecclesiastical wealth and the need for celibacy was established early on, and in Justinian's legislation we find it in its strictest form, prohibiting not only wives but also any descendants.

This prohibition against the existence of descendants was never repeated in Byzantine ecclesiastical legislation. Legitimate children were not an obstacle to ordination to the episcopate. Even the Council in Trullo, which made episcopal celibacy compulsory, had nothing to say about children or the problems that they might cause to ecclesiastical finances.[10] The discrepancy between Byzantine civil and canon law was resolved by a novel of Emperor Leo VI (r. 886–912), which explained but also rejected Justinian's motives. The novel stated that previous legislation had aimed to protect the Church against the excessive love of some parents which could lead them to the misappropriation of ecclesiastical property. However, the absence of children could not guarantee that bishops would not squander the property of their church on their brothers, nephews, or other relatives, as family love was not restricted to paternal love.[11] After Leo's legislation, children were no longer an impediment to ordination to the episcopate in Byzantine civil law. Balsamon too stated explicitly that Justinian's novel was no longer valid, quoting instead Leo's decree.[12]

Similarly in the West, what was eventually demanded of bishops was celibacy, and there were no binding stipulations about legitimate episcopal children. Gratian's *Decretum* (D.28 c.13) did include a letter of Pope Pelagius I (556–561) stating that clerics who had been married or had a child should preferably not be promoted to the episcopate, but the canonist pointed out the contradiction with other decrees which allowed clerics to form families while in minor orders.[13] The decretists responded in various ways. Master Honorius stated that for him such restrictions were special provisions applying solely to the given context of the time of their promulgation.[14] The author of the *Summa Lipsiensis*, on the other hand, adopted a harsher stance: he reminded his readers of Justinian's laws and argued that a cleric with a family should be elected to the episcopate only if there was no other acceptable candidate and after due precautions were taken.[15] In the twelfth century, Justinian's ideals fitted better in a Western than in a Byzantine context, as they resonated with contemporary views about the evils of clerical marriage.[16]

In practice, episcopal families were becoming the exception in England, but in the second half of the twelfth century we could still find bishops with children, such as Hugh du Puiset, bishop of Durham (1154–1195), and Richard of Ilchester, bishop of Winchester (1173–1188).[17] In fact, some of these episcopal fathers were committing double transgressions: not only were they falling short of the *Summa Lipsiensis*' Justinianic aspirations but also they were failing to adhere to basic chastity rules. The children they produced were often illegitimate, either because they were born after their father's ordination or because their parents had not been married in the first place. That was the case for Hugh du Puiset, who had at least two illegitimate children with his long-term mistress Alice de Percy.[18] The exact extent of such transgressions is not clear, as often details including the mother's name, whether there was a marriage, or when the children were conceived simply have not survived.[19]

Episcopal resources

Given the existence of episcopal families, the next question to address is what kinds of resources English and Byzantine bishops had at their disposal and how easy it was for them to misappropriate these resources for the sake of their wives and children.

England

Twelfth-century English bishops could draw on a variety of ecclesiastical revenues from both lands and levies. Their main item of income was the estates of the bishopric, while other sources included payments from judicial proceedings in church courts, rights of hospitality when conducting visitations, payment for the consecration of churches, and synodal dues. Parochial dues as well as payments for the provision of pastoral care would also provide an income, but only during vacancies.[20]

Furthermore, from the late eleventh century onwards, the bishops' control over parish churches changed, bringing with it changes for their own finances. Under the influence of the Gregorian reforms lay patrons began to grant away their advowson to monastic communities. This meant that monastic communities rather than lay patrons would have the right to present a candidate for a benefice to the bishop for approval. Once a religious house had the advowson, it might then decide to take over the rectory itself – that is to say, to appropriate the church. Therefore, instead of belonging to laymen in a proprietary way – as a possession comprising not only the advowson but also the church with its contents, its land, buildings, and stock, its tithes, dues, and offerings – all these rights were transferred to monastic houses, reducing secular interference and dominion over the Church. Both the granting of advowson and appropriation required episcopal approval. As a result, bishops could ask for compensation in return for issuing a charter that showed their agreement. In spite of rules against simony, bishops could receive benefits in the form of money, or could put pressure on the monks in order to have one of their own clerics presented to the appropriated church. Having the right of presentation was in itself an important financial benefit, as by the end of the twelfth century advowson had become a saleable right, completely separate from the estate to which it was originally attached.[21]

Episcopal revenues could vary widely from one diocese to another. Two of the poorest dioceses were those of Rochester and Carlisle.[22] The latter was indeed so poor that that no one could be found to occupy it between 1157 and 1204.[23] Its income *sede vacante* from 1 November 1186 to Michaelmas 1188 was £52 19s. 6d., a meagre sum compared to the more or less steady income of about £1,500 extracted annually from Canterbury by the same king, Henry II (r. 1154–1189), between 1164 and 1172, or the £1,555 1s. 6d. extracted from Winchester between Michaelmas 1171 and 1172.[24] More generally, however, thirteen out of seventeen cathedrals made at least £250 a year, while nine of them had an estimated average income of at least £400 in the late twelfth century.[25] Given that the average income of a baron between 1160 and 1220 has been estimated at around £200, the position of bishop would have made for a very profitable career in twelfth-century England.[26]

How much of the church's income a bishop could spend on himself depended both on how the property of the bishopric had been divided and on what we consider 'personal expenses'. Bishops had to pay out large sums to employ, feed, house, and move around the clerks and lay servants in their household and had to provide for the upkeep of the buildings on episcopal estates. These kinds of payments were necessary for the supervision of the diocese, but the bishop had some choice in how much he lavished on these aspects of his daily lifestyle. More importantly, the bishop's part of the overall income differed from one diocese to another and even in the same diocese at different periods. The separation of episcopal property from property supporting the cathedral community had been a long, drawn-out process, often beginning in the tenth century or before and becoming finalised after about 1150.[27] Part of this entailed the creation of individual prebends for the cathedral canons.[28] In twelfth-century England, most of these prebends were endowed with land and could have one or more parish churches.[29] Prebends were managed by cathedral canons and were in effect their benefices with their material appurtenances, in tithes, income from lands, and donations from the laity for the performance of liturgical duties.[30] The creation of prebends gave more control to the canons themselves. They were responsible, for example, for making the most out of their manors by using them as food farms, by leasing them out to individuals (sometimes other canons) who could yield a higher return, or by managing them directly through their own officers, bearing all the risk but also taking all the profits.[31]

Prebends could be established from the lands of the chapter or the lands of the bishop, through royal grants, or through the grants of aristocratic families.[32] Their establishment happened at different speeds in different cathedral chapters. It was a process which took place in several stages, with most prebends gaining further endowments, as well as supplementary estates, churches, and tithes, over time. At Salisbury, for example, the property of the church was divided into twenty-seven prebends in the mid-twelfth century; later in the same century this extended to forty-two. Bishop Jocelin (1142–1184) also took the step – not taken by any other English bishop – of assigning a prebend to himself, the *Major Pars Altaris*, which was ranked as the most profitable. By 1226, the number had increased to a total of fifty-two.[33] Although this division of cathedral property limited the direct control that bishops had over ecclesiastical wealth, it opened up other ways of increasing episcopal power: cathedral prebends were in the gift of the bishop during his episcopate.[34] He could use them to advance men close to him, rewarding them in this way for their service. We see, for example, that in Hereford during the episcopate of Bishop William de Vere (1186–1198) the intake of episcopal clerics into the chapter increased substantially, with five or six out of a total of fourteen newly appointed canons being the bishop's own clerics.[35]

Further confusion regarding the division of episcopal and cathedral property could ensue when a bishop brought personal assets with him to the see upon his appointment, or was given them during his term on an individual capacity. Gratian's *Decretum* (C.1 q.2 c.9) stated that only bishops who had given up their personal property, either by distributing it to the poor or giving it over to their cathedral, were worthy of supporting themselves through the money of the Church. This rule, however, does not seem to have been maintained even at the level of prescription. The author of the *Summa Lipsiensis* commented that decrees which advocated that clergymen should receive no ecclesiastical stipends if they could maintain themselves from their own property were to be taken as advice and not as a rule, unless they referred to churches that were too poor or to clerics who completely neglected their duties. Others among his contemporaries, he tells us, followed current custom and claimed that this canon had been altogether abolished.[36]

Byzantium

Similarly to their English counterparts, Byzantine bishops acted as the administrators of Church finances.[37] Contributions in cash and kind formed one source of income available to them. The latter included oil for the lamps and incense for the liturgy, as well as fruits and vegetables to be shared by the bishop and his clergy.[38] The bulk of these revenues came from the *kanonikon*, a levy paid to the bishop by clerics, monks, and laymen.[39] Priests were formally asked to pay a *kanonikon* to the bishop in the eleventh century. Its payment was instituted by Patriarch Alexios the Studite (1025–1043) and confirmed by Patriarch Nikolaos III Grammatikos (c. 1087). According to Herman, it was meant as a form of compromise which institutionalised and regularised the long-standing abuse of bishops receiving money from their clerics. It amounted to 1 *hyperpyron* per year and by the end of the twelfth century it was considered an established custom.[40] The *kanonikon* of the monasteries was also considered a long-standing abuse and was condemned by Patriarch Sisinios II (996–999), but without success.[41] In addition to the *kanonikon*, abbots and clerics had to pay certain dues to the bishop on the occasion of their consecration, despite several prohibitions on this matter.[42] Following a decree of Patriarch Nikolaos III Grammatikos, readers were required to pay 1 *hyperpyron*, while deacons and priests paid 3 *hyperpyra*.[43] In the case of the laity, bishops had always received voluntary donations, and the payment of the *kanonikon* became compulsory only briefly in the eleventh century. It was meant to be paid annually and its exact amount was determined based on the population of the village. According to a law of Emperor Isaak I Komnenos (r. 1057–1059), in a village of thirty families the bishop would receive 1 *hyperpyron*, two silver coins, one ram, six *modioi* of barley, six measures (*metra*) of wine, six *modioi* of wheat flour, and thirty chickens as *kanonikon* per year.[44] This corresponded roughly to the payment of tithes in the West, but was paid to the bishop rather than the parish priest as there were no parishes *per se* in Byzantium. Already by the end of the twelfth century, however, payment of the *kanonikon* had reverted to being optional, and depended on what the village or family wished to donate.[45] A further charge was levied on the laity for obtaining a marriage licence.[46]

The majority of episcopal wealth came from cathedral lands and their appurtenances – meadows, vineyards, mills, fisheries, and so on.[47] These lands were exploited indirectly through dependent peasants (*paroikoi*) or, if they were not particularly profitable, they were rented out through emphyteutic leases.[48] They could belong directly to the bishopric or to diocesan monasteries – that is to say, monasteries under the control of the bishop.[49] These could be episcopal foundations or monasteries within the diocese whose written rule, their *typikon*, did not exclude episcopal supervision. Such an exclusion could be achieved through an imperial or patriarchal exemption; through continuing provisions for the founder and his/her heirs; or by obtaining independent status. If no exclusion had been put in place, any surplus revenues would go to the bishop, after the needs of the monastery had been met.[50] Given the importance of monastic landed property for episcopal finances, as well as its potential for misappropriation, I will explain here briefly what challenges it posed and how the bishop could benefit from it.[51]

Although monasteries represented a particularly important source of revenue, the imposition of episcopal authority over them had a troubled history.[52] As bishops pushed for more control, monasteries and their founders fought for greater independence. The state also got involved, supporting one side or the other. We read, for example, in a well-known novel of Emperor Basil II of 996 that bishops were no longer to abuse their rights by appropriating small houses of prayer which had been endowed by peasants in village communities; these were not big enough to be properly considered monasteries and as such were to be exempt from episcopal control.[53] In the twelfth century, the most important challenges to episcopal control were presented by the patriarchal *stauropegia*, the institution of the *charistike*, and the prevalence of the *autodespota* monasteries.

Stauropegia were patriarchal grants which provided concerned private founders with the opportunity to protect their interests by transferring the supervisory rights of the local bishop to the more distant patriarch. It meant that their monastery would inscribe the patriarch in its diptychs, a list of people dead and living to be commemorated by the community, and would pay him the *kanonikon*.[54] This represented a significant loss for bishops, who fought back. In 1191, Patriarch Georgios Xiphilinos agreed that dependencies of *stauropegia* – that is to say, monasteries or chapels built as extensions to a stauropegial monastery – would remain under the control of the local bishops. This applied to new and existing foundations.[55]

Starting in the eleventh century, episcopal revenues from monasteries were also threatened by the institution of the *charistike*, which involved granting the financial administration of monasteries to laymen. This could be detrimental to episcopal finances, as bishops were no longer able to draw an income from the monasteries they had granted in *charistike*, which now belonged to the *charistikarios*. A famous example comes from an 1118 patriarchal synod which recounted the complaints of Constantine, metropolitan of Cyzicus: Constantine's predecessors had granted away the monasteries of his cathedral to *charistikarioi*, leaving his church in such poverty that it was apparently unable to even provide the candles and oil needed for liturgical services.[56] Suffragan bishops could be doubly affected by this, as they were obliged to support their metropolitan, if he happened to suffer financial hardship, by giving back any monasteries they held from him. This was decreed by Patriarch Alexios the Studite (1025–1043) as part of the measures taken to alleviate the problems caused to bishoprics by the *charistike*.[57]

By the end of the twelfth century, the institution of the *charistike* was largely abolished, but as a reaction to its abuses a different challenge took its place: the independent and self-governing (*autodespota kai eleuthera*) monasteries.[58] Their founders aimed to insure their institutions against outside ecclesiastical control while at the same time protecting them from subsequent financial exploitation by their own heirs. In order to achieve this, they set up foundations that were intended to be independent and self-governing from the start rather than after the death of the founder's descendants. It was the abbot of the monastery that would now hold most of the power. This form of government allowed for complete freedom from episcopal and patriarchal control and was adopted by most important monasteries and philanthropic institutions in the twelfth century.[59]

One interesting example is that of the Areia monastery (c. 1149), a new foundation of Bishop Leo of Nauplia, set up in his private capacity, not as a diocesan foundation but on the contrary as an independent monastery endowed with revenues from other diocesan monasteries.[60] The Areia produced no income for the incumbent or his successors, and even reduced episcopal revenues by using the surplus of diocesan monasteries as part of its endowment. It is this kind of landed property that a bishop could most easily alienate for the benefit of himself or his family and to the detriment of his diocese.

More generally, great disparities existed between the wealth of different bishoprics.[61] According to Morrisson and Cheynet, in the middle Byzantine period (843–1204) most metropolitans were lower in the scale of payments than high-ranking officials.[62] But the bishop of a large and prosperous diocese could control very significant sums of money as well as landed property. For example, in the early 1040s, Theophanes, archbishop of Thessalonike, was found to have in his possession 33 *kentenaria* of gold, the equivalent of 237,600 *nomismata*.[63] This was surely exceptional. When the same archbishop was asked by Emperor Michael IV for a loan of 1 *kentenarion* (7,200 *nomismata*), he claimed to have had only 30 pounds of gold (2,160 *nomismata*) on hand.[64] Although the emperor did not believe Theophanes, this could have been because of his reputation for avarice, not because metropolitan sees, even as large as Thessalonike, were expected to have greater liquidity.[65] In any case, 2,000 *nomismata* was still a very substantial amount of money to have available in ready cash, if we compare it, for example, to the patrimony worth 7,000 to 10,000 *nomismata* that Attaleiates, an eleventh-century civil official, accumulated throughout his long career. Being a bishop could be a very profitable career in Byzantium.

We also need to keep in mind regional and chronological variations. Before the Turkish raids and settlements of the eleventh and twelfth centuries, the European sees, with the exception of Thessalonike, had been poorer and their metropolitans had had fewer suffragans compared to their Anatolian counterparts.[66] This changed towards the end of the eleventh century, when it became difficult to fill the now impoverished episcopal seats in the East. The Turkish raids left religious institutions abandoned and their lands appropriated, while the local population was reduced to poverty due to heavy taxation and administrative abuses.[67] In such cases, the state could intervene to help the bishops in need. In 1094 Alexios I

Komnenos issued a novel giving permission to the bishops of the afflicted areas to keep any revenues that they held from previous positions as abbots or *oikonomoi* or from ecclesiastical dignities, for as long as the situation persisted.[68] Similarly, in the twelfth century Emperor Manuel Komnenos promised life-long state support to bishops who were elected to provinces under Turkish control, due upon their taking up residence in their seats.[69]

The revenues thus far described were all held by the bishop in his official, rather than personal, capacity. This was made clear in canonical sources by the name they were assigned: they were often called *Κυριακά*, meaning belonging to the Lord, or *πτωχικά*, belonging to the poor.[70] Byzantine bishops were expected to preserve the remainder of their cathedral revenues for their successor, after all necessary expenses had been deducted. This included money used for the maintenance of the bishop himself, who, unlike other clerics, did not receive a salary.[71] How much the bishop was allowed to spend on himself was open to debate. In his commentary on these canons, Zonaras advised bishops to use ecclesiastical resources to cover their bare necessities, such as food and clothing, 'not for anything superfluous, or involving luxury or slackness'.[72] Balsamon elsewhere added that episcopal poverty was not to be taken to extremes, as that would cause shame to the dignity of the bishop as well as to God: 'it will go against God's honour that a bishop may go on foot or deprive himself of what is necessary because of poverty.'[73] Nonetheless, the canonist believed that bishops should be free from avarice (ἀφιλάργυροι) and should provide for themselves from their private property if they happened to be wealthy. More specifically, he stated,

> a bishop is not allowed to use for his personal advantage any of the resources of the diocese, except for what is absolutely necessary and on the occasion when he does not have a sufficient store of these things from his own financial resources.[74]

Bishops were strongly encouraged to preserve the resources of their church, although, or perhaps because, their personal spending was to be drawn directly from them.

The episcopal family: lawful beneficiaries?

Leaving aside their personal expenses, English and Byzantine bishops were expected to spend money on the fabric of the church as well as the clergy, monks, and laity within their diocese.[75] More specifically, laws and their commentaries often singled out four categories of laypeople as worthy beneficiaries of Church resources: widows, orphans, foreigners, and the weak.[76] Another, more controversial, beneficiary of financial provisions was the episcopal family. We read in the late eleventh-century *Strategikon* of Kekaumenos (d. after the 1070s) the advice he gave his sons on how to behave, were they ever to become bishops, metropolitans, or patriarchs:

> don't become grandiose, escorted by guards, and heaping up money, and concerned with gold and silver and expensive meals; let your concern be for

> supporting orphans, and sustaining widows, and for hospitals, and ransoming captives, and for making peace, and standing up for the powerless and not for joining house to house and attaching field to field, and taking away your neighbour's property, while you make the excuse: 'I am not offering this to my children, but to God and my church'.[77]

Kekaumenos paints here the image of the ideal bishop. In doing so, he emphasises the risk of misappropriation of Church resources and links it both to the highest echelons of the ecclesiastical hierarchy – bishops, metropolitans, and patriarchs – and to a father's desire to provide for his children. This desire, he warns, can be disguised as piety, but God has no need for earthly possessions; it is the bishop himself and his children who are presented here as the real recipients of the accumulated wealth, with God and the Church as mere excuses for the appropriations.[78]

In England, much more so than in Byzantium, ecclesiastical propaganda tied concerns about the misappropriation of Church property to the image of the doting clerical father and husband. Negative depictions of clerical marriage had been a commonplace long before the Gregorian reforms, which only increased the fear that clerics might lavish on their spouses and children resources destined for the upkeep of the church and the support of the poor. Many of these concerns focused on priests rather than bishops as the problem of incontinence was greater at that level.[79] But examples of episcopal misbehaviour can also be found.

The early eleventh-century bishop of Durham, Aldhun (990–1018), gave six episcopal vills as dowry to his daughter Ecgfrida (c. 995). Although it was stressed that the estates were not to be permanently alienated but to remain with Ecgfrida and her husband as long as they were married, this did not happen in practice. By the end of Ecgfrida's second marriage, the vills had already been fragmented (c. 1018). While three were temporarily returned to the church, the other three remained under the control of Ecgfrida's daughter, Sigrid. All six vills were again in secular hands after they were seized by Siward, earl of Northumbria, who argued that they belonged by hereditary right to his wife Ælfflaed, Ecgfrida's granddaughter (c. 1041).[80]

Such practices continued in the twelfth century. A similar example comes from neighbouring Wales, where David fitz Gerald, bishop of St Davids (d. 1176) and uncle of Gerald of Wales, used episcopal lands to provide for his family members, also granting part of them as dowry to his daughters.[81] The unknown author of the bishop's *Life* set up Bishop David as a villain figure in contrast to St David, the patron saint of the diocese. He gave a long list of the beneficiaries of the bishop's misappropriations and emphasised his inappropriate episcopal behaviour by commenting that he 'distributed all these properties despite the canons' opposition and protests'.[82] The author is thought to have been one of the cathedral clerics who would have preferred to see a pure Welshman elected to the episcopate and as such was intentionally hostile to Bishop David.[83] The alienation of Church property was always an offence which could be used to show a clergyman in a bad light. The fact that David was doing this for his sons-in-law made the offence even more scandalous in contemporary eyes, even among Welsh clergy, who had a reputation for higher incidence of clerical marriage throughout the Middle Ages.

Gerald of Wales was also vocal against the financial impact of clerical marriage, despite having received his early education from his uncle. In his *Gemma ecclesiastica*, he states,

> How much do you think is necessary for his women's pride, for his maidservants' extravagances, for the expensive cost of keeping his boys – for their education and their preferments? [. . .] These are the things, then, which give rise to greed in the clergy and banish charity. These are the things which cause doves to be sold in the temple again and the sacraments to be prostituted for money. These are the things which prompt the hierarchy to sell Holy Orders, benefices, and consecrations, and the minor clergy to sell weddings, and burials, and even baptisms, to duplicate masses, to triple and quadruple gospels, and to accept tricenaries.[84]

All grades were negatively affected and in the case of bishops clerical marriage could lead to simony. The great two evils against which the Gregorian reforms fought were here united in Gerald's mind.

Nonetheless, according to both Byzantine and Anglo-Norman canon law, wives and children could be lawful beneficiaries of episcopal benefaction. In the Byzantine context, canon 48 of Trullo allowed the bishop's wife to continue to enjoy the help of her former husband after her removal to a monastery.[85] But the twelfth-century canonists added a further requirement: to receive this provision the bishop's wife had to be poor.[86] More specifically, Zonaras stated,

> For if even the bishop is not allowed to spend on himself more than is necessary from the revenues of the bishopric, and that when he does not have sufficient for necessities at home, how much more shall he be prevented from providing anything from the goods of the Church for the woman with whom he was formerly living, if she can obtain from elsewhere what she needs for her keep? At any rate, when she has nothing he will provide for her from the property of the bishopric on the grounds of her poverty.[87]

The bishop's wife could receive financial support from the bishopric's resources only if she was unable to support herself. Balsamon also emphasised the parallel between the episcopal wife and the bishop himself: he could not provide for her unless she was in need, just as he could not provide for himself.[88] Both canonists followed the canons in further suggesting that if the bishop's wife was of good character she could join the order of deaconesses.[89] This was as close as an episcopal spouse could get to her former husband's ecclesiastical grade, maintaining her status within the Church.[90]

Episcopal children were also expected to be under the care and supervision of their father. They are not mentioned explicitly in discussions about clerical marriage or celibacy, but the canonists talk about their situation when they comment on canon 35 of Carthage. This canon asked bishops and other clerics not to let their children become independent through an act of emancipation without first having informed themselves adequately about their character and maturity (εἰς τοὺς τρόπους καὶ εἰς τὴν ἡλικίαν); otherwise, their children's sins would fall upon them.[91] The association of sinning with finances is not surprising. With financial independence came the potential of mismanagement and debt, a situation which could then compromise a child not only materially but also spiritually. Byzantine children were under paternal authority (ὑπεξούσιοι) up to the age of 25, so long as their father or grandfather was still alive and they had not obtained an act of emancipation or established an independent household. This meant that they could not conclude contracts independently and without their father's or grandfather's permission.[92] Zonaras and Balsamon commented that bishops should make sure their children were virtuous (ἀγαθοί) and could manage their affairs suitably and piously (δεόντως καὶ εὐλαβῶς τὰ κατ' αὐτοὺς οἰκονομεῖν).[93] Balsamon added that independence from paternal authority should not be decided solely by the father but also by a judge.

Furthermore, he pointed to the difference between clerics and laymen. According to civil law (Book 31 Title 2 chapter 4 of the *Basilika*), laymen who had tolerated their children acting independently from them for two years or more lost their authority over them. However, according to canon 35 of Carthage, bishops and other clerics could not do the same, since if their children were to live in wantonness, it would be an insult (περιϋβρίζωνται) to clerical dignity. Excepted from this rule were the children of clerics and bishops who held an office at the Hagia Sophia. In that case, they were considered independent from parental supervision, and conversely their fathers were not deemed responsible for any potential wrongdoing on their part.[94] This, then, is an instance where Balsamon shows consideration for the family of the bishop. If his children are in need of help, he wants to prevent the father from easily freeing himself from his financial obligations, as the episcopal father should provide for his children until they are emancipated; if, however, the children become clerics themselves, the canonist wants them to have the necessary independence to be able to run their lives.

Similarly, Anglo-Norman ecclesiastics accepted that bishops could support their families, at least under certain circumstances. One of the key texts for this question was a letter written by Cardinal Humbert of Silva Candida (d. 1061) and addressed to the Studite monk Niketas Stethatos (c. 1005–c. 1085) as part of the discussions surrounding the 1054 schism. This is one of the rare occasions where we can see direct interaction between East and West on the topic of clerical celibacy (D.31 c.11):

> We altogether confess that it is not allowed for a bishop, priest, or deacon to cast away his own wife from his care on account of religion. On the contrary he is to supply her with food and clothing, but without lying with her carnally as before. We read that the holy apostles acted thus, with St Paul saying: 'Do we not have the ability to travel around with a woman who is a sister, just as the brothers of the Lord, and Cephas?' [1 Cor. 9:5] Look, fool, because he did

> not say: Do we not have the ability to 'embrace' a woman who is a sister, but to 'travel around' with her, that is to say so that she may be supported by them out of the profits of preaching, not however that between them there may also be a carnal union.[95]

Although Cardinal Humbert put more emphasis on the fact that clerics should not sleep with their wives, their obligation to provide for them was also clearly stated. The rule applied not only to bishops but also to priests and deacons, and presumably to subdeacons, although this is not explicitly stated, as it was at the level of the subdiaconate that the separation was meant to take place. The author of the *Summa Lipsiensis* agreed that former wives could not be abandoned and raised the question of where the funds for their upkeep should come from:

> According to this chapter it is manifestly held that a man who enters into sacred orders ought to provide to his wife the necessary things of life. But should he do so from the goods of the Church or from his own goods? From his own goods, if he has any, as is stipulated in C.12 q.1 c.21 [canon 40 of the Apostles]. Otherwise, he can give from the goods of the Church, just as [he gives] to the poor, as it is stipulated in D.86 c.14.[96]

Similarly to the Byzantine commentators, the *Summa Lipsiensis* considered the wife's poverty a prerequisite in cases where the funds of the Church were involved, as did also Master Honorius.[97] What this meant for the clerical wife depended on contemporary ideas about poverty and especially the deserving poor.[98] For example, the author of the *Summa Lipsiensis* seems to have taken quite a harsh stance when it came to helping family members. He believed that being good to one's relatives could not be taken as a manifestation of a person's kindness, as even bad people bring relief to their families.[99] By contrast, Master Honorius emphasised that kindness and nature could both be combined, when one helped a relative who was a worthy person.[100]

In the case of the clerical wife, expenses could be avoided if she entered a nunnery at the point when her husband acceded to sacred orders (D.77 c.6). According to Master Honorius, this was always the preferred line of action.[101] The author of the *Summa Lipsiensis*, on the other hand, was willing to accept that monastic conversion could be avoided if there was absolutely no suspicion that the wife could be unchaste due to her old age. To support this claim he directed the reader to a decretal of Pope Alexander III which advised the bishop of Exeter that 'if a wife is old and barren' he could allow her to remain in the secular world.[102] Unfortunately, he gave here no further details about the alternative financial measures to be taken.

Episcopal children were also to be provided for. Gratian's *Decretum* (D.30 c.14) included canon 15 of Gangra, which stated,

> If anyone abandons his own children, not feeding them or supplying them with the necessities that are part of the familial duties, but thinks that under the pretext of continence they ought to be neglected, let him be anathema.[103]

Master Honorius commented on this chapter, adding that both good and bad children had to be supported when they were in need.[104] The author of the *Summa Lipsiensis* also commented on this topic, but under D.93 c.23. This chapter had made only an incidental mention of children in the context of a reference to Deuteronomy 33:9, which described deacons as men who ceased to 'recognise' their family because of their devotion to God. As the *Summa Lipsiensis* explained, the reference was to be taken figuratively rather than literally. Deacons were indeed meant to 'recognise' their children, in the sense that they were meant 'to love them and not despise them', but without allowing human affection to distract them from their real duties.[105] Like Master Honorius, the *Summa Lipsiensis* maintained that parents had an obligation to take care of their offspring.

These provisions applied only to legitimate families – that is to say, women who had been married to clerics before their accession to the subdiaconate, had children with them during that time, and then separated from them following their ordination. By contrast, the *Summa Lipsiensis* reminds us that concubines or women who had unlawfully married a cleric after his ordination were threatened to be sold into servitude if they did not wish to enter a monastery.[106] Equivalent laws existed on the subject of illegitimate children, but these were largely theoretical.[107] The author of the *Summa Lipsiensis*, commenting on D.56 c.4, affirmed that the law which expected children born to clerical fathers not only to be unable to inherit but also to be held in perpetual 'servitude' in their father's church (C.15 q.8 c.3) had been abolished and was no longer followed in his time.[108] In practice, bishops could, and often did, take care of their families, even illegitimate ones. One late example comes from the family of Richard of Ilchester, whose two illegitimate sons, Herbert Poore (d. 1217) and Richard Poore (d. 1237), became successive bishops of Salisbury and inherited parts of their father's land, in Winchester, Hampshire, and London.[109]

Conclusion

In the twelfth century, the Byzantine and Anglo-Norman Churches operated within a legal tradition that linked clerical marriage to the potential for ecclesiastical misappropriations. Most notably, Justinian's laws required bishops to be not only celibate but also without direct descendants so that they would not squander the Church's resources on them. Although this extreme legal position did not survive intact in either East or West, it was still a point of reference, and current practices were explained against it.

Both Byzantine and Anglo-Norman canon lawyers conceded that legitimate children did not constitute an impediment to episcopal ordination, and episcopal families could be provided for, either through the bishop's personal property or through the Church if they were thought to be too poor. But in the West, Justinian's decrees could be used to support an existing climate of suspicion around clerical families and to encourage the selection of celibate men for the episcopate. In Byzantium, on the other hand, although rules requiring episcopal celibacy remained, they were no longer explained with reference to wives and direct descendants. It was acknowledged that bishops could misappropriate ecclesiastical property, but they could do so for the sake of a variety of people who did not need to be limited to the smallest familial circle; the beneficiaries could include other relatives and friends.

We will see in the following chapters that the greater focus on wives and sons in England is in fact a recurring theme in legal sources relating to clerical marriage. To some extent, this can be explained by contrasting attitudes to clerical families. In the general climate of hostility in England, rules about ecclesiastical property, such as a preference for bishops without families, acted as a disincentive towards marriage, whereas in Byzantium the respect for clerical marriage meant that there was no such appetite for attacking it by targeting wives and children as potential beneficiaries of ecclesiastical misappropriations.

Despite this difference in the interpretation of the rules of celibacy, a basic similarity remains: both Eastern and Western bishops could have an enviable financial position within society and considerable control over ecclesiastical assets, especially landed property; as such their spending had to be controlled. The rules of clerical celibacy represented one measure among others deployed in an effort to limit episcopal misappropriations, regardless of whether the Byzantines chose to emphasise this at different periods.

Given that it has been my contention that it was this great episcopal access to ecclesiastical wealth which gave rise to a number of legal restrictions, some of which concerned the bishop's familial status, in the next chapter I will turn to a different group of clerics, those below the episcopate, to see what impact their different access to ecclesiastical property may have had on the legislation that controlled their spending and how this related to their marital status.

Notes

1 See also S.N. Troianos, 'Zölibat und Kirchenvermögen in der früh- und mittelbyzantinischen kanonischen Gesetzgebung', in *Eherecht und Familiengut in Antike und Mittelalter*, ed. D. Simon (Munich, 1992), 133–46, at 135–8.

2 *Syntagma* 3.168: 'μεταβάλλοι δὲ τὰ πράγματα εἰς οἰκείας αὐτοῦ χρείας, καὶ τοὺς πόρους τῆς ἐκκλησίας ἢ τοὺς τῶν ἀγρῶν καρποὺς μὴ μετὰ γνώμης τῶν πρεσβυτέρων ἢ τῶν διακόνων χειρίζοι, ἀλλ᾽ οἰκείοις αὐτοῦ καὶ συγγενέσιν ἢ ἀδελφοῖς ἢ υἱοῖς παράσχοιτο τὴν ἐξουσίαν, ὥστε διὰ τῶν τοιούτων λεληθότως βλάπτεσθαι τοὺς λόγους τῆς ἐκκλησίας'.

3 *Syntagma* 2.52: 'μὴ ἐξεῖναι δὲ αὐτῷ σφετερίζεσθαί τι ἐξ αὐτῶν, ἢ συγγενέσιν ἰδίοις τὰ τοῦ Θεοῦ χαρίζεσθαι· εἰ δὲ πένητες εἶεν, ἐπιχορηγείτω ὡς πένησιν, ἀλλὰ μὴ προφάσει τούτων τὰ τῆς ἐκκλησίας ἀπεμπολείτω'. See also *Syntagma* 3.593.

4 *Syntagma* 2.55: ''Ἔστω φανερὰ τὰ ἴδια τοῦ ἐπισκόπου πράγματα (εἴγε καὶ ἴδια ἔχοι) καὶ φανερὰ τὰ Κυριακά· ἵνα ἐξουσίαν ἔχῃ τὰ ἴδια τελευτῶν ὁ ἐπίσκοπος οἷς βούλεται καὶ ὡς βούλεται, καταλεῖψαι· καὶ μὴ προφάσει τῶν ἐκκλησιαστικῶν πραγμάτων διαπίπτειν τὰ τοῦ ἐπισκόπου, ἐσθ᾽ ὅτε γυναῖκα καὶ παῖδας κεκτημένου, ἢ συγγενεῖς ἢ οἰκέτας. Δίκαιον γὰρ παρὰ Θεῷ καὶ ἀνθρώποις τὸ μήτε τὴν ἐκκλησίαν ζημίαν τινὰ ὑπομένειν ἀγνοίᾳ τῶν τοῦ ἐπισκόπου πραγμάτων, μήτε τὸν ἐπίσκοπον ἢ τοὺς αὐτοῦ συγγενεῖς προφάσει τῆς ἐκκλησίας δημεύεσθαι, ἢ καὶ εἰς πράγματα ἐμπίπτειν τοὺς αὐτῷ διαφέροντας, καὶ τὸν αὐτοῦ θάνατον δυσφημίαις περιβάλλεσθαι.' The same idea was expressed in canon 24 of the synod of Antioch (341). See *Syntagma* 3.166–7.

5 See 1.3.41 §5 in *The Codex of Justinian* 1.106–7. See also Novel 131 c. 13 in W. Kroll and R. Schöll (eds.), *Corpus iuris civilis*, vol. III (Berlin, 1895; repr. 1968), 661–2.
6 For a list of alienations of Church property committed by fifth- and sixth-century bishops, see P. Allen and B. Neil, *Crisis Management in Late Antiquity (410–590 CE)* (Leiden, 2013), 153–4.
7 See 1.3.41 §2–3 in *The Codex of Justinian* 1.106–7.
8 See also P. L'Huillier, 'The First Millennium: Marriage, Sexuality, and Priesthood', in *Vested in Grace: Priesthood and Marriage in the Christian East*, ed. J.J. Allen (Brookline, MA, 2001), 23–65, at 34–6.
9 See, for example, Novel 6 c. 1 §7, where we are told again that bishops must not have a wife, children, or even grandchildren, in Kroll and Schöll (eds.), *Corpus iuris civilis*, 3.37. See also Sp. Troianos, 'Le célibat épiscopal dans la "civitas augescens"', in *Roman Law as Formative of Modern Legal Systems: Studies in Honour of Wieslaw Litewski*, eds. J. Reszczyński, P. Ściślicki, and J. Sondel, vol. II (Cracow, 2003), 185–95, at 191.
10 *Syntagma* 2.330–1. See also Troianos, 'Le célibat épiscopal', 193.
11 Novel 2 in *Leo VI*, 16–19.
12 *Syntagma* 2.422: 'λέγομεν ὡς τὰ τῆς τοιαύτης νεαρᾶς ἠπράκτησαν'.
13 Winroth, *Making of Gratian's Decretum*, 199. See also D.61 c.17.
14 *Magistri Honorii* 1.194. D.61 c.17 s.v. *nec uxorem nec filios*: 'Hoc speciale, ut illud supra di.xxviii De Siracusane (D.28 c.13).'
15 *Summa Lipsiensis* 1.108, D.28 c.13 s.v. *uxor uel filii*: 'Hinc habes quod uxorem habens et filios non debet promoueri, etsi reperiatur idoneus, ut di.lxi. Cathinensis (D.61 c.17).' *Summa Lipsiensis* 1.109, D.28 c.13 s.v. *cautionem*: 'Nota quod in Autentico predicto precipitur ut non eligatur presbiter habens uxorem et filios.' *Summa Lipsiensis* 1.285, D.61 c.17 s.v. *nec uxorem habeat*: 'Tales enim non debent eligi, si alius dignus reperiatur. Si tamen eligantur, cautio ab eis debet exigi eo modo quo dicitur supra di.xxviii (D.28 c.13).'
16 Other decretists also mention Justinian's laws on this topic and in particular Novel 6. See, for example, *Summa des Stephanus*, 44; *Summa Parisiensis*, 28.
17 C.N.L. Brooke, '1. The Gregorian Reform in Action: Clerical Marriage in England, 1050–1200', *Cambridge Historical Journal*, 12 (1956), 1–21, at 7; C.N.L. Brooke, '2. Married Men Among the English Higher Clergy, 1066–1200', *Cambridge Historical Journal*, 12 (1956), 187–8.
18 G.W.S. Barrow, 'Puiset, Hugh du, earl of Northumberland (c. 1125–1195)', *Oxford Dictionary of National Biography*. https://doi.org/10.1093/ref:odnb/22871. Accessed 2/12/2017.
19 For example, while we know that Robert Bloet, bishop of Lincoln, fathered his son Simon when he was royal chancellor – that is to say, before his consecration – we do not know whether at the time Simon's mother was Robert's wife or his concubine. Our only evidence about Simon's parentage comes from a letter written by Henry of Huntingdon. See D.E. Greenway (ed. and trans.), *Henry, Archdeacon of Huntingdon: Historia Anglorum* (Oxford, 1996), 596–7.
20 Bishops were also in charge of the collection of Peter's Pence. This money was payable to the pope but there is good evidence to suggest that collectors could keep some of it for themselves and their bishoprics. See Brett, *The English Church*, 161–73.
21 On this topic, see C. Harper-Bill, 'The Struggle for Benefices in Twelfth-Century East Anglia', in *Anglo-Norman Studies XI: Proceedings of the Battle Conference 1988* (Woodbridge, 1989), 113–32, at 130–2; M. Burger, *Bishops, Clerks, and Diocesan Governance in Thirteenth-Century England* (Cambridge, 2012), 169–85.
22 M. Brett, 'The Church at Rochester, 604–1185', in *Faith and Fabric: A History of Rochester Cathedral, 604–1994*, ed. N. Yates (Woodbridge, 1996), 1–27, at 14–15.
23 A. Oakley, 'Rochester Priory, 1185–1540', in *Faith and Fabric: A History of Rochester Cathedral, 604–1994*, ed. N. Yates (Woodbridge, 1996), 29–55, at 37–8; H.

Summerson, 'Medieval Carlisle: Cathedral and City From Foundation to Dissolution', in *Carlisle and Cumbria: Roman and Medieval Architecture, Art and Archaeology*, eds. M. McCarthy and D. Weston (Leeds, 2004), 29–38, at 31.

24 Since these figures correspond to vacancy profits, they cannot accurately represent the revenues a bishop would have had. Strictly speaking, the king was meant to receive the temporalities (e.g., agricultural profits and rents) but not the spiritualities – that is, income that came from religious sources and which was meant to go only to the clergy (e.g., Peter's Pence); but the very definitions of what constituted spiritualities and what temporalities changed during the period. See M. Howell, *Regalian Right in Medieval England* (London, 1962), 39, 110–16, 214–15.

25 These figures come from Crosby, *Bishop and Chapter*, 70. In turn his calculations were based on the table of enrolled accounts of episcopal vacancies to the year 1307, found in Howell, *Regalian Right*, 212–33. They can be compared with the value of pre-Conquest episcopal endowments in the Domesday Book, where we find Canterbury at the top with £1,330 and the average value at £362. The episcopal Church as a corporate body controlled about 8 per cent of the kingdom's landed wealth in 1066. Its estates were valued at around £5,400. This was less than the £7,185 held by monastic communities at the time, without including the monastic cathedrals of Christ Church, Canterbury, Old Minster, Winchester, St Mary's of Worcester, and Sherborne. See M.F. Giandrea, *Episcopal Culture in Late Anglo-Saxon England* (Woodbridge, 2007), 125–6. Glastonbury was at the top of the rankings of monastic houses according to their gross income in Domesday with £827, followed by Ely with £768. See Appendix VI in D. Knowles, *The Monastic Order in England* (Cambridge, 1963, 2nd edn.), 702–3.

26 For a more extensive analysis and comparison between secular and clerical incomes, see Thomas, *Secular Clergy*, 56–7.

27 Cf. the leases of Bishop Oswald of Worcester in F. Tinti, *Sustaining Belief: The Church of Worcester From c. 870 to c. 1100* (Farnham, 2010), 33–8.

28 In France it was not before the twelfth century at the earliest that individual prebends were created from lands taken from the mass of the ecclesiastical property and assigned to individual canons. See E. Lesne, 'Les origines de la prébende', *Revue historique de droit français et étranger*, Ser. 4, 8 (1929), 257. In England, territorial division occurred earlier, although the term *praebenda* was not used until the late eleventh century. An exception to the usage of the word *praebenda* can be found in connection with Exeter, where the term signified a share in the communal revenues. See J. Barrow, 'Cathedrals, Provosts and Prebends: A Comparison of Twelfth-Century German and English Practice', *The Journal of Ecclesiastical History*, 37:4 (1986), 536–64, at 538.

29 Some prebends corresponded to cash payments. There are three such examples from Lincoln cathedral: *Decem Librarum*, *Centum Solidorum*, and *Sexaginta Solidorum*. See *Fasti*, III, ix–xiii. Cathedral communities with secular clergy would often have property they ran communally in addition to separate holdings for individual canons. At St Paul's in London, Domesday evidence shows that the canons communally owned large estates in Essex and Hertfordshire, but the bulk of the individual territorial holdings created for the canons, the future prebends, was created on estates run by the bishop in Middlesex. See S.E. Kelly (ed.), *Charters of St Paul's, London* (Oxford, 2004), 103–6.

30 See also S.P.J. Harvey, 'The Extent and Profitability of Demesne Agriculture in England in the Later Eleventh Century', in *Social Relations and Ideas: Essays in Honour of R.H. Hilton*, eds. T.H. Aston et al. (Cambridge, 1983), 45–72, at 54–5; P.D.A. Harvey, 'English Cathedral Estates in the Twelfth Century', in *The Medieval English Cathedral: Papers in Honour of Pamela Tudor-Craig*, ed. J. Backhouse (Donington, 2003), 1–14.

31 Harvey, 'English Cathedral Estates', 12–14.

32 Chapter lands were used for the establishment of prebends in St Paul's and royal grants for some of the prebends in Lincoln. See Barrow, 'Cathedrals, Provosts and Prebends', 559.

33 *Fasti*, IV, xxi–xxxix. For another example, see the establishment of prebends in Lincoln, which began with twenty-one prebends founded by Remigius (1067–1092) and reached fifty-six prebends by around 1187. See *Fasti*, III, ix–xiii.

34 In around the mid-twelfth century, prebends and benefices in England were also assigned to specific clerics under the influence of the pope. This situation was the result of the papacy asserting its supremacy on a local level, but was also a reflection of the desire of bishops, abbots, and English kings to foster good relations with Rome as a means of defending their political, legal, and economic interests. See C.R. Cheney, *Pope Innocent III and England* (Stuttgart, 1976), 80–96, at 91–5. Papal influence on the bestowal of prebends was not sizeable until the thirteenth century and peaked in the fourteenth century. See G. Barraclough, *Papal Provisions: Aspects of Church History, Constitutional, Legal and Administrative in the Later Middle Ages* (Westport, CT, 1971).

35 J. Barrow, 'Clergy in the Diocese of Hereford in the Eleventh and Twelfth Centuries', in *Anglo-Norman Studies XXVI: Proceedings of the Battle Conference 2003*, ed. J. Gillingham (Woodbridge, 2004), 37–53, at 44.

36 The *Summa Lipsiensis* pointed out the contradiction between C.1 q.2 c.6, which asked clerics not to receive stipends from their church if they could afford to use their own money, and C.12 q.1 c.21, which acknowledged that bishops could have access to both their own funds and those of the church, but should try to keep the two separate. See *Summa Lipsiensis* 2.77.

37 They had help in this from the so-called *oikonomoi*. For more on this, see the next chapter.

38 Such payments in kind could be given to clerics of all grades. Balsamon mentions how the faithful at the Church of Blachernai would offer grapes to the patriarch after the celebration of the Dormition of the Mother of God. See *Syntagma* 2.4–7. Balsamon also calls such donations 'κανίσκια' in *Syntagma* 2.6.

39 E. Herman, 'Das bischöfliche Abgabenwesen im Patriarchat von Konstantinopel von XI. bis zur Mitte des XIX. Jahrhunderts', *OCP*, 5 (1939), 434–513, at 437–57; Moulet, *Évêques*, 299.

40 It is difficult to establish which priests were meant to pay this levy; it was probably compulsory for all priests, whether they were part of a cathedral, a parish, or a private religious foundation. See Herman, 'Abgabenwesen', 445, 446–7. Cf. *Les regestes de 715 à 1206*, 322 n. 808. See also Thomas, *Private Religious Foundations*, 240.

41 S. Troianos, 'Ein Synodalakt des Sisinios zu den bischöflichen Einkünften', *Fontes Minores*, 3 (1979), 211–20. See also Herman, 'Abgabenwesen', 448–52, at 449.

42 Herman, 'Abgabenwesen', 457–60. On the *synetheiai* which abbots had to pay, see Thomas, *Private Religious Foundations*, 215.

43 *Syntagma* 5.60.

44 *JGR* 1.275–6. This law was confirmed by Alexios I Komnenos in September 1100. See *JGR* 1.311–2. For an idea of the value of the different Byzantine currencies during this period, see C. Morrisson and J.-C. Cheynet, 'Prices and Wages in the Byzantine World', in *The Economic History of Byzantium: From the Seventh Through the Fifteenth Century*, ed. A.E. Laiou (Washington, DC, 2002), 815–78. See also Angold, *Church and Society*, 61, 144–5.

45 See Balsamon's answer to question 59, of Mark Patriarch of Alexandria in *Syntagma* 4.492.

46 This seems to have been legally constituted for the first time during the reign of Emperor Constantine IX Monomachos (r. 1042–1055) and was later confirmed by Emperor Alexios I Komnenos. See Herman, 'Abgabenwesen', 465.

47 Herman, 'Abgabenwesen', 158. Through the correspondence of bishops and particularly through the gifts that accompanied their letters, we can get an idea of the goods produced in their bishoprics. See B. Moulet, 'Le goût des autres. Correspondances gourmandes et culture du goût à Byzance', in *L'échange: Journées de maison des Sciences de l'homme Ange-Guépin*, ed. J. Tolan (Paris, 2009), 163–77.
48 Emphyteutic leases were long-term, covering possibly two or three generations, and gave more rights to the tenant, who could transfer the lease as a dowry or sell it. See M. Kaplan, 'The Producing Population', in *A Social History of Byzantium*, ed. J. Haldon (Oxford, 2009), 143–67, at 146–7; E. Papagianni, 'Legal Institutions and Practice in Matters of Ecclesiastical Property', in *The Economic History of Byzantium: From the Seventh Through the Fifteenth Century*, ed. A.E. Laiou (Washington, DC, 2002), 1059–69, at 1061.
49 We can see, for example, that the list of properties of the metropolis of Athens drawn up in 1209 by Pope Innocent III included episcopal estates in twenty-five villages around Athens as well as at least twenty monasteries. See PL 215.1560–1. For the possessions of another well-documented bishopric, see D. Papachryssanthou, 'Un évêché byzantin: Hierissos en Chalcidique', *Travaux et mémoires*, 8 (1981), 373–96, at 383–4.
50 M. Kaplan, *Les hommes et la terre à Byzance du VIe au XIe siècle* (Paris, 1992), 283–6.
51 For an example of how episcopal and monastic financial interests could clash, see G. Merianos, 'More than a Shepherd to his Flock: Eustathios and the Management of Ecclesiastical Property', in *Reading Eustathios of Thessalonike*, eds. F. Pontani, V. Katsaros, and V. Sarris (Berlin, 2017), 309–30.
52 C.A. Frazee, 'Late Roman and Byzantine Legislation on the Monastic Life From the Fourth to the Eighth Centuries', *Church History*, 51:3 (1982), 263–79.
53 P. Charanis, 'The Monastic Properties and the State in the Byzantine Empire', *DOP*, 4 (1948), 51–118, at 63–4.
54 Monasteries could also be entirely free of supervision, including that of the patriarch. The way for this was paved through Emperor Nikephoros Phokas' chrysobull to St Athanasios for the monastery of Lavra on Mount Athos in 964. See Thomas, *Private Religious Foundations*, 215–6.
55 Angold, *Church and Society*, 124; *Les regestes de 715 à 1206*, 592–3 nn. 1179–80.
56 *Les regestes de 715 à 1206*, 458–9 n. 1000; Th. Uspenskij, 'Mnemija i postanovlenija Konstantinopol'skikh pomestnykh soborov', *Izvestija russkago arkheologicheskago instituta v Konstantinopole*, 5 (1900), 1–48, at 16–17. See also Charanis, 'Monastic Properties', 78–79; Angold, *Church and Society*, 144.
57 *Syntagma* 5.23–4; Thomas, *Private Religious Foundations*, 170.
58 *Syntagma* 2.310. See also Angold, *Church and Society*, 149, 333–7; E. Herman, 'Ricerche sulle istituzioni monastiche bizantine. Typika kletorika, caristicari e monasteri liberi', *OCP*, 6 (1940), 361–72; J.P. Thomas, 'The Rise of the Independent and Self-governing Monasteries as Reflected in the Monastic Typika', *Greek Orthodox Theological Review*, 30 (1985), 21–30.
59 Thomas, *Private Religious Foundations*, 209.
60 J. Thomas and A. Constantinides Hero (eds.), *Byzantine Monastic Foundation Documents* (Washington, DC, 2000), 860, 954–72.
61 Angold and Whitby commented that 'major metropolitan sees were relatively wealthy, but the general run of Byzantine bishoprics were, when compared with their Western counterparts, decidedly poor.' See Angold and Whitby, 'Church Structures and Administration', 580. Although this is interesting in its own right, for the purpose of this comparison it is more important to establish the relative position of bishops within their own society.
62 Morrisson and Cheynet, 'Prices and Wages in the Byzantine World', 869.

63 Later on in the twelfth century when another archbishop of Thessalonike, Eustathios, was ransomed, the Normans demanded 4,000 gold coins for his release under the pretext that his metropolis had the exceedingly large income of 100 *kentenaria*, or 720,000 *nomismata*. See Melville-Jones, *The Capture of Thessaloniki*, 109, 212.

64 J. Wortley, *John Skylitzes: A Synopsis of Byzantine History, 811–1057: Translation and Notes* (Cambridge, 2010), 379; I. Bekker (ed.), *George Cedrenus, Historiarum Compendium*, vol. II (Bonn, 1839), 518–19.

65 Cf. M.F. Hendy, *Studies in the Byzantine Monetary Economy c. 300–1450* (Cambridge, 1985), 240.

66 Even Thessalonike had only twelve suffragans, while Ephesos had thirty-eight and Sardis twenty-five. See Angold and Whitby, 'Church Structures and Administration', 579.

67 Especially in frontier regions, raids by Turkish marauders were still a daily occurrence in the twelfth century. Some areas, such as the bishopric of Chonai, appear to have been less affected, but others, such as the bishopric of Ephesos, were hit particularly hard. For more information on the situation in Asia Minor, see Magdalino, *Empire of Manuel*, 128–32.

68 *JGR* 1.326. See also E. Herman, 'Les bénéfices dans l'église orientale', in *Dictionnaire de droit canonique*, ed. R. Naz, vol. II (Paris, 1937), 706–35, at 714.

69 Such measures would allow areas which were only scarcely populated by Christians to receive the necessary pastoral care and would encourage non-Christian populations to convert. See *Syntagma* 3.246. See also V. Tiftixoglu, 'Gruppenbildungen innerhalb des konstantinopolitanischen Klerus während der Komnenenzeit', *Byzantinische Zeitschrift*, 62 (1969), 25–72, at 50.

70 See, for example, *Syntagma* 3.51; 2.76.

71 See Herman, 'Les bénéfices', 718. Cf. Moulet, *Évêques*, 298 n. 53.

72 Zonaras' comment on canon 41 of the Apostles in *Syntagma* 2.57: 'οὐ μὴν εἰς περιττόν τι, καὶ πρὸς τρυφὴν ἢ βλακείαν ἀνῆκον'. See also his comment in *Syntagma* 3.169. In a lay context, Kekaumenos also stressed that the necessities of life included primarily food: 'Essential things are those by which we are sustained; extras are things like expensive furniture, and soft bedding, and gilded couches, etcetera.' See C. Roueché, *Kekaumenos, Consilia et Narrationes*. www.ancientwisdoms.ac.uk/folioscope/greekLit%3Atlg3017.Syno298.sawsEng01%3Adiv3&viewOffsets=-5573. Accessed 18/06/2014.

73 *Syntagma* 3.223: 'οὐκ ἔσται πρὸς τιμὴν τοῦ Θεοῦ τὸ πεζῇ βαδίζειν ἀρχιερέα διὰ πενίαν καὶ στερεῖσθαι τῶν ἀναγκαίων'. The canonist was referring here to the churches in the East in the areas under Turkish control, which in his opinion had become unsafe and had too small a population of Christians to support a bishop.

74 *Syntagma* 4.350: 'οὐδὲ εἰς οἰκείαν χρῆσιν τοῖς τῆς ἐπισκοπῆς πράγμασι κεχρῆσθαι τῷ ἐπισκόπῳ συγκεχώρηται, εἰ μὴ εἰς τὰ πάνυ ἀναγκαῖα, καὶ τότε, ὅτε οἴκοθεν οὐκ εὐπορεῖ τούτων ὁ ἐπίσκοπος'.

75 See, for example, D.L. Douie and H. Farmer (eds.), *The Life of St. Hugh of Lincoln*, vol. I (London, 1961), xxxvi. For Byzantium, see how Michael Choniates, archbishop of Athens (1182–1205), proudly commemorated his actions in favour of his church and clergy in a poem, in A. Kaldellis, *The Christian Parthenon: Classicism and Pilgrimage in Byzantine Athens* (Cambridge, 2009), 151. Such obligations were also codified in canon law. Canon 59 of the Apostles excommunicated bishops who did not provide what was necessary for life (τὰ δέοντα, τὰ ζωαρκῆ) to poor clerics in their diocese. See *Syntagma* 2.76. Canon 4 of Chalcedon asked bishops to 'take appropriate care of the monasteries' in *Syntagma* 2.226; 2.228.

76 See Balsamon's comment on canon 10 of Theophilos of Alexandria in *Syntagma* 4.350: 'Τὴν δὲ εἰς δέον δαπάνην, τὸ ἑξῆς δηλοῖ κεφάλαιον, ἥτις ἐστὶ τὰ εἰς χήρας καὶ ξένους καὶ πένητας ἀναλώματα'. For the sick, see Aristenos' comment on canon 6 of the Apostles in *Syntagma* 2.9: 'Κοσμικὰς φροντίδας ἐπίσκοπος ἢ πρεσβύτερος ἢ διάκονος ἀναδέχεσθαι οὐ συγκεχώρηται δι' αἰσχροκέρδειαν οἰκείαν, εἰ μή που ὑπὸ νόμων

καλεῖται εἰς πραγμάτων ἀφηλίκων διοίκησιν, ἢ ἄλλως πως ἀπαιτεῖται ἀντιλαβέσθαι χηρῶν καὶ ὀρφανῶν καὶ ἀσθενῶν διοικήσεως'. See also Gratian's *Decretum* D.87 cc.1–4.

77 Roueché, *Kekaumenos, Consilia et Narrationes*.

78 See also C. Roueché, 'The Literary Background of Kekaumenos', in *Literacy, Education and Manuscript Transmission in Byzantium and Beyond*, eds. C. Holmes and J. Waring (Leiden, 2002), 111–38, at 123–4.

79 For an early example, see Wulfstan the Homilist's description of clerics who 'decorate their wives with what they should the altars' in B. Thorpe, *Ancient Laws and Institutes of England*, vol. II (London, 1840), 328–9.

80 C.J. Morris, *Marriage and Murder in Eleventh-Century Northumbria: A Study of the 'De Obsessione Dunelmi'* (York, 1992), 12–18. See also W.M. Aird, *St Cuthbert and the Normans: The Church of Durham, 1071–1153* (Woodbridge, 1998), 116.

81 M. Richter, 'A New Edition of the So-called Vita Dauidis Secundi', *Bulletin of the Board of Celtic Studies*, 22 (1966–68), 248.

82 Richter, 'Dauidis secundi', 248: 'Et hec omnia distribuit canonicis contradicentibus et reclamantibus.'

83 J.W. Evans, 'Transition and Survival: St David and St Davids Cathedral', in *St David of Wales: Cult, Church and Nation*, eds. J.W. Evans and J.M. Wooding (Woodbridge, 2007), 20–40, at 32, 37.

84 *Gemma Ecclesiastica*, 212–3; *Gir. Camb. opera* 2.281. Tricenaries are thirty-day commemorations of a dead member of the community.

85 *Syntagma* 2.419–20.

86 The fact that poor bishops should be able to help their poor relatives was also pointed out by Emperor Leo VI in his law which allowed bishops to have descendants. See Novel 2, in *Leo VI*, 16–19, at 19: 'Ἀλλὰ προειδότες τοῦτο οἱ θεῖοι κανόνες ἔδοσαν τοῖς ἐπισκόποις ἐξουσίαν, εἰ συγγενεῖς εἶεν ἄποροι, ἐκ τῆς ἱερᾶς ὑπάρξεως τούτων παραμυθεῖσθαι τὴν ἀπορίαν.'

87 *Syntagma* 2.419–20: 'Εἰ γὰρ αὐτὸς ὁ ἐπίσκοπος οὐ συγκεχώρηται περαιτέρω τῶν ἀναγκαίων εἰς ἑαυτὸν δαπανᾶν ἐκ τῶν τῆς ἐπισκοπῆς εἰσόδων· καὶ τοῦτο, ὅτε μὴ οἴκοθεν εὐπορεῖ τῶν ἀναγκαίων, πῶς οὐ μᾶλλον τῇ πρώην συνοικησάσῃ αὐτῷ κωλυθήσεται χορηγεῖν τι ἐκ τῶν τῆς ἐκκλησίας, δυναμένῃ πορίζεσθαι τὰ πρὸς διοίκησιν ἄλλοθεν; Ὡς γοῦν ἐνδεεῖ κἀκείνῃ, ὅτε μὴ ἔχει, παρέξει ἐκ τῶν τῆς ἐπισκοπῆς'.

88 *Syntagma* 2.420: 'Οὕτω δὲ τούτου γινομένου, ἀξιοῦσθαι τὴν γυναῖκα παρὰ τοῦ ἐπισκόπου προνοίας σωματικῆς, ἐνδεῆ οὖσαν. Εἰ γὰρ εὐπορεῖ, οὐδέν τι δοθήσεται αὐτῇ παρὰ τοῦ ἐπισκόπου, ὅτι οὐδὲ αὐτὸς εὐπορῶν δύναταί τι εἰς ἑαυτὸν δαπανᾶν ἐκ τῶν εἰσόδων τῆς ἐπισκοπῆς.'

89 *Syntagma* 2.420; 2.422.

90 On the duties of the deaconess during this period in Byzantium, see V. Karras, 'Female Deacons in the Byzantine Church', *Church History*, 73:2 (2004), 272–316. On the decline of the role of deaconesses, see J. Herrin, 'Public and Private Forms of Religious Commitment Among Byzantine Women', in *Women in Ancient Societies*, eds. L.J. Archer, S. Fischler, and M. Wyke (London, 1994), 181–203, at 191. In the Western Church references to deaconesses were rare. They appear to have lost their sacramental role and to have survived only in monastic communities. See G. Muschiol, *Famula Dei: Zur Liturgie in merowingischen Frauenklöstern* (Münster, 1994), 295–300. For a more optimistic suggestion in terms of the survival of the office of the deaconess, see G. Macy, *The Hidden History of Women's Ordination* (New York, NY, 2007).

91 *Syntagma* 3.396–7.

92 See G. Prinzig, 'Observations on the Legal Status of Children and the Stages of Childhood in Byzantium', in *Becoming Byzantine: Children and Childhood in Byzantium*, eds. A. Papaconstantinou and A.-M. Talbot (Washington, DC, 2009), 15–34; B. Caseau, 'Too Young to Be Accountable: Is 15 Years Old a Threshold in Byzantium?',

in *Coming of Age in Byzantium Adolescence and Society*, ed. D. Ariantzi (Berlin, 2018), 19–28.

93 *Syntagma* 3.397.

94 *Syntagma* 3.398.

95 D.31 c.1: 'Omnino confitemur, non licere episcopo, presbitero, diacono, propriam uxorem causa religionis abicere a cura sua, sed ut ei uictum et uestitum largiatur, sed non ut cum illa ex more carnaliter iaceat. Sic et sanctos apostolos legimus egisse, B. Paulo apostolo dicente: "Numquid non habemus potestatem sororem mulierem circumducendi, sicut frater Domini et Cephas?" Vide insipiens, quia non dixit: numquid non habemus potestatem sororem mulierem "amplectendi?" sed "circumducendi," scilicet ut mercede predicationis sustentaretur ab eis, nec tamen deinceps foret inter eos ulterius carnale coniugium.' This chapter is present in both recensions. See Winroth, *Making of Gratian's Decretum*, 199.

96 *Summa Lipsiensis* 1.119, D.31 c.11 s.v. *sustentaretur*: 'Ex hoc capitulo habetur manifeste quod uir ad sacros ordines transiens necessaria debet ministrare uxori. Set utrum de bonis ecclesie uel de propriis? De propriis, si propria habet, ut xii. q.i Sint manifeste (C.12 q.1 c.21); uel de rebus ecclesie potest dare, tamen ut pauperi, ut di.lxxxvi. Non satis (D.86 c.14), in xii. q.ii Quisquis (C.12 q.2 c.19).'

97 Master Honorius also asked this question: 'thence would it be allowed to a priest to provide for such a wife from the goods of the Church?' He answered simply 'yes, as he would do for the poor'. See *Magistri Honorii* 1.109, D.31 c.11 s.v. *de mercede*: 'Vnde liceret presbitero de bonis ecclesie talem uxorem exhibere? Resp.: Sic, ut pauperem.'

98 D.86 c.14 dealt with the issue of the deserving poor and received extensive commentary in *Summa Lipsiensis* 1.361–2. Contemporary theologians and canon lawyers idealised poverty and paupers, who just like monks became sanctified through association with Christ. Those in the circle of Peter the Chanter (d. 1197) discussed the obligation of the entire Christian community to provide for those in need. See J. Taliadoros, 'Law, Theology, and Morality: Conceptions of the Rights to Relief of the Poor in the Twelfth and Thirteenth Centuries', *Journal of Religious History*, 37:4 (2013), 474–93, at 482, 486–7. Brodman has called the twelfth century 'a watershed in medieval Europe's concept and practice of charity'. See J. Brodman, *Charity and Religion in Medieval Europe* (Baltimore, MD, 2009), 14–15. For a fuller discussion of the late twelfth- and early thirteenth-century canonical treatises and their recognition of the right of the poor to relief and the obligation of society to provide it, see B. Tierney, *Medieval Poor Law: A Sketch of Canonical Theory and Its Application in England* (Berkeley, CA, 1959).

99 *Summa Lipsiensis* 1.363, D.86 c.16 s.v. *natura non gratia*: 'Nam non propter gratiam humani fauoris, set propter naturalem affectum beneficiendum est parentibus, qui pre ceteris nobis coniuncti sunt; uel 'non' alia 'gratia' etiam apposita; nam et mali homines subueniunt, qui tamen gratia extorres probantur.' Cf. *Summa Parisiensis*, 68: 'i.e. pro natura sibi subuenire debeo non priuata dilectione'; *Magister Rufinus*, 177: 'i.e. quod nos subuenimus parentibus, non debemus hoc facere affectu carnalis gratie sed intuitu nature, scil. quia nobis ipsi magis ceteris coniuncti sunt'.

100 *Magistri Honorii* 1.241, D.86 c.16 s.v. *causam prestat natura, non gratia*: 'Supple "tantum", quia ubi datur consanguineo bono hec dant causam natura et gratia'.

101 *Magistri Honorii* 1.222; 1.231.

102 *Summa Lipsiensis* 1.119, D.31 c.11 s.v. *sustentaretur*: 'nec ordinari debet uir nec ad religionem transire, nisi illa similiter conuertatur, preterquam in casu ut si senex fuerit, ut in extrau. Cum sis.' Pope Alexander's decretal was eventually included in the *Liber Extra*, X.3.32.4: 'Verum si ita uxor senex est et sterilis, quod sine suspicione possit esse in saeculo, dissimulare poteris, ut, ea in saeculo remanente et castitatem promittente, ad religionem transeat uir eiusdem.' See also *Summa Lipsiensis* 1.334.

103 D.30 c.14: 'Si quis dereliquerit proprios filios, et non eos aluerit et (quod pietatis est) necessaria non prebuerit, sed sub occasione continentiae negligendos putauerit, anathema sit.' See also B. Schimmelpfennig, 'Ex fornicatione nati. Studies on the Position of Priests' Sons from the Twelfth to the Fourteenth Century', *Studies in Medieval and Renaissance History*, 2 (1980), 3–50, at 31.

104 *Magistri Honorii* 1.107, D.30 c.14 s.v. *non aluerit*: 'Tam causa boni quam mali in necessitate sunt alendi'.

105 *Summa Lipsiensis* 1.387, D.93 c.23 s.v. *dicentes patri et matri: 'non nouimus'*: 'Verba sunt Moysi, que in benedictionibus <tribus Leui> protulit, cum singulis tribubus in Deuteronomio benedixit. Leuite autem patrem et matrem non nouisse dicuntur, quando in ultione idolatrie, que in adoratione uituli comissa est, precepto Moysi a porta castrorum usque ad portam pertranseuntes idolatras interfecerunt parentibus aut filiis non parcentes. Mistice diaconi non nosse parentes et filios, quia non ita eos carnali affectu diligunt, ut pro ipsis a ueris auocentur. Eos tamen noscere debent, idest diligere et non contempnere, ut xxx.di. c.i. et Si quis filios.'

106 *Summa Lipsiensis* 1.128, D.32 c.10 s.v. *principibus indulgemus licentiam ut eorum feminas*: 'Vnde nota quod si fuerint libere, si admonite recedere noluerint, per principes debent mancipari seruituti, ut hic dicitur; si uero fuerint ancille et aliene et ignorantibus dominis coniuncte, dominis debent reddi, quia nullum dampnum patitur ecclesia; si que sunt aliena, reddantur, ut di.liiii. Generalis; si uero ancille proprie uel aliene et dominis scientibus coniuncte, si timeatur quod ad eas redire uelint clerici, uendi debent ad alienas prouincias, ut di.lxxxi. Quidam; si uero non habeatur timor, retrudi debent in monasterium, ut di.xxxiiii.'

107 See canon 10 of the Ninth Council of Toledo (655), which was included in Gratian's *Decretum* C.15 q.8 c.3.

108 *Summa Lipsiensis* 1.271, D.56 c.4 s.v. *crimine*: 'Set contra reperitur infra xv. q. ult. Cum multe (C.15 q.8 c.3). Set illud est speciale uel non habet locum hodie, quia ei derogatur'.

109 P. Hoskin, 'Poor [Poore], Richard', *Oxford Dictionary of National Biography*. https://doi.org/10.1093/ref:odnb/22525. Accessed 2/12/2017.

4 Finances of clergy below the episcopate

In the previous chapter, I discussed some similarities between Byzantine and English bishops: their revenues were substantial and involved both landed and movable properties, and their expenditure was controlled by laws, some of which imposed limitations upon their familial status. Here I turn to clergy below the episcopate, where we notice a great difference: this time it is only in England that laws created a link between clerical finances and marital status. With few exceptions, Byzantine clerics below the episcopate were free to dispose of their revenues in any way they saw fit, independently of whether they were married. I argue that the severity of these laws depended on the access that clerics of different grades had to ecclesiastical resources, and I discuss the impact this has on our understanding of attitudes towards clerical marriage in twelfth-century England and Byzantium.

Byzantium

In contrast to the many ecclesiastical laws regulating episcopal revenues and expenses, it is rare for canons or the canonists to mention the financial responsibilities of priests, deacons, or subdeacons. One example can be found in Balsamon's commentary on canon 39 of the Apostles, where he stated that priests and deacons were not allowed to take over episcopal functions, such as the alienation of ecclesiastical lands or the collection of church revenues, without the bishop's permission.[1] But most often such rules focused on clerics who had access to Church resources through their ecclesiastical offices. These clerics could be heads of religious institutions, including orphanages and old people's homes, or clerics who acted as *oikonomoi* of a monastery, a large public church, an imperial foundation, or a bishopric.[2]

In the case of bishoprics, *oikonomoi* were elected to assist with, and to a great extent check, the bishop's management, safeguarding the reputation of the episcopal dignity against accusations of misappropriation. As Zonaras put it, they were there to assure 'that no scandals would arise against the bishop by leaving his administration without witnesses.'[3] They were usually deacons, and as such could be married and have a family.[4] In theory they were expected to be clerics of the church which they helped administer, but in practice laymen often ended up taking on the role.[5] Zonaras, commenting on the situation at his time, added that the *oikonomoi* should not be recruited from among those close to the bishop, his relatives or servants.[6] Close familiarity with the bishop could place them in a subordinate position, diminishing their ability to control the bishop's actions and criticise his management.[7]

The *oikonomoi* played a particularly important role during episcopal vacancies when they were expected to govern the property of the church and preserve its income for the bishop's successor.[8] It is not surprising then that they were targeted by certain financial regulations. In his commentary on canon 38 of the Apostles, Balsamon quoted chapter 5 of Justinian's Novel 120:

> We forbid, under the same penalty as for those in Constantinople, the *oikonomoi*, the administrators, and the record-keepers of venerable houses, wherever these may be, as well as their parents, children, and others related to them through blood or proper marriage, to obtain secretly leases, *emphyteuses*, sales, or hypothecations of immovable property belonging to these venerable houses, either personally or through a third person.[9]

This is particularly interesting, as canon 38 of the Apostles talked only of bishops. The fact that Balsamon chose to include this novel on the *oikonomoi* and other administrators shows that they too had significant access to Church funds. It was further assumed in their case that their families could profit from access to ecclesiastical resources. The same assumption can be found elsewhere in civil law. According to a Justinianic decree issued in 528, the *oikonomos* was to render an annual account to the bishop to inform him whether the church had made a financial gain or loss. If he were to die before he could render this account, it became the responsibility of his heirs to do so and to make restitution for any damages incurred.[10] Although Balsamon tells us that this law was not included in the *Basilika*, a decree promulgated in 1028 by Patriarch Alexios the Studite made a similar connection between the *oikonomoi* and their family members. It stated that if those in charge of Church finances refused to provide their accounts, they were to be punished according to the canons and were to be subjected to fines together with their heirs and their descendants. The fact that their families were involved in the punishment suggests that they were presumed to be the beneficiaries of the *oikonomos*' appropriations.[11]

The majority of the clergy, however, did not hold an administrative position and as such did not handle ecclesiastical property. This is reflected in Balsamon's commentary, which often diverged from the canons on this issue. Canon 59 of the Apostles decreed that not only bishops but also priests were responsible for the provision of other clerics. Balsamon, however, drew an important distinction. He maintained that the canon did not punish *all* priests who did not distribute their private property to other clerics in need; rather, the rule applied only to priests who were in charge of ecclesiastical property, such as those who held the dignity of *chorepiskopos* or *protopapas*.[12] The *protopapades* had indeed an important financial role to play. This can be seen from the instructions which

Demetrios Chomatenos, archbishop of Ohrid (1216–1236), drew up for a cleric newly appointed to that position. He would be in charge of annually gathering the ecclesiastical taxes from the laity and clergy in the bishopric and forwarding them to the local bishop. He had the power to increase or decrease these taxes, but Chomatenos discouraged him from doing either.[13] The dignity of *chorepiskopos*, on the other hand, had long disappeared, as Balsamon informs us elsewhere.[14] This used to be a rank of country bishop, which was initially endowed with full episcopal power. *Chorepiskopoi* would still have existed at the time of the promulgation of the canon of the Apostles on which Balsamon was commenting. By mentioning them here the canonist emphasised that the law did not apply to the priests of his time.

The distinction between ordinary priests and those with administrative powers needed to be made because only the latter were in charge of Church property and could misappropriate it.[15] Ordinary clerics below the episcopate were only in possession of their own property, which they were allowed to accrue and keep for themselves.[16] This can be clearly seen if we compare canon 32 of Carthage with Balsamon's commentary on it. The canon states,

> It also seemed good that if bishops, priests, deacons, and all other clerics who had no property [before their ordination], having prospered during their episcopate or during their time among the clergy, buy in their own names fields or any other estates, they will be held guilty of the crime of having encroached upon the Lord's goods, unless, when they are later asked to do so, they shall give these properties to the Church.[17]

The canon imposed the same rules on all clergymen, not only bishops but also priests, deacons, subdeacons, readers, and singers. All clerics who acquired possessions after their accession to their grade would be held guilty of appropriation of the Lord's goods if they did not place these possessions at the disposal of the Church when asked to do so. This position was rejected by Balsamon, who argued that although it applied to bishops, it could not possibly apply to all clerics:

> But if after their entrance to the clergy, clerics buy things not using the resources of the church but through other means, they are not to be forced to transfer these to the church. For if a cleric happened to become a teacher or a calligrapher or amanuensis for some great man, and thence became rich, why shall he be forced to transfer to the church the things which he had acquired in such ways?[18]

According to Balsamon this applied both to movable and immovable property. Ordinary clerics below the episcopate could consider their own the wages they earned from their ecclesiastical and other occupations.

These clerics were divided into two categories in terms of their ecclesiastical wages: the *embathmoi*, who had a remunerated position and the *perissoi*, who did not but were in line to secure a paid post once one became vacant.[19] The latter performed their liturgical duties in the same way as the *embathmoi* but needed to wait for a promotion because the maximum number of clerics in the church in which they were enrolled had already been reached.[20] Alternatively it was possible for a cleric to become *embathmos* instead of *perissos* if he could find a patron who would provide the church with enough resources to finance his ecclesiastical career.[21] The main income of the *embathmoi* was an annual payment in kind and money which they received from their church, their patron, or the emperor for their ecclesiastical services. For example, the highest annual salary for a priest at the church of the Theotokos Eleousa of the Pantokrator monastery in Constantinople (1136) was 15 *hyperpyra nomismata* and 25 *modioi thalassioi* of grain, which comes to about 19 *nomismata* in total.[22] Deacons, subdeacons, and other clerics lower down the hierarchy were paid less, depending on their grade and time of appointment.[23] The patriarchal clergy would have been better off than most, especially due to their political role in the legitimation of emperors.[24] The average salary of an *embathmos* cleric who was not newly appointed at the Hagia Sophia in the tenth century was 24 to 28 *nomismata*.[25] But even the patriarchal clergy would occasionally be in financial trouble. Although we are not well informed about the salaries they received at different periods, we know that in the eleventh century, Emperor Konstantinos IX Monomachos (r. 1042–1055) had to increase their revenue so that they could celebrate the liturgy on a daily basis.[26] By comparison, a mid-eleventh-century professor of law (*nomophylax*) in Constantinople received about 230 *nomismata*, and a twelfth-century provincial judge received between 936 and 1,872 *nomismata* per year.[27]

Clerical income from pastoral duties was also limited. Byzantine priests did not as a rule receive baptismal dues or fees for burials.[28] They were allowed to accept donations from the laity for communion and other liturgical functions, but these had to be within reason and completely voluntary.[29] As such, clerical revenues from one church were often insufficient and were supplemented by serving two or more churches. This practice of pluralism was generally forbidden by the canons, but in certain cases it was allowed due to the scarcity of priests.[30] In Constantinople during Balsamon's period, it was commonplace to find priests serving not only one or two churches but even three or more at the same time. The canonist stated that the law against pluralism was not being observed 'because those who transgressed it were not punished, or because of the great number of churches and the straits of truly worthy men and of their affairs'.[31]

Clerics further supplemented their income through the exercise of worldly professions (πράγματα κοσμικά; φροντίδες κοσμικῶν πραγμάτων) or the possession of secular dignities (ἀξίωμα κοσμικόν). Secular dignities did not always carry a regular function.[32] That is to say that at any given time several individuals may have held the dignity of *protospatharios*, for example, but only few among them would have had to perform the military or judicial services that the office implied; the rest simply enjoyed the income and honour that was conveyed through the title.[33] Nonetheless, secular dignities were thought to be altogether incompatible with clerical status. Some secular professions, on the other hand, were allowed by the canons.[34] For example, clerics were permitted to work as teachers and scribes.[35] But they were explicitly forbidden from managing the landed estates of others, from becoming doctors, from serving in the army, from keeping a tavern (καπηλικὸν ἐργαστήριον), or more generally from gaining a living through any shameful or dishonest occupation.[36]

Zonaras noted in his commentary on canon 3 of Chalcedon that despite the numerous prohibitions clerics continued to occupy themselves with worldly affairs in an effort to increase their profits. As the canonist put it, 'no cure for this disease was effected'; indeed he lamented that in his day even patriarchs and bishops co-celebrated with clerics who broke the rules.[37] Despite Zonaras' indictment, there were at least three twelfth-century patriarchs who issued laws regulating clerical activity in secular affairs: John Agapetos (1111–1134), Luke Chrysoberges (1156–1169), and Michael Anchialos (1170–1178).[38] The legislation of Patriarch Chrysoberges in fact had a famous victim: following an 1157 decree which reiterated the prohibition of clerical engagement in worldly professions, the canonist Alexios Aristenos was forced to abandon his secular position as *dikaiodotes*, or high-ranking judge of one of the Constantinopolitan tribunals.[39] Although for certain individuals engaging in such worldly occupations might have been the result of greed, for others – and especially the *perissoi* – it was a necessary evil which helped them to sustain themselves and their families.[40] In any case, what clerics managed to earn from their ecclesiastical or secular occupations would have been theirs to keep.

Given the way that clerics below the episcopate were remunerated, it is easy to see that, unless they held an administrative function, they would have had little access to ecclesiastical lands.[41] It was mainly the movable goods of their church which could become the object of misappropriation. We can get an idea of the items which were found in a private religious institution by looking at the sacred objects which Eustathios Boilas, a court functionary of senatorial rank and an important landowner, donated to one of his foundations in 1059.[42] According to his will, Boilas dedicated to his church of the Theotokos numerous liturgical vessels, including two chalices, one silver-gilt and one wooden, a strainer, an asterisk, two spoons, a paten, an incense holder, and a silver candlestick; items of clerical clothing, including seven sacerdotal robes with the stola and belts; many items of worship, such as silver and golden crosses, eight gilt icons, twelve other icons of copper, thirty assorted icons painted in gold, and reliquaries full of holy relics; as well as other items necessary for the fabric of the church, such as hanging lamps, two large candelabra of bronze and five iron ones, and six chandeliers with their chains.[43] These movable items, donated for use at Boilas' private religious institution, represent the types of objects that could be misappropriated by the incumbent clergy and their family. Canon 33 of Carthage prohibited the appropriation of such property by the clergy, making a distinction between bishops who should not alienate land (χωρία) and priests who should not alienate the objects (πράγματα) of the church.[44] To do so bishops needed the approval of the priests, and priests needed the approval of the bishop. Balsamon commented on this canon, emphasising that the need for such bilateral approval did not mean that bishops and priests had equal power over ecclesiastical affairs. Bishops needed approval only when the transaction involved Church estates, whereas for anything else they could proceed even against the opinion of their priests. Clerics needed episcopal approval for any kind of transaction they might have wanted to perform, whether it concerned movable or immovable property or even perishable goods, such as wine and grain.[45] It was because they were not meant to have any control over the wealth of their church that they were allowed to have complete control over their own income and spending.

Opportunities for clerics to gain greater access to ecclesiastical resources came with episcopal vacancies, but were again objectionable. Canon 15 of Ankyra decreed that Church property sold by clerics during a vacancy could be reclaimed by the bishop's successor if the sale was deemed unprofitable.[46] Canon 22 of Chalcedon prohibited clerics from seizing the property of the bishop after his death.[47] These regulations were still relevant in the twelfth century, when Patriarch Luke Chrysoberges (1156–1169) issued a decree to prohibit such appropriations after complaints from Constantine, the metropolitan of Thessalonike, that clerics in his cathedral had unlawfully seized the property of the church as well as some of the property of the previous bishop during the vacancy.[48]

Overall, the majority of Byzantine clerics did not have any significant control over the finances of the Church and were not particularly well off. Indeed Papagianni in her in-depth study of the finances of the married clergy in Byzantium states that she does not know of even one Byzantine cleric who became rich from the exercise of his ecclesiastical duties.[49] Of course, some among them would have come to the clergy with an already substantial fortune, but private property and family connections are different from gains earned through ecclesiastical services. These relatively poor clerics were free to spend their money on their family members in any way they wished. Their sons and wives were not targeted as potential beneficiaries. Even in the case of the *oikonomoi*, whose heirs would come under pressure to reimburse any damages to the Church, the issue was not addressed in terms of their marital status; parents as well as more distant relations were mentioned alongside children as heirs and potential beneficiaries.

England

Canons

In contrast to the situation in Byzantium, in England there were clerics below the rank of bishop who could lay claim to substantial Church resources. As we saw in the previous chapter, cathedral canons were often provided with prebends endowed with land, churches, or, in some cases, rents. Hugh Thomas has argued that even a fairly average prebend was likely to allow its holder to lead a lifestyle similar to that of both the knightly and non-knightly landowning classes. The evidence from the long twelfth century suggests that prebends of the value of £5 were reasonably common, while larger prebends of £10 were also recorded. Although the income from most prebends would have been smaller than that of any but the poorest knights, canons had fewer expenses (having no need for armour, weaponry, etc.) and the revenues of those residing in the cathedral would have been supplemented by food distributions.[50] A canon's right to his prebend was expected to end at his death, or in certain cases to continue for another year.[51] After that time, it would be assigned to a different canon. The most profitable prebends would have gone to priests and deacons, and when clerics lower down the hierarchy were given one, they would have been strongly encouraged by the bishop to be ordained in a higher grade.[52] In the early twelfth century it was still possible for canons to transfer their prebends to their sons. According to Brooke the positive evidence on the canons of St Paul's cathedral in London proves that down to the death of Richard de Belmeis I (d. 1127) at least a quarter of them were married and the succession of their sons to their prebends was often recognised as some sort of prescriptive right.[53] Indeed, we know that at least eight dignities and prebends were transmitted from father to son between 1090 and 1127.[54]

Parish clergy

Just as cathedral canons were supported by prebends, parish clergy were supported by benefices. The income they produced could differ significantly depending on the region where their parish was situated as well as its size. Unfortunately it is not until the thirteenth century that we start to have detailed records of the value of parishes in different parts of the country, but it is worth giving an example of the potential disparity in their valuation. Based on taxation records from either 1217 or 1229, there were 202 churches in the archdeaconry of Leicester with an average income of £6 per church. This meant, however, that while some churches made more than £10, others made as little as 5s.[55]

The situation was further complicated by the fact that these revenues would occasionally need to be divided between different people who had a stake in the church. A parish church would usually come with a variety of revenues, such as the great and lesser tithes, altar offerings, burial dues, a house, and a plot of land called the glebe. These belonged to the rector, the cleric who was responsible for the cure of souls of his parishioners. But the rector could not always perform the *cura animarum*, either because he was not present or because he was not in the right orders. For example, clerics below the grade of priest could become rectors of parish churches, but being unable to perform the necessary sacramental functions, they would need a vicar who was ordained into the priesthood to stand in for them. Arrangements differed from one case to the next, but rectors would often keep the great tithes – that is to say, tithes of grain – while the vicar kept the house, the glebe, the altar offerings, burial dues, and the lesser tithes, which consisted of tithes of everything else, but principally animals and animal produce.[56]

A slightly different financial arrangement was involved when a monastery or cathedral acquired the right of advowson from a lay landowner, as began to happen from the last quarter of the eleventh century.[57] The religious house who held the advowson would choose a rector for the church and would receive a pension from him. This payment could vary from a small sum to the greater proportion of the total revenues.[58] Such donations of local churches to monasteries had been sanctioned by the Gregorian reformers with the expectation that it would help eliminate hereditary succession to benefices.[59] This belief was misplaced, however, as monks, nuns, and canons treated these churches as a source of revenue and were often willing to tolerate hereditary succession in order to maximise their profits. As Harper-Bill has shown in the case of the diocese of Norwich, in the face of often openly fiscal rather than pastoral monastic interests, many laymen tried to recover their previously alienated advowsons through litigation, while the king and bishops continued to divert them to the needs of their increasingly demanding bureaucracies.[60]

Often religious houses would not be satisfied with the advowson only and would also try to acquire the rectory – that is to say, they would try to appropriate the churches. This meant that the cleric who was chosen as a vicar could either receive a stipend from the religious house which had appropriated the church – with the religious house keeping the benefices in its own hands – or he would receive a vicarage formed from part of the endowment of the appropriated church.[61] Although in the 1160s and 1170s there was an increase in grants of appropriation, these were not to become the norm until the 1180s.[62] Roughly from the middle of the twelfth century, bishops insisted on licensing appropriations, as far as they could, and a normal feature of these licences from early on was the stipulation that any vicar should be 'perpetual' and ought to have a suitable vicarage.[63] This meant that he could not be dismissed by the religious house and that he would receive sufficient income to live on.[64] Hugh Thomas examined the volumes of the English Episcopal Acta Series until 1216 and found thirty-six vicarages with a fixed income of an average of approximately £4 9s, and another eleven of £2 or less.[65] This can give us an idea of the income of a vicar in an appropriated church.

Unbeneficed clergy

Initially bishops ordained clergy in proportion to the number of places available in churches, but by the thirteenth century the numbers ordained had become unhitched from any places available. There was some effort to insist on 'title', a document which guaranteed financial support for the ordinand, especially for the major orders. This title would normally represent the cleric's benefice, but could also correspond to the private property of the cleric or his patron. 'Unbeneficed' clergy would be ordained to a title of patrimony which consisted of private income, such as lands, rents, and pensions, belonging either to them or to the person or religious house presenting them. It is hard to know how serious the problem of unbeneficed clergy was in the twelfth century, as most information dates from the mid-thirteenth century. In principle, a bishop who knowingly ordained a cleric without a title became liable for his upkeep and preferment. In the thirteenth century many clerics are known to have perjured themselves, swearing they had the necessary income, in order to be ordained. This suggests that sufficient opportunities in the form of work as assistant clergy in parish churches, or in chantries, oratories, and private chapels, were available to them.[66]

Overall, unbeneficed clergy and many vicars would have been worse off compared to parish rectors and prebendaries, and the values of different parishes and prebends could vary significantly. But it is clear that there existed in England a stratum of wealthy clerics below the episcopate. The opportunities for making money were further increased by the fact that many of these clerics held benefices, prebends, and churches in plurality.[67] Indeed, Hugh Thomas commented on the chances available to English clerics in the long twelfth century, stating that through an ecclesiastical career

> far more individuals could gain incomes equivalent to those of knights or even barons. A younger son from the secular elites could conceivably end up better off than his older brother, and for clerics of ordinary background the possibilities must have been astonishing.[68]

This is in stark contrast to the pessimistic comments made by Papagianni about the financial opportunities offered by clerical careers in Byzantium.

Legal restrictions on expenditure

The greater access to ecclesiastical resources which English clerics enjoyed in comparison with their Byzantine counterparts is reflected in the legislation regulating their finances and has often been linked to their marital status. Clerics in sacred orders were warned that having a wife meant the loss of their ecclesiastical benefice. Three Westminster councils dealt with this issue. The 1127 council forbade the association of priests, deacons, subdeacons, and all canons with women: 'but if they cling to concubines (God forbid!) or perhaps wives, let them be excluded from their ecclesiastical order, in terms of both honour and benefice.'[69] Similarly the 1138 Council of Westminster threatened to deprive married priests from their office and benefice and encouraged the laity to boycott their liturgical services.[70] Still in 1175 the first canon of the council stated,

> if some priest or cleric established in sacred orders and holding a church or an ecclesiastical benefice openly keeps his harlot and having been warned one, two, and three times has not sent his harlot away and disowned her completely, but has rather decided to persist in his filth, he is to be deprived of every office and ecclesiastical benefice.[71]

Such threats were difficult to put into practice due to the great number of married clerics in England, but the association created in law between ecclesiastical remuneration and marital status is interesting for our purposes. These sanctions were to a large extent punitive in character: clerical marriage was forbidden, so clerics in major orders who contravened the law were being punished. But the same link is also visible in the case of clerics in minor orders, who were allowed to marry provided that they were not members of cathedral communities. Canon 1 of the 1175 Council of Westminster continued:

> If some clerics established in the grades below the subdiaconate contract matrimony, they are under no circumstances to be separated from their wives, unless by common consent they wish to turn to religion and to continue there constantly in the service of God. But if they live with their wives, they are in no way to gain ecclesiastical benefices.[72]

This restriction cannot be considered a punitive measure; rather, it was a manifestation of ecclesiastical uneasiness about accepting the spending of Church property on wives and children, and it was meant to act as a deterrent against clerical marriage at any level of the hierarchy. Such measures were not easy to enforce nor were they universally accepted as good solutions. Indeed, the financial prospects of married clerics in minor orders attracted considerable attention in the twelfth century. Here I will focus on the treatment of this topic by Gratian and some of the decretists.

Gratian's *Decretum* (D.32 c.3) included a letter of the sixth-century pope, Gregory the Great, to Augustine of Canterbury in which the pope advised Augustine and his community to lead a common life and to possess no private property.[73] Gregory made an exception, however, when it came to married clerics in minor orders:

> But if there are any clerics in minor orders who cannot be continent, they should marry and receive their stipends outside the community; for we know that it is written concerning those Fathers whom we have mentioned that 'division was to be made to each according to his need' [Acts 4:35]. Care must also be taken and provision made for their stipends and they must be kept under ecclesiastical rule, living a moral life and attending to the chanting of the psalms and, under God's guidance, keeping their hearts, their tongues, and their bodies from all things unlawful.[74]

Although there were distinct provisions for married clerics below the subdiaconate, according to Gregory, they were still expected to receive some kind of remuneration from the Church. Indeed it had been normal in the Late Antique period and into the early Middle Ages for the income of each church to be divided in such a way that all clerics would receive stipends.[75] As we have seen, financial arrangements for the remuneration of clerics were different in twelfth-century England. But what is of interest to our discussion is the reaction that canon lawyers had towards the idea that married clerics in minor orders should continue to be remunerated by the Church in one way or another.

Gratian used this letter to emphasise not the rule, which was to lead a common life, but the exception, the right of married clerics in minor orders to receive a stipend. He placed Gregory's advice among chapters which aimed to convince clerics in major orders to remain continent, or to remain in minor orders, if they wished to marry. This can be seen also in the chapter rubric, which reads, 'Clerics not received into holy orders may take wives and may receive stipends from the church.'[76] Although Gratian accepted that married clerics below the subdiaconate had a fair claim to a stipend, other twelfth-century commentators questioned this. A continental writer, the author of the *Summa Parisiensis*, saw Pope Gregory's leniency towards married clerics as a special concession granted to the English when they were new to the faith.[77] He said, 'Nowhere in this corpus [of canon law] do we find again this concession, that acolytes and other married clerics of that rank should have incomes.'[78] Instead the commentator maintained that 'today nothing would be given from the stipends of the church to those who have wives.'[79]

This meant that although the marriage of clerics in minor orders was allowed, those among them who chose to take wives would lose any ecclesiastical revenues they might have received and would need to find alternative ways of supporting themselves and their families financially. These alternative means included the performance of secular occupations, such as administering justice or writing charters. Clergy in minor orders performing secular occupations would not have been unusual in England. Indeed, based on the complaints of Gervase of Chichester, a cleric of Thomas Becket (1162–1170), there seem to have been many men in minor orders who made a living out of such secular activities and who even abandoned their ecclesiastical careers to pursue them more fully.[80] Many of them, however, would have been remunerated for their secular activities through an ecclesiastical benefice. Indeed, Turner has argued that many men who wished to engage themselves in royal service were tonsured so that they could be paid through ecclesiastical resources which would not otherwise have been accessible to them as laymen. This made it possible for the king to gain their service at the Church's expense.[81] For them, losing their ecclesiastical benefice for taking a wife would have been a particularly harsh punishment. In any case, the views advocated by the author of the *Summa Parisiensis* would have acted as a deterrent. To take away the ecclesiastical stipend of a cleric in minor orders because he chose to take a legitimate wife was effectively to create a disincentive towards such a marriage.

Not all commentators, however, believed that married clergy in minor orders should be completely cut off from the Church's financial care. According to another continental canonist, Stephen of Tournai, married clerics were not prohibited from receiving a portion of income from the Church (*partem ab ecclesia*) as long as they did not advance to major orders. Stephen interpreted Pope Gregory's letter in a way that allowed for clerics to live from the common resources of an ecclesiastical community but not in common (*de communi, non tamen in communi*). This meant that they were not allowed to eat with other clerics at the refectory, but had instead to eat at their own houses. It did not mean, however, that they had to give up their rights to a stipend from the church to which they were attached.[82] Stephen of Tournai was describing a situation common in eastern French and German cathedrals, where prebendal payments were still made in the form of food distribution as late as the later twelfth century. The custom was in fact dying out by the time he was writing (c. 1164xc. 1166), but it represented an old tradition.[83] Stephen took a strong interest in the state of the secular clergy, but being himself a regular canon, he did so as an outsider. In his attitude, we see reflected Augustinian views on property and common eating.

The Anglo-Norman author of the *Summa Lipsiensis* also discussed this issue, recognising that this was a contemporary topic of debate.[84] He presented the reader with three different options on the financial fate of married clerics in minor orders. The first was the one we have already seen in the *Summa Parisiensis*: Pope Gregory's rule no longer applied and no married cleric should receive remuneration from the Church.[85] The second option was that all clerics below the subdiaconate could lawfully take a wife and have a prebend, as long as no cure of souls was attached to that prebend. The decretist suggested the church of York as an example where this took place, and he considered this solution to be the best.[86] Certain cathedral prebends were endowed only with lands or rents and could as such be held by clerics of any ecclesiastical grade.[87] But even in the case of prebends endowed with parish churches, canons would not have been expected to provide cure of souls themselves; they would, however, be receiving revenues from them. Despite the decretist's preference for this solution, it was rare for clerics in minor orders to have a prebend, especially a very profitable one. The third option involved what is known as a simple benefice. Philippa Hoskin has described a simple benefice as 'an annual payment granted from the income of a particular church to be paid to a named individual who has no apparent connection to the church in question'.[88] In thirteenth-century England simple benefices were found most frequently in patronage disputes, where they were offered as a consolation prize to a losing patron or presentee. They could also provide an income for unsuitable rectors, such as those who were married or under the age of canonical ordination. In this case, they acted as a financial incentive for them to resign the cure of souls.[89] If a patron insisted on presenting a married cleric to a benefice as rector, a compromise could be reached by presenting another candidate in major orders as rector while the original presentee would receive a simple benefice.[90] The author of the *Summa Lipsiensis* described the simple benefice of the married cleric in minor orders as a form of pension, 'a fixed measure of grain or wine per month'.[91] Although in this present case the payment was monthly rather than annual, we are talking about a similar principle of remuneration to the one we find in Byzantium. After giving these three options, the author of the *Summa Lipsiensis* complained that allowing married clerics in minor orders to sustain their wives from the property of the church was unfair towards celibate clerics. Married ones, he said, were provided with stipends enough for two people rather than one: double the amount continent clerics received.[92]

A similar comment was made by Master Honorius, who offered two options: married clerics in minor orders could receive a prebend with no cure of souls; or a stipend, such as a fixed payment of wheat and wine, from a church whose title they did not hold.[93] However, unlike the author of the *Summa Lipsiensis*, Master Honorius did not find fault with the fact that clerical wives needed to be financially supported. He said,

> since the wives of such men are to be provided for from the property of the Church [. . .], a greater part is to be given to those who are incontinent than to those who are continent, since they always have need for their family, the others only for themselves.[94]

The use of the contrasting words *continentibus* and *incontinentibus* initially suggests that Honorius would be against this provision. However, he directed the reader towards Cardinal Humbert's letter to Niketas Stethatos which commanded bishops, priests, and deacons who had been married while in minor orders to continue to provide financially for their wives (D.31 c.11). The implication was that if wives were canonically allowed to receive financial support after their husband's elevation to sacred orders, they would have also been allowed to receive support before, when the couple was still living together. The two Anglo-Norman commentators agreed that married clerics in minor orders could continue to receive some form of ecclesiastical stipend. Master Honorius seems to have been more accepting of the situation, but the author of the *Summa Lipsiensis* shows us, through his begrudging acceptance, that such arrangements – even when they were achieved – were likely to be met with criticism.

The same begrudging acceptance of the rights of clerics below the subdiaconate to care for their families without giving up their claim to a stipend is also found in contemporary papal decretals addressed to English bishops. The decretists were clearly aware of these letters and referred to them to lend support to their argument. We read, for example, in a decretal sent by Alexander III (1159–1181) to Gilbert Foliot, bishop of London (1163–1187),

> We have learnt that a large number of those living in your bishopric, after having been constituted in the office of the acolyte or below, have taken wives, and nevertheless presume to retain the churches which they previously held. Thence because they have taken wives, they cannot concentrate solely on divine things, since they are pulled in two directions and it is necessary for them to think how they can please their wives and perform their duties. We order you, our brother, through the reception of these apostolic writings to compel without appeal the aforementioned men to renounce their churches freely and absolutely and to concede them to other suitable clerics who have been constituted in sacred orders. But if some among them have previously held a simple benefice in the same churches, you can silently let them keep this benefice without control of the churches.[95]

As we learn from the pope's letter, the reason why clerics in minor orders should ideally be celibate, despite being allowed to marry, was that the cares of a family would distract them from their ecclesiastical duties. The pope suggested that it was preferable for churches to be served by clerics in major orders, for whom celibacy was required by canon law. They would perform their duties with undivided attention. However, despite the generally negative tone of the letter, it was used by Master Honorius to *support* the right of married clerics in minor orders to a church stipend. The decretist chose to emphasise the decretal's final sentence, which concedes their retention of simple benefices.[96]

Other papal decretals also show relative leniency by placing the emphasis on *future* prohibitions. This can be seen in a letter (1174x1181) sent by Alexander III to Robert Foliot, bishop of Hereford (1174–1186). The pope advised Robert to put up with the current situation and to allow married clerics in minor orders to keep the benefices they already possessed. He was, however, to make sure that 'from now on no married cleric may be admitted to ecclesiastical benefices, or sacred orders or the ecclesiastical administration, unless he has vowed perpetual chastity, and had had only one wife who was a virgin.'[97] Alexander III described Robert's parishioners as 'barbarous and numerous', and this was, according to the pope, the reason why the married clerics of Hereford had for such a long time held benefices 'from which they could not be deprived without [causing] a great crisis and effusion of blood'.[98] This 'barbarous and numerous' people probably referred to the Welsh as much as the English. The south-western part of the diocese of Hereford was Welsh-speaking until the eighteenth century, and it is likely that Robert Foliot himself had emphasised the Welshness of his clerics in a prior letter to the pope in order to gain some sympathy for his difficulties in dealing with them.[99] Such leniency, however, was not to become law. The general rule was expressed in a letter of Alexander III to the archbishop of Canterbury and his suffragans known as *Sicut ad extirpanda* (X.3.3.1). There the pope condemned clerical concubinage and marriage among clerics in major orders and asked that clerics below the subdiaconate who had been married relinquish their benefice and keep their wives.[100] Such decretals were bound to discourage currently celibate clerics in minor orders from getting married.

Despite the steady flow and increasing severity of papal letters on the subject, these regulations continued to be resisted by some English ecclesiastics. For example, Thomas of Chobham reminded the clerical audience of his *Summa confessorum* of Pope Gregory's order that financial provisions ought to be made for married clerics in minor orders.[101] He lamented that, despite this, in his day the custom prevailed that when an acolyte contracted a marriage he was immediately deprived of all ecclesiastical benefices. As an answer to this problem, Thomas maintained that if an acolyte was to approach a priest during private confession and to confide in him that he could not observe continence, the priest would not commit a great sin if he advised the acolyte to contract a secret wedding and if he hid this incident from the bishop.[102] Through a secret wedding clerics in minor orders could keep both their wife and their benefice.

The debated nature of this topic can also be seen in Gerald of Wales' *Gemma Ecclesiastica*, where he accepted it as reasonable that married clerics in minor orders could on certain occasions hold churches, but acknowledged the uncanonical nature of the situation, suggesting ideally that the cleric in question should seek consultation with the pope:

> As regards the question of clerics in minor orders who hold churches, certain noteworthy men feel (and not improperly so) that married men hold churches more tolerably than men living in concubinage, as long as they have honest and prudent vicars who take care of external affairs and who are paid modest but sufficient stipends out of the small tithes and offerings to the sanctuary. [. . .] If it is objected that this arrangement is contrary to what is stated in the canons and decretals and people complain that it is more fitting for a cleric to

> be continent, some may reply that the ancient decretals seem to permit marriage. But in fact the decretals oppose it. [. . .] But it would be better for such clerics, if they cannot remain continent (that is, if they will not strive to), to consult with the pope on this matter, either personally or through a trustworthy messenger.[103]

Overall, having examined twelfth-century canons and decretals on clerics in minor orders, we see that this was a question that divided people at the time. At one extreme, some maintained that no remuneration at all was due to married clergy in minor orders; at another extreme, some thought that such clerics should keep their benefice even if it meant lying about their wives. What becomes clear, however, is that even when clerics in minor orders were not required to remain celibate, they were strongly encouraged to do so through financial incentives. Interestingly, this seems to have worked the other way around too: not being given a benefice provided some, even among the sacred orders, with licence to neglect their vow of chastity. At least this is what Richard Poore, bishop of Durham (1228–1237), suggested when he wrote that 'whether beneficed or not' clerics had to live honourably and chastely.[104]

Conclusion

This chapter has focused on one important difference between England and Byzantium regarding the laws on clerical expenditure in England and Byzantium, and their impact on attitudes towards clerical marriage. Byzantine clerics below the episcopate were allowed to spend as they pleased any property they owned before joining the clergy, as well as any goods they obtained since, through ecclesiastical or secular occupations. It was only when they assumed positions of financial responsibility in the Church, such as that of *oikonomos*, that Byzantine clerics needed to be kept in check. In England, fears of misappropriation were linked to all ecclesiastical grades. Even clerics in minor orders were the subject of debate and were presented with financial disincentives to marry. As such, there seems to have been an association between their ecclesiastical income and their marital status.

Why were acolytes generating such discussion in England, when in Byzantium there were no restrictions even for priests and deacons? This was the only stage in the ecclesiastical career of a Western cleric when he could contract a lawful marriage. Such a marriage could then result in legitimate children who could make legitimate claims on their father's property even after his accession to sacred orders. But that was also true for Byzantine priests and deacons: they too could and did have legitimate children who laid claims to their father's property. So this must be only part of the answer. A great difference between England and Byzantium had to do with the way that clerics were remunerated and how much they earned. First, clerical positions in the West could provide much more lucrative opportunities than corresponding positions in Byzantium. Second, Byzantine clerics below the episcopate received their income in the form of an annual salary and unlike their Western counterparts did not hold a benefice or prebend. So Byzantine clerics below the episcopate did not earn enough to pose a threat and did not have any ecclesiastical lands to alienate. Exactly the opposite was true for English clerics: clerics in major orders, and even some acolytes, could earn a great deal, and part of what they earned was in the form of lands which could be appropriated. It is this greater access to ecclesiastical resources which English clerics enjoyed that we see reflected in the legislation regulating their finances. The fear of misuse of Church property was one of the factors which contributed to the different attitudes towards clerical marriage in twelfth-century England and Byzantium.

Notes

1 *Syntagma* 2.54.

2 Nomokanon Title 10 Chapter 5 in *Syntagma* 1.240. The Great Church had nine *oikonomoi*, who were eventually placed under the *Grand Oikonomos*. See Angold and Whitby, 'Church Structures and Administration', 576. The *Pantokrator* had four, see P. Gautier, 'Le typikon du Christ Sauveur Pantocrator', *REB*, 32 (1974), 1–145, at 112–3. The St Mokios in Constantinople had one. See I. Bekker (ed.), *Theophanes Continuatus* (Bonn, 1838), 365.21–3. But the bishopric of Hierissos does not seem to have had an *oikonomos* during the tenth century or before the second half of the eleventh. See Papachryssanthou, 'Un évêché byzantin: Hierissos en Chalcidique', 385–6.

3 *Syntagma* 3.390: 'δεῖ γὰρ τῶν διοικήσεων τῶν ἐκκλησιαστικῶν πραγμάτων εἴδησιν ἔχειν αὐτούς, ἵνα μὴ ἀμαρτύρου οὔσης τῆς οἰκονομίας σκάνδαλα κατὰ τοῦ ἐπισκόπου φύωνται.' See also Troianos, 'Le célibat épiscopal', 189.

4 For example, we learn of an *oikonomos* who needed a dispensation in order to marry off his daughter in a case of consanguinity. See *Les regestes de 715 à 1206*, 331 n. 822; *Syntagma* 5.25–32. See also Darrouzès, *Offikia*, 16–17.

5 See Title 10, chapter 1 of the Nomokanon in *Syntagma* 1.236; canon 26 of Chalcedon in *Syntagma* 2. 277. Balsamon said that during his time some people claimed that it was allowed for laymen to become *oikonomoi*, but he himself was against this. See *Syntagma* 2.592.

6 *Syntagma* 2.277. An example of the violation of this rule comes from the bishopric of Hierissos, where in the 1080s the bishop's grandson was acting as his grandfather's *oikonomos*. See Papachryssanthou, 'Un évêché byzantin: Hierissos en Chalcidique', 389. We find similar considerations in the case of monasteries. The *typikon* of the Virgin Kecharitomene nunnery in Constantinople stipulated that 'the men who are sent to take care of the properties of the convent must not be selected for any family connection or affinity or any other reason of that sort.' See R. Jordan (trans.), 'Kecharitomene: Typikon of Empress Irene Doukaina Komnene for the Convent of the Mother of God Kecharitomene in Constantinople', in *Byzantine Monastic Foundation Documents*, eds. J. Thomas and A. Constantinides Hero (Washington, DC, 2000), 649–724, at 685. See also J. Lefort, 'The Rural Economy, Seventh-Twelfth Centuries', in *The Economic History of Byzantium: From the Seventh Through the Fifteenth Century*, ed. A.E. Laiou (Washington, DC, 2002), 231–315, at 293–5.

7 Zonaras laments the fact that the rules were rarely observed in his time, neither in bishoprics nor in monasteries, in *Syntagma* 2.278. See also a synodal act of Patriarch John IX Agapetos (1028) which authorised metropolitans to appoint their own *oikonomoi* if they deemed that the bishops were causing great financial damage to their cathedral and by extension to their metropolitan church. See *Les regestes de 715 à 1206*, 342 n. 835 (1).

8 See canon 25 of Chalcedon in *Syntagma* 2.273. In particular, they needed to protect the bishopric's income from potential appropriations by the metropolitan. See canon 35 of Trullo, in *Syntagma* 2.383–4.

9 *Syntagma* 2.53: 'Τοῖς δὲ οἰκονόμοις καὶ διοικηταῖς καὶ χαρτουλαρίοις τῶν ὁπουδήποτε ὄντων εὐαγῶν οἴκων, καὶ τοῖς αὐτῶν γονεῦσί τε καὶ παισὶ καὶ τοῖς ἄλλοις ἢ κατὰ γένος ἢ κατὰ γαμικὸν δίκαιον αὐτοῖς συναπτομένοις, μισθώσεις ἢ ἐμφυτεύσεις ἢ ἀγορασίας ἢ ὑποθήκας πραγμάτων ἀκινήτων τοῖς αὐτοῖς εὐαγέσιν οἴκοις προσηκόντων ὑπεισιέναι, ἢ δι' ἑαυτῶν ἢ διὰ παρενθέτου προσώπου, καθὰ καὶ τοῖς ἐν τῇ βασιλίδι τῶν πόλεων οὖσιν, ἐπὶ ταῖς αὐταῖς ποιναῖς ἀπαγορεύομεν.' On the institution of the *emphyteusis*, see Papagianni, 'Legal Institutions', 1061–2.

10 *Syntagma* 1.236. See also 1.3.41 §10 in *The Codex of Justinian* 1.108–9.

11 *Les regestes de 715 à 1206*, 342 n. 835 (11).

12 Zonaras applied the rule specifically to 'those who are at the head of churches' ('οἱ τῶν ἐκκλησιῶν προεστῶτες'), probably referring to bishops, rather than priests, deacons, or subdeacons. See *Syntagma* 2.76. Aristenos, on the other hand, did talk of priests. See *Syntagma* 2.77.

13 Angold, *Church and Society*, 249; G. Prinzing (ed.), *Demetrii Chomateni Ponemata diaphora* (Berlin, 2002), 432–3. There is, however, no evidence for the involvement of the *protopapas* in transactions concerning lands, which fell more strictly within the domain of episcopal duties. For more on this position and for a prosopographical list, see also Leontaritou, *Εκκλησιαστικά αξιώματα*, 490.

14 *Syntagma* 3.47: 'Περὶ μέν τοι τοῦ παρόντος κανόνος ἠθέλομεν γράψαι τινά· ἐπεὶ δὲ ὁ τῶν χωρεπισκόπων βαθμὸς παντελῶς ἠπράκτησεν, οὐδὲ ἡμεῖς ματαιοπονῆσαι ἠθελήσαμεν.'

15 *Syntagma* 3.388–9.

16 *Syntagma* 2.77: 'οὐ συνορῶ ποίῳ τρόπῳ ἀφορισθήσεται, ἢ καθαιρεθήσεται πρεσβύτερος, μὴ διδοὺς οἴκοθεν τὰ χρειώδη τῷ πενομένῳ συγκληρικῷ αὐτοῦ.'

17 *Syntagma* 3.386–7: 'Ὁμοίως ἤρεσεν ἵνα ἐπίσκοποι, πρεσβύτεροι, διάκονοι ἢ καὶ οἱοιδήποτε κληρικοί, οἱ μηδὲν ἔχοντες, ἐὰν προκόψαντες τῷ καιρῷ τῆς ἐπισκοπῆς ἢ τῆς κληρώσεως αὐτῶν ἀγροὺς ἢ οἱαδήποτε χωρία ἐπ' ὀνόματι αὐτῶν ἀγοράσωσιν, ὡς κατὰ δεσποτικῶν πραγμάτων ἔφοδον πεποιηκότες ἐνέχωνται, εἰ μὴ ἄρα λοιπὸν ὑπομνησθέντες τῇ ἐκκλησίᾳ ταῦτα εἰσκομίσουσιν.'

18 *Syntagma* 3.389: 'Οἱ δὲ κληρικοί, ἐὰν μετὰ τὴν κλήρωσιν ἀπὸ ἑτέρων τρόπων, οὐχὶ ἀπὸ τῶν τῆς ἐκκλησίας, ἀγοράσωσι πράγματα, οὐκ ἀναγκασθήσονται ταῦτα προσκυρῶσαι τῇ ἐκκλησίᾳ. Ἐὰν γὰρ τυχὸν παιδοδιδάσκαλος γένηταί τις κληρικὸς ἢ καλλιγράφος ἢ ὑπογραφεὺς μεγιστᾶνός τινος, καὶ ἐντεῦθεν πολυκτήμων καταστῇ, ἵνα τί καταναγκασθήσεται τὰ ἀπὸ τοιούτων τρόπων ἐπικτηθέντα αὐτῷ τῇ ἐκκλησίᾳ προσκυρῶσαι;'

19 E. Papagianni, *Τὰ οἰκονομικά τοῦ ἔγγαμου κλήρου στό Βυζάντιο* (Athens, 1986), 78. On this topic, see also the edict of Alexios I Komnenos, in P. Gautier, 'L'édit d'Alexis Ier Comnène sur la réforme du clergé', *REB*, 31 (1973), 165–201; P. Magdalino, 'The Reform Edict of 1107', in *Alexios I Komnenos, I: Papers*, eds. M. Mullett and D. Smythe (Belfast, 1996), 199–218.

20 We know, for example, that in the twelfth century there were sixty paid deacons in the Hagia Sophia, but we do not know how many unpaid ones served at the same time. For the maximum number of clerics during different periods, see Papagianni, *Οἰκονομικά*, 87, 92–4.

21 Papagianni, *Οἰκονομικά*, 64.

22 This church had its own clerical personnel, independent from the monastic community. See Papagianni, *Οἰκονομικά*, 95–7, n. 86. A *hyperpyron* between 1092 and 1204 was equivalent to four fifths of a *nomisma*. In Constantinople c. 1170 1 *modios thalassios* would have been equivalent to one third of an *hyperpyron*. The *typikon* of the Pantokrator dates from 1136. As the dates do not match, the calculations can only be approximate, but can give us an idea of relative wages. For a table of monetary

equivalencies, see Morrisson and Cheynet, 'Prices and Wages in the Byzantine World', 816.

23 For example, deacons of the Eleousa received 13 *hyperpyra nomismata* and 24 *modioi thalassioi* of grain, which comes to 17 *nomismata*, and a servant of the same church made 6 *hyperpyra* and 30 *modioi thalassioi*, which comes to about 13 *nomismata*. For more on the income of ecclesiastics, see also Morrisson and Cheynet, 'Prices and Wages in the Byzantine World', 868.

24 For example, in the twelfth century Manuel Komnenos safeguarded his claim to the throne by buying the compliance of the clergy of the Great Church through a grant of 200 silver pieces a month. See Angold, *Church and Society*, 77–8.

25 Papagianni, *Οἰκονομικά*, 102.

26 Skylitzes, writing towards the end of the eleventh century, stated with reference to Konstantinos IX Monomachos, 'Until his time the holy Eucharist was only offered to God on greater feast days, Saturdays and Sundays in that place and not at all on the other days, for want of revenue. This the emperor generously augmented in such a way that the sacred liturgy could be celebrated every day, as it continues to be until our time.' See Wortley, *John Skylitzes*, 444.

27 For consistency I have turned all values into *nomismata*. Here 230 *nomismata* correspond to 288 *hyperpyra nomismata* and 936 and 1,872 *nomismata* correspond to 13 and 26 pounds of gold. See Morrisson and Cheynet, 'Prices and Wages in the Byzantine World', 865. For more examples of salaries attached to civil positions, see N. Oikonomides, 'Title and Income at the Byzantine Court', in *Byzantine Court Culture from 829 to 1204*, ed. H. Maguire (Washington, DC, 1995), 199–215.

28 The Hagia Sophia had at its disposal 1,100 workshops (ἐργαστήρια) which were exempt from taxes and it was from their income that burial costs were covered. Nine hundred and fifty of them were instituted by Constantine the Great (306–337) and another 150 by Anastasios (491–518). Leo VI (Novel 12) confirmed this privilege in the tenth century, although by this time funeral services were covered through other sources of income, such as money set aside for this purpose by confraternities. See *Leo VI*, 50–51; Papagianni, *Οἰκονομικά*, 58–9; N. Oikonomides, 'Quelques Boutiques de Constantinople Au Xe S.: Prix, Loyers, Imposition (Cod. Patmiacus 171)', *DOP*, 26 (1972), 345–56, at 353–4; A. Talbot, 'A Monastic World', in *The Social History of Byzantium*, ed. J. Haldon (Chichester, 2009), 257–78, at 263–4.

29 *Syntagma* 4.471–3; Papagianni, *Οἰκονομικά*, 241.

30 Nicaea II (787), for example, had allowed priests in the countryside to serve more than one church. See *Syntagma* 2.620–1.

31 'Ὡς ἔοικε δὲ κατεφρονήθησαν τὰ τοῦ παρόντος κανόνος, διὰ τὸ μὴ κολάζεσθαι τοὺς τούτου καταφρονητάς· ἢ διὰ τὸ πλῆθος τῶν ἐκκλησιῶν, καὶ τὴν στενοχωρίαν τῶν ἀξιολογωτέρων καὶ τῶν πραγμάτων.' *Syntagma* 2.621.

32 See also E. Papagianni, 'Επιτρεπόμενες και απαγορευμένες κοσμικές ενασχολήσεις του βυζαντινού κλήρου', in *Δ΄ Πανελλήνιο Ἱστορικό Συνέδριο. Πρακτικά* (Thessalonike, 1983), 143–66.

33 See, for example, canon 7 of Chalcedon in *Syntagma* 2.232. See also P. Magdalino, 'Court Society and Aristocracy', in *A Social History of Byzantium*, ed. J. Haldon (Chichester, 2009), 212–32, at 224. The attraction that such dignities had for clerics can also be seen from a story included in the *De administrando imperio*. Ktenas, an aged cleric of great wealth living in the time of Emperor Leo VI, wanted to buy for himself the secular title of *protospatharios*, but found the emperor very reluctant. He managed to acquire it only through the aid of the patrician and chamberlain Samonas after increasing the price he was willing to pay. This was, however, a bad investment. Ktenas did not live long enough to enjoy the benefits and made a loss. As such the story could be read as a cautionary tale against the possession of secular dignities by the clergy. See G.Y. Moravcsik (ed.) and R.J.H. Jenkins (trans.), *Constantine Porphyrogenitus De administrando imperio* (Washington, DC, 1967), 244–5. See also

R. Guilland, 'Vénalité et favoritisme à Byzance', *REB*, 10 (1952), 35–46, at 40–1. On the dignity of *protospatharios*, see R. Guilland, *Recherches sur les institutions byzantines,* vol. II (Berlin, 1967), 99–131.

34 On this topic, see also D. Constantelos, 'Clerics and Secular Professions in the Byzantine Church', *Byzantina*, 13:1 (1985), 375–400; E. Herman, 'Le professioni vietate al clero bizantino', *OCP*, 10 (1944), 23–44; A.E. Laiou, 'God and Mammon: Credit, Trade, Profit and the Canonists', in *Byzantium in the 12th Century: Canon Law, State and Society*, ed. N. Oikonomides (Athens, 1991), 261–300.

35 See Zonaras on canon 10 of Nicaea II in *Syntagma* 2.588: 'παιδεύειν δὲ καὶ διδάσκειν παῖδας ἀρχόντων καὶ δούλους, καὶ τὰ τούτων ἤθη ῥυθμίζειν, οὐ κωλύονται'.

36 See Zonaras on canon 16 of Carthage in *Syntagma* 3.342: 'μὴ γίνεσθαί τινας τῶν ἱερωμένων ἀλλοτρίων κτημάτων ἐκλήπτορας, ἤγουν μισθωτάς'. Patriarch Luke Chrysoberges (1159–1169/70) linked the prohibition against clerics becoming doctors to their consequent change of clothes, in *Syntagma* 3.344: 'Ἀλλ' οὐδὲ ἀρχιητροὺς παρεχώρει γίνεσθαι τοὺς διακόνους ἢ τοὺς ἱερεῖς, λέγων ἀνένδεκτον εἶναι τοὺς μετὰ φαινολίων καὶ στιχαρίων τὰ ἅγια μεταχειριζομένους κοσμικὰς στολὰς ἐνδιδύσκεσθαι καὶ μετὰ λαϊκῶν ἀνδρῶν, τῶν ἰατρῶν δηλαδή, προπομπεύειν.' See also *Les regestes de 715 à 1206*, 532 n. 1092; S. Troianos, 'Ιατρική επιστήμη και γιατροί στο ερμηνευτικό έργο των κανονολόγων του 12ου αιώνα', in *Byzantium in the 12th Century: Canon Law, State and Society*, ed. N. Oikonomides (Athens, 1991), 477–81. On the incompatibility of the clerical dignity with war, see P. Viscuso, 'Christian Participation in Warfare: A Byzantine View', in *Peace and War in Byzantium: Essay in Honor of George T. Dennis, S.J.*, eds. T.S. Miller and J. Nesbitt (Washington, DC, 1995), 33–41, at 38–9. On clerics keeping taverns, see *Syntagma* 2.326–8. On more general shameful occupations, see canon 16 of Carthage in *Syntagma* 3.342: 'μηδὲ ἔκ τινος αἰσχροῦ ἢ ἀτίμου πράγματος τροφὴν παρίζωνται'.

37 *Syntagma* 2.222: 'τὸ κακὸν ἀθεράπευτον ἔμεινε'; 'καὶ οὐδ' οὕτως ἴασις τῆς νόσου ταύτης ἐγένετο'. Indeed, it was possible for a cleric to obtain a dispensation from the patriarch. Evidence that these regulations were both taken seriously and circumvented when necessary comes from Niketas Choniates' description of how, at the time of Alexios III Angelos, Constantinos Mesopotamites was given such a dispensation that allowed him to acquire both secular and ecclesiastical dignities. See H.J. Magoulias (trans.), *O City of Byzantium: Annals of Niketas Choniates* (Detroit, MI, 1984), 269.

38 John promulgated his law in 1115 under the reign of Alexios, prohibiting clerics from pleading in either ecclesiastical or civil courts. See *Syntagma* 3.349. The list of prohibited professions in Patriarch Luke Chrysoberges' 1157 law included curators and overseers of aristocratic houses and properties, collectors of public taxes, executors of fiscal surveys and accounts, dignitaries and magistrates of the civil establishment. See *Syntagma* 3.346. The 1171 law of Michael Anchialos targeted readers and is mentioned by Balsamon on two occasions, but also survives independently. See *Syntagma* 1.159; 3.344; V. Laurent, 'Réponses canoniques inédites du patriarcat byzantin', *Échos d'Orient*, 33 (1934), 298–315, at 310–11.

39 *Syntagma* 2.9; Darrouzès, *Offikia*, 82; *Les regestes de 715 à 1206*, 505 n. 1048. Alexios Aristenos presents us with a typical example of a cleric who accumulated both ecclesiastical and secular dignities: after acceding to the diaconate, he acquired the positions of *hieromnemon*, *nomophylax*, *protekdikos*, *orphanotrophos*, *megas oikonomos*, and *dikaiodotes*. See also Troianos, 'Twelfth to the Fifteenth Centuries', 179. The office of *dikaiodotes* is attested for the first time in 1094. See N. Oikonomides, 'L'évolution de l'organisation administrative de l'empire byzantin au XIe siècle (1025–1118)', *Travaux et mémoires*, 6 (1976), 125–52, at 135. Other well-known examples of individuals who amassed both ecclesiastical and secular titles are those of Nikolaos Agiotheodorites and Nikolaos Katafloron. See E. Madariaga, 'Η βυζαντινή οικογένεια των Αγιοθεοδωριτών (I): Νικόλαος

Αγιοθεοδωρίτης, Πανιερώτατος Μητροπολίτης Αθηνών και Υπέρτιμος', *Βυζαντινά Σύμμεικτα*, 19 (2009), 147–81, at 155 n. 27.

40 In some cases, both *perissoi* and *embathmoi* might have also received a daily allowance of bread or money for food. See Papagianni, *Οικονομικά*, 144–5.

41 A limited segment of the clergy, the so-called *klerikoparoikoi*, would have had some access to lands, but their financial condition was worse than that of most clerics. For more on this, see the next chapter.

42 Boilas was probably residing near Edessa in 1059 at the time when his will was composed. See P. Lemerle, 'Le testament d'Eustathios Boïlas (avril 1059)', in his *Cinq études sur le XIe siècle byzantin* (Paris, 1977), 15–63, at 49.

43 S. Vryonis, 'The Will of a Provincial Magnate, Eustathius Boilas (1059)', *DOP*, 11 (1957), 267–70.

44 *Syntagma* 3.390.

45 *Syntagma* 3.394.

46 *Syntagma* 3.50.

47 *Syntagma* 2.267–8.

48 *Syntagma* 5.98–9.

49 Papagianni, *Οικονομικά*, 294. Hussey makes a more reserved statement: 'It would be rash to generalize about the economic position of parish priests. Evidence from the thirteenth century onwards, from sources such as Chomatianus's rulings, Athos archives, patriarchal registers, shows considerable variation in their material circumstances. In both city and countryside there were instances of wealthy parish clergy as well as others living on the poverty line.' See Hussey, *The Orthodox Church*, 334. For the case of an exceptionally wealthy village priest in the thirteenth century, see A.E. Laiou, 'Priests and Bishops in the Byzantine Countryside, Thirteenth to Fourteenth Centuries', in *Church and Society in Late Byzantium*, ed. D.G. Angelov (Kalamazoo, 2009), 45–57, at 44, 47–8.

50 Based on the twelfth-century treatise *Dialogue of the Exchequer*, knights were paid 8 *d* a day compared to the 5 *d* received by the treasurer's scribe, because they needed to maintain horses and arms. With 8 *d* a day, their income would come to about £12 a year, but with 5 *d* it would come to about £7.5. For more on how lucrative different prebends were, see Thomas, *Secular Clergy*, 58–9.

51 In Chichester, for example, in the mid-twelfth century a canon could make provisions for the disposal of the revenues generated from his prebend for a year and a day after his death. The money could be used to pay off his debts and provide support for his family and friends. For how this changed in the later twelfth century, see Crosby, *Bishop and Chapter*, 266. Similarly, for Salisbury and Exeter, see Brett, *The English Church*, 195.

52 Many acolytes would be young and still supported by their parents. See Barrow, 'Grades of Ordination', 48, 60–1. For an example of the pressure put on clerics in minor orders to get themselves ordained into the priesthood, see a letter (c. 1102) from Gerard, archbishop of York, to Anselm, archbishop of Canterbury, asking for help to force his canons to do so, in W. Fröhlich (ed. and trans.), *The Letters of Saint Anselm of Canterbury*, vol. II (Kalamazoo, MI, 1990), 245.

53 C.N.L. Brooke, 'I. The Composition of the Chapter of St Paul's, 1086–1163', *Cambridge Historical Journal*, 10:2 (1951), 111–32, at 125.

54 Brooke, 'I. The Gregorian Reform in Action', 17.

55 Thomas, *Secular Clergy*, 62.

56 G.W.O. Addleshaw, *Rectors, Vicars and Patrons in Twelfth- and Early Thirteenth-Century Canon Law* (London, 1956), 13; C.R. Cheney, *From Becket to Langton: English Church Government 1170–1213* (Manchester, 1956), 131–9.

57 The grants of parish churches to monasteries become well-documented only after c. 1120 and more especially after c. 1130. This can be traced in the volumes of the English Episcopal Acta Series dealing with the twelfth century. For examples of the granting of advowsons, see *EEA*, I, 29; *EEA*, XXXI, 44, 149.

58 Harper-Bill, 'Struggle', 119.
59 Harper-Bill, 'Struggle', 126. In the diocese of Norwich in the twelfth century more than 270 parish churches were transferred to monastic patronage. See Harper-Bill, 'Struggle', 119.
60 Harper-Bill, 'Struggle', 113–32.
61 Addleshaw, *Rectors, Vicars and Patrons*, 8–9.
62 U. Rasche, 'The Early Phase of Appropriation of Parish Churches in Medieval England', *Journal of Medieval History*, 26:3 (2012), 213–37, at 223.
63 An early example of a perpetual vicarage was that of Aynho, Ralph de Diceto's church, established by Bishop Robert de Chesney (1148–64). See Cheney, *From Becket to Langton*, 132.
64 Addleshaw, *Rectors, Vicars and Patrons*, 8–9.
65 Thomas, *Secular Clergy*, 68. In the late thirteenth century, 28 per cent of the churches in Lincoln diocese were appropriated. See Thomas, *Secular Clergy*, 63.
66 On this topic more generally, see S. Townley, 'Unbeneficed Clergy in the Thirteenth Century: Two English Dioceses', in *Studies in Clergy and Ministry in Medieval England*, ed. D.M. Smith (York, 1991), 38–64; R.N. Swanson, 'Titles to Orders in Medieval English Episcopal Registers', in *Studies in Medieval History Presented to R.H.C. Davis*, eds. Henry Mayr-Harting and R.I. Moore (London, 1985), 233–45.
67 For example, Godfrey de Lucy was dean of St Martin-le-Grand in London; archdeacon of Derby and later of Richmond; canon of Exeter, Lincoln, York, and St Paul's cathedrals; as well as vicar of two parish churches. See R.V. Turner, *The English Judiciary in the Age of Glanvill and Bracton, c. 1176–1239* (Cambridge, 1985), 57.
68 Thomas, *Secular Clergy*, 71. Clerics from ordinary backgrounds stood a better chance of advancement because sons of earls rarely became clerics in the twelfth century. There are only two examples of aristocratic clerics among twelfth-century bishops: a son of the earl of Gloucester and a brother of the earl of Oxford. See D. Crouch and C. de Trafford, 'The Forgotten Family in Twelfth-Century England', *Haskins Society Journal*, 13 (2004), 41–63, at 47.
69 *Councils & Synods* 2.743–9: 'Quod si concubinis (quod absit) uel forte coniugibus adheserint, ecclesiastico priuentur ordine, honore simul et beneficio.'
70 *Councils & Synods* 2.768–79: 'Sanctorum patrum uestigiis inherentes, presbiteros, diaconos, subdiaconos uxoratos aut concubinarios ecclesiasticis officiis et beneficiis priuamus, ac ne quis eorum missam audire presumat, apostolica auctoritate prohibemus.'
71 *Councils & Synods* 2.984: 'Si quis sacerdos uel clericus in sacris ordinibus constitutus ecclesiam uel ecclesiasticum beneficium habens publice fornicariam suam habeat, et semel, secundo et tertio commonitus fornicariam suam non dimiserit, et a se prorsus non expulerit, sed potius in immunditia sua duxerit persistendum, omni officio et beneficio ecclesiastico spolietur.'
72 *Councils & Synods* 2.984: 'Si qui uero infra subdiaconatum constituti matrimonia contraxerint, ab uxoribus suis nisi de communi consensu ad religionem transire uoluerint et ibi in Dei seruicio iugiter permanere, nullatenus separentur, sed cum uxoribus suis uiuentes ecclesiastica beneficia nullo modo percipiant.'
73 This part of Gregory's letter appears also in a *causa* about ecclesiastical property (C.12 q.1). But its inclusion in the *causa* was only incidental and cannot tell us much about the financial fate of married clerics. It was used to emphasise the need for the clergy to lead a common life. Its rubric reads, 'Let clerics possess no private property.' The sentences pertaining to the married clergy were included here only because Gratian did not leave out from his quotations any intervening passages which might have been of lesser interest. We learn much more from the inclusion of Gregory's letter in D.32, a discussion on the sexual continence of clerics in holy orders. Both chapters were part of Gratian's first recension. See Winroth, *Making of Gratian's Decretum*, 200, 212.

74 D.32 c.3: 'Siqui uero sunt clerici extra sacros ordines constituti, qui se non possunt continere, sortiri uxores debent, et stipendia sua exterius accipere, quia et de eisdem Patribus nouimus scriptum: "quod diuidebant prout cuique opus erat." De eorum quoque stipendio cogitandum atque prouidendum est, et sub ecclesiastica regula sunt tenendi, ut bonis moribus uiuant, et canendis psalmis inuigilent, et ab omnibus illicitis cor, et linguam, et corpus Deo auctore conseruent.' For a translation, see B. Colgrave and R.A.B. Mynors (eds. and trans.), *Ecclesiastical History of the English People* (Oxford, 1991), 78–81.

75 In principle all clergy were paid by the bishop out of diocesan income. From the later fifth century attempts were made to divide this income into four or three parts, for the bishop's use, the clergy, the fabric of the church, and perhaps the poor. See S. Wood, *The Proprietary Church in the Medieval West* (Oxford, 2006), 10; D. Ganz, 'The Ideology of Sharing: Apostolic Community and Ecclesiastical Property in the Early Middle Ages', in *Property and Power in the Early Middle Ages*, eds. W. Davies and P. Fouracre (Cambridge, 1995), 17–30, at 20.

76 D.32 c.3: 'Extra sacros ordines constituti ducant uxores et ab ecclesia stipendia accipiant.'

77 *Summa Parisiensis*, 31, 151. See also *Magister Rufinus*, 321.

78 *Summa Parisiensis*, 31, D.32 c.3 s.v. *Si qui*: 'Alibi in hoc corpore non inuenitur hoc concessum ut acolythi et similes conjugati habeant redditus'.

79 *Summa Parisiensis*, 156, C.12 q.1 c.8 s.v. *Quia*: 'Hodie enim habentibus uxores nihil daretur de stipendiis ecclesiae'.

80 B. Smalley, *The Becket Conflict and the Schools* (Oxford, 1976), 226.

81 R.V. Turner, 'The Miles Literatus in Twelfth- and Thirteenth-Century England: How Rare a Phenomenon?', *The American Historical Review*, 83:4 (1978), 928–45, at 932.

82 *Summa des Stephanus*, 47.

83 In English cathedrals common funds were established in the later twelfth century to provide extra top-up payments to encourage some canons to reside and to attend services. The payments were often made in money, though sometimes money payments could be combined with or substituted by food payments. See Barrow, 'Cathedrals, Provosts and Prebends', 552. Exeter represented an exception in England, as throughout the Middle Ages the estates of its cathedral remained communally managed and the prebends of its canons consisted of a share of the annual revenues. See D. Blake, 'The Development of the Chapter of the Diocese of Exeter 1050–1161', *Journal of Medieval History*, 8:1 (1982), 1–11.

84 He commented on this issue primarily under D.32 c.3 in *Summa Lipsiensis* 1.122. In C.12 q.1 c.8, he simply redirects the reader to his other, fuller comment. *Summa Lipsiensis* 3.72.

85 *Summa Lipsiensis* 1.122, D.32 c.3 s.v. *Si qui*: 'Hoc capitulum dicunt quidam locale esse et tantum Anglicis specialiter concessum, quia noui erant in fide.'

86 *Summa Lipsiensis* 1.122, D.32 c.3 s.v. *Si qui*: 'Alii dicunt et melius quod omnes in minoribus ordinibus licite possunt uxores ducere et stipendia exterius accipere. Vnde dicunt quod talis posset prebendam habere in ecclesia Eboracensi uel alia, dum tamen talis esset, ad quem cura animarum non spectaret.'

87 We can indeed find such examples among the prebends of the York cathedral. For one, the prebend of Apesthorpe initially consisted of a hamlet in Nottinghamshire, which was probably part of the archbishop's manor of Laneham. It was later (1143x1147) augmented to include twenty bovates in Barkston and Grimston in the parish of Kirkby Wharfe as well as tithe of demesne and the mill of North Milford. It was not, however, endowed with a church. See *Fasti*, VI, 54–6.

88 P. Hoskin, 'Robert Grosseteste and the Simple Benefice: A Novel Solution to the Complexities of Lay Presentation', *Journal of Medieval History*, 40:1 (2014), 1–20, at 6.

89 Hoskin, 'Robert Grosseteste and the Simple Benefice', 7.

90 Hoskin, 'Robert Grosseteste and the Simple Benefice', 11.

91 *Summa Lipsiensis* 1.122, D.32 c.3 s.v. *Si qui*: 'Alii dicunt quod simplex beneficium posset talis habere, ut certam mensuram frumenti uel uini singulis mensibus percipiant, et hoc ita, si consuetudo illius ecclesie non refragetur, arg. illius capituli infra di. e. Placuit; et hec stipendia uocantur simplex beneficium secundum eos ab Alexander III. in extrau. Vniversalis.'

92 *Summa Lipsiensis* 1.122, D.32 c.3 s.v. *accipere*: 'Hinc uidetur posse haberi quod uxores eorum de rebus ecclesie debeant sustentari, set secundum hoc melior uidetur condicio eorum quam continentium: Illi enim percipiunt stipendia que sufficiunt duobus, quod non faciunt continentes.'

93 *Magistri Honorii* 1.110, D.32 c.3 s.v. *Si qui uero clerici stipendia accipere*: 'uel *stipendia exterius* quasi dicat exteriora eiusmodi, illa quibus cura animarum siue spiritualium non est adnexa. Talia uxorati habere possunt, alia non, ut in decretali Vniversalis. Vel exteriora uocat non attitulata, quorum scilicet ratione non dicatur titulum haberi in ecclesia, ut scilicet sit canonicus, ut modium frumenti et uini.' Master Honorius discusses titles in more detail in his comment on D.70 c.2, in *Magistri Honorii* 1.209–11.

94 *Magistri Honorii* 1.110, D.32 c.3 s.v. *singulis annis prout cuique opus*: 'Hinc arg. cum uxores talium sint de rebus ecclesie exhibende, ut supra di. prox. Omnino (D.31, c.11), maiorem partem incontinentibus quam continentibus dandam cum opus quandoque habeant ad familiam, alii sibi tantum.'

95 1 Comp. 3.3.2: 'Accepimus autem, quod plerique in tuo episcopatu degentes, cum essent in acolitatus offitio et infra constituti, uxores duxerunt, et nichilominus ecclesias quas prius habebant detinere presumunt. Vnde quoniam uxorati, cum diuisi sint et eos cogitare oporteat, quo modo uxoribus placere ualeant et seruire obsequiis, non solummodo possunt intendere diuinis: fraternitati tuae per ap. scripta precipiendo mandamus, quatinus predictos uiros ecclesias libere et absolute dimittere appellatione cessante compellas et eas aliis personis idoneis in sacris ordinibus constitutis concedas. Verum si qui eorum aliquod in eisdem ecclesiis simplex prius benefitium habuerunt, ipsum eis excepto magisterio ecclesiarum sub dissimulatione dimittere poteris.' There were a substantial number of clerics in the diocese of London who took wives while in minor orders during the time of Gilbert Foliot and he seems to have been lax when it came to clerical marriage. This is supported by the fact that Gilbert was personally admonished not only by the pope but also by Thomas Becket in 1166 in a letter that the archbishop addressed to the whole of the English clergy. See A. Morey and C.N.L. Brooke (eds.), *The Letters and Charters of Gilbert Foliot* (Cambridge, 1967), 221. See also C. Duggan, 'Equity and Compassion in Papal Marriage Decretals to England', in his *Decretals and the Creation of the 'New Law' in the Twelfth Century: Judges, Judgements, Equity and the Law* (Aldershot, 1998), 59–87, at 64–5.

96 *Magistri Honorii* 1.110, D.32 c.3 s.v. *Si qui uero clerici stipendia accipere*: 'Talia uxorati habere possunt, alia non, ut in decretali Vniversalis.'

97 X.3.3.2: 'Prouideas attentius, ne deinceps clericus coniugatus ad ecclesiastica beneficia, uel sacros ordines aut administrationes ecclesiasticas admittatur, nisi forte castitatem uoueret perpetuam, et qui unicam et uirginem habuisset uxorem.' See also Duggan, 'Equity and Compassion', 65–6.

98 X.3.3.2: 'quia ibi natio et gens barbara et multitudo in causa'; 'a quibus sine magno discrimine ac effusione sanguinis non possunt priuari'.

99 Barrow, 'Clergy in the Diocese of Hereford', 41.

100 See also Duggan, 'Equity and Compassion', 63–4.

101 Broomfield, *Thomae de Chobham*, 376.

102 Broomfield, *Thomae de Chobham*, 377.

103 *Gemma Ecclesiastica*, 143–4.

104 *EEA*, XXIX, 232: 'ut omnes ministri ecclesie parochie in sacris ordinibus constituti, siue sint beneficiati siue non, honeste et caste uiuant'.

5 Clerical dynasties

As discussed in the two previous chapters, one of the criticisms commonly levelled against clerical marriage was that it could lead to the alienation of Church resources. Another potential by-product with financial implications was the restriction of ecclesiastical positions and lands to specific families. Clerical marriage contributed to the growth of clerical dynasties, by adding sons to the list of male relatives, such as nephews or brothers, whose careers a cleric may have wished to advance. Attitudes towards such familial arrangements were influenced by, and could in turn influence, contemporary views on clerical marriage, especially when combined with accusations of illegitimacy.

As we shall see, this was the case in England, where hostility towards married priests intensified the dislike of clerical dynasties and led to harsher denunciations of illegitimacy, and where conversely the banning of hereditary succession to churches was used as a weapon against clerical marriage. In Byzantium, on the other hand, hereditary succession *per se* was not problematic. When it occurred, it did so with the support of the bishop and the sanction of the Church. It was not seen as an abuse or a potential threat, but as a way to further fund the poorest part of the clergy. The issue of illegitimacy was not raised in this context, and nor was the question of clerical marriage more generally. Only in the case of bishops were rules put in place to regulate their succession, but these were addressed more widely to relatives and friends, rather than episcopal sons.

Byzantium

Ecclesiastical dynasties and hereditary succession to clerical positions were neither unusual nor unwanted in Byzantium.[1] Indeed they occurred in different ecclesiastical settings, from cathedrals to private religious foundations, and among clerics of all grades.

At the episcopal level, John Mauropous, Michael Psellos' teacher, presents a famous eleventh-century example. When he became metropolitan of Euchaita (c. 1050–1075), he was following in the footsteps of two of his uncles who had taken care of him in his early years, the archbishop Leo of Bulgaria (1037–1056) and the bishop of Claudiopolis.[2] Another example of a bishop who promoted a family member's clerical career was Georgios, bishop of Hierissos, whose grandson, also called Georgios, was acting as *oikonomos* of his bishopric in 1080. We know of the connection between the two men because Georgios the younger was proud of it and did not hesitate to advertise it in his signature: 'Georgios the grandson and *oikonomos* of the most beloved to God bishop of Hierissos'.[3]

A later example is that of Nikephoros Chrysoberges (d. after 1213?), who succeeded his uncle Theodore Galenus as metropolitan of Sardis (c. 1204).[4] Nikephoros wrote two poems commemorating his uncle's death, from which we learn that Theodore was a highly educated man who took upon himself the instruction of his nephew in grammar, rhetoric, history, and philosophy.[5] But Nikephoros and Theodore were not the only members of their dynasty to have obtained episcopal positions. One of their relatives held the metropolitan see of Naupaktos at the turn of the twelfth century, and another was archbishop of Corinth (c. 1170–1204).[6] More importantly, the Chrysoberges family could boast of two patriarchs of Constantinople, Nicholaos II (979–991) and Luke Chrysoberges (1157–1170), and a patriarch of Antioch, Theodosios, who served in the mid-eleventh century.[7]

Another example, this time of an episcopal father and son, is that of Georgios Bardanes, metropolitan of Kerkyra (1219–c. 1240), and his father Demetrios, bishop of Karystos.[8] Georgios was educated by Michael Choniates, archbishop of Athens (1182–1205), who was a friend but also the metropolitan of his father.[9] Michael Choniates himself counted many of his nephews among his archiepiscopal entourage. Although they do not seem to have occupied regular positions in his cathedral church, they participated actively in ecclesiastical affairs.[10] They were also personally important to Michael, who lamented the departure of one of them, the deacon Niketas, who had been his companion on the island of Keos.[11]

The Parthenon in Athens offers us many more examples of clerical dynasties among cathedral clergy, which can be found inscribed onto the very fabric of the building. The columns of the Parthenon have been carved with over 230 inscriptions, many of which record the deaths of the clergy who served the church.[12] One inscription jointly commemorates the metropolitan of Athens, Philip (d. 981), and his father, the *chartophylax* Theodegios (d. 959); another talks of the death of *protopapas* Ioannes (d. 1041), who was the son of Pothos, deacon and *oikonomos* (d. 918).[13]

At the level of private religious foundations, direct hereditary succession can be found in the will of Eustathios Boilas (1059) and the provisions for his church of the *Theotokos tou Salem*. Boilas actively supported the formation of clerical dynasties, by first ordaining into the clergy one of his freed slaves, Gregory, and then requesting that all male children who were born of his freed slaves and servants 'be brought up in the church of the *Theotokos* in the learning of the holy letters and be made clerics, being provided for by the church'.[14] Boilas was happy to have both Gregory and any sons he might produce serve at his religious foundation.

As these examples suggest, clerical dynasties and hereditary succession to ecclesiastical positions were not problematic in Byzantium; on the contrary, they could be proudly embraced or encouraged.[15] It is easy to imagine that such family networks would also have been important among the priests, deacons, and subdeacons who served the public churches, the most numerous part of the Byzantine clergy, about whom unfortunately we are the least well informed.

Legitimate children

In Byzantine law, regulations regarding clerical hereditary succession avoided extremes, advocating instead a middle path: it should not be compulsory but neither should it be forbidden. Hereditary succession was to take place only when a suitable candidate was available. Canon law dealt with this issue in the case of bishops in canon 76 of the Apostles:

> It is not permitted to a bishop to show favour to a brother or a son or another relative, and to ordain whomever he wishes to the episcopal dignity. For it is not right to make heirs of the bishopric, gifting the things of God out of human affection. It is not proper to make the Church of God subject to one's heirs. But if anyone shall do this, let the ordination be void and the person himself punished with excommunication.[16]

Balsamon commenting on this canon emphasised that it was for the synods to elect bishops, not for the bishops themselves to appoint their successors.[17] He gave the recent example of the metropolitan of Philippopolis, Michael Italikos (c. 1143–1146), who had tried to make it a condition that his *oikonomos* would take his place when he renounced his metropolis.[18] The synod rejected his request, 'because they knew that the things that the bishop acquires after his ordination from Church revenues are not his to gift or bestow upon whom he wills, let alone the bishopric itself'.[19] Similarly, Zonaras pointed out that episcopal authority was a gift of the Holy Spirit: 'how can someone transfer to another the grace of the Holy Spirit as a favour, like a bequest?'[20] The problem seems to have been twofold: the bishop was the leader and spiritual father of his community, but also the administrator of the bishopric's finances. The high degree of responsibility of both of these functions might explain why it was specifically forbidden to *bishops* to select their successor, with no reference made to clerics lower down the ecclesiastical hierarchy.

The second point to note about canon 76 of the Apostles is that although it explicitly mentions sons, it talks equally of brothers and other relations. The problem is not posed here in terms of a specific pattern of succession, but more generally, in terms of who has the responsibility for the appointment. To the already extensive list of the canon, Zonaras added friends among the people who should not be appointed to a position 'out of human affection', a phrase which he explained as 'a friendship or a familial relation'.[21] This is not surprising as in Byzantium familial networks were often combined with networks of friendship when it came to the advancement of individuals.[22] An example of this can be found in a letter of the twelfth-century scholar Ioannes Tzetzes where he attempts to advance the career of a priest whom he does not know personally but who was the brother of one of his friends. The way these relationships were meant to work can be seen in the phrasing of Tzetzes' request to his addressee:

> I beg you, with the freedom of speech that you have allowed me to ask you what I want freely and without constraint, to take care and to honour that priest, Leo, as if he were I myself, with the honour, protection and love that you surround me with, because of the love that I nourish towards his brother, both now and in the future.[23]

Friends were part of a network of patronage which dominated professional advancement, not only in the Church but also in the army and the bureaucratic administration.[24] Such a wide network is likely to have taken away the emphasis from clerical dynasties when they occurred in Byzantium, leading to broader regulations rather than singling out fathers and children.

Below the episcopal level more generally, and in the case of the father-to-son pattern in particular, hereditary succession was deemed problematic only when it was made compulsory; this was seen in Byzantium as a Judaic custom.[25] As canon 33 of Trullo emphasised, clerics needed to possess certain requirements which could not be substituted by a right of birth:

> Since we know that, in the region of the Armenians, only those who are of priestly descent are appointed to the clerical orders, following in this Jewish customs [. . .], we decree that henceforth it shall not be lawful for those who wish to bring anyone into the clergy, to pay regard to the descent of him who is to be ordained; but let them examine whether they are worthy (according to the decrees set forth in the holy canons) to be placed on the list of the clergy, so that they may be ecclesiastically promoted, whether they are of priestly descent or not.[26]

This extreme example was condemned by the canonists and was presented as a custom which was alien to Byzantium. Both the canon itself and Zonaras mentioned this as an Armenian practice. As such they did not refer to the father-to-son succession that was occurring among Byzantine clerics of all ranks, but were referring in the abstract to the idea of compulsory succession as something that 'others' wrongly practised, be they Armenians or Jews. Balsamon began his commentary in the same way, but then switched the discussion to a current *Byzantine* practice which was taking place in the churches of Athens and Mesembria.[27] There the descendants of the cathedral canons claimed a hereditary right to be enrolled in the clergy, even if they remained members of the laity:

> there has often been discussion about various bishops, who keep clerics made through chrysobulls – that is to say the bishops of Athens, Mesembria, and others – that the offspring of the old clerics force them to enlist them in the clergy (and often they are even laymen) instead of those who are worthy, and to let the ecclesiastical work be performed by others assigned by them.[28]

Balsamon stated that a similar practice was followed in Constantinople in the churches of the *Forty Martyrs* and the *Theotokos Kyrou*, where the culprits were not only laymen but also monastic houses.[29] According to Papagianni, Balsamon wrote here of two different abuses. In the case of Constantinople, the passage referred to the distribution of ecclesiastical positions: members of the laity and monasteries seem to have held something similar to a right of advowson to these churches – that is to say, they had the right to nominate a cleric to a specific church.[30] Given the context in which this comment appears, we can infer that these laymen and/or members of religious houses chose to appoint to the priesthood relatives who might not have been suitable candidates. It is these unworthy appointments that Balsamon criticises. In the case of Athens and Mesembria, on the other hand, the canonist referred specifically to hereditary succession and to a special category of clerics, *klerikoparoikoi*.[31]

Klerikoparoikoi were members of the clergy who, on top of receiving a salary for their ecclesiastical duties, were given a piece of land, called a *klerikato*. In exchange for this land they paid a fee to the bishop. *Klerikata* appear for the first time in the eleventh century, but much of what we know about them comes from the thirteenth and fourteenth centuries. The clerics who had use of these *klerikata* could be 'donated' to the bishopric by the emperor or could be gathered together by the bishop himself.[32] One of the reasons for establishing *klerikoparoikoi* in an area was to provide for the pastoral needs of the population in cases when clerical salaries were too low.[33] *Klerikoparoikoi* had an advantage compared to other dependent agricultural workers (*paroikoi*), as they paid a smaller fee to the bishop for their lands. Not all *paroikoi* who were clerics would have been considered *klerikoparoikoi*; *paroikoi* who decided to be ordained clerics later in their lives and who belonged to a monastery or a private religious foundation, rather than the bishopric, might not have enjoyed the same advantages.[34]

In some sense these *klerikata* were similar to Western benefices: both contributed to the sustenance of the cleric and both involved the exploitation of a piece of ecclesiastical land. A great difference, however, was that unlike a benefice, a *klerikato* was expected to be passed down to the descendants of the cleric who held it, provided that there were male sons who could perform the ecclesiastical duties and would continue the exploitation of the land under the same provisions.[35] An episcopal charter issued in 1339 by Neilos, metropolitan of Lakedaimonia, stated explicitly that clerics were not to sell the land, use it as surety, or give it out as a dowry; instead they should 'transmit it to sons worthy of serving the church'.[36] Another difference had to do with the actual profitability of benefices and *klerikata*. Byzantine *klerikoparoikoi* were expected to work on the land themselves, rather than have it exploited by others, as would have been the case in England.[37] They were effectively dependent agricultural workers. We can see this in an 1163 document for the bishopric of Stagoi in Thessaly. The thirty-six *klerikoparoikoi* who had been established there by the imperial authorities were settled around the cathedral and held ecclesiastical roles from deacon to *protekdikos* and *skeuophylax*; clearly, they formed the cathedral clergy. They were also divided, however, into the fiscal categories of *zeugaratos*, *boidatos*, and *aktemon*, which were used for peasants.[38] The category they belonged to and the tax they paid to the bishop depended on the size of their holdings. A *zeugaratos* was the most prosperous among them, holding a pair of oxen and/or the quantity of land that could be cultivated by them. A *boidatos* had only one ox, while an *aktemon* (or *pezos*) possessed no plough animals and little or no land but could own other livestock, such as sheep, goats, and bees.[39] The situation of *klerikoparoikoi* was not enviable and Angold has stated that 'there was a danger that they would be reduced to the condition of episcopal serfs.'[40]

Although Balsamon was complaining about potential abuses, reminiscent of the forced succession of the Armenians and the Jews, the practice itself was clearly accepted by the Church, as bishops were involved in both gathering and managing *klerikoparoikoi*. It was the involvement of laymen that caused problems: if in one generation there were only daughters, and as a result no member of the family was capable of filling the office, or if the sons did not choose to follow in the footsteps of their father, some families could still keep the ecclesiastical property and hire a priest to carry out the ritual functions. Balsamon's complaint here was not so much about restricting access to ecclesiastical lands and positions to specific clerical families but about putting them into the hands of laymen.[41]

Illegitimate children

The Byzantine examples discussed so far have involved the legitimate children of clerics in major orders. Given that clerical marriage was lawful in Byzantium but equated with adultery, fornication, or incest in twelfth-century England, it is important for the sake of comparison to look also at the illegitimate children of Byzantine clerics. Such would be the children of a cleric at any rank and any woman apart from one he had legitimately married before his accession to the subdiaconate; or a bishop and any woman after his accession to the episcopate.[42]

Legislation targeting clerics and their illegitimate children appeared early on in Byzantium. In 530, Emperor Justinian decreed that priests who fathered illegitimate children were to lose their priesthood.[43] Justinian punished not only the priests but also their children, whom he wished to be 'contaminated by the disgrace which accompanies this kind of procreation' and to whom he denied any right of inheritance:

> We make such children the same as the laws define those begotten of incestuous or nefarious marriages: they shall be considered neither natural nor spurious, but utterly destitute and unworthy to inherit from their parents; nor can they or their mothers receive a gift from the fathers or through third parties, but all munificence made on their behalf by the fathers shall fall to the holy church to which they who commit this sin belong.[44]

Justinian's law about the illegitimate children of clerics was included in Title 9, Ch. 29 of the *Nomokanon*, and was commented on by Balsamon, who added that those daring such a thing, after having lost the priesthood, would not be allowed to attain any secular office, or to be part of the army, but were to remain private individuals (ἰδιωτεύοντας) for all time.[45] This was overall a harsh punishment that was addressed to all the persons involved: the father, the mother, and the child. However, Balsamon finished his commentary by lamenting that at least part of that injunction was not kept in his own day.[46] It is not clear whether this referred to the loss of the inheritance for the children and the prohibition of gifts towards them, and/or to the strict punishment of the priestly father, who was forbidden from pursuing secular and military careers.

In any case, although the punishment in question purported to restrict the inheritance rights of illegitimate clerical children, it did not affect their ability to join the clergy. It did not create an impediment to ordination. The same was true for all illegitimates. Balsamon said so explicitly in one of his answers to a question of Patriarch Mark of Alexandria, where he noted that no impediment had ever existed for the children of third marriages, even before the *Tome of Union* of 920, when third marriages had not yet become acceptable by civil law. At that time, such children would have been debarred from their father's inheritance but would have been permitted – if found worthy – to become clerics.[47] Even the sons of prostitutes, the canonist tells us, were allowed to accede to the priesthood, as it was their mothers who had sinned and should be under penance, not the children themselves.[48] On the contrary, as we saw in Chapter 3 in the case of emancipation from parental authority, it was the sins of the children which could have a detrimental impact upon their episcopal father.

What is more, illegitimacy had not been raised as an issue in Title 1, Chapter 23 of the *Nomokanon*, which set forth the impediments to clerical ordination.[49] It was the sins that the individual himself had committed that could form an impediment, rather than the sins of his parents. This was in accordance with patristic teaching.[50] John Chrysostom said so explicitly in his third homily on Matthew 1:3:

> For such a man, although he may have a foreigner or a prostitute or whatever else she might be as his parent, will be able to suffer no damage from it. For if the former life of a fornicator who has transformed himself does not disgrace him, how much less will the wickedness of his ancestors be able to disgrace him who is virtuous but born to a harlot or an adulteress.[51]

Similar comments were made in the eleventh century by Theophylact of Ohrid and in the twelfth by Euthymios Zigabenos in their own commentaries on Matthew.[52] The main punishment of illegitimate children was of a civil rather than a religious nature: they were threatened with the loss of their inheritance, but were not prohibited from joining the clergy.

England

Despite the rules against clerical marriage, hereditary succession and clerical dynasties remained common in the Anglo-Norman kingdom in the early twelfth century.[53] Many well-documented examples can be found among English cathedral clergy.[54] Thurstan, archbishop of York (1114–1140), his brother Audoen, bishop of Evreux (1113–1139), and their father, Ansger, had all been canons of

St Paul's. Ansger held the prebend of Kentish Town, which was passed down to Audoen after his death some time after 1104.[55] Another example of a very successful clerical family comes from Bayeux. The brothers Thomas and Sampson, the children of a priest called Osbert and his wife Muriel, were successive treasurers of Bayeux and both won English bishoprics, with Thomas becoming archbishop of York (1070–1100) and Sampson bishop of Worcester (1096–1112).[56] What is more, Sampson started his own family, having at least two sons, one of whom, Thomas II, also became archbishop of York (1109–1114) while another, Richard de Douvres, became canon and bishop of Bayeux (c. 1107–1133). Samson also had a daughter, Isabelle de Douvres, known for her later liaison with Robert, first Earl of Gloucester. The son of Robert and Isabelle was Richard, bishop of Bayeux (1135–1142).[57] At a parish level, hereditary succession remained common in some areas until the thirteenth century.[58] Kemp, for example, has shown that the benefice of Eye, in Herefordshire, remained from c. 1150 to as late as 1254 in the hands of the same clerical dynasty.[59]

In contrast to the situation we have seen in Byzantium, in England the issue of hereditary succession to churches became directly linked to the question of clerical marriage. Western laws on this topic evolved during the twelfth century: conciliar canons became harsher, papal decretals multiplied, but dispensations also became more numerous. These developments affected both the illegitimate and the legitimate children of clerics. Although we do not know the proportion of the two in each society, in Byzantium even a very ambitious cleric had ten more years to form a lawful family compared to his English counterpart.[60] Byzantine clerics could produce legitimate children until they became bishops, for which the minimum canonical age was 30. In England, on the other hand, one could become subdeacon, and so rule oneself out of legitimate fatherhood, at the much younger age of 20. The illegitimate children of these English clerics were attacked in two main ways: they were forbidden from joining the clergy and from succeeding their father in his church and benefice. The second presupposed a failure of the first, and both proved difficult to enforce. It is these two lines of attack that will form the focus of this section.

Hereditary succession

Although as early as the mid-seventh century councils had decreed against illegitimate clerical children inheriting their father's ecclesiastical position, twelfth-century conciliar legislation from England became stricter only progressively.[61] At the 1102 Council of Westminster the sons of priests were prohibited from becoming heirs to their fathers' churches, but no punishment was attached to this canon.[62] Similarly the 1125 Council of Westminster decreed that

> no one is to claim a church or prebend by inheritance from his father or to constitute himself a successor in any ecclesiastical benefice. If such a presumption is made, we allow it to have no force, saying with the psalmist, 'My God, make them like a wheel', who have said, 'let us possess the sanctuary of God through inheritance'.[63]

A further clarification of the rules of hereditary succession came at the 1175 Council of Westminster:

> We decree also by the authority of the same epistle that the sons of priests are not in the future to be instituted as parsons in the churches of their fathers, nor are they to obtain them by any means, without another parson coming in between.[64]

This conciliar canon was influenced by Pope Alexander III's letter *Inter cetera sollicitudinis*, sent on 26 November 1164 to Bishop Roger of Worcester (1163–1179).[65] But it appears more lenient compared to the original letter. The prohibition of hereditary succession to ecclesiastical benefices was to apply only in the future, despite the fact that the decretal had been sent more than ten years prior to the council and was meant to have immediate effect. What is more, clerical dynasties were not altogether forbidden; it was direct hereditary succession that was not allowed.[66] In fact, this rule created a loophole that clerics at the time exploited: by acquiring the advowson of another church and presenting their son to it, they respected the law, while ensuring the continuation of their clerical dynasty. This was quickly recognised as an abuse and in the 1170s Robert Foliot, bishop of Hereford, obtained a papal decretal against it (X 3.38.6).[67]

These prohibitions of direct hereditary succession to the same church were primarily addressed to the illegitimate children of clerics, but affected also legitimate sons. In a letter to the archbishop of Canterbury, Alexander III wrote that

> if some sons of priests in your province were to hold churches, in which their father had ministered as parson or vicar, without another person intervening, you should not delay to remove them from these churches without appeal or opposition, whether they were born after ordination or before.[68]

This is in contrast to other decretals where before deciding whether a cleric was to be removed from his office, it had to be examined whether he had been born while his father was in major orders – '*in sacerdotio genitus*', as Alexander III had put it in his letter to Geoffrey Fitzroy, bishop-elect of Lincoln (c. 1170–1173) (X 1.17.2).[69] Indeed, in principle a distinction was to be made between legitimate and illegitimate clerical sons. Children whose parents were married and whose father had occupied a grade below the subdiaconate at the time of their conception were considered legitimate and were not prohibited from pursuing an ecclesiastical career. This is explicitly said by the author of the *Summa Lipsiensis* and other decretists: 'But it ought to be noted that there are some priests who produce offspring before they accede to sacred orders and some who do so after. Those sons who are conceived before can lawfully be promoted.'[70]

Nonetheless, there is further evidence that clerical sons born from lawful marriages and conceived at the right time had to struggle to keep their positions. Within this context of accusations of illegitimacy, some legitimate children of clerics were also attacked and it was up to them to prove their status from under a cloud of suspicion.[71] One such example was Reginald, bishop of Bath

(1174–1191), son of Jocelin de Bohun, bishop of Salisbury (1142–1184), whose right to his bishopric was attacked on account of his father's clerical status. In his defence, Arnulf, bishop of Lisieux (1141–1181), emphasised in a letter to Peter, archbishop of Tarentaise, and Richard, archbishop of Canterbury, that Reginald had been born before his father's accession to holy orders and that this false accusation stemmed from hatred and envy.[72]

The reasons for such attacks were partly financial: celibate clerics could claim an already occupied church and benefice by accusing the current incumbent of being the son of a priest. In fact, success in limiting the father-to-son pattern should be attributed to a great extent to such individuals in whose interest it was to enforce the law. It was often the claimants who made the complaints, not the bishops who were supposed to be disciplining the clergy, and it was primarily when a church was being disputed that a priest would be 'discovered' to be married or the son of the previous incumbent. We hear, for example, of a poor cleric who had been in possession of his church for almost thirty years before he was harassed by accusations of being the son of the previous incumbent. He lamented that his accuser had ample means, while he had none other than appealing to the pope. His poverty was made worse by his disability: he had lost sight in one eye and hearing in one ear. He was eventually allowed to keep his church and benefice, but his example shows the difficult situation in which some clerics below the episcopate found themselves, especially those who lacked the means and networks to defend themselves, and as such would have formed the easiest targets.[73]

The importance of personal interest can further be seen through an example of the malleable attitudes that people exhibited towards father-to-son succession, depending on the individual circumstances. The chronicler of Battle Abbey accused Alan, the son of Richard I of Beaufou, bishop of Avranches (1134–1142), of hereditary succession to the church of Brantham in Suffolk.[74] He stated that Alan dared to appropriate the church 'on the sole and uncanonical authority of his father' and was 'clearly in possession of a sanctuary of God by inheritance'.[75] This invective was closely followed by the description of the hereditary succession of Nicholas, son of Withgar, to the church of Mendlesham. The chronicler stated that Nicholas was confirmed in the presence of the monks, the abbot, many knights, clerics, and laymen, none of whom seemed concerned by the fact that he was acceding to his father's church. We do not learn whether Nicholas had been born before his father had received holy orders; we are told only that he agreed to pay 40s. annually in his church's name instead of the 10s. that his father had previously been paying, possibly as a form of penance for his illegitimate status. This case is an example of how the laws themselves were manipulated to suit one's interests: the same author could discredit one priest's claim to property for having a clerical father, while in the same breath acknowledging as proper the wish of another priest 'to provide for his children after him'.[76] When it suited the interests of the accuser, the laws against hereditary succession could be used as a tool against married priests and their children, even legitimate ones.[77]

This negative climate must have been partly responsible for the change in the system of hereditary succession which can be detected in this period: the father-to-son pattern was gradually replaced by an uncle-to-nephew pattern.[78] This alternative had already been well established by the eleventh century in Western Europe, although it was much less frequent among Anglo-Saxon bishops.[79] Statistics are difficult to obtain for England, but based on Spear's prosopographical study on the personnel of the Norman cathedrals between 910 and 1204, Barrow calculates that from the sixty-three clerical fathers and sons found among a total of 900 Norman canons, two thirds can be dated to the eleventh century and only one third to the twelfth, with the majority of the latter coming from the early part of that century. In contrast, of the eighty-eight clerical uncles traced during the same period, only twelve occur during the eleventh century, with the vast majority being dated to the twelfth century. Although kinship seems to have mattered more in Normandy, England would have shown a similar trend.[80] Clerical succession in the form of the uncle-to-nephew pattern was not theologically problematic or canonically condemned.[81] As such, it could not be used as a weapon by those who wished to free up access to ecclesiastical positions and lands for themselves. Nonetheless, Gerald of Wales' quotation of Pope Alexander III's statement 'the Lord deprived bishops of sons but the Devil gave them nephews' suggests that once direct hereditary succession had come under the microscope, more extended familial arrangements came to be seen as suspect.[82]

Ordination

Another line of attack against clerical children involved their right to be ordained. Although in Byzantium illegitimate sons were not prohibited from joining the clergy, in the West such prohibitions can be found already in the Carolingian era, with one of the first canons on this topic coming from the council of Meaux-Paris (845/6). This canon made it into the ninth-century collection of Regino of Prüm and eventually into Gratian's *Decretum* (C.1 q.7 c.17), but not into the eleventh-century collections of Burchard of Worms and Ivo of Chartres.[83] The extent to which such canons were previously enforced is uncertain, but prohibitions against the taking of sacred orders by illegitimate children became more common in the later eleventh century, as part of the attacks against clerical marriage.[84] Importantly, canons promulgated at Poitiers (1078), Melfi (1089), and Clermont (1095) stated that the sons of priests and anyone born of fornication should not be promoted to sacred orders unless they became monks or joined a community of regular canons.[85] In the 1180s, these eleventh-century conciliar decrees were consolidated through their inclusion in canonical collections.[86] But it is only during the pontificate of Clement III (1187–1191) that we find one of the first examples of an illegitimate clerical son asking for a dispensation to be ordained into sacred orders. This suggests that for a long time there was a gap between what church legislation said and what actually happened.[87]

In the case of bishops, an important canon was promulgated at Lateran III (1179) enjoining that episcopal candidates should be of legitimate birth.[88] We can see the issue raised in practice in England in a letter sent by the chapter of Lincoln to Pope Innocent III, after the death of Bishop Hugh of Avalon (1200). When the chapter was about to elect a new bishop, they asked the pope whether they were allowed to choose a candidate of illegitimate birth, as Hugh had selected many among them to join the chapter 'more for the merits of their life than by their right of birth, more for the verve of their character than the regularity of their origin'. The pope replied that no one with a defect of birth should be put forward without compelling reasons, but agreed to act as he deemed expedient should that happen.[89] This example shows both the challenges that the illegitimate sons of priests could face and the opportunities that were still open to them. Lincoln was a secular cathedral which still in the early thirteenth century was populated by illegitimate canons, presumably many of them clerical sons, but even they were aware of the prohibitions which came with such an irregularity and thought it necessary to inform the pope of the situation.

These restrictions regarding ordination were also discussed by Gratian and the decretists under *distinctio* 56. Gratian began with the aforementioned canon of the Council of Melfi held by Urban II in 1089, which commanded that the sons of priests should be removed from the ministry of the sacred altar unless they became monks or joined a community of regular canons.[90] In his *dictum* (D.56 d.p.c.1), he mitigated the harshness of this decree by stating that the rule applied only to the sons of priests who imitated their father's incontinence. Those who displayed honest morals and made themselves commendable could become not only priests but even popes.[91] Chapter 2 of Gratian's second recension supported this argument further by adding a list of popes who had clerical fathers.[92] This was followed by a series of canons (cc.3–9) which stated that the parents' sins should not be visited upon their offspring. The *distinctio*, however, took a more negative turn with chapter 10, an extract from St Boniface which suggested that parental sinful characteristics could pass down to children – with offspring produced through intercourse with harlots (*commixtione meretricum*) being described as 'degenerate', 'vulgar', and 'crazy with lust'.[93] This was followed by the suggestion that the sons of priests could join the clergy only in exceptional circumstances (cc.12–13). More specifically, Gratian (D.56 d.p.c.12) commented that a letter of Alexander II (1061–1073) (D.56 c.12), which stated that the son of a priest should be elected if he is more worthy than other candidates, was meant only as a dispensation and not as a general rule.[94] The pope had explicitly stated that 'this is not to be taken as precedent for the future, but is designed against the danger to the Church at this time.'[95] Gratian (D.56 d.p.c.13) went on to note that the popes he had previously mentioned (D.56 c.2) had not in fact been illegitimate at all, as the prohibition of clerical marriage had not been instituted at the time of their conception. In the end, despite Gratian's own *dictum* and the large number of chapters arguing that children should not be punished for their parents' sins, we are left with the impression that avoiding their father's errors was certainly important but not quite enough for the illegitimate sons of priests, who would need a dispensation in order to join the secular clergy.[96]

Master Honorius and the author of the *Summa Lipsiensis* also found a middle ground between following the canon of Melfi and completely absolving the illegitimate children of clerics of any irregularity. They maintained that those among them who lived in the world, rather than in a monastery or a community of regular canons, could still be ordained priests without dispensation, as long as they lived a very meritorious life.[97] Admittedly, this is a vague statement that could have worked in favour of clerical children, but it is one that also added to the malleable attitudes towards them, which, as we have seen, depended to a large extent on the personal circumstances of all parties involved. Given this flexibility, it is not surprising that so many clerical sons managed to go past the initial prohibition of ordination and were found grappling with the further prohibition of hereditary succession.

But the two decretists also set some limitations. Both maintained that illegitimate children could not become bishops without a papal dispensation.[98] Master Honorius added that they were barred from ministering their father's church unless they obtained a dispensation or unless they had previously taken monastic vows, commenting on the financial aspects behind this regulation: monastic life meant that clerical sons would not beget children themselves, thus ending hereditary succession; it also meant that by leading a communal life they would renounce their rights to property.[99] In fact, it was often encouraged not only for the children but also for the married clerical father to join monastic orders. One such example is that of the family of Nicholas Breakspear (d. 1159). His father, a parish priest, became a monk at St Albans; his brother, Ralph, also a parish priest, holding his church from Westminster Abbey, became a regular canon at Great Missenden; and Nicholas himself became a regular canon of Saint-Ruf in the South of France, and even ended up as pope.[100]

These prohibitions against clerical sons joining the clergy were also explicitly said to be a punishment directed at the priests themselves and a deterrent to further transgression.[101] Master Honorius stated as a reason for such laws 'hatred for the father's incontinence' and saw them as preventive measures: 'so that others may be called back from a similar sin'.[102] As such they were meant to help eliminate clerical marriage, and the punishment of the illegitimate sons was most likely the means rather than the ultimate goal of the legislation.[103] This would explain the leniency we often see in dispensations: what mattered was that the Church maintained control over the processes of ordination and appointment to benefices. As has been pointed out by Taglia, dispensations allowed the ecclesiastical authorities to find a balance between controlling clerical misbehaviour and meeting their recruitment needs, while at the same time reinforcing the power structure that was trying to impose clerical celibacy by reminding everyone that profaners of the system could not take part in it until they had been formally reinstated.[104] In the twelfth century, bishops were still allowed to grant dispensations, but calls to the papal *curia* increased.[105]

A further point of interest involves the way that the decretists understood 'sin' in the case of illegitimate clerical children. As we have seen, Master Honorius considered their punishment to be a deterrent for clerical fathers, who, as he continued to say, 'in this way see their offspring being punished for their own sin'.[106] The idea of a double punishment, affecting both father and son, contrasts with the Byzantine attitude towards parental sin discussed earlier. But the two decretists did not put much emphasis on sinfulness *per se*. Instead they interpreted the word 'peccatum' as 'impedimentum' and noted that there were occasions when people were punished through no fault of their own, not because they had sinned but because of an impediment.[107] The *Summa Lipsiensis* offered a historical example of such a case based on C.27 q.2 c.20, a letter of Gregory the Great I (594) in which we learn that, during the time of his predecessor, subdeacons, for whom it had been previously lawful to enjoy sexual intercourse with their wives, had been given two choices: either to abstain from their spouses or to give up their ecclesiastical office. The author of the *Summa Lipsiensis* commented that in this case the subdeacons were being punished, either with loss of their office or with loss of their wife, despite the fact that they had not sinned.[108] An impediment had simply been created that made their situation untenable. But the most common example given by the two decretists in such discussions of sin and punishment involved cases of simony: children whose parents bought them an ecclesiastical office were punished – for example, by losing their benefice or by being cast away from the church – despite not having personally sinned.[109] Such cases made the punishment of illegitimate clerical children more acceptable and reinforced the idea that canons advocating that the sins of parents should not be imputed to their children did not apply to punishments in this world, but only the next.[110] We can see, then, that although Eastern and Western canon lawyers shared and quoted some of the same religious texts absolving children from parental sin, in England attempts to accommodate for specific circumstances, such as the fight against simony, made it admissible for a child to be held accountable for a parental transgression, even if this was sometimes presented as an impediment rather than a sin.

Another factor which is not mentioned here by the decretists but is worth keeping in mind is the Western tradition of monastic oblation, which, although in decline in the twelfth century, had previously made it possible for children to share in parental penance as a live expiatory offering.[111] If children could be offered to monasteries as an atonement for their parents' sins, was it too much of a stretch to ask that priests' sons should also join a monastery or a regular community as a result of their father's incontinence, when they too wished to enter the clergy?

Conclusion

In England, as in Byzantium, we find twelfth-century examples of fathers and sons, and uncles and nephews, as well as brothers, serving churches at the same time or in succession to each other. While clerical dynasties were not, strictly speaking, prohibited in either society, restrictions applied in both. In Byzantium, bishops were particularly singled out and were forbidden from choosing the successor to their sees. This prohibition did not refer specifically to episcopal sons, but more generally to relatives and even friends. A son was legally allowed to succeed his father as long as he was a suitable candidate. Lower down the hierarchy, direct hereditary succession could be controversial when it was made compulsory, or when it meant the devolvement of ecclesiastical positions and lands to laymen. The latter could happen in the case of *klerikoparoikoi*, if no male heirs were available to perform the ecclesiastical duties and to cultivate the land. In

Byzantium as in the West, laymen were not supposed to hold church lands and distribute ecclesiastical positions. Even in the case of the *klerikoparoikoi*, however, the holders of the *klerikato* did not enjoy the same financial benefits as their Western counterparts. They were mostly poorer clerics who needed further financial support. As such, although criticised by Balsamon, this system of compulsory hereditary succession was not only tolerated but encouraged by the Church. Overall, in Byzantium – even when hereditary succession was not approved – clerical sons were not attacked and their position was not threatened. This applied both to legitimate and to illegitimate sons, as illegitimacy did not form an impediment to sacred orders nor did it limit the kind of ecclesiastical office that a clerical child could attain. More generally, the issue of hereditary succession to churches and lands was not linked to clerical marriage in the minds of Byzantine ecclesiastics. Clerical dynasties were simply one component of a wider friendship network which formed an integral part of how society was expected to function.

In the West, attitudes towards clerical sons changed in the course of the twelfth century. Initially, the situation was similar to what we find in Byzantium, and father-to-son succession was common. However, as part of the efforts to eradicate clerical marriage, clerical sons and particularly the sons of priests came under attack. In England, the laws on father-to-son succession were made progressively harsher, with initial councils remaining vague on the topic and forgoing punishments. When stricter decretals were promulgated, with them also came the possibility of dispensation, allowing the Church to secure enough ordinands while still taking control of ordination and appointment back into its own hands. By the end of the twelfth century, however, clerical sons were facing harsh opposition. They were prohibited from succeeding their father to his church and even from receiving sacred orders unless they wished to join a monastery or the regular canons. These prohibitions applied primarily to illegitimate sons, but the general climate of disapproval of clerical marriage meant that legitimate sons too faced the same challenges. They could be accused of being illegitimate and the burden was upon them to prove their status. Clerical sons began to be seen as a manifestation of their father's sin and their illegitimacy was emphasised, especially when there was an opportunity for financial gain. This created a vicious cycle: negative attitudes towards clerical marriage fed into ideas about illegitimacy and illicit succession, and these ideas in turn exacerbated the existing negative attitudes towards clerical marriage.

Overall, we can conclude that hereditary succession could but did not have to be important in determining attitudes towards clerical marriage. Other factors contributed to the transformation of a relatively normal aspect of medieval life into something unlawful and spiritually damaging. First, there was a different understanding about who stood to gain from clerical familial networks. Contrary to the situation in Byzantium, in England sons were particularly singled out, as there were no laws about more distant relatives or friends. Western society expected clergy to look after nephews, especially those who were themselves clerics. Similarly, older brothers were expected to look after younger brothers. Sons had initially formed part of the same process, but the association of hereditary succession with clerical marriage made the father-to-son pattern problematic. In Byzantium, on the other hand, laws referred more generally to family and friends. In fact, as we saw in Chapter 3, the Byzantines understood that familial love extended far beyond the love of a parent for his children and friendship networks had an important part to play in the making of one's career. Secondly, East and West developed different attitudes towards illegitimacy. In Byzantium, illegitimacy was not a reason to deny someone access to holy orders and men continued to be judged on their own merits. In England, the illegitimate nature of clerical children was progressively highlighted, to the extent that even legitimate ones suffered through association. Thirdly, hereditary succession in England brought about problems which were not directly applicable in a Byzantine context: restricting ecclesiastical positions and lands to specific families could diminish the authority of the bishop and lead to Church lands falling into the hands of the laity. In Byzantium, the bishops were in control of the hereditary succession in *klerikata*, and although lay appropriations were problematic, their value was not such that it could cause serious damage. A further difference involves the frequency of such abuses. *Klerikoparoikoi* do not seem to have been common in twelfth-century Byzantium, where clerics were primarily remunerated through yearly salaries. These differences meant that although in both England and Byzantium canon law attempted to protect the inviolability of ecclesiastical property, there was a stark difference in focus. Byzantine law aimed to create a meritocratic succession at the episcopal level, whereas legal discourse in England came to be driven by an ideal of clerical superiority over the laity, manifested in their celibacy and purity standards which were incompatible with the existence of clerical offspring.

Notes

1 For more examples, see Magdalino, 'Enlightenment and Repression', 371 n. 54. For extended familial networks of ecclesiastical office-holding in earlier periods, see C. Rapp, *Holy Bishops in Late Antiquity: The Nature of Christian Leadership in an Age of Transition* (Berkeley, CA, 2005), 195–9; Moulet, *Evêques*, 216–21. Generally, family ties are more difficult to detect in these earlier periods due to the lack of family names.

2 A. Karpozilos, *Συμβολή στη μελέτη του βίου και του έργου του Ιωάννη Μαυρόποδος* (Ioannina, 1982), 24–5. We do not have much information about Mauropous' uncle who was the bishop of Claudiopolis. Based on evidence from seals, he has been identified with an Ioannes, metropolitan of Claudiopolis, in the early eleventh century. See D.A. Karpozilos, *The Letters of Ioannes Mauropous, Metropolitan of Euchaita: Greek Text, Translation, and Commentary* (Thessalonike, 1990), 10.

3 Papachryssanthou, 'Un évêché byzantin: Hierissos en Chalcidique', 389 n. 158: 'Γεώργιος ὁ ἔγκων καὶ οἰκονόμος τοῦ θεοφιλεστάτου ἐπισκόπου Ἱερισσοῦ.'

4 A. Kazhdan and S. Franklin, 'Nicephorus Chrysoberges and Nicholas Mesarites: A Comparative Study' in their *Studies on Byzantine Literature of the Eleventh and Twelfth Centuries* (Cambridge, 1984), 224–36; R. Browning, 'An Unpublished Address of Nicephoros Chrysoberges to Patriarch John X Kamateros of 1202', *Byzantine Studies*, 5 (1978), 37–68.

5 C. Foss, *Byzantine and Turkish Sardis* (London, 1976), 66–89, at 84–5; S.G. Mercati, 'Poesie giambiche di Niceforo Chrysoberges, metropolita di Sardi', in *Collectanea Byzantina*, vol. I (Bari, 1970), 574–94, at 587–9.

6 M. Mullett, *Theophylact of Ochrid: Reading the Letters of a Byzantine Archbishop* (Farnham, 1997), 306–7; V. Laurent, 'Etienne Chrysobergès, archevêque de Corinthe', *REB*, 20 (1962), 214–8.

7 A.P. Kazhdan, 'Chrysoberges', *The Oxford Dictionary of Byzantium*. www.oxfordreference.com/view/10.1093/acref/9780195046526.001.0001/acref-9780195046526-e-1087#. Accessed 5/01/2018.

8 The fact that Georgios Bardanes was the son of the bishop of Karystos is now widely accepted. For the reasons for and against this identification, see A. Galone, *Georgios Bardanes: A Contribution on the Study About His Life, His Work and His Time* (Thessalonike, 2008), 89–93.

9 Galone, *Georgios Bardanes*, 97–117; Angold, *Church and Society*, 200.

10 Angold, *Church and Society*, 199. For more recent work on Michael Choniates and Athens, see S. Efthymiadis, 'Michael Choniates' Inaugural Address at Athens: Enkomion of a City and a Two-Fold Spiritual Ascent', in *Villes de toute beauté, l'ekphrasis des cités dans les littératures byzantine et byzantino-slaves*, eds. P. Odorico and C. Messis (Paris, 2012), 63–80.

11 F. Kolovou (ed.), *Michaelis Choniatae Epistulae* (Berlin, 2001), 127–8, 216–9.

12 A.K. Orlandos and L. Branouses, *Τα χαράγματα του Παρθενώνος* (Athens, 1973). For examples from the Propylaia, see Archimandrite Antonin, *O drevnikh khristianskikh nadpisakh v Athinakh* (St Petersburg, 1874), 33, no. 4; 35, no. 8.

13 See nos. 61, 56, 188, in Orlandos and Branouses, *Χαράγματα*, 50, 43, 151.

14 Vryonis, 'Eustathios Boilas', 271; Lemerle, 'Le Testament d'Eustathios Boïlas', 27.

15 Such criticism can be found, however, in relation to monasticism. See, for example, D.C. Hesseling and H. Pernot, *Poèmes prodromiques en grec vulgaire* (Amsterdam, 1910), 50, 66.

16 *Syntagma* 2.97–8: 'Ὅτι οὐ χρὴ ἐπίσκοπον τῷ ἀδελφῷ ἢ τῷ υἱῷ ἢ ἑτέρῳ συγγενεῖ χαριζόμενον εἰς τὸ ἀξίωμα τῆς ἐπισκοπῆς χειροτονεῖν ὃν βούλεται· κληρονόμους γὰρ τῆς ἐπισκοπῆς ποιεῖσθαι οὐ δίκαιον, τὰ τοῦ Θεοῦ χαριζόμενον πάθει ἀνθρωπίνῳ· οὐ γὰρ τὴν τοῦ Θεοῦ ἐκκλησίαν ὑπὸ κληρονόμους ὀφείλει τιθέναι. Εἰ δέ τις τοῦτο ποιήσει, ἄκυρος μενέτω ἡ χειροτονία· αὐτὸς δὲ ἐπιτιμάσθω ἀφορισμῷ.' Similarly, canon 23 of Antioch decreed that the bishop could not appoint his successor, even if he was on the verge of dying. See *Syntagma* 3.465–6.

17 It was not only bishops who tried to pass down their position to relatives and friends. Laymen too felt that they could benefit from placing their friends in ecclesiastical positions of power. See, for example, J. Koder (trans.), *Syméon le Nouveau Théologien: Hymnes 41–58, Texte critique et index*, vol. III (Paris, 1973), 290–3. Contrast, however, Theophylact of Ohrid's refusal to appoint to a bishopric the nominee of John Taronites, doux of Skopje: 'Bishops have been appointed by me either for their work in this church and their discretion and dignity, like the bishops of Morava and Prisdiana, or they are chosen from those who in Constantinople have been brilliant in thought and teaching, or those who were conspicuous in the monastic life, like the bishop of Triaditsa.' See M. Mullett, 'Patronage in Action', in *Church and People in Byzantium*, ed. R. Morris (Birmingham, 1990), 125–50, at 140.

18 P. Gautier (ed.), *Michel Italikos, Lettres et Discours* (Paris, 1972), 56.

19 *Syntagma* 2.99: 'ὡς εἰ τὰ πράγματα, ἅτινα ἐπικτᾶται ὁ ἐπίσκοπος μετὰ τὴν χειροτονίαν ἐκ τῶν τῆς ἐκκλησίας εἰσόδων, οὐ δύναται δωρεῖσθαι, ἢ παραπέμπειν πρὸς οὓς βούλεται, πολλῷ μᾶλλον τὴν ἐπισκοπήν.' According to Angold, this refusal was 'another snub administered by the patriarchal synod'. Italikos was having problems with members of his own clergy but also with the patriarchal synod, which had failed to give him support in his dealings with the heretics within his diocese. See Angold, *Church and Society*, 175.

20 *Syntagma* 2.98: 'Πῶς οὖν τις τὴν χάριν τοῦ Πνεύματος ὡς κλῆρον μεταβιβάσει πρὸς ἕτερον, αὐτῷ χαριζόμενος;' Zonaras' comment on canon 29 of the council of Chalcedon is indicative of his great respect for the sanctifying powers of the bishop. See *Syntagma* 2.287: 'Διὰ γὰρ τῆς ἐπικλήσεως τοῦ ἀρχιερέως, οἱ ναοὶ καθιεροῦνται τῇ τοῦ

ἁγίου Πνεύματος ἐπιφοιτήσει, καὶ τὰ ἱερὰ ἁγιάζονται, καὶ μεῖζον πάντως τὸ ἁγιάζον τοῦ ἁγιαζομένου.'

21 *Syntagma* 2.98: 'καὶ διὰ πάθος ἀνθρώπινον, φιλίαν δηλαδὴ ἢ σχέσιν συγγενικήν, τὰ τῷ Θεῷ ἀφιερωθέντα οἷς βούλονται, χαριζόμενοι.' Similarly, Symeon the New Theologian (d. 1022) in his hymns refers to his friends along with his family as reminders of the secular world that one needs to escape. See Koder, *Hymnes 41–58*, 3.146–7. A special kind of friend was an ex-pupil, and teachers were often very eager to secure positions for their former students. In his old age, Michael Choniates was still anxious to obtain good positions for his pupils at Nicaea and in Epirus. See J. Herrin, 'Realities of Byzantine Provincial Government: Hellas and Peloponnesos, 1180–1205', *DOP*, 29 (1975), 253–84, at 263; S. Lampros, *Μιχαὴλ Ἀκομινάτου τοῦ Χωνιάτου τὰ σωζόμενα*, vol. II (Athens, 1880), 337, 350.

22 M.E. Mullett, 'Byzantium: A Friendly Society?', *Past and Present*, 118 (1988), 3–24, at 13–14. For the difference between instrumental friendship and personal patronage, see Mullett, 'Patronage in Action', 134, 138.

23 I. Gregoriades, *Ιωάννης Τζέτζης, ΕΠΙΣΤΟΛΑΙ: Εισαγωγή-Μετάφραση-Σχόλια* (Athens, 2001), 102–5: 'δέομαι τοίνυν ὡς παρρησιαστικωτέρως ἡμῖν ἐξεχώρησας ἐλευθέρῳ καὶ ἀκαταδουλώτῳ τῷ λόγῳ ζητεῖν ὅπερ δὴ καὶ βουλοίμεθα, ἵνα τὸν ἱερέα τουτονὶ Λέοντα, ἄλλον ἐμέ πεφυκότα, δι' ἣν τετήρηκα καὶ εἴθε τηροίην πρὸς τὸν ἀδελφὸν τούτου στοργήν, καὶ ὁρᾷς ὥσπερ ἡμᾶς καὶ τιμᾷς διὰ τῆς σῆς πρὸς ἡμᾶς κηδεμονίας καὶ ἀντιλήψεως'.

24 Ahrweiler noted the importance of such friendships for career advancement in the case of Psellos' network: 'Être *φιλόφιλος* – l'expression est de l'époque – c'est un réflexe spontané; au nom de la *φιλία* et de la *οἰκείωσις* la cooptation pour la nomination dans les postes administratifs et même ecclésiastiques devient la règle, des *συντεκνίαι* et des *ἀδελφοποιήσεις* rehaussent les solidarités et consolident les liens entre amis: ils est caractéristique que Psellos désigne comme "frère" un nombre important de ses correspondants et, chose encore plus significative, il n'hésite pas à s'identifier à ses amis au point de prendre à son compte et de faire siens les liens de parenté qui les unissent à diverses personnes; c'est du moins ainsi, me semble-t-il, qu'il faut expliquer le nombre important de ses neveux.' See H. Ahrweiler, 'Recherches sur la société byzantine', *Travaux et mémoires*, 6 (Paris, 1976), 103–23, at 109.

25 The father-to-son succession to the priestly office in Judaism is documented in 1 Chronicles 6. Although both Zonaras and Balsamon agree here with the canon that this was a Judaic custom, elsewhere Zonaras states that compulsory hereditary succession was even forbidden to the Jews: 'for Moses called it a sin that Aaron promoted his own sons to the priesthood, and unless God confirmed their ordination by signs, they were quickly removed from it'. See *Syntagma* 2.98–9.

26 *Syntagma* 2.379: ''Επειδὴ περ ἔγνωμεν ἐν τῇ Ἀρμενίων χώρᾳ, μόνους ἐν κλήρῳ τοὺς ἐκ γένους ἱερατικοῦ κατατάττεσθαι, Ἰουδαϊκοῖς ἔθεσιν ἑπομένων τῶν τοῦτο πράττειν ἐπιχειρούντων, [. . .] συνείδομεν, ὥστε ἀπὸ τοῦ νῦν μὴ ἐξεῖναι τοῖς εἰς κλῆρον βουλομένοις προάγειν τινὰς εἰς τὸ γένος ἀποβλέπειν τοῦ προχειριζομένου, ἀλλὰ δοκιμάζοντες εἰ ἄξιοι εἶεν κατὰ τοὺς τεθέντας ἐν τοῖς ἱεροῖς κανόσιν ὅρους ἐν κλήρῳ καταλεγῆναι, τούτους ἐκκλησιαστικοὺς προχειρίζεσθαι, εἴτε καὶ ἐκ προγόνων γεγόνασιν ἱερέων, εἴτε καὶ μή.' For Balsamon's claim that the Armenian Church practised strict hereditary succession, see S. Payaslian, *The History of Armenia: From the Origins to the Present* (New York, NY, 2007), 36–7.

27 Mesembria was a city on the Bulgarian Black Sea coast, 35 km north-east of Burgas. At the end of the twelfth century it became part of the Second Bulgarian Empire; in the following two centuries it would frequently go back and forth between the Byzantines and the Bulgarians.

28 *Syntagma* 2.380: 'ἐλαλήθη πολλάκις περὶ διαφόρων ἀρχιερέων, ἐχόντων ἀπὸ χρυσοβούλλων κληρικούς, ἤγουν τοῦ Ἀθηνῶν, τοῦ Μεσημβρίας, καὶ ἑτέρων, ὡς οἱ ἀπόγονοι τῶν ἀρχαίων κληρικῶν καταναγκάζουσιν αὐτοὺς μὴ τοὺς ἀξίους τῷ

κλήρῳ κατατάττειν ἀλλὰ τούτους, πολλάκις ὄντας καὶ λαϊκούς, καὶ τὴν δουλείαν τῆς ἐκκλησίας δι' ἑτέρων παρ' ἐκείνων διδομένων γίνεσθαι.' Chrysobulls were imperial documents for granting privileges. For what follows, see Angold, *Church and Society*, 232–9 and Papagianni, *Οἰκονομικά*, 186–216.

29 Angold, *Church and Society*, 153.

30 Papagianni, *Οἰκονομικά*, 206.

31 Although the canonist talked of 'clerics made through chrysobulls' (ἀπὸ χρυσοβούλλων κληρικούς), the context makes it clear that he is referring to *klerikoparoikoi*. See Papagianni, *Οἰκονομικά*, 200–2.

32 Papagianni, *Οἰκονομικά*, 283.

33 For example, Papagianni has argued that if there were so many *klerikoparoikoi* in the Despotate of Epiros in the time of John Apokaukos, metropolitan of Naupaktos (1199/1200–1232), it was because the money-grabbing attitude of Constantine Doukas, brother of the ruler of the despotate, combined with low annual salaries, had made many non-dependent clerics lose their own lands and abandon the area. See Papagianni, *Οἰκονομικά*, 193, 195.

34 Papagianni, *Οἰκονομικά*, 198.

35 Papagianni, *Οἰκονομικά*, 289; E. Herman, 'Die kirchlichen Einkünfte des byzantinischen Niederklerus', *OCP*, 8 (1942), 378–442, at 412–3.

36 G. Millet, 'Inscriptions byzantines de Mistra (Pl. XIV-XXIII)', *Bulletin de correspondance hellénique*, 23:1 (1899), 97–156, at 125: 'παραπέμψῃ δὲ ταῦτα εἰς παῖδας ἀξίους ἐκδουλεύειν τὴν ἐκκλησίαν'.

37 For rare exceptions to this in England, see Thomas, *Secular Clergy*, 70.

38 Angold, *Church and Society*, 234; E. Vranouse, 'Τὸ ἀρχαιότερο σωζόμενο ἔγγραφο γιὰ τὴ θεσσαλικὴν ἐπισκοπὴ Σταγῶν', *Σύμμεικτα*, 7 (1987), 19–32.

39 A. Laiou-Thomadakis, *Peasant Society in the Late Byzantine Empire* (Princeton, NJ, 1977), 161–4, 153 n. 27; Kaplan, *Les hommes et la terre*, 507–9.

40 Angold, *Church and Society*, 236.

41 Another example of clear hereditary succession to ecclesiastical positions which did not raise objections can be found in Corfu, where there were at least two colleges of priests whose membership was strictly hereditary. These colleges might have existed since the time of Manuel I, but the earliest evidence of them survives only in a chrysobull of 1246 issued in the name of Michael II Angelos. See Angold, *Church and Society*, 232–3, 236.

42 Nomokanon Title 9, chapter 29; see *Syntagma* 1.211–2.

43 For the wider context of Justinian's promotion of monogamous relations through his laws on illegitimate children, see J. Evans-Grubbs, 'Illegitimacy and Inheritance Disputes in the Late Roman World', in *Inheritance, Law and Religions in the Ancient and Mediaeval Worlds*, eds. B. Caseau and S. Huebner (Paris, 2014), 1–25, at 20–5.

44 See 1.3.44 §3 in *The Codex of Justinian* 1.118–9. For a definition of the different types of illegitimate children in law, see C. Van de Wiel, 'Les différentes formes de cohabitation hors justes noces et les dénominations diverses des enfants qui en sont nés dans le droit romain, canonique, civil et byzantin jusqu'au treizième siècle', *Revue internationale des droits de l'antiquité*, 3rd ser. 39 (1992), 327–58.

45 *Syntagma* 1.211–2.

46 *Syntagma* 1.212: 'Ὅπως δὲ σήμερον οὐ φυλάττεται τοῦτο ἀγνοῶ.'

47 *Syntagma* 4.404–5.

48 *Syntagma* 4.494: 'αἱ γὰρ μητέρες αὐτῶν ἐπιτιμίοις πορνευόντων ὑπέπεσον, αὐτοὶ δὲ οὐδὲν ἥμαρτον, καὶ διὰ τοῦτο οὐδὲ ἐπιτιμίοις ὑπόκεινται'. The same answer is given by John Kastamonites. See M. Gedeon, 'Λύσεων Κανονικῶν Διάφοροι Γραφαί', *Ἐκκλησιαστικὴ ἀλήθεια*, 24 (1915), 185–9, at 187. For example, Maria, the mother of the seventh-century saint Theodore of Sykeon, was according to his hagiographer an innkeeper and prostitute. Such unlikely origins were meant to emphasise the holiness of the saint himself, who managed to lead a virtuous life despite his humble

beginnings. See A.J. Festugière (ed.), *Vie de Théodore de Sykéon*, vol. I (Brussels, 1970), 3. See also J. Witte, *The Sins of the Fathers: The Law and Theology of Illegitimacy Reconsidered* (Cambridge, 2009).

49 *Syntagma* 1.59–60: 'Κληρικοὺς δὲ οὐκ ἄλλως χειροτονεῖσθαι συγχωροῦμεν εἴ μὴ γράμματα ἴσασι, καὶ ὀρθὴν πίστιν καὶ βίον σεμνὸν ἔχουσι, καὶ οὐδὲ παλλακήν, οὐ φυσικὸν ἔσχον ἢ ἔχουσι παῖδα, ἀλλὰ ἢ σωφρόνως βιοῦντας ἢ γαμετὴν νόμιμον, καὶ αὐτὴν μίαν καὶ πρώτην ἐσχηκότας ἢ ἔχοντας, καὶ μηδὲ χήραν μηδὲ διαζευχθεῖσαν ἀνδρὸς μηδὲ ἄλλως τοῖς νόμοις ἢ τοῖς θείοις κανόσιν ἀπηγορευμένην.' There were, however, other considerations which formed an impediment to ordination, not mentioned by the foregoing canon. For example, there was the question of a possible disability, such as being deaf or blind, which would not allow the candidate to perform his duties. See *Syntagma* 2.99–101.

50 See also Witte, *The Sins of the Fathers*, 36–47.

51 PG 57.34: 'Ὁ γὰρ τοιοῦτος, κἂν ἀλλόφυλον ἔχῃ πρόγονον, κἂν πεπορνευμένην, κἂν ὁτιοῦν ἕτερον οὖσαν, οὐδὲν παραβλαβῆναι δυνήσεται. Εἰ γὰρ αὐτὸν τὸν πόρνον μεταβληθέντα οὐδὲν ὁ πρότερος αἰσχύνει βίος, πολλῷ μᾶλλον τὸν ἐκ πόρνης καὶ μοιχαλίδος ἐνάρετον ὄντα οὐδὲν ἡ τῶν προγόνων κακία καταισχῦναι δυνήσεται.'

52 C. Stade (trans.), *The Explanation by Blessed Theophylact of The Holy Gospel According to St. Matthew* (House Springs, MO, 1994), 15–16; Euthymios Zigabenos in PG 129.121–4.

53 Hereditary succession from father to son was also widespread in the eleventh century among clerics below the episcopate. There is evidence, for example, for the communities of Durham, Hereford, Hexham, and St Paul's. See D. Rollason (ed. and trans.), *Symeon of Durham, Libellus de Exordio atque Procursu istius hoc est Dunhelmensis Ecclesie* (Oxford, 2000), 146–7; *Fasti*, I, 14–15, 18, 34, 45, 49, 55, 65, 67–9, 71, 77, 83, 87–9; *Fasti*, VIII, 148. See also V.D. Oggins and R.S. Oggins, 'Richard of Ilchester's Inheritance: An Extended Family in Twelfth-Century England', *Medieval Prosopography*, 12 (1991), 57–128; E.J. Kealey, *Roger of Salisbury, Viceroy of England* (Berkeley, CA, 1972), 272–6; Bartlett, *England under the Norman and Angevin Kings*, 384–6; chapter entitled 'A Network of Nephews' in Crosby, *The King's Bishops*, 51–8. For a detailed study focused on Normandy, see E. van Houts, 'The Fate of Priests' Sons in Normandy', *The Haskins Society Journal*, 25 (2013), 57–105. On the married clergy in Hereford and an explanation for the persistence of clerical marriage there as late as 1200, see J. Barrow, 'Hereford Bishops and Married Clergy c. 1130–1240', *Historical Research*, 60 (1987), 1–8.

54 Brooke, 'St Paul's, 1086–1163', 125; Brooke, 'Clerical Marriage in England, 1050–1200', 17.

55 J. Burton, 'Thurstan (c. 1070–1140)', *Oxford Dictionary of National Biography*. www.oxforddnb.com/view/article/27411. Accessed 8/12/2017.

56 For the obits of Thomas' parents, see J. Raine (ed.), *Liber Vitae ecclesiae Dunelmensis* (London, 1841), 139–40; for Sampson, see V.H. Galbraith, 'Notes on the Career of Samson, Bishop of Worcester (1096–1112)', *English Historical Research*, 82 (1967), 86–101, at 86–97; *Fasti*, II, 99.

57 The patterns of hereditary succession among Norman canons can be reconstructed using Spear's list, which notes their names and first occurrence in the sources, as well as their family connections. See D. Spear, *The Personnel of the Norman Cathedrals During the Ducal Period, 911–1204* (London, 2006).

58 Brooke, 'Married Men among the English Higher Clergy', 187–8.

59 B.R. Kemp, 'Hereditary Benefices in the Medieval English Church: A Herefordshire Example', *Bulletin of the Institute of Historical Research*, 43 (1970), 1–15.

60 Twenty years of age as the minimum was proposed in D.28 c.5 and D.77 c.4 of Gratian's *Decretum*. However, in the eleventh century and particularly in Italy there was pressure for minimum ages for the various grades to drop. The Synod of Ravenna (1014), for example, decreed that clerics could be ordained subdeacons at the age of 12. See J.St.H.

Gibaut, *The Cursus Honorum: A Study of the Origins and Evolution of Sequential Ordination* (New York, NY, 2000), 248–50. In 546, Justinian had fixed the minimum age for elevation to the episcopate at 35 years. In 565 the limit was brought down to 30. The minimum age for the priesthood was also 30 years of age. See Nomokanon, Title 1 Chapter 28, in *Syntagma* 1.65–8; Moulet, *Evêques*, 244. There have been, however, examples of extremely young patriarchs, such as Theophylact Lekapenos (933–956), who was only 16 at the time of his accession. See Moulet, *Evêques*, 192–4.

61 Canon 10 of the Ninth Council of Toledo (655) was the first regulation against father-to-son succession to ecclesiastical office. The assembled bishops condemned anyone in holy orders, 'from bishop to subdeacon', who had procreated sons from a 'detestable union' with either a maidservant (*ancillae*) or a free woman (*ingenuae*). They decreed that children 'born from such pollution' not only were unable to inherit but also were to be held in perpetual 'servitude' in their father's church. This law was included in Gratian's Decretum (C.15 q.8 c.3). Slavery, however, was in decline in the twelfth century and most decretists focused on how to explain the now-changed conditions with regard to this canon. The author of the *Summa Lipsiensis* affirmed that the law had already been abolished; it was to be understood as a special case, no longer followed, or otherwise 'servitude' (*servitutem*) was to be taken more broadly as some kind of 'obligation' (*obnoxietate*). See *Summa Lipsiensis* 1.271. See also D.A.E. Pelteret, *Slavery in Early Mediaeval England: From the Reign of Alfred Until the Twelfth Century* (Woodbridge, 1995), 251–9.

62 *Councils & Synods* 1.668–88, at 675: 'Vt filii presbyterorum non sint heredes ecclesiarum patrum suorum.' Cf. Melfi (1089), c. 14 and Clermont (1095), cc. 9, 23 in R. Somerville, *The Councils of Urban II*, vol. I (Amsterdam, 1972), 76, 79–80, 95.

63 *Councils & Synods* 1.733–41, at 739: 'Sancimus praeterea ne quis ecclesiam sibi siue prebendam paterna uendicet hereditate aut successorem sibi in aliquo ecclesiastico constituat beneficio. Quod si presumptum fuerit, nullas uires habere permittimus, dicentes cum psalmista "Deus meus, pone illos ut rotam", qui dixerunt, "Hereditate possideamus sanctuarium Dei".'

64 *Councils & Synods* 1.965–92, at 984: 'Decernimus etiam eiusdem epistole auctoritate ne filii sacerdotium in paternis ecclesiis modo persone instituantur; nec eas qualibet occasione media non intercedente persona optineant.'

65 M.G. Cheney, *Roger, Bishop of Worcester 1164–1179* (Oxford, 1980), 73. On Pope Alexander III more generally, see P.D. Clarke and A.J. Duggan (eds.), *Church, Faith and Culture in the Medieval West: Pope Alexander III (1159–81): The Art of Survival* (Farnham, 2012). On his contribution to canon law, see A.J. Duggan, 'Master of the Decretals: A Reassessment of Alexander III's Contribution to Canon Law', in *Pope Alexander III (1159–1181): The Art of Survival*, eds. P.D. Clarke and A.J. Duggan (Burlington, VT, 2012), 365–417.

66 The 1195 legatine council at York Minster does not mention clerical marriage, nor does the 1200 Council of Westminster or the diocesan statutes attached to it. See *Councils & Synods* 2.1055–1074.

67 See also Barrow, 'Hereford Bishops', 6.

68 X 1.17.11: 'si qui filii presbyterorum prouinciae tuae teneant ecclesias, in quibus patres eorum tanquam personae uel uicarii nulla persona media ministrarunt, eos, siue geniti sint in sacerdotio, siue non, ab eisdem ecclesiis, contradictione et appellatione cessantibus, non differas amouere.'

69 This is an interesting case, as Bishop Geoffrey himself was the illegitimate son of King Henry II.

70 *Summa Lipsiensis* 1.270, D.56 d.a.c.1 s.v. *Presbiterorum filii*: 'Set notandum est quod sacerdotum quidam suscipiunt filios ante sacros ordines, quidam post. Qui ante suscepti sunt, licite possunt promoueri'. Similarly in the other decretists, see *Magister Rufinus*, 149; *Summa des Stephanus*, 84. By contrast, Thibodeaux has argued that the laws which barred clerical children from ordination applied to both illegitimate

and legitimate children: 'One important component of these statutes that scholars have vastly overlooked is that these canons, unlike the Bourges statutes, never distinguished the time of birth as a requirement for entry into Holy Orders. In other words, it did not matter if a clerical son was born before his father became a priest or afterward, for in either scenario he was barred from ordination to the priesthood. The dissemination of the Poitiers, Melfi, and Clermont canons led to a blanket refusal of all who were born of men in Holy Orders.' See J.D. Thibodeaux, *The Manly Priest: Clerical Celibacy, Masculinity, and Reform in England and Normandy 1066–1300* (Philadelphia, PA, 2015), 77.

71 For more examples of legitimate sons who were unjustly accused of being born while their father was in major orders, see Duggan, 'Equity and Compassion', 66.

72 F. Barlow (ed.), *The Letters of Arnulf of Lisieux* (London, 1939), no. 98, 157–8: 'didicimus nauitatem huius, de qua queritur, sacros patris ordines precessisse' and 'constabit uobis nichil esse nisi odii et inuidie questionem'.

73 Duggan, 'Equity and Compassion', 68.

74 Spear, *Personnel of the Norman Cathedrals*, 4. For the clerical positions of the de Beaufou family members see J. Fournée, 'Notes sur un évêque d'Avranches au XII siècle: Richard de Beaufou (1134–1143)', *Revue de l'Avranchin et du pays de Granville*, 33 (1946), 359–64.

75 E. Searle, *The Chronicle of Battle Abbey* (Oxford, 1980), 239. See also Harper-Bill, 'Struggle', 126–7.

76 Searle, *Battle Abbey*, 241.

77 The same was true in the case of wives and concubines. A famous example is that of Gerald of Wales, who obtained his position as archdeacon of Brecon by accusing his predecessor of having a concubine. See *Gir. Camb. opera* 2.34 (1.6); Bartlett, *Gerald of Wales, 1146–1223*, 30–5, at 32. On this specific controversy, see F.M. Powicke, 'Gerald of Wales', *Bulletin of the John Rylands Library*, 12 (1928), 389–410, at 394–5.

78 Another pattern was brother-to-brother. See, for example, F. Barlow, 'John of Salisbury and His Brothers', *Journal of Ecclesiastical History*, 46 (1995), 95–109.

79 One pre-Conquest example is Oda, archbishop of Canterbury (d. 958), and his nephew Oswald, bishop of Worcester and archbishop of York (d. 992). On this topic, see also R. Stone, 'Spiritual Heirs and Families: Episcopal Relatives in Early Medieval Francia', in *Celibate and Childless Men in Power: Ruling Eunuchs and Bishops in the Pre-Modern World*, eds. A. Hofert, M.M. Mesley, S. Tolino (London, 2018), 129–48.

80 Several of the cases of clerical kinship we find in England involve in fact Norman clergymen. See Barrow, *Clergy in the Medieval World*, 149–50.

81 Western medieval society expected uncles to take care of their nephews. But sometimes relationships broke down, with greedy nephews turning against their uncles. The complaints of the uncles show the similarities between the uncle-to-nephew and father-to-son patterns. See, for example, Bishop Arnulf of Lisieux's (1141–1184) complaint to Pope Alexander III about his two nephews, Silvester and Hugh of Nonant, in Barlow, *The Letters of Arnulf of Lisieux*, 201. We can find the same idea in a letter written by Peter of Blois, archdeacon of Bath (1182–1212), for his two nephews shortly after 1205. See E. Revell (ed.), *The Later Letters of Peter of Blois* (Oxford, 1993), 37 no. 6. Similarly, Gerald of Wales (c. 1146–1220x1223) reminded his nephew that he was to him more of a father than an uncle. See Y. Lefèvre and R.B.C. Huygens (ed.), *Speculum Duorum, or A Mirror of Two Men*, trans. B. Dawson (Cardiff, 1974), 72–3. See also J.S. Barrow, 'Gerald of Wales' Great-Nephews', *Cambridge Medieval Celtic Studies*, 8 (1984), 101–6; Barrow, *Clergy in the Medieval World*, 115–57.

82 *Gemma Ecclesiastica*, 230; *Gir. Camb. opera* 2.304.

83 P. Landau, 'Das Weihehindernis der Illegitimität in der Geschichte des kanonischen Rechts', in *Illegitimität im Spätmittelalter*, ed. L. Schmugge (Munich, 1994), 41–53, at 43.

84 But we can find earlier instances of such views among ecclesiastics in Anglo-Saxon England. For example, Ælfric in his letter to Wulfstan, archbishop of York

(1002x1005), asked that priests who were the sons of adulterous parents be demoted. See *Councils & Synods*, II, 248.

85 Canon 8 of Poitiers was included in the *Liber Extra* (X 1.17.1): 'Vt filii presbyterorum et ceteri ex fornicatione nati ad sacros ordines non promoueantur, nisi aut monachi fiant, uel in congregatione canonica regulariter uiuentes.' For Melfi, see R. Somerville and S. Kuttner, *Pope Urban II, the Collectio Britannica, and the Council of Melfi (1089)* (Oxford, 1996), 117–20, 262. Canon 25 of the council of Clermont expanded this rule to include the sons of deacons and subdeacons who were canons, in PL 162.719B: 'ne filii presbyterorum, diaconorum uel subdiaconorum canonicorum ad ordines uel alios honores ecclesiasticos promoueantur, nisi monachus uel canonicus fuerit.'

86 The *Liber Extra* contains eighteen such letters on the topic of clerical sons and whether they should be ordained (Title 17, *De filiis presbyterorum ordinandis uel non*). Of those, ten had already been included in Bernard of Pavia's *Compilatio Prima* (c. 1191). See 1 Comp. 1.9.1–4; 1.9.6–8; 1.9.10–12.

87 Landau, 'Weihehindernis', 51. In 1107 Pope Paschal II permitted Anselm to admit the sons of priests to holy orders if he considered them suitable. Although dispensations for ordination may have been given out at this stage too, the fact that the issue of priests' sons was not raised at all in the 1108 Council of Westminster suggests that Anselm preferred to focus on clerical marriage, and priests' sons probably continued to be ordained without much change. See Fröhlich, *The Letters of Saint Anselm of Canterbury*, 3.194–5.

88 Canon 3 of Lateran III in Tanner, *Decrees of the Ecumenical Councils*, 212–3.

89 C.R. Cheney and M. Cheney, *Letters of Pope Innocent III (1198–1216) Concerning England and Wales* (Oxford, 1967), 119. For the Latin text, see PL 215.1011–12. There are also earlier examples of clerical sons needing dispensation to accede to the episcopate. See R. Génestal, *Histoire de la légitimation des enfants naturels en droit canonique* (Paris, 1905), 13.

90 D.56 c.1: 'Presbiterorum filios a sacris altaris ministeriis remouendos decernimus, nisi aut in cenobiis aut in canonicis regularibus religiose probati fuerint conuersari.'

91 This chapter is found in both recensions. See Winroth, *Making of Gratian's Decretum*, 202.

92 Gratian's D.56 c.2 was not part of the first recension, but d.p.c. 2 was. See Winroth, *Making of Gratian's Decretum*, 202.

93 D.56 c.10: 'Si gens Anglorum (sicut per istas prouincias diuulgatum est, et nobis in Francia et in Italia inproperatur, et ab ipsis paganis inproperium nobis obicitur), spretis legalibus conubiis adulterando et luxuriando ad instar Sodomiticae gentis fedam uitam uixerit, de tali commixtione meretricum estimandum est degeneres populos et ignobiles, et furentes libidine fore procreandos, et ad extremum uniuersam plebem ad deteriora et ignobiliora uergentem, et nouissime nec bello seculari fortem, nec in fide stabilem, et nec honorabilem hominibus, nec Deo esse amabilem uenturam, sicut aliis gentibus Ispaniae et Prouinciae et Burgundionum populis contigit, que sic a Deo recedentes fornicatae sunt, donec iudex talium criminum ultrices penas per ignorantiam legis Dei, et per Sarracenos, uenire et seuire permisit.'

94 The letter was expressing Alexander II's assent to the consecration of the son of a priest to the episcopate of Le Mans. See also Schimmelpfennig, 'Ex fornicatione nati', 21.

95 D.56 c.13: 'non tamen, ut pro regula in posterum assumatur, sed ad tempus ecclesiae periculo consulitur'.

96 Contrast Schimmelpfennig's statement that 'Gratian regarded obedience to the precepts of celibacy as the crucial point in suitability for clerical office. The defect of birth thus became irrelevant for Gratian.' Schimmelpfennig bases his argument primarily on d.p.c. 1. See Schimmelpfennig, 'Ex fornicatione nati', 22. By contrast, Landau highlights Gratian's reinforcement of the rule through his use of the biblical verse 'Adulterorum filii abominatio sunt Domino' from the Liber Sapientiae 3.16–19.

'The sons of adulterers are an abomination to God.' See Landau, 'Weihehindernis', 46–7.

97 *Magistri Honorii* 1.185, D.56 c.1 s.v. *Presbiterorum*: 'Si autem excellentiori, siue in seculo siue in cenobio, de iure communi promouentur'. *Summa Lipsiensis* 1.270, D.56 d.a.c.1 s.v. *Presbiterorum filii*: 'Tunc autem pre ceteris excellenter dicuntur uiuere, si priuilegio honestatis pre turba prefulgeant, et tunc maxime, si in cenobio aut canonica regulari religiose fuerit conuersatus'. Note, however, that elsewhere the author of the *Summa Lipsiensis* expresses that this is a hotly debated topic and seems more reluctant to accept that in certain cases no dispensation is necessary. See *Summa Lipsiensis* 2.107.

98 *Magistri Honorii* 1.185, D.56 c.1 s.v. *Presbiterorum*: 'Set num tales citra dispensationem in episcopum ordinantur? Resp.: Non, ut in extra. ex concilio Lateran. Cum in cunctis.' See also *Summa Lipsiensis* 1.273.

99 *Magistri Honorii* 1.185–6, D.56 c.1 s.v. *Presbiterorum*: 'Set num citra dispensationem in paterna ecclesia ministrare? Resp.: Sic, cenobite, in quibus non est causa successionis que omnia abdicarunt.'

100 However, this did not immediately put an end to the family tradition of appointment to clerical office. Ralph's son was holding a fee from St Albans in the early 1170s. See C. Egger, 'The Canon Regular: Saint-Ruf in Context', in *Adrian IV The English Pope (1154–1159)*, eds. B. Bolton and A.J. Duggan (Aldershot, 2003), 15–28, at 18–19.

101 The illegitimate sons of priests were in a worse position compared to sons born of concubinage, as the latter could become fully legitimate if their parents married, given that there was no diriment impediment to that marriage. See *Summa Lipsiensis* 1.273, lines 11–13. Note, however, that their legitimation was only on an ecclesiastical level, not a civil one, and they were not allowed to succeed to their parents' secular estates. See R. Southern, *Robert Grosseteste: The Growth of an English Mind in Medieval Europe* (Oxford, 1986), 252–7; Crouch and Trafford, 'The Forgotten Family in Twelfth-Century England', 41–63 and 42–53. On this topic, England was a particularly harsh example, as the regulations that developed there were some of the 'strictest and most discriminatory policies against illegitimate children found in Western Europe'. See S. McDougall, *Royal Bastards: The Birth of Illegitimacy, 800–1230* (Oxford, 2017), 184–5.

102 *Magistri Honorii* 1.186, D.56 c.1 s.v. *Presbiterorum*: 'Est autem causa huius edicti odium paterne incontinentie et ut alii a consimili peccato reuocentur'.

103 The same argument has been made about the civil laws which restricted the hereditary rights of illegitimate children. Their main aim at least before the thirteenth century was to encourage monogamous relations, not to punish the illegitimate children themselves. See McDougall, *Royal Bastards*, 4, 166–89.

104 Taglia interprets this situation through Mary Douglas' theory. Clerical children did not conform to the classificatory systems of marriage/celibacy, laity/priest, impurity/purity. They were 'anomalous events' that needed to be controlled lest they threaten the integrity of the cultural system. See K.A. Taglia, '"On Account of Scandal . . .": Priests, Their Children, and the Ecclesiastical Demand for Celibacy', *Florilegium*, 14 (1995–96), 57–70, at 66. See also L. Wertheimer, 'Children of Disorder: Clerical Parentage, Illegitimacy, and Reform in the Middle Ages', *Journal of the History of Sexuality*, 15:3 (2006), 382–407.

105 See, for example, X 1.17.9. Eventually, Pope Boniface VIII (1294–1303) decreed that bishops would be allowed to grant dispensations to sons of priests only in minor orders, and reserved to the pope the right to grant it to those in major orders. L. Schmugge, *Kirche, Kinder, Karrieren: Päpstliche Dispense von der unehelichen Geburt im Spätmittelalter* (Zürich, 1995), 38–42. Cf. Wertheimer's argument that dispensations were more readily accessible than has previously been suggested, in L. Wertheimer, 'Illegitimate Birth and the English Clergy, 1198–1348', *Journal of Medieval History*, 31 (2005), 211–29. See also Broomfield, *Thomae de Chobham*, 67.

106 *Magistri Honorii* 1.186, D.56 c.1 s.v. *Presbiterorum*: 'cum sic etiam prolem propter suum peccatum puniri uideant'.

107 *Summa Lipsiensis* 1.273; *Magistri Honorii* 1.187.

108 *Summa Lipsiensis* 1.272, D.56 c.7 s.v. *Satis* usque *quem sua culpa*: 'ibi enim dicitur quod subdiaconus qui licite contraxit ante prohibitionem sine culpa sua debet cogi unum duorum eligere, scilicet utrum uelit uxorem relinquere an in ordine stare, et sic unum amittit'.

109 *Summa Lipsiensis* 1.271, D.56 c.4 s.v. *opprobriis*: 'Tamen quandoque propter delictum patris beneficium aufertur'. *Summa Lipsiensis* 1.272, D.56 c.7 s.v. *Satis* usque *quem sua culpa*: 'si enim pater pro filio pecuniam dedit eo etiam inscio, abiciendus est de ecclesia'. See also *Magistri Honorii* 1.186.

110 *Summa Lipsiensis* 1.270, D.56 d.a.c.1 s.v. *Presbiterorum filii*: 'Denique quod dicitur parentum uitia filiis non imputari, hoc non de pena temporali qua sepe puniuntur, set de pena eterna intelligendum est'. See also *Summa Lipsiensis* 2.87. *Magistri Honorii* 1.186, D.56 c.5 s.v. *Vndecumque*: 'In sequentibus dicitur non imputari filiis peccati parentum. Quod uerum est ad gehennam'. Similarly, for a discussion of the punishment of the orthodox children of heretic parents, see K. Pennington, '"Pro Peccatis Patrum Puniri": A Moral and Legal Problem of the Inquisition', *Church History*, 47 (1978), 137–54.

111 See, for example, Orderic Vitalis and his brothers, who all joined monastic communities to atone for their father's sins, in E. van Houts, 'Orderic and His Father, Odelerius', in *Orderic Vitalis: Life, Works, and Interpretations*, eds. C.C. Rozier, D. Roach, G.E.M. Gasper, and E. van Houts (Woodbridge, 2016), 17–36, at 27. On oblation more generally, see M. de Jong, *In Samuel's Image: Child Oblation in the Early Medieval West* (Leiden, 1996).

6 Bodily secretions and the sacred

Introduction

A common argument against clerical marriage was that sexual intercourse and the celebration of the Eucharist were incompatible because sexual thoughts and acts rendered clerics in major orders impure and unfit for their service at the altar. This line of reasoning had already been suggested in Late Antiquity, and in the next chapter I will examine to what extent it was also followed in twelfth-century England and Byzantium. But before I do so, I would like to discuss the similar example of nocturnal emissions. Like sexual intercourse, wet dreams involved seminal secretions as well as sexual thoughts, and could thus make one unfit for liturgical service. Given that in both England and Byzantium the focus of this much-discussed topic centred on the concept of purity in relation to the sacred, this case study will allow us to establish whether the two societies had comparable ideas on these issues, and will put into perspective their very different treatments of clerical marriage. At the same time, it will foreshadow several issues that will play a key role in our understanding of clerical continence, including the different treatment of clerics and laymen in canon law, given their different access to the sacred.

In what follows I will make a distinction between two types of impurity: physical and moral.[1] I use the term 'physical' to refer to an impurity that arises from contact with substances which are the by-product of natural events that were not considered sinful, such as menstruation, and the term 'moral' to refer to an impurity that is a direct consequence of sin, such as heresy or fornication.[2] Both could potentially lead to ritual exclusion, and, as such, fall under the broader category of 'ritual impurity'. Nocturnal emissions, which combined physiology and psychology, could be considered both physically and morally polluting.[3]

Nocturnal emissions: East

Nocturnal emissions sparked off a multiplicity of opinions among Eastern ecclesiastics.[4] Dionysios, bishop of Alexandria (d. 265), recommended that men should examine their own conscience and decide for themselves whether they could receive communion after experiencing a wet dream.[5] Timotheos, bishop of Alexandria (d. 385), advised that a cleric should allow a layman to receive the Eucharist if his wet dream had been the result of Satan tempting him so as to keep him away from communion, but not if he had experienced it out of sexual desire for a woman.[6] The topic had also been more extensively discussed by Athanasios, bishop of Alexandria (d. 373), in his letter to Ammoun. For Athanasios, the emissions themselves were always sinless, and like other natural secretions, such as nasal mucus and saliva, they were created by God.[7] As such, they were good and pure. What could be bad was our own misuse of God's creation.[8] These views had continuing significance for Byzantine canon law as they were ratified by the Council in Trullo and commented on by the twelfth-century canonists.

Zonaras devoted a lengthy treatise to the topic, entitled 'A Speech by the Former Great *Droungarios* of the *Vigla* and *Protasekretis* Against Those Who Think That the Natural Emission of Semen Is an Impurity'. In it, he refuted the view put forward by some monks of his time that all nocturnal emissions were impure, even when they occurred in the absence of sexual thoughts.[9] The monks in question, he tells us, had failed to distinguish between the different causes of nocturnal emissions and expected men who suffered from them to abstain not only from communion but also even from touching the holy icons.[10] The canonist saw the monks' views as Judaic vestiges and accused them of following Jewish customs (ἰουδαΐζειν).[11] This was something that he himself had done in his comments on menstruation, where he was happy to acknowledge the Judaic roots of the rules that kept women from the sacred because of their 'uncleanness'.[12] Zonaras did not take this line here, but rather considered nocturnal emissions to belong among those 'impurities' that had been treated as such in the Old Testament but were no longer considered impurities in the New, such as leprosy and the touching of the dead.[13] Importantly, in his defence of nocturnal emissions Zonaras made reference to marital sex and the purity of semen more generally:

> But you, I suppose, will also judge impure the man who has had intercourse with his own wife, when he rises from his bed; and you will not admit him for prayer, but you will even close the doors of the temple against him. You will not take into account that it is stated that marriage is honourable and the bed undefiled, but you will condemn the innocent man because in this case too there is an emission of sperm, indeed a pleasurable one.[14]

For Zonaras, the flux of semen was not impure, neither in the case of involuntary emissions nor in the case of marital sex. Arguing that semen was impure implied that the body from which it came was impure; our bodies, then, would be a creation of the Devil:

> Those who believe that emissions are impure give the impression of being like the Manicheans, or that they partake of the heresy of the Bogomils. Since by introducing twofold powers and by saying that the body is a creation of evil, they too clearly act like Manicheans.[15]

In opposition to this, Zonaras followed Athanasios in arguing that everything created by God was sinless and pure.[16] There could, then, be no question of physical pollution.

What could potentially be blameworthy was the mental state that accompanied the emissions. A man was to blame if he had caused his wet dream through gluttony or indecent thoughts.[17] Zonaras stated explicitly that a man who drank and ate in excess was responsible for his predicament and as such had to abstain from communion.[18] Similarly, a man who welcomed sexual thoughts, turning them over in his mind, was 'most responsible' for what happened to him, and again needed to abstain from the Eucharist.[19] This kind of thinking would have to take place while the man was awake, since the canonist maintained that consent could not exist in a dream: as you do not call a person a martyr for having shown exceptional piety in his dream, in the same way you do not punish him for having dreamt of committing murder.[20] Consent was important because it was seen as the third out of four steps that led to sin. According to the canonist, the first two, temptation (προσβολή) and struggle (πάλη), were not sinful. It was only the latter two, consent (συγκατάθεσις) and action itself (πρᾶξις), which constituted sin.[21] So, a man who was tempted during the day by indecent thoughts but chose to fight them off was not seen as polluted even if he experienced a nocturnal emission, because he had not consented.[22] A man would be considered polluted only if he accepted these thoughts happily (ἀσμένως) and chose to dwell upon them and take pleasure in them (ἐνηδυνόμενος). The pleasure mentioned here is not the physical pleasure that resulted from the emission but the pleasure of the mind which dwelled on indecent thoughts. In this case, a man was considered polluted even without experiencing a nocturnal emission.[23]

Zonaras described this state of moral impurity clearly through a variety of words, such as μεμιασμένος, ἀκάθαρτος, and μεμολυσμένος, and he asserted that men were 'polluted through this emission of semen not with respect to their body (for this excretion is not impure), but with respect to their mind, because of their consent to carnal desire'.[24] They would have to perform penance and were not considered fit to receive the Eucharist: 'for such a man does not have a good conscience, and therefore cannot communicate with God freely (οὐδ' εὐπαρρησίαστος) because of the weight upon his mind. So how will he approach God if he is wavering?'[25] The reception of communion implied participating in the body and blood of the resurrected Son of God. One could not be in a distracted state of mind if one was to do so effectively. This meant dwelling upon thoughts about God, not lewd thoughts. As we shall see, the same justification was given by the canonists in favour of sexual continence before receiving communion or performing the Eucharist.[26]

For Balsamon too nocturnal emissions did not cause physical pollution.[27] He treated erotic dreams entirely as a problem of the mind. This becomes clear in his comment on the *Questions and Answers* of Timotheos of Alexandria, where he began by saying, 'this Father talks about things seen during dreams after which an emission of sperm *may* also occur.'[28] The emission itself was not necessary. Instead it was pleasurable thoughts of sexual desire (ἐπιθυμίᾳ . . . ἐνεφιλοχώρησε) which were blameworthy, as they represented consent to sin.[29] Contrary to Zonaras, however, Balsamon assigned penance – albeit mild – to men who experienced a nocturnal emission only because of temptation and without consent.[30] As we have seen, such emissions were deemed sinless by Zonaras, whose views represent one of the most forgiving positions on the topic to be found in twelfth-century Byzantium.[31]

Nocturnal emissions: West

Similarly in the West, nocturnal emissions were primarily associated with moral, rather than physical, pollution; the issue was not so much the emission itself but the cause that brought it about.[32] Pope Gregory the Great had identified the same three causes as Byzantine ecclesiastics: an infirmity or superfluity of nature, drunkenness or gluttony (*crapula*), and impure thoughts.[33] Those who suffered nocturnal emissions due to infirmity or superfluity were not assigned any sin by Gregory, and as such were not barred from communion.[34] Those who experienced them due to excessive drinking were considered to be 'partially at fault', but could still receive the Eucharist, especially on feast days.[35] Those who had entertained indecent thoughts while awake were excluded from the sacred mysteries.[36] Therefore, in terms of receiving the Eucharist, it was only the last group who were ritually impure, and their impurity was moral rather than physical. In terms of *performing* the Eucharist, the rules associated with the second type of emissions were different: clerics in major orders who had experienced an emission due to gluttony or drunkenness could celebrate mass, but it was preferable for them to abstain out of humility if there was someone else to officiate in their place.[37]

Pope Gregory's views, through their inclusion in Burchard of Worms, Ivo of Chartres, and Gratian's second recension, had varying influence on later ecclesiastics.[38] In the penitential of Bartholomew of Exeter, a compilation of older and newer canonical authorities, nocturnal emissions were discussed under two different headings: *De Illusione Nocturna* and *De Ministris et Ministerio Altaris*. Under the former we find Gregory's threefold classification of nocturnal emissions, which treated both lay and clerical penitents.[39] Under the latter we find further specific rules for the clergy taken from the *Decretum* of Burchard of Worms, where nocturnal emissions had been discussed in two sections both covering clerical affairs. The first dealt with priests engaging in immodest speech and gaze. Here, Burchard meted out different penances to clerics who had experienced a nocturnal emission depending on their grade, the place where it happened, and whether it had been preceded by impure thoughts.[40] This canon punished the very fact of having an emission regardless of whether the priest was meant to celebrate communion. The second reference was in a section devoted to clerical negligence with respect to the Eucharist. There, Burchard stated that a priest who celebrated communion after a nocturnal emission should be subject to seven days' penance.[41] The cause of the emission in this case was not important and penance was assigned even if it had occurred without impure thoughts. Bartholomew decided to include the latter provision in his penitential.[42] His inclusion of indiscriminate penance in the case of priests suggests that, despite Gregory's influence, Bartholomew was somewhat reluctant to consider any association of nocturnal emissions with the celebration of the Eucharist as entirely sinless.

Robert of Flamborough also included the same Burchardian canon in Book 5 of his penitential under the heading *De sacerdote negligenter tractante eucharistiam*.[43] Apart from this, nocturnal emissions came up only once in a fictional dialogue between a priest and a penitent, who in this case was revealed to be a subdeacon who suffered frequently from wet dreams. The priest instructed the subdeacon that if his dreams occurred because of customary drunkenness or impure thoughts, they constituted a mortal sin. If they occurred for some other reason – presumably infirmity or a natural superfluity – they constituted a venial sin.[44] For Robert, all nocturnal emissions were sinful.[45]

Thomas of Chobham devoted four chapters to this topic under the heading of lust (*De luxuria*).[46] He treated it as a sexual sin and examined whether it was venial or mortal, but did not explicitly discuss whether it barred laymen from communion. It was only in the case of clerics in major orders that Thomas gave specific instructions about approaching the sacred. He advised that priests who had been 'polluted' by mental images during the night after having drunk and eaten in excess should abstain from the divine office the following day, until they had performed penance.[47] He did, however, make a special mention of feast days, where practical considerations had to be taken into account: 'because the people would be scandalised if they had to leave without listening to mass'.[48] Thomas was very insistent on the need for penance so that the priest could atone for his wet dream. This included ablutions with cold water, fasting with Lenten food, and wearing woollen clothes against the skin.[49] This way 'the filth of the nocturnal emission would be wiped away from his body before, on the following day, he approached the sacraments at the altar.'[50]

An emphasis on the clergy can also be found in some of the commentaries on Gratian's *Decretum*. Master Honorius and the *Summa Lipsiensis* highlighted the special responsibility attached to the liturgical function: celebrating the Eucharist required higher standards than receiving it.[51] In the context of emissions experienced because of drunkenness, Honorius noted that it would be a great sin to celebrate mass, not because of the enormity of the crime but because of the existence of the prohibition itself and the 'excellence' of the Eucharistic mass; such an act would be considered irreverent.[52] The *Summa Lipsiensis* added that there were many who were allowed to receive the Eucharist but forbidden to offer it, such as priests who had been twice married or deposed.[53] Nonetheless, both extended Gregory's rule and permitted the celebration of the Eucharist to priests who had experienced a nocturnal emission due to impure thoughts, under specific circumstances. The *Summa Lipsiensis* allowed for such a priest to celebrate only if he was forced by his bishop and after private confession.[54] Master Honorius focused on the impact this could have on the community and stated that according to some of his contemporaries such priests were expected to serve on Easter Day after first having confessed. Although he considered that they had committed a mortal sin, Honorius feared that cancelling the Easter mass would cause too great a scandal.[55]

Perhaps the faithful who did not know the reason behind the priest's withdrawal from the liturgy could begin to imagine sins far worse than nocturnal emissions.

Master Honorius' commentary and the *Summa Lipsiensis* also discussed more generally the kind of sin, venial or mortal, contracted through the different types of emissions. This was a topic of contemporary canonical interest, as can be seen through the competing interpretations that they reported. They both quoted, for example, the opinion of G., which was Master Honorius' favourite, and which emphasised that the secretion itself was not impure, as a man fell into pollution not during his sleep but before he fell asleep, when he was gorging himself with food and drink.[56] But it also suggested that a man who experienced a sexual wet dream had to abstain from communion, even if this had come about due to excessive eating or drinking.[57] This allowed for little difference between the second and third causes of nocturnal emissions that we have seen in Gregory's classification: emissions due to gluttony and emissions due to impure thoughts.[58] Master Honorius pointed also to another interpretation, that of S., according to which there *was* a difference between the two emissions. The kind caused by gluttony was venial and a man was prevented only from the everyday reception of the Eucharist, from which even monks who were worthier than laymen could abstain. The other, caused by impure thoughts, was mortal and as such would justify complete abstention from the Eucharist, even during feast days, such as Easter, Christmas, and Pentecost.[59]

Overall, in the West there were many slightly different rules about what a man had to do in the case of a wet dream. This seems to have been a popular topic, and the two decretists, in particular, discussed different interpretations about when and how one sinned and whether one should receive communion. These were questions which aligned with their legal interests and allowed them to make sense of Gregory's views in conjunction with other canons on drunkenness (C.15 q.1 c.9), communion (De con. cc.13, 15), and so on. Bartholomew's, Robert's, and Thomas' practical manuals had more to say about clerics than they did about laymen and they were generally stricter than Gregory's advice.

Where are the Byzantine clerics?

In Byzantine canon law on nocturnal emissions, ecclesiastics were not treated separately from the laity, nor was particular emphasis laid on them. In his long treatise on the subject, Zonaras focused on the spiritual children of monks (τοῖς ὑφ' ὑμᾶς), presumably both monastic and lay, who confessed to them and received from them excessively strict advice.[60] He did not talk about clerics in major orders, as he did not discuss whether a man should perform the Eucharist after a nocturnal emission, but only whether he should receive it.[61] Zonaras mentioned that Ammoun, Athanasios' addressee, had been a monk, and was well aware of the patristic tradition of writing about nocturnal emissions in the context of monasticism.[62] However, he used Athanasios' monastic letter alongside the canon of Dionysios, which did not differentiate based on religious status, and the canon of Timotheos, which referred specifically to laymen. Zonaras made no explicit distinction between monks and laymen and the rules they should follow. He certainly did not advocate higher standards for the monastic addressees of his writings, and in fact rejected the stringent standards that they were advocating for their spiritual children and were presumably keeping themselves.[63] In some sense, he was following Athanasios, who in his day had tried to diminish the divide between monks and laity that was building up in Late Antique Egypt, where some had posited voluntary absence from the Eucharist after a nocturnal emission as a sign of the superiority of ascetic life and the exceptional care that monks took for their spiritual health.[64] Zonaras too was trying to bring his monastic addressees down to earth, by showing that the stricter standards they were imposing on their spiritual children were unnecessary.

Fögen has placed Zonaras' reaction within the context of the competition between monks and secular clergy for the title of guardians of orthodoxy: Zonaras was aligning himself against the uneducated monks who were usurping and misusing the right to receive confession and assign penance, which belonged to the ordained clergy.[65] True as that may be, the secular clergy was conspicuously absent from the discussion. Contrary to what we have seen in the West, Zonaras does not seem overly interested in separate rules for clerics. While safeguarding the role of priests as confessors, he does not assert their superiority in terms of purity.

Balsamon too in his commentaries kept his focus on the laity, as he explicitly took the advice given by Dionysios, Timotheos, and Athanasios to refer to laymen.[66] He did, however, refer specifically to clerics in one of his answers to Patriarch Mark, which asked whether priests were allowed to perform their liturgical duties on the day they had experienced a nocturnal emission. While Master Honorius and the *Summa Lipsiensis* emphasised the exclusive nature of the priesthood, Balsamon pointed towards the commonality between priests and laymen. His answer began by highlighting the human weakness of the clergy:

> The sacred letter says that the bishop who offers gifts and sacrifices is taken from amongst the men and as he offers to God for the people, in the same way he also offers for himself, because the weight of carnal disease is also laid upon him.[67]

He then went on to quote Dionysios' canon on this topic, regarding what ought to happen in the case of laymen:

> If he is subject to desire for a woman, he should not [receive the Eucharist]; but if Satan is tempting him, so that under this pretext he may alienate him from communion with the holy mysteries, he should receive communion. Because the enemy will not stop tempting him, attacking him during that time.[68]

Balsamon's choice to quote Dionysios' advice for the laity in full was not accidental. It gave him the chance to compose an answer about the clergy which paralleled Dionysios' own:

> We too decree the same things about laymen, but we do not judge the same rule to hold for bishops, deacons, and priests who have had a dream entirely under Satanic influence. We decree that the act of performing the sacred rites should rather be shut to them on the day of their dream alone, out of the reverent nature of the priesthood, unless by any chance the postponement is dangerous, either because the day is particularly important, or because their duty is particularly useful. For in that case let the trap of the temptation be crushed and the power of the sacrifice be elevated.[69]

Balsamon made a distinction between clerics and laymen only when it came to emissions of one kind – namely, those influenced by Satanic temptation – and his advice for the clergy followed closely the advice he had just quoted concerning the laity. Both focused on the different traps that Satan lays for priests and laymen: he tempted laymen to keep them away from communion, as such harming them personally, but he tempted priests to prevent the whole congregation from receiving their 'useful' priestly duties. Balsamon's advice took into consideration these two different targets and ensured that they would suffer no damage: in the case of the layman this meant receiving the Eucharist every time there was Satanic temptation; in the case of the cleric this meant officiating when his congregation needed it (e.g., on feast days or for last rites), but abstaining out of reverence from celebration when there was no particular need to perform it.

Balsamon did not specify what was to happen if a cleric's temptation had not come from the Devil. By comparing the rules of the laity, we can infer that such a priest would need to abstain from celebrating. But the fact that this is not discussed in Balsamon's or Zonaras' writings is indicative of their relative lack of interest in clerics, or perhaps their assumption that they could use or adapt the rules for the laity. More generally, we can say that neither of the two Byzantine canonists went out of his way to talk about clerics, let alone to emphasise their special need for purity. Balsamon's comment does highlight that reverence is due to the Eucharist, but gives precedence to practical considerations, without any hint that the priest himself was being compromised: there was no need for him to confess before celebrating.

Conclusion

We can see, then, that English and Byzantine ecclesiastics held comparable views on nocturnal emissions. In both societies there were avoidance rules about approaching the sacred and debates about when a secretion of semen could disqualify a man from receiving or celebrating the Eucharist. Both Eastern and Western canonical sources used the language of impurity to reinforce, or sometimes negate, these avoidance rules. In both societies, we find the belief that such emissions were caused by a superfluity of nature, excessive drinking and eating, or sexual thoughts. In both, we encounter great respect for the Eucharist, which led to different provisions for communion depending on the importance of the day, with more pragmatic considerations prevailing: the faithful could not be prevented from receiving communion for too long; the priest could not miss the Easter mass. Importantly for the question at hand, both Byzantine and Western ecclesiastics emphasised the moral impurity that stemmed from the mind rather than any physical impurity that could come from the secretion itself.

There were also some important differences. In the Anglo-Norman sources there was a greater emphasis on the need for priests to perform penance regardless of whether they celebrated the Eucharist. In the Byzantine ones, some of the personal responsibility was reduced by reference to Satanic influence. More generally, the Western categorisation of sins into venial and mortal, which was not mirrored in Byzantium, led Western discussions down different paths, allowing for more precise and subtle rules and regulations. Finally, the Anglo-Norman sources seem to have placed more emphasis on clerics rather than laymen, while the Byzantine sources largely treated all men together. When Balsamon was asked to make a distinction he seemed more ready to acknowledge that clerics too were human and prone to weakness.[70]

Some of the arguments used in this chapter will resurface in discussions of clerical marriage. Both in the case of nocturnal emissions and in that of sex within clerical marriage, the Byzantine canon lawyers argued that everything created by God was sinless and that it was heretical to say otherwise; in both cases, the two Anglo-Norman decretists emphasised the importance of respecting a canonical prohibition: breaking the law was sinful in itself. Similarly, the idea that one needed to be in a certain state of mind in order to receive communion will prove pivotal to our understanding of abstinence from sex in the next chapter. When it came to both emissions and sexual intercourse, the emphasis was on the fact that in order to pray or receive the Eucharist one should not distract one's thoughts away from God.

Another argument, however, will be conspicuous by its absence in Byzantium: Zonaras has here firmly denied that semen emitted with pleasure is impure, but his very denial hints at the existence of contemporary opposition to this view. When it comes to clerical marriage, the purity or impurity of semen is not explicitly discussed, but we are told again that 'marriage is honourable and the bed undefiled.' More generally, the difference in the treatment of laymen and clerics which we have seen in the Western sources continues and is intensified in the case of clerical marriage. Clergy in major orders were supposed to distinguish themselves from the laity through their purity. This is not something that is emphasised in Byzantium, where, as we have seen in this chapter, there was little distinction between men of different religious statuses in the canonical commentaries or in Zonaras' treatise. As we will see in the next chapter, the same is true in the case of clerical marriage, and is, I think, indicative of the place of Byzantine clergy within society. As Michael Angold put it, 'Ideally, the bishop and clergy formed a spiritual elite above, but not entirely separate from, lay society.'[71]

Notes

1 Historical analyses of the concepts of purity and impurity have been greatly influenced by Mary Douglas' *Purity and Danger*, which argues that pollution avoidance rules

are not relics of earlier taboos imposed by a 'primitive' mind, but can be rationally explained and systematised as part of a coherent system of things prohibited and things permitted. As such, purity 'taboos' are a means of drawing sharp social lines, protecting the boundaries through rituals of separation. See M. Douglas, *Purity and Danger: An Analysis of Concepts of Pollution and Taboo* (London, 2nd ed., 2002 [orig. 1966]). More recently, Frevel and Nihan have emphasised that ideas about purity and impurity have a complex history; they may have been adopted and adapted from diverse origins in centuries-long processes or they may have been directly imported from one culture to another. As such, although they probably hold a function in the society in which they are observed, they may not always reflect that society's cultural values. See C. Frevel and C. Nihan, 'Introduction', in their *Purity and the Forming of Religious Traditions in the Ancient Mediterranean World and Ancient Judaism* (Leiden, 2013), 1–46, at 7.

2 The need for such a distinction was already made in the context of Judaism by Klawans, who questioned Douglas' statement that 'a polluting person is always in the wrong.' See J. Klawans, *Impurity and Sin in Ancient Judaism* (Oxford, 2000), 23.

3 On the topic of nocturnal emissions in the West, see also J. Murray, 'Men's Bodies, Men's Minds: Seminal Emissions and Sexual Anxiety in the Middle Ages', *Annual Review of Sex Research*, 8 (1997), 1–26; Chapter 1: 'Pollution, Illusion, and Masculine Disarray: Nocturnal Emissions and the Sexuality of the Clergy' in D. Elliott, *Fallen Bodies: Pollution, and Demonology in the Middle Ages* (Philadelphia, PA, 1999), 14–34; M.R. Godden, 'Were It Not That I Have Bad Dreams: Gregory the Great and the Anglo-Saxons on the Dangers of Dreaming', in *Rome and the North: The Early Reception of Gregory the Great in Germanic Europe*, eds. R.H. Bremmer Jr, K. Dekker, and D.F. Johnson (Paris, 2001), 93–113. For erotic dreams in Byzantium, see C. Messis, 'Fluid Dreams, Solid Consciences: Erotic Dreams in Byzantium', in *Dreaming in Byzantium and Beyond*, eds. C. Angelidi and G.T. Calofonos (Farnham, 2014), 187–205; C. Angelidi, 'Αισθήσεις, σεξουαλικότητα και οπτασίες', in *Ανοχή και καταστολή στους μέσους χρόνους*, ed. K. Nikolaou (Athens, 2002), 221–9.

4 For the Late Antique period, see D. Brakke, 'The Problematisation of Nocturnal Emissions in Early Antiquity', *Journal of Early Christian Studies*, 3:4 (1995), 419–60, which discusses a series of texts on nocturnal emissions written around the Mediterranean from the third to the fifth centuries, and interprets them as arguments about the boundaries of Christian and particularly monastic communities. See also C. Leyser, 'Masculinity in Flux: Nocturnal Emission and the Limits of Celibacy in the Early Middle Ages', in *Masculinity in Medieval Europe*, ed. D.M. Hadley (London, 1999), 103–20, which argues that fourth- and fifth-century writings on nocturnal emissions can be seen as part of an aggressive bid for public authority and moral superiority on behalf of an ascetic movement which was far from cloistered.

5 *Syntagma* 4.12. This was also his attitude with regard to marital intercourse and communion. See *Syntagma* 4.9.

6 *Syntagma* 4.338.

7 *Syntagma* 4.67–8.

8 Athanasios asserted that the same was true of the genitals: their proper usage was in marital sex, and their misuse in adultery. See *Syntagma* 4.69–70.

9 *Syntagma* 4.598: 'Πολλοὶ τῶν ἀκριβέστερον τάχα μετιέναι δοκούντων τὴν μοναχικὴν πολιτείαν, καὶ ῥεπόντων οἷον πρὸς τὸ πνευματικώτερον, ὡς μίασμά τι τὴν φυσικὴν τῆς γονῆς νομίζουσιν ἐκροήν· καὶ οὐ μόνον ὅτε μετά τινος φαντασίας συμβῇ, ἀλλ' ὁπηνίκα καὶ φαντασίας χωρίς.' See also Theophylact of Ohrid's fictional dialogue in defence of eunuchs, in which one of the interlocutors points out the superiority of eunuchs, who no longer experience nocturnal emissions, in C. Messis, 'Public hautement affiché et public réellement visé dans certaines créations littéraires byzantines: le cas de l'*Apologie de l'eunuchisme* de Théophylacte d'Achrida', in *La face cachée de la littérature byzantine*, ed. P. Odorico (Paris, 2012), 41–85, at 80–1; P. Gautier (ed. and trans.), *Théophylacte d'Achrida, I, Discours, traités, poésies* (Thessalonike, 1980), 328–9.

10 *Syntagma* 4.598: 'ὡς μὴ μόνον τῆς τῶν ἁγιασμάτων εἴργειν αὐτὸν μεταλήψεως, ἀλλ' ἤδη τινὲς καὶ προσψαύειν αὐτὸν εἰκόνος θείας ἀπείργουσιν [. . .] Διαλεκτέον δὴ τούτοις, καὶ δεικτέον, ὡς οὔτ' ἀεὶ τὸ πάθος ἀνέγκλητον, οὔτ' ἀδιαφόρως ὁ τοῦτο παθὼν ὑπὸ ἐπιτίμησιν'.

11 *Syntagma* 4.601–2: 'Οὐδὲ συνίετε κατά γε τὴν γνώμην ταύτην ἰουδαΐζοντες, καὶ τὰς τῆς Παλαιᾶς Διαθήκης ἀνανεοῦντες διαταγὰς ἅς περ ὁ Σωτὴρ ἐνανθρωπήσας κατήργηκεν;'

12 *Syntagma* 4.7–8: 'Αἱ Ἑβραΐδες γυναῖκες, ὅτε γένηται αὐταῖς ἡ τῶν ἐμμήνων ῥύσις, ἐν τόπῳ μεμονωμένῳ καθήμεναι, οὐδενὸς προσάπτονται ἕως ἂν ἑπτὰ ἡμέραι παρέλθωσιν· ὅθεν εἴληπται τὸ ἐν ἀφέδρῳ, δηλοῦν τὸ κεχωρίσθαι αὐτὰς ἀπὸ τῆς τῶν λοιπῶν ἕδρας ὡς ἀκαθάρτους.' Fögen has argued that the difference in Zonaras' views regarding menstruation and nocturnal emissions might be due to the fact that in the latter case he was trying to attack a group of monks who were assuming priestly functions by receiving confessions using the penitential of John the Faster. See M.T. Fögen, 'Unto the Pure All Things Are Pure: The Byzantine Canonist Zonaras on Nocturnal Pollution', in *Obscenity: Social Control and Artistic Creation in the European Middle Ages*, ed. J. Ziolkowski (Leiden, 1998), 260–78, at 274.

13 *Syntagma* 4.602: 'καὶ τὸν νεκροῦ προσαψάμενον οὐκ ὀκνήσετε μεμιασμένον ἡγήσασθαι· καὶ οὗ ἐν τῷ σώματι λέπρα ἐξήνθησε, τῆς πόλεως ἐξωθήσετε'.

14 *Syntagma* 4.602: 'Ὑμεῖς δ' οἶμαι καὶ τὸν συνευνασθέντα τῇ ἑαυτοῦ γαμετῇ τῆς κοίτης ἐξανιστάμενον κρινεῖτε ἀκάθαρτον, καὶ εἰς προσευχὴν οὐ προσήσεσθε, ἀλλὰ καὶ τὰς τοῦ ναοῦ θύρας τούτῳ ἐπιζυγώσετε· οὐδ' ὅτι τίμιος ὁ γάμος εἴρηται λογιεῖσθε, καὶ ἡ κοίτη ἀμίαντος, ἀλλ' ὅτι κἀνταῦθα σπέρματος ἐκροή, καὶ μᾶλλον σὺν ἡδονῇ, καταδικάσετε τὸν ἀναίτιον'.

15 *Syntagma* 4.609: 'Οἷς δὲ ἀκαθαρσία νενόμισται ἡ γονή, μανιχαΐζειν ὑπόληψιν δώσουσιν, ἢ τῆς τῶν Βογομίλων μετέχειν αἱρέσεως· ἐπεὶ καὶ οὗτοι κατά γε τὸ διττὰς εἰσάγειν ἀρχὰς καὶ τὸ σῶμα κτίσμα λέγειν τοῦ πονηροῦ, προδήλως μανιχαΐζουσι'. On the Manicheans and the Bogomils, see D. Gress-Wright, 'Bogomilism in Constantinople', *Byzantion*, 47 (1977), 163–85; D. Angelov, 'Ursprung und Wesen des Bogomilentums', in his *Les Balkans au Moyen Age: la Bulgarie des Bogomils aux Turcs* (London, 1978), VI 144–56; A. Rigo, 'Il processo del bogomilo Basilio (1099 ca.). Una riconsiderazione', *OCP*, 58 (1992), 185–211; Y. Stoyanov, *The Other God: Dualist Religions From Antiquity to the Cathar Heresy* (London, 2000), 161–9; Angold, *Church and Society*, 468–501.

16 *Syntagma* 4.609; 4.75: 'τῶν δ' ὑπὸ Θεοῦ κτισθέντων οὐδὲν ὑπάρχει ἀκάθαρτον'. In fact, Zonaras insisted upon this point so much that he used it in his interpretation of St Basil's view of nocturnal emissions. See Fögen, 'Zonaras on nocturnal pollution', 267–70. This is an argument that he would also use in the case of marital sex. See *Syntagma* 2.67–8.

17 Food and drink in general could symbolise both good and evil, as seen, for example, in the Eucharistic meal that brings about man's salvation and in the apple that brought about his fall. See A. Eastmond and L. James, 'Eat, Drink . . . and Pay the Price', in *Eat, Drink and Be Merry (Luke 12:19): Food and Wine in Byzantium*, eds. L. Brubaker and K. Linardou (Aldershot, 2007), 175–89, at 175, 177–8. On desire in Byzantium, see also M.B. Cunningham, '"Shutting the Gates of the Soul": Spiritual Treatises on Resisting the Passions', in *Desire and Denial in Byzantium Papers from the 31st Spring Symposium of Byzantine Studies, Brighton, March 1997*, ed. L. James (Farnham, 1999), 23–32.

18 *Syntagma* 4.611: 'Ὅς ἐξ ἀκρασίας τῆς περὶ βρῶσιν καὶ πόσιν, καὶ τὴν γαστέρα ἐβάρυνε, καὶ τὸν νοῦν συνεθόλωσε, καὶ ὕπνον ἀδελφὸν ὑπνώττων θανάτῳ, φαντασίᾳ περιπέπτωκε, καὶ σπέρμα ἐξέκρινε· καὶ οὗτος γὰρ αὐτὸς ἑαυτῷ διὰ τὴν ἀκρασίαν τοῦ φαντάσματος ὁ αἴτιος· καὶ ὁ τὰ κατ' ἐκεῖνον οἰκονομῶν, ὡς συνίδῃ συμφέρειν τῷ ἀνθρώπῳ, ἐπενέγκῃ τὴν ἐπιτίμησιν.' Zonaras also discusses this in his commentary on canon 4 of Dionysios, although the original canon does not mention excessive food and

drink as a cause of nocturnal emissions. Balsamon does the same and this is the only time that he makes this association. See *Syntagma* 4.12–13.

19 *Syntagma* 4.602: 'Εἰ μὲν ὁ τοῦτο παθών, ὦ ἀντίθετε, προϋκειμένην εἶχεν ἐμπάθειαν, κἂν τοῖς λογισμοῖς ἐπιθυμίαν ἔτρεφε γυναικὸς καὶ ταύτην ἔστρεφεν ἐπὶ νοῦν, καὶ οὕτως ἡ φαντασία καθ' ὕπνους ἐπηκολούθησεν, οὐδ' αὐτὸς κρινῶ τὸν τοιοῦτον ἀναίτιον· αὐτὸς γὰρ ἑαυτῷ τοῦ πάθους ἐστὶν αἰτιώτατος'.

20 *Syntagma* 4.603–4: 'Σύ μοι δοκεῖς [. . .] καὶ τὸν ἐν ὕπνοις δόξαντα πεφονευκέναι τινὰ φόνου κρινεῖν, καὶ φονικοῖς ἐπιτιμίοις ὑποβαλεῖν, ἢ καὶ τῇ ἀρχῇ παραδοῦναι πρὸς κόλασιν· καὶ γνώμης αὖθις ἐξ ἀντιρρόπου, τὸν ἐν ὀνείροις ὑπὲρ εὐσεβείας ἀθλήσαντα, συγκαταλέξαι τοῖς μάρτυσι· [. . .] Εἰ δὲ μὴ ταῦτα τῶν τιμωμένων, οὐδ' ἐκεῖνα τῶν ἐπιτιμωμένων'. See also Fögen, 'Zonaras on Nocturnal Pollution', 260.

21 *Syntagma* 4.605: 'Τεσσάρων γὰρ ἐπὶ τῆς ἁμαρτίας λεγομένων συμβαίνειν, προσβολῆς, καὶ πάλης, φημί, συγκαταθέσεώς τε καὶ πράξεως, τὰ μὲν τῶν προηγουμένων ἀμφοῖν, παρὰ τοῖς θεοφόροις Πατράσιν ἀνέγκλητα· ἡ συγκατάθεσις δ' ὑπ' αἰτίασιν, ὡς τὴν κατὰ διάνοιαν ἁμαρτίαν εἰσάγουσα· ἡ δέ γε πρᾶξις, καὶ ὑπὸ κόλασιν.' Zonaras also refers to this in his commentary on canon 22 of Nicaea II: although he does not mention the four steps, he says that one can be considered an adulterer without having actually committed the act itself and emphasises again the importance of desire. He uses the language of impurity and says that such desire can pollute the mind. See *Syntagma* 2.644. This doctrine of sin was also discussed by the Church Fathers, including Maximos the Confessor (d. 662). See Question I.31 in J.H. Declerck, *Maximi Confessoris quaestiones et dubia* (Turnhout, 1982), 149–50.

22 *Syntagma* 4.605. Fighting against such urges was praiseworthy and seen as a feat in itself. See *Syntagma* 4.76.

23 *Syntagma* 4.605: 'Εἰ μὲν γὰρ τοῦ λογισμοῦ προσβαλόντος, καὶ πρὸς ἀσελγεῖς ἐπιθυμίας κινήσαντος, ὁ πάσχων ἀσμένως ἐδέξατο τὸ ἐνθύμιον, καὶ τὸν νοῦν ἔσχε τούτῳ ἐνδιατρίβοντα, καὶ οἷον ἐνηδυνόμενον, καὶ μελετῶντα τὰ περὶ αὐτοῦ, οὕτω τε τἀνθρώπου διακειμένου, ἡ φαντασία νυκτὸς ἐπελήλυθεν, οὐκ ἀνέγκλητος, κἂν ἴσως καὶ τὴν ἔκκρισιν τῆς γονῆς διαπέφευγεν'.

24 *Syntagma* 4.602–3: 'καὶ μεμόλυνται οὐ τὸ σῶμα, διὰ τὴν ἔκκρισιν τὴν σπερματικήν (οὐ γὰρ ἀκαθαρσία τουτὶ τὸ περίττωμα), ἀλλὰ τὸν λογισμὸν διὰ τὴν συγκατάθεσιν τῆς ἐπιθυμίας τῆς σαρκικῆς'. See also *Syntagma* 4.13.

25 *Syntagma* 4.13: 'ὁ γοῦν τοιοῦτος οὐκ εὐσυνείδητος, κἀντεῦθεν οὐδ' εὐπαρρησίαστος διὰ τὸ ἴδιον ἐνθύμιον· πῶς οὖν προσελεύσεται τῷ Θεῷ διακρινόμενος;' This is also repeated in *Syntagma* 4.74.

26 *Syntagma* 4.13–14.

27 *Syntagma* 4.77: 'Ἡ δὲ ἀπὸ νόσου νεφριτικῆς γινομένη ἐκροὴ τοῦ σπέρματος, οἵα ἐστὶν ἡ τῶν γονορροιῶν, καὶ τῆς λιθιάσεως, πάντη ἐστὶν ἀκατέγκλητος. Κἂν γὰρ ἀπὸ τοῦ Μωσαϊκοῦ νόμου οἱ γονορρυεῖς ἀκάθαρτοι ἐλογίζοντο, ἀλλὰ καθ' ἕτερον τρόπον, ὅσον πρὸς τὸν ἡμέτερον νόμον, καθαροὶ λογίζονται'.

28 *Syntagma* 4.338: 'Περὶ τῶν ἐν ὀνείροις φανταζομένων, οἷς καὶ σπέρματος *ἴσως* ἐπιγίνεται ἐκροὴ φησὶν ὁ Πατὴρ οὗτος' (my emphasis).

29 *Syntagma* 4.338: 'εἰ μὲν πρὸ τούτου προσέβαλε τῷ ὀνειρασθέντι ἐπιθυμίας γυναικὸς λογισμὸς καὶ ἐνέμεινεν ὁ νοῦς ἐπὶ τῇ ἐπιθυμίᾳ, καὶ ἐνεφιλοχώρησε ταύτῃ, κἀντεῦθεν ἡ φαντασία ἐπῆλθε καὶ ἡ ῥύσις τοῦ σπέρματος, οὐκ ὀφείλει μεταλαβεῖν'.

30 *Syntagma* 4.76: 'εἰ μὲν ἀπὸ μόνης προσβολῆς φαντασία γένηται νυκτερινὴ μετριώτερον ἐπιτιμηθῶμεν'.

31 Fögen, 'Zonaras on Nocturnal Pollution', 270–4; P. Magdalino, 'Enlightenment and Repression in Twelfth-Century Byzantium. The Evidence of the Canonists', in *Byzantium in the 12th Century: Canon Law, State and Society*, ed. N. Oikonomides (Athens, 1991), 357–74, at 361–2.

32 We do, however, find a passing comment in Thomas of Chobham which suggests that, for some, nocturnal emissions were still treated as an issue of physical impurity. See Broomfield, *Thomae de Chobham*, 333: 'licet alii dicant, nullo modo peccat aliquis

dormiendo sed contrahit quamdam immunditiam propter quam se mundare debet antequam accedat ad altare uel sumat eucharistiam'.

33 D.6 c.1: 'Aliquando enim ex crapula, aliquando ex naturae suae superfluitate aut infirmitate, aliquando ex cogitatione contingit pollutio.' Unlike most commentators, Master Honorius interpreted *crapula* as excessive drinking rather than excessive eating. Rufinus interprets *crapula* as overeating. See *Magister Rufinus*, 18.

34 D.6 c.1: 'Et quidem cum ex naturae superfluitate uel infirmitate euenerit, omnimodo hec illusio non est timenda, quia hanc animus nesciens pertulisse magis dolendus est, quam fecisse.'

35 D.6 c.1: 'Cum uero ultra modum appetitus gulae in sumendis alimentis rapitur, atque idcirco humorum receptacula grauantur, habet exinde animus aliquem reatum, non tamen usque ad prohibitionem sacri misterii percipiendi.'

36 D.6 c.1: 'Sin uero ex turpi cogitatione uigilantis oritur illusio in mente dormientis, patet animo reatus suus.'

37 D.6 c.1: 'cum fortasse aut dies festus exigit, aut exhibere ministerium pro eo, quod sacerdos alius deest, ipsa necessitas compellit. Nam si adsunt alii, qui implere ministerium ualeant, illusio per crapulam facta a perceptione sacri misterii prohibere non debet, sed ab immolatione sacri misterii, ut arbitror, abstinere debet humiliter, si tamen dormientem turpi imaginatione non concusserit.' In some manuscripts this is followed by c. 2, which breaks the sin down to three stages – namely, suggestion, delight, and consent: 'For although an evil spirit might suggest a sin to the mind, if no delight in the sin follows, sin is in no way committed because sin comes to birth only when the flesh begins to delight in sin. If consent arises after deliberation, then the sin is complete. Therefore, in suggestion is the seed of sin, in delight its nurture, in consent its completion.' Thompson, Gordley, and Christensen, *The Treatise on Laws*, 20. This is similar to the Byzantine understanding of the steps that lead to sin that we have seen in Zonaras.

38 The fuller version of Gregory's response (D.6 cc.1, 2) is found in Burchard's *Decretum* 5.43 in PL 140.760–1; and in Ivo of Chartres' *Decretum* 2.52. https://ivo-of-chartres.github.io/decretum/ivodec_2.pdf. Accessed 8/12/2017. However, only D.6 d.p.c.3, which discusses natural and customary law, was included in Gratian's first recension. See Winroth, *Making of Gratian's Decretum*, 198. Master Honorius and the *Summa Lipsiensis* provided comments for D.6 c.1 and c.3, but not c.2.

39 This includes D.6 c.1 but not c.2. See Morey, *Bartholomew of Exeter*, 269.

40 Burchard's *Decretum* 17.41 in PL 140.927.

41 Burchard's *Decretum* 5.51 in PL 140.762.

42 Morey, *Bartholomew of Exeter*, 267.

43 Firth, *Robert of Flamborough*, 268: 'Si uero celebrata missa presbyter neglexerit accipere sacrificium, quadraginta dies poeniteat; et qui accipit sacrificium pollutus nocturno tempore septem dies poeniteat.'

44 Firth, *Robert of Flamborough*, 298, 13. Venial sins were relatively minor faults which could be forgiven without private confession through prayer, charity, genuflexions, or aspersions with holy water, or through the reception of communion. Mortal sins could be forgiven only after private confession and penance. See J. Goering, 'The Internal Forum and the Literature of Penance', in *The History of Medieval Canon Law in the Classical Period, 1140–1234: From Gratian to the Decretals of Pope Gregory IX*, eds. W. Hartmann and K. Pennington (Washington, DC, 2008), 379–428, at 397. See also Broomfield, *Thomae de Chobham*, 17–20.

45 See also Murray, 'Men's Bodies, Men's Minds', 12.

46 Broomfield, *Thomae de Chobham*, 330–3.

47 Broomfield, *Thomae de Chobham*, 331: 'Sed in secundo casu dicit beatus Gregorius quod sacerdos si tali modo fuerit pollutus de nocte, debet in crastino abstinere a diuinis officiis, nec debet celebrare donec aliquam fecerit penitentiam.'

48 Broomfield, *Thomae de Chobham*, 331: 'Verumtamen si sit dies sollemnis et populus conueniat ad missam audiendam, melius est quod cum proposito penitendi celebret si non sit alius sacerdos presens, quia populus scandalizetur recedendo sine missa.'

49 Broomfield, *Thomae de Chobham*, 331: 'Debet autem penitere pro tali illusione uel suspiciendo disciplinam, uel abluendo se in aqua frigida, uel ieiunando in cibis quadragesimalibus, uel induendo se laneis ad carnem'.

50 Broomfield, *Thomae de Chobham*, 331: 'ut sordes nocturne illusionis abstergantur a corpore suo antequam die crastina accedat ad sacramentum altaris'.

51 *Magistri Honorii* 1.22, D.6 c.1 s.v. *a perceptione ab immolatione*: 'Set quare potius ab immolatione quam a simplici perceptione? Quia plus est illud quam istud'.

52 *Magistri Honorii* 1.22, D.6 c.1 s.v. *a perceptione ab immolatione*: 'Hinc tamen colligitur non propter criminis enormitatem, set propter rei excellentiam hanc fieri prohibitionem; peccatum tamen enorme esse immolare citra necessitatem non ratione criminis, set prohibitionis.' The author of the *Summa Lipsiensis* gives the same justification. See *Summa Lipsiensis* 1.25.

53 *Summa Lipsiensis* 1.25, D.6 c.1 s.v. *suo iudicio*: 'Multi enim possunt percipere quibus illicitum est immolare, ut bigamus, depositus, laicus, quibus immolatio illicita est, set non acceptio.'

54 *Summa Lipsiensis* 1.23–4, D.6 d.a.c.1 s.v. <*Quia uero de natura*>: 'Item et tertio modo oritur, cum ex cogitatione precedente prouenit; tunc a sacro ministerio siue percipiendo siue conficiendo abstinere debet, nisi cogatur a prelato; tunc enim facta ei priuata confessione poterit celebrare'. The same statement can be found in Rufinus' *Summa Decretorum*. See *Magister Rufinus*, 18.

55 *Magistri Honorii* 1.23, D.6 c.1 s.v. *Sin uero reatus*: 'Quia ex consensu mortali peccat. Set num in hoc casu propter scandalum diei Paschali hi debent celebrare? Resp.: Sic secundum quosdam, post priuatam secum factam confessionem.' Master Honorius stated that he would wait a day if it meant confessing to a cleric instead of a layman. Indeed, he asserted that the validity of confession to laymen was doubted by many. Cf. Morey, *Bartholomew of Exeter*, 172, 181.

56 *Summa Lipsiensis* 1.24, D.6 c.1 s.v. *suo iudicio*: 'G. aliter legit: "Qua in re" idest in pollutione. Et hic est sensus: Nec dormiens nec excitatus delinquit, set ante dormitionem se ingurgitando.' *Magistri Honorii* 1.22, D.6 c.1 s.v. *Qua in re*: 'Cum uariis modis exponatur hec clausula magis placet expositio G., que talis est: Et est sensus in pollutione que contingit per ymaginum concussiones, ostenditur mentem polluti reatum contraxisse, quoniam tunc non contraxit, quando pollutio accidit, quia cum dormiebat, set nec post dormitionem, set ante dormitionem quando in crapula cedidit.' On G. or Gandulph, see Pennington and Mueller, 'The Decretists: The Italian School', 139.

57 *Summa Lipsiensis* 1.25, D.6 c.1 s.v. *suo iudicio*: 'Item nota: si mens turpiter concussa fuerit, licet ex crapula, deberet abstinere, ut hic dicitur secundum hoc.'

58 *Summa Lipsiensis* 1.25, D.6 c.1 s.v. *suo iudicio*: 'Secundum hoc nulla est distinctio inter secundum casum et tertium, nisi hec sola quod in secundo casu abstinet propter cogitationem que precessit crapulam, in tertio casu habetur respectus ad cogitationem simplicem ex qua sola processit pollutio.'

59 *Magistri Honorii* 1.23, D.6 c.1 s.v. *cecidisse*: 'Vel secundum S. ut omnimodo differentia huius ad posterius membrum habeatur dicatur hoc esse ueniale et agitur hic de cotidiana perceptione, ut infra de con. di.ii. Cotidie, a qua si abstineat propter tale peccatum nichil deperit, cuius proposito ad quod claustrales tenentur, qui potius quam alii possunt cotidie comunicare, ut de con. di.ii. Si non sunt. Agitur de trina sollempni a qua propter peccatum ueniale non debet quis prohiberi.'

60 *Syntagma* 4.598–9: 'Εἰ μὲν οὖν, βέλτιστοι, τῶν κανόνων ἀγνοίᾳ ταῦθ' ὑμῖν νενομοθέτηταί τε καὶ ᾠκονόμηται, τὸ καθηγεῖσθαι καὶ δέχεσθαι λογισμοὺς καὶ τοῖς σφαλλομένοις ἐπιτιμᾶν, ὑμῖν οὐκ ἐπέοικεν· [. . .] ὑφ' ἑαυτῶν δ' ἐπιτιμᾶτε τοῖς ὑφ' ὑμᾶς.'

61 Although sometimes the expression used is vaguer and could apply to both, most often it is very clear that what is being discussed is whether a layman should receive communion. There is no explicit mention of whether a cleric should perform the Eucharist after a nocturnal emission.

62 Syntagma 4.600: 'Ὁ δὲ μέγας καὶ ἱερὸς Ἀθανάσιος, πρὸς Ἀμμοῦν ἐπιστέλλων περὶ τούτου μονάζοντα, πολύστιχον ἔθετο τὴν ἐπιστολήν·' and *Syntagma* 4.603: 'ἢ καὶ

ἐξ ἐπηρείας σατανικῆς ἐπενήνεκται, κατὰ τοὺς θείους Πατέρας, τοῦ δυσμενοῦς τοῖς ἀσκηταῖς ἐνεδρεύοντος'.

63 *Syntagma* 4.603: 'οὐ μιμήσομαί σου τὴν ἀνευλαβῆ περὶ ταῦτα εὐλάβειαν'.

64 Brakke, 'The Problematisation of Nocturnal Emissions in Early Antiquity', 442.

65 Fögen, 'Zonaras on Nocturnal Pollution', 272. For the gulf between the sacerdotal and monastic Church, see Magdalino, *Manuel*, 318, 374, 388.

66 *Syntagma* 4.455: 'τέως τὰ περὶ τῶν λαϊκῶν ἀκολούθως ταῖς θείαις ταύταις Γραφαῖς διηλύτωσαν'.

67 *Syntagma* 4.455: 'Ὁ προσφέρων, φησὶ τὸ γράμμα τὸ ἱερόν, δῶρα καὶ θυσίας ἀρχιερεὺς ἐξ ἀνθρώπων λαμβάνεται, καὶ καθὼς περὶ τοῦ λαοῦ προσφέρει τῷ Θεῷ οὕτω δὴ καὶ περὶ αὐτοῦ· ἐπεὶ καὶ αὐτῷ βάρος σαρκικῆς ἀσθενείας ἐπίκειται.'

68 *Syntagma* 4.455: 'Φησὶ γὰρ ἡ τοῦ ἁγίου Διονυσίου ἀπόκρισις· Εἰ μὲν ὑπόκειται ἐπιθυμίᾳ γυναικός, οὐκ ὀφείλει· εἰ δὲ ὁ σατανᾶς πειράζει αὐτόν, ἵνα διὰ τῆς προφάσεως ταύτης ἀπαλλοτριώσῃ τῆς κοινωνίας τῶν μυστηρίων, ὀφείλει κοινωνῆσαι· ἐπεὶ οὐ παύσεται ὁ ἐχθρὸς πειράζων αὐτὸν κατ' ἐκεῖνον τὸν καιρὸν ἐπιτιθέμενος αὐτῷ.'

69 *Syntagma* 4.455: 'Διὸ καὶ ἡμεῖς τὰ αὐτὰ περὶ λαϊκῶν διοριζόμενοι, περὶ ἐπισκόπων, διακόνων, καὶ ἱερέων φανταζομένων κατὰ σατανικὴν καὶ μόνον ἐπήρειαν, τὸν αὐτὸν τύπον κρατεῖν οὐ διαγινώσκομεν· ἐπιζυγωθῆναι δὲ μᾶλλον αὐτοῖς τὴν τῆς ἱεροτελεστίας ἐνέργειαν κατὰ μόνην τὴν ἡμέραν τῆς ὀνειρώξεως ψηφιζόμεθα, διὰ τὸ τῆς ἱερωσύνης σεβάσμιον· εἰ μὴ τυχὸν κινδυνώδης ἐστὶν ἡ ὑπέρθεσις, ἢ διὰ τὸ τῆς ἡμέρας περιφανέστατον, ἢ διὰ τὸ τοῦ πράγματος χρησιμώτατον· τηνικαῦτα γὰρ συντριβείη μὲν ἡ παγὶς τοῦ ἐπηρεαστοῦ, ὑψωθείη δὲ τῆς ἱερουργίας ἡ δύναμις.' Subdeacons are missing from this list. This points to their limited liturgical duties. As we shall see in the next chapter, subdeacons were often also absent from the lists of clerics who had to be continent.

70 A change in emphasis from monastic to lay has also been noted by Angelidi in the context of sexual fantacies recorded in middle Byzantine hagiographies. See Angelidi, 'Αισθήσεις, σεξουαλικότητα και οπτασίες', 227–8.

71 Angold, *Church and Society*, 150.

7 Was clerical marriage polluting?

As we have seen, bodily fluids such as nocturnal emissions carried with them the potential for physical and/or moral pollution. Was that also the case for marital sex? In this chapter, I explore why clerics were expected to abstain from sexual intercourse with their spouses and how the rules of abstinence related to twelfth-century ideas on marriage, sexuality, and purity. I argue that despite the basic similarity inherent in the shared view that sex and service should not mix, the temporary continence imposed on Byzantine clerics cannot be understood in the same way as the Western need for celibacy. Sex within marriage was not called impure by the Byzantines, even when it occurred outside the bounds set by law. Rather it was the need to avoid distractions that was emphasised by the Byzantine canon lawyers. I will start by explaining why a case for purity concerns could be made for Byzantium, before I continue to argue against it. Then I will turn to the situation in England to highlight the difference in the vocabulary used to describe clerical marriage. Finally, I will give two reasons for the contrast between the two societies: (1) the discrepancy between law and practice was greater in England than in Byzantium, eventually triggering a need for change, which brought with it a further need to draw sharp social lines by means of pollution discourse; (2) in Byzantium there was less of a drive to firmly divide clerics from laymen and as such less of an imperative to present clerics as purer.

Byzantium

Clerical marriage and purity

In the *Oxford Handbook of Byzantine Studies* we read that 'the canons dealing with the marital status of clergy [. . .], especially in the higher orders, stress the issue of ritual purity more than the ethical implications of personal behaviour.'[1] According to this statement temporary abstinence would be linked to fears of pollution. This is not an unreasonable assumption given that Byzantine canons associated the need for continence with the liturgical duties of the cleric. Already in 419, canon 4 of the Council of Carthage stated that bishops, priests, and deacons and 'all those who handle the holy [mysteries]' should abstain from their wives.[2]

In 691/2, canon 13 of Trullo explicitly added subdeacons to this list and described them as 'those who handle the holy mysteries'.[3]

If we look more closely, however, at the reasons put forward for clerical marital abstinence, we will see that, in the twelfth century at least, the issue of purity was never explicitly raised. In what follows, I will focus on subdeacons and bishops who occupied liminal positions: subdeacons were the lowest ecclesiastical grade expected to observe temporary abstinence and bishops the only grade required to lead a celibate life. These are two cases where one might expect purity to receive particular emphasis if it presented an issue of concern. The same is true for occasions when the law was not followed; we would expect the consequences of any potential pollution to be highlighted. As we shall see, this did not happen.

Subdeacons

Canon 25 of the council of Carthage (419), which explicitly included subdeacons in the list of those who needed to abstain from their wives, described them as τὰ ἱερὰ μυστήρια ψηλαφῶντας.[4] Aristenos in his commentary did not make any special reference to subdeacons, but talked more generally of 'those who presided over the altar' and used the words χειριζόμενοι (those who handle) and μεταχειρίσεως (handling) to gloss the term ψηλαφῶντας. Although these terms have their root in the word for hand (χείρ), the canonist emphasised the intercessory role of the ministers rather than any physical aspect of their duties: they needed to abstain 'so that they might be able to obtain what they ask frankly from God'.[5] This was the same justification that had been given by canon 3 of Carthage, which again asked for abstinence but without including the subdiaconate.[6] The other two canonists showed special interest in subdeacons and what facet of their duties the word ψηλαφάω specifically referred to.

Zonaras interpreted it to mean the same as ἅπτεσθαι and believed that it denoted a high degree of participation in the Eucharistic sacrifice. He took this to be unusual and perhaps a Carthaginian custom and noted its contradiction with canon 21 of Laodicea (before 380), which stated that subdeacons should not enter the *diakonikon* or ἅπτεσθαι (touch) sacred objects.[7] Despite his interest in the word, he made no attempt to justify why subdeacons were included in the list of those who were to observe continence. After all, for Zonaras the expression used in the canon did not apply to all subdeacons, but peculiarly to those of Carthage. Therefore, no particular weight can be placed on the expression 'those who handle the holy' in his case. Zonaras was simply repeating it.

Balsamon, on the other hand, explained that the two words had different meanings:

> So note that subdeacons too handle (μεταχειρίζονται) the holy mysteries; and do not say that the present canon goes against canon 21 of the synod of Laodicea, which decrees that subdeacons do not have a place in the *diakonikon* and do not take part in (ἅπτεσθαι) the holy mysteries. But say that ψηλαφᾶν is different from ἅπτεσθαι: ψηλαφᾶν, that is to say moving something from

> place to place, is a service and not even the subdeacon will be prevented from doing that; but ἅπτεσθαι is only allowed to priests and to those who assist in the sacrifice, that is to say the deacons. According to this present canon, not only those who take part in the consecration (ἁπτόμενοι) of holy mysteries but also those who transfer sacred objects (ψηλαφῶντες) ought to be continent during the time of their service.[8]

According to Balsamon, despite their relatively inferior role in the liturgy, subdeacons needed to observe continence because they moved the ceremonial instruments. This interpretation appears to emphasise the physical contact between the subdeacon and the holy vessels, so it could suggest that although the language of impurity was not explicitly used, the avoidance rule set in place was motivated by fears of pollution. This rule, however, had been fixed in the fifth century. Whether at the time it was meant to protect the holy mysteries against potential pollution is a separate question. For the twelfth century at least, there is no proof that Balsamon, just like Zonaras, was doing anything more than simply repeating the words of the fifth-century canon when using expressions such as τὰ ἱερὰ μυστήρια ψηλαφῶντας. In fact, it is likely that the only reason why Balsamon went on to explain the meaning of the word was because he was 'replying' to Zonaras' comment about the contradiction between the two canons (canon 21 of Laodicea and canon 25 of Carthage). He was making a point here about the harmony of the law, rather than a point about purity and clerical marriage.

What is more, the expression τὰ ἱερὰ μυστήρια ψηλαφῶντας did not necessarily represent for Balsamon a firmly fixed and meaningful category. In his comment on canon 70 of Carthage, he used this same phrase to refer again to those who needed to observe abstinence, but this time made no mention of subdeacons, rather taking τὰ ἱερὰ μυστήρια ψηλαφῶντας to refer only to bishops, priests, and deacons.[9] The canonist was again simply following the canon, rather than making a deliberate and thoughtful statement about who should or should not be included.

Given the uncertainty of what this fifth-century phrase meant for the canonists, it is difficult to use it in order to draw any conclusions about twelfth-century fears of impurity. It is possible that rather than being invested with loaded connotations it was simply taken as a convenient shorthand meant to remind the reader of the rules of temporary abstinence.

Bishops

Episcopal celibacy had already been decreed by civil legislation in the sixth century.[10] Canon 12 of Trullo was the first ecclesiastical law to repeat this command and to emphasise that bishops were not allowed to cohabit with their former wives, 'creating offence (πρόσκομμα) and scandal (σκάνδαλον) for the people'.[11] For this, it gave the following justification:

> we say this, not to abolish and overthrow things established through the authority of the Apostles, but because we are taking thought for the salvation

> of the people and their advance to better things, and for not bringing any reproach (μῶμον) upon the ecclesiastical state.[12]

Although the word μῶμος has a history of associations with impurity, it is clear from Zonaras' commentary that in the case of episcopal celibacy it was the bishop's reputation that was in question.[13] The canonist wrote,

> when the faith was new and the holy preaching had not yet been widely spread, the holy Apostles were more leniently disposed towards those who were joining the faith and did not demand from them perfection in all, but made concessions for their weakness and for the customs of the Gentiles and the Jews. For the high priests of the Jews were allowed by law to live with wives, and to the high priests of the Greeks marriage was not forbidden. But now, when preaching has been spread far and wide, and the faithful have come to a better state and order and the evangelical city is growing, they say that it is necessary also for the bishops to direct their domestic life towards perfect chastity, such that they abstain not only from the wives of others, but also from their former bedfellows; and that they not only do not share their bed or have intercourse with them, but do not even live with them or dwell in the same house. For even if some might live in chastity, they will be a source of offence and scandal to others.[14]

In their discussion of episcopal celibacy neither the canons nor the canonists mentioned abstinence as a means of attaining purity. Instead, it was the need to avoid scandal and enhance the Church's reputation that was put forward as a justification for continence. All clerics were expected to lead their flocks by example and maintain the superiority of the Christian faith vis-à-vis heretics and the heterodox.[15] This was even more the case for bishops, who were the leaders of the flock within their diocese as well as high-ranking representatives of the Orthodox Church. The 'offence and scandal' mentioned by the canon would ensue from the cohabitation of the bishop and his former wife after their separation. The canonists indeed expressed great doubts about the ability of men to avoid temptation when directly faced with it. When discussing the customs of 'barbarian' Churches which imposed celibacy upon their clergy in major orders, Balsamon insisted that those who wished to be celibate should be forbidden from cohabiting with women; otherwise they would not lead a truly celibate life, but would only pretend to do so (καθ' ὑπόκρισιν).[16] Bishops, then, were expected to maintain higher standards than the rest of the clergy, and it was acknowledged that celibacy constituted a harsh demand. Perfect chastity was put forward as a state preferable to marriage, but one that could not be attained by everyone. Nonetheless, this was done without denigrating the marital union or implying that it compromised the purity of the spouses.

The same attitude can be seen in a law promulgated by Emperor Isaak II Angelos (1186/7) which asked the former wives of bishops to embrace monastic life before their husband's accession to the episcopate.[17] The law tells us that some metropolitans and archbishops had refused to separate from their wives and continued to live with them openly (ἀνυποστόλως) in the same house as before. According to Angold this decree had a political motivation; it was intended to embarrass the emperor's opponents on the episcopal bench and formed part of a different scandal, concerning the rigging of episcopal elections.[18] The fact that this issue came to light only incidentally suggests that it was not of great importance in its own right. Nonetheless, it is unlikely that it would have carried much weight if the accusation had been baseless. There must have been bishops at the time who continued to cohabit with their former wives. What the emperor emphasised as problematic was the fact that these bishops were contravening the law.[19] This contravention was particularly bad as no one had forced (μὴ ἐξ ἐπιτάγματος) these men to become bishops: each one of them had been given a free choice (αὐθαιρέτῳ γνώμῃ) between a life of abstinence as a bishop on the one side and the 'undefiled intercourse' (τὴν ἀμίαντον συνάφειαν) of honourable (τίμιον) marriage on the other.[20] The choice of words here is telling. The emperor and the bishops gathered to promulgate this law had no intention of diminishing marriage in order to safeguard episcopal celibacy. On the contrary, the reader was reminded that sex within marriage cannot render spouses impure; even bishops who had unlawful intercourse with their former wives were not called polluted. Instead Isaac's decree emphasised that being a bishop, as well as being an emperor, was a gift from God (θεόσδοτον χρίσμα καὶ ἀξίωμα) meant to set in order (κατακοσμοῦντα) human life; bishops in particular were expected to intercede to God on behalf of the faithful and to act as divine anchors (ἱεραί τινες ἄγκυραι) to steady the empire. They were expected to uphold the laws, not to ignore and break them (παραθεωρεῖσθαι καὶ παραθραύεσθαι); episcopal dignity had to remain free of scandal and reproach (ἀσκανδάλιστα, καὶ ἀπρόσκοπα, καὶ μώμου παντὸς ἀπεξενωμένα).[21] We find here the same stems (σκάνδαλον, πρόσκομμα, and μῶμος) used by the canons and the canonists. Maintaining the dignity and reputation of the episcopacy was key for both emperor and Church.

Bishops also came up in the context of older canons in favour of clerical marriage, dating from a period when episcopal celibacy had not yet been instituted. For example, canon 51 of the Apostles stated that

> if any bishop, presbyter, or deacon, or any one of the sacerdotal list, abstains from marriage, or meat, or wine, not for the sake of asceticism, but because he abhors them (διὰ βδελυρίαν), having forgotten that God made all things very good and that he made humans male and female, and thus blaspheming the work of creation, let him be corrected, or else deposed and cast out of the Church.[22]

Zonaras added that God would not have created women if they were a source of evil.[23] This was very similar to his argument against the impurity of nocturnal emissions, which was discussed in the previous chapter: abhorring marriage was a calumny towards God's creation, which was wholly natural and pure. Neither Zonaras nor Balsamon made any further comment about the fact that this canon no longer applied to bishops. They were simply content to affirm more generally the purity of clerical marriage.

We find a more detailed response in the commentaries on canon 5 of the Apostles (c. 380), which asked bishops, priests, and deacons not to put away their wife under the pretence of piety. Zonaras stated that to dismiss one's spouse would look like 'slander towards marriage' and would falsely suggest that 'intercourse created impurity', whereas the scriptures stated that 'marriage is honourable and the bed undefiled' (Hebrews 13:4).[24] Then he hastened to add that since the Council in Trullo (691/2) bishops had no longer been allowed to keep their wives.[25] But this was not an apologetic comment intended to patch up a contradiction between the canons. Rather, canon 5 of the Apostles was understood by Zonaras and Balsamon within the context of valid reasons for divorce.[26] The bishop's separation from his wife had become part of canon law, and as such did not constitute a 'pretence of piety' or slander against marriage. Instead, it was the only lawful and pious thing for a married cleric to do before his accession to the episcopate. More generally, the two canonists did not dwell much on the reasons that had brought about episcopal celibacy in the first place, but were happy to accept the laws as they found them and to emphasise the value of marriage as an option for the clergy.

Breaking the rules

Impurity was not explicitly invoked as a reason for temporary abstinence for priests and deacons, not even when the rules were blatantly disregarded. This was the case in Constantinople during Balsamon's time, when it was common for clerics to hold more than one ecclesiastical post, a pluralism which was necessary in areas lacking ecclesiastical personnel, but which was detrimental to the rules of temporary abstinence.[27] According to Balsamon, in his day it was not unusual in Constantinople to find priests serving three or more churches at a time.[28] This meant that many of them would have performed their ecclesiastical duties daily, not following their prescribed shifts.[29] Priests, deacons, and subdeacons were not expected to serve the altar daily, but rather to take regular time away from their ecclesiastical duties, when they could engage in sexual intercourse with their wives. Clerics who wished to follow the canons and perform their duties on a daily basis would have needed to observe absolute continence. It is unlikely that all these clerics remained in a state of complete abstinence, although, as Balsamon noted, it was impossible to know 'because [the act] is not manifest and cannot be proven'.[30] The canonist lamented the situation and asked for its correction.[31] This is a rare glimpse of the transgression of the rules of temporary continence, and I have found only one other example in the canonical commentaries, again a comment by Balsamon but this time on canon 13 of Trullo, which affirmed the right of priests, deacons, and subdeacons to keep their wives. The comment, which is found only in some manuscripts and as a marginal note, reads, 'How will they defend themselves, those who always and almost every day serve at the altar and transfer the holy vessels (ψηλαφῶντες τὰ ἅγια)?'[32] Apart from his two brief remarks, clerical incontinence did not attract much attention in the canonical commentaries.

Other reasons for temporary abstinence

Given that the language of pollution was not used in Byzantium to justify or reinforce the rules of temporary abstinence, how are we to understand the restrictions imposed on priests, deacons, and subdeacons? I argue that the reason for abstinence was the need to focus on prayer and intercession: sexual intercourse represented for the Byzantines a distraction to be avoided in order to communicate effectively with God.[33]

Canon 13 of Trullo decreed that it was necessary for those who assisted at the divine service to observe abstinence 'so that they may be able to obtain what they ask frankly (ἁπλῶς) from God'.[34] The same expression is found in canon 3 of Carthage and was repeated verbatim by Aristenos and Zonaras in their commentaries.[35] But the commentators also paraphrased and expanded upon this justification. Zonaras stated that the purpose of abstinence was that clerics

> may be able to obtain those things which they ask frankly (ἁπλῶς) from God, that is to say without hesitation and without doubt. For these are the intermediaries between God and people, appeasing the divine for others and asking salvation for the faithful and peace for the world. Therefore, [the canon] says, if they practise every virtue and so have free speech (παρρησιάζονται) with God, He may respond to their prayers. If they were not to have free speech, how would they act as ambassadors for others?[36]

Similarly, Balsamon stated that the canon asked for clerics in major orders

> to practise every virtue and to be continent not only through moderation [in sensual desires], but also through every deed and occurrence; for this way, [the canon] says, they will be listened to when they pray to God on behalf of the people.[37]

The same idea was expressed in interpretations of Paul's 1 Corinthians 7:5: 'Do not deprive one another, except perhaps by agreement for a limited time, so that you may devote yourselves (σχολάσητε) to prayer; but then come together again, so that Satan may not tempt you because of your lack of self-control'. This verse was invoked in a variety of Byzantine sources, including biblical and canonical commentaries, as well as *questions and answers*, and it was applied to both clerical and lay marriage. An influential starting point can be found in the writings of John Chrysostom, where it was stated that the reason for the abstinence demanded by Paul was not that marital intercourse created ἀκαθαρσία, impurity, but that it created ἀσχολία, occupation or distraction.[38] The word ἀσχολία is a direct reference to Paul's σχολάσητε, with which it shares its stem. This clearly shows that what was at stake here was the most useful way to occupy one's time.

This view was repeated in the late eleventh century by Theophylact, archbishop of Ohrid (d. 1107), in his commentary on the same verse: 'so that your prayer may become greater, he says, abstain from each other, because the union will create occupation, not impurity.'[39] It surfaces yet again in the twelfth-century commentary on this verse by the Constantinopolitan monk Euthymios Zigabenos (c. 1100):[40]

> For if marriage is truly honourable [. . .], because it is lawful and has been entrusted from God, it does not pollute, but it does create occupation for those who have intercourse, when the pleasure (ἡδονῆς) that results from it scatters the mind and weakens the soul (χαυνούσης τὴν ψυχήν). It is necessary for us in the aforementioned times to be collected and careful and roped off from every bodily relaxation.[41]

All three extracts use very similar language to talk about the reasons behind abstinence. Echoes of their phrases can also be found in Zonaras' canonical commentaries. Compare, for example, the comment on canon 5 of the Apostles (c. 380), which we have already discussed. There Zonaras stated that it would constitute slander to marriage for clerics to leave their wives 'as if intercourse created impurity'.[42] Zonaras' 'ὡς ἀκαθαρσίαν τῆς μίξεως ἐμποιούσης' recalls Chrysostom's 'ὡς ἀσχολίαν ἐμποιοῦντος τοῦ πράγματος, ἀλλ' οὐκ ἀκαθαρσίαν', Theophylact's 'ὡς τῆς μίξεως ἀσχολίαν, οὐκ ἀκαθαρσίαν, ποιούσης', and even Zigabenos' 'ἀσχολίαν δὲ ἐμποιεῖ'. Still clearer is the connection between Zigabenos' views and those of Zonaras in the canonist's comment on canon 3 of Dionysios of Alexandria, where reflecting again on Paul's 1 Corinthians 7:5 in the context of lay marriage, he said, 'those fasting should keep away from all luxury, since the enjoyment of physical pleasures (ἡδονῶν) by nature weakens one's soul (χαυνοῦν τὴν ψυχήν) and confounds one's reasoning.'[43] Not only do Zonaras' and Zigabenos' comments express the same ideas but also they do so using some of the same phrases. Similar language was employed by another twelfth-century ecclesiastic, John Kastamonites, metropolitan of Chalcedon (fl. 1195), in reference to lay abstinence during the week.[44] Kastamonites quoted Timotheos' advice that lay couples should abstain on Saturday and Sunday, and suggested that if it was pleasing to some they could also abstain on Wednesday and Friday. As part of his justification, he stated explicitly that marital intercourse was free from stain (διὰ τὸ τῆς κοινωνίας ἀμίαντον) and that the reason for abstinence was concentration on prayer (διὰ τὸ σχολάσαι τῇ προσευχῇ).[45]

In these passages sexual intercourse was interpreted as an occupation likely to distract the mind from prayer. In doing so, it was posited as one form of luxury among others and was not singled out. As such, it is useful to think of sexual abstinence as part of a group of restrictions, including rules against working or going to the hippodrome on feast days, which ensured that there were specific times especially reserved for worship.[46]

A final example from the twelfth century comes from Michael Glykas, in the letters of spiritual direction he wrote after becoming a monk (after 1164):[47]

> [St Paul] orders us to be completely rid of our marriage bed during the time of prayer and fasting, lest we give great offence to God through such a futile prayer, when we are trying instead to make him gracious towards us. For

> what reason? So that the eyes of the mind may not be fanned into flame from every direction because of affection for our wife, hence making our prayer inadmissible. For if when we want to appease human anger we employ all our energy and self-restraint to this end, what should we do, or in what state of mind should we be, when we want to appease God himself for our crimes?[48]

This is how Glykas explained both the temporary abstinence of clerics in sacred orders and that of lay couples before the reception of communion:

> Thence also the synod convened in Carthage in its different canons commanded those in sacred orders to abstain from their spouses during the time when they handle the sacred mysteries. In the same way also the second ecumenical synod decreed that laymen should abstain from their wives on Saturdays and Sundays, because the spiritual sacrifice is offered in those days.[49]

We can see, then, that there was no substantial dividing line between clerics and laymen when it came to temporary abstinence from sex: both were understood, following Paul's instruction, as means of increasing one's ability to communicate with God. Clerics were not asked to observe greater standards and impurity language was avoided in their case.

In fact, impurity language was generally also avoided in the case of the laity. But it is telling that the one explicit example we do have of a twelfth-century canonist referring to marital intercourse as a polluting activity referred to lay rather than clerical marriage.[50] The passage in question is offered in some manuscripts as an alternative interpretation of canon 4 of Carthage, which decreed which clerics ought to abstain from sex with their wives. But the alternative interpretation turned the discussion away from the clergy and addressed all couples: 'Abstaining from women is decreed by the Apostle not only for those in orders, but for all faithful at the time of communion.'[51] In its explanation of the phrase 'The Holy things unto the Holy' from the Eucharistic prayer of the Divine Liturgy, it is stated, 'for if they are polluted through sexual intercourse with a woman, or if through some other foul way they are not holy, that is to say worthy, they should not receive communion'.[52] Within the context of this argument the 'women' in question must be wives.[53] As such, this sentence represents an instance in which sex within marriage is described as polluting. This is a rare example of such language being used about marital intercourse, and in any case it was not addressed to clerics. There was no attempt in Byzantium to use pollution discourse in the case of clerical marriage to separate clerics from laymen.

England: clerics and the language of pollution

The language used in twelfth-century England to refer to the marriage of clerics contrasts starkly with the language we have just seen in Byzantine legal sources. A preoccupation with the ritual purity of the clergy in the West had been particularly prominent since the pontificate of Gregory VII (1073–1085).[54] In his letters to Siegfried, archbishop of Mainz (1060–1084), and Otto, bishop of Constance (1071–1086), the pope referred to clerical marriage as 'the foul defilement of polluting lust' (*fedam libidinosae contagionis pollutionem*).[55] Similarly, in his letter to William the Conqueror he equated it with evil and uncleanness. Discussing the marriage of Judhael of Dol (1040–c. 1076), he wrote that the bishop had dedicated 'his body in shame to the devil by his lewd and foul lust' (*foedae libidinis*).[56]

In the case of clerics, the distinction between marital and non-marital sex was less important than one might initially suppose, as sexual intercourse between a cleric and his wife could be considered 'fornication' and even 'incest'. Similarly, clerical wives would often be called harlots or concubines, and when the term 'uxor' (wife) was used it is difficult to know whether it referred to women whom the clerics had lawfully married before their accession to the subdiaconate and illicitly kept thereafter, or to wives they had taken uncanonically while in sacred orders. The latter would have been highly problematic in Byzantium, but the two states were equally reprehensible in the West, where clerics in major orders had to be celibate. This means that the terms 'focaria', 'fornicaria', 'scortum', 'concubina', 'sponsa', and 'uxor' could refer to the same kinds of women. Indeed, in his aforementioned letter to William of Conqueror, Pope Gregory stated that Bishop Judhael 'was not ashamed to enter openly into marriage and to take a harlot rather than a wife'.[57] Here a woman who had openly been married is emphatically called not a 'sponsa' but a 'scortum'.

This kind of language was used not only by the papacy but also by ecclesiastics in England. For one, Gerard, archbishop of York (1100–1108), in a letter (1102) to Anselm, archbishop of Canterbury (1093–1109), stated that he thirsted 'for the purity of [his] clerics' and asked for sanctions to be imposed on those who refused to profess chastity, making special reference to their service at the altar:

> But how can I entrust the consecration of the body and blood of the Lord and the ministry to them without a profession of chastity? Their presumption has long carried out these things within the filth of lust so that they repeatedly go back and forth, publicly, from the beds of their concubines to the altar, and then from the altar to the beds of wickedness.[58]

In fact, even those who resisted the legislation against clerical marriage knew and repeated the language of impurity which was used to justify it.[59] The description of the 1102 Council of London by Henry, archdeacon of Huntingdon (c. 1088–c. 1154), in his *Historia Anglorum* (c. 1129) is telling. He wrote,

> In the same year Archbishop Anselm held a council in London at Michaelmas in which he forbade English priests to have wives, which had not been prohibited before. This seemed to some to be the greatest purity, but to others there seemed a danger that if they sought a purity beyond their capacity, they might fall into horrible uncleanness, to the utter disgrace of the Christian name.[60]

This was a personal issue for Henry, who had a clerical father, whom he had uncanonically succeeded as archdeacon of Huntingdon, and at least one clerical son, probably still in minor orders at the time of his writing.[61] His argument is particularly interesting, as he contrasted marriage with fornication and stated that it was the latter that needed to be avoided due to its impurity. Marriage was effectively a protection against greater uncleanness. This was a usual argument of Western proponents of clerical marriage.[62]

Pope Alexander III (1159–1181) also sent several decretals to English ecclesiastics addressing this issue. He called clerical fornication 'an abominable and long-standing custom which prevailed in corrupt England', and described it as 'filthy'.[63] In a letter to the archbishop of Canterbury and his suffragans he referred to the fornication of priests as *immunditia* and ordered that if they persist in their filth, they should be removed from their office and their benefice (1 Comp. 3.2.6). In another letter, Alexander stated that many among the English clergy kept their concubines in their houses and expressed his amazement that the archbishop of Canterbury allowed them 'to remain in the filth of their vices' (1 Comp. 3.2.9).[64] In yet another decretal to the bishop of Worcester, the pope commented that 'it is indecent and against reason that those who serve at the altar may be stained by the embraces of women or may wander into taverns, when they ought to be chaste and sober' (1 Comp. 3.2.11).[65] These references to 'fornication' and 'concubines' would have applied to both married clerics and their wives and unmarried ones who were carrying out illicit affairs.

These decretals, although addressed by the pope to English bishops, to a great extent reflect local circumstances. The argument has particularly been made in the case of Roger, bishop of Worcester (1164–1179). Cheney has shown that one of the first of the hundreds of decretals issued by Pope Alexander, the *Inter cetera* (1164), which dealt with clerical marriage and hereditary succession, was almost certainly the result of a request made by the bishop to the pope on the occasion of a short visit at Sens.[66] It was the bishop's wish to prevent the holding of benefices by married clergy in the diocese of Worcester and it was his understanding that the older authorities were not enough to enforce such legislation. The new statements of law which he obtained from Pope Alexander allowed him not only to settle legal uncertainties but also to impose the law upon his unwilling clerics more easily.[67] Although it would be difficult to establish to what extent the vocabulary of impurity found in the papal letters was the bishop's own, its extensive use in both decretals and conciliar legislation guaranteed that it became part and parcel of the problem of clerical marriage.[68]

Even ecclesiastics such as Thomas of Chobham and Gerald of Wales, whom we have seen to support the relaxation of the rules of clerical celibacy, used this kind of language when referring to clerical marriage.[69] Thomas argued that a priest who did not desist from his concubine should not perform mass 'because he kills his soul as long as he celebrates after having been polluted'.[70] Indeed he instructed the laity to avoid requesting the services of such a priest unless it was urgent, and advised them, if possible, to find another 'pure priest' (*mundum sacerdotem*).[71]

Similarly, Gerald of Wales, despite having urged clerics in major orders to observe absolute continence, resigned himself and demanded that

> the priest who lives and rolls about as if in his own pig-pen of impurity show at least this reverence to the sacred altar and to the Eucharist – that he keep his body cleansed from sexual intercourse at least three days and three nights before he presumes to consecrate the body of Christ.[72]

This is similar to the requirement of temporary continence that we find in Byzantium, but with the important difference that here the language of pollution is used: Gerald allowed sexual intercourse for clerics despite its impurity, and only as a concession.

But not everyone in the Anglo-Norman realm was as keen to employ pollution discourse in the case of clerical marriage. Master Honorius and the author of the *Summa Lipsiensis* seem remarkably reluctant to use such vocabulary in their commentaries to Gratian's *Decretum*. This is particularly surprising as the language of impurity is found on numerous occasions in Gratian, who used it himself and quoted canons which used it: when talking about the duty of priests always to be ready to pray (D.31 d.p.c.1) and serve at the altar (D.84 d.a.c.3); when discussing clerics who take concubines (D.34 d.p.c.8), commit fornication (D.81 c.1), cohabit with women (D.81 c.23), or marry (D.28 c.2); when talking about clerical children (D.81 c.6), and so on. When commenting on these distinctions, Master Honorius chose to bring up the issue of impurity in relation to only two of them: D.81 c.6 and D.81 c.23. The former claims that priests who had begotten children should 'become strangers to the ministry that they defiled (*polluerunt*) through an illicit life'.[73] The latter prohibits priests from cohabiting with women and contains two quotations based on Zephaniah 3:4 ('My priests contaminate (*contaminant*) my holy things (*sancta*) and reject the law') and Malachi 1:6–7, where God explains that priests have disappointed his name by 'offering at my altar bread that has been polluted (*pollutos*)'.[74] On both of these distinctions, Master Honorius makes the same brief comment in his glosses of the words 'polluerunt', 'contaminant', and 'pollutos': 'Quantum in ipsis est'.[75] This expression comes from an extract of Augustine's *Contra epistolam Parmeniani* (Book 2, chapter 30), also included in Gratian under C.1 q.1 c.97, which emphasises that no matter whether the priest is polluted himself, the sacraments that he performs are not affected by his impurity; there is no contagion. So here Master Honorius' concern is not so much to emphasise that clerical marriage is bad because it is polluting, but to reassure the reader that the sacraments are safe even in the hands of unworthy priests.

With regard to the above distinctions, the author of the *Summa Lipsiensis* made only one comment concerning purity, under D.81 c.23, repeating the same brief expression as Master Honorius and directing the reader to his comment under a similar distinction (D.49 c.2), where he stated,

> Here it is held that the sacrament is not polluted with respect to itself, even if sometimes it may be found to be polluted. This ought to be understood, as it is said here, with respect to the person who offers it in a polluted way.[76]

A more explicit statement is made under D.31 c.1, where the author of the *Summa Lipsiensis* explains that Pope Gregory the Great extended celibacy to subdeacons 'out of reverence for the sacraments and for the sake of the purity of ministers'.[77] Such statements, however, are relatively rare, given the length of the two decretists' comments and how often the topic of clerical celibacy came up. What concerned these decretists more was how clerics came to be bound to celibacy both as a group and as individuals.[78] As such, a question that recurred time and again was whether the vows of abstinence for clerics in major orders were annexed to the vows of ordination. There was no need to use purity language to discuss such issues. Purity discourse was more the domain of propaganda and a means of enforcing the Gregorian agenda.

The Gregorian reforms

Starting in the eleventh century, efforts to eliminate clerical marriage were intensified. Conciliar legislation and papal decretals strove to extinguish any difference between clerical marriage and fornication, making both equally reprehensible.[79] Already at the Council of Poitiers (1078), canon 8 placed the sons of priests in the same category as those born of fornication (*ex fornicatione nati*).[80] This effectively denied the validity of their mother's marriage to their clerical father. An even starker declaration was made in canon 7 of Lateran II (1139):

> Indeed, that the law of continence and the purity pleasing to God might be propagated among ecclesiastical persons and those in holy orders, we decree that where bishops, priests, deacons, subdeacons, canons regular, monks, and professed lay brothers have presumed to take wives and so transgress this holy precept, they are to be separated from their partners. For we do not deem there to be a marriage which, it is agreed, has been contracted against ecclesiastical law.[81]

For the papacy, then, it was no longer a question of 'clerical marriage' but only of 'clerical concubinage' or 'clerical fornication'.[82] This trickled down progressively. Gratian's *Decretum* did not emphasise the fact that clerical marriage had been declared null and void.[83] The aforementioned canon 7 of Lateran II (1139), which nullified marriage, was included in the second recension of the *Decretum* (C.27 q.1 c.40), but was placed in a rather unexpected section, C.27 q.1, which discussed the vow of chastity taken by widows and virgins.[84] By the time Bartholomew of Exeter was writing in the 1160s, he would treat sexual intercourse in the case of the clergy, both marital and extra-marital, as fornication. Canons concerning clerical marriage are found in his penitential under the heading 'On the fornication of clerics' (*De fornicatione clericorum*).[85] The same can be said about Robert of Flamborough, who under the same title included canons on fornication, adultery, and the marriage of priests.[86]

Not only would a married priest be thought of as a fornicator but also his marriage would be associated with the most serious type of fornication. The word 'fornicatio' had a wider meaning compared to the modern use of the term.[87]

According to one of Gratian's *dicta*, the term applied to any type of intercourse apart from that between legitimate spouses and was used especially in the cases of widows, prostitutes, or concubines.[88] Importantly, fornication could be divided into two types: simple and double. Simple fornication included sexual intercourse outside wedlock when both partners were unmarried. Double fornication took place if at least one of the two partners was married. Augustine's hierarchical scale of sexual offences, which was repeated in Gratian's *Decretum*, ranked simple fornication as the basic offence, followed in order of increasing seriousness by adultery (double fornication), incest, and unnatural sex.[89]

In the case of clerical marriage we cannot talk of simple fornication, as becomes evident in Thomas of Chobham's detailed definition:

> Simple fornication is when a single man knows a single woman in the natural manner. And he should be understood here to be free from the bond of marriage, the bond of consanguinity, the bond of affinity, the bond of orders, the bond of religion, the bond of any vow; because if he had been bound by any of these bonds, he does not commit simple fornication, but adultery or incest.[90]

In the case of the marriage of clerics in major orders, the existence of a vow would immediately exclude simple fornication. Indeed, Thomas of Chobham discussed the issue of clerical continence (*De continentia clericorum*) under the heading of incest (*De incestu ordinatorum*).[91] More specifically, he identified four forms of 'incest', expanding beyond our modern definition. Those arose not only from consanguinity but also from baptismal sponsorship, affinity, and the breaking of continence vows. Clerical marriage entailed the violation of the last.

As we have mentioned, the link between vows of continence and ordination was a hotly debated issue at the time. Some thought that during their ordination to major orders, clerics made an implicit vow of continence; others argued that this vow needed to be made explicitly. Thomas believed that the definitive decision on this topic, binding to continence all Western clerics (including those who did not make an explicit vow), had been taken at Nicaea I (325).[92] Thomas stated that some people in his time questioned the validity of this council.[93] He continued to wonder how it was possible for lawful marriage, which had been constituted by God, to be broken by the decisions of men, but ultimately he accepted that continence had become the law of the Church and as such needed to be obeyed; it was frivolous, he said, to argue against it.[94] Clerical marriage had become incest – albeit due to a man-made law.

According to Thomas' definition, the marriage of clerics could also be considered incestuous when it violated the rules of spiritual affinity. In fact, in that case priests were doubly incestuous (*duplicem incestum*) by not only breaking their vows of continence but also by doing so with one of their spiritual daughters. Although Thomas lamented that there were few people at the time who understood the difference (*quem pauci intelligunt*), this topic had been brought up in Gratian's *Decretum* as well as the writings of Bartholomew of Exeter and Robert of Flamborough.[95] Different authors could have slightly different ideas about which women were a priest's spiritual daughters, but the list certainly included women who had been received in baptism or penance.

Marriage, then, in the case of clerics in major orders was no better than illicit affairs and could sometimes be punished more harshly. In the case of public marriages, Thomas quoted a canon from the Eleventh Council of Toledo (675) which stated that the children of clerics (from bishops to subdeacons) ought to be reduced to servitude at the church where their father served. This canon applied specifically to children who had contracted matrimony *in facie ecclesie*, not to their children from concubines.[96] Marriage *in facie ecclesie* could refer to a church service, but it also had the wider significance of a public wedding in the presence of the local community or 'in the eyes of the Church'.[97] It seems that despite the prohibitions, some priests preferred this more official way of marrying, probably in an effort to garner more legitimacy for their families. Thomas reprimanded them for thinking that they could get married just like everyone else (*sicut alii homines*).[98] The problem was that such public marriages caused scandal. Elsewhere he recommended that clerics in minor orders contract secret marriages instead of keeping concubines. Even if the same clerics were later to accede to sacred orders, Thomas asserted that 'it was less of a sin for them to use their wife than to fornicate with someone else, if they could not contain themselves altogether.'[99] Although for Thomas clerical marriage still retained some of its religious value and was preferable to concubinage as long as it remained secret, it is clear that by the end of the twelfth century it was considered worse than many illicit affairs.

Explaining the difference

As we have seen, in both England and Byzantium there were avoidance rules about approaching the sacred which disqualified clerics in major orders from performing the Eucharist at least for a period of time. In the case of nocturnal emissions this enforced abstinence was temporary; it could not have been otherwise, as no man is immune to wet dreams or able to control them.[100] In the case of clerical marriage, meanwhile, it was possible to demand absolute abstinence from sexual intercourse and that is what was required in the West. In Byzantium, on the other hand, the rule in this case too was that only temporary abstinence was necessary. This difference was partly due to the fact that since about the fifth century Western clerics in major orders had been expected to perform the Eucharist on a daily basis, while in Byzantium they celebrated following prescribed shifts.[101] An obligation of daily service would automatically have turned temporary abstinence into absolute abstinence. Nonetheless, Byzantine clerics are known to have celebrated daily by uncanonically serving more than one church at the time, and as such were bound to have transgressed their rules of clerical continence, just as Western clerics were transgressing their own rules of clerical celibacy.

The first question that we can ask, then, is why these legal transgressions were treated differently by Western and Eastern ecclesiastics. In one case, they led to loud and clear messages of condemnation and in the other to much more muted and infrequent complaints. Although in both West and East there was a discrepancy between the rules of clerical continence and its practice, it was only in the West that this discrepancy had reached a critical point in this period, meaning that change was overdue.[102] One could argue that this was due to the existence of a more 'reformist' attitude towards the law in the West and a more 'conservative' attitude in Byzantium. Certainly such general arguments have been made, and more comparative study of the laws in East and West would be useful to properly substantiate them.[103] But in the particular case of clerical marriage, we need to consider that the discrepancy in the West was greater than that found in the East. It was easier to spot that a cleric who was meant to be observing absolute continence was not doing so: he would only need to have a child. With temporary abstinence, however, sexual habits were harder to police. As Balsamon put it, the act was not manifest and could not be proven.[104] Bishops of course were in a more similar situation, as in both East and West they were expected to observe complete abstinence after ordination to the episcopate. Still, I believe that the discrepancy would have been smaller in Byzantium. First, clerics could form legitimate families throughout their years as subdeacons, deacons, and priests.[105] As such, there might have been fewer illegitimate episcopal children. But also the image of the bishop still living with his wife (something that in principle was not allowed) might have been less offensive in Byzantium, where the laity was used to seeing their priests, deacons, and subdeacons doing exactly this. Nonetheless, some discrepancy did exist, and in fact we do see a small 'reform' on this topic in this period. As we have said, Isaac II Angelos (1186/7) decried the fact that some bishops continued to live with their wives and asked that the latter not simply live in a monastery but fully embrace monastic life.[106] It was partly, then, this greater discrepancy between law and practice in the West that eventually brought about the need for change and concomitantly the need for purity language as a means of enforcing that change.

Therefore, one reason behind the different language used in England and Byzantium was the topicality of clerical marriage in the twelfth-century West. The Gregorian reforms had raised awareness about the marital status of the clergy and encouraged a language that would help enforce the neglected rules, fixing the glaring discrepancy between law and practice. Many of the legal sources we have mentioned from the West have the avowed purpose of doing so. This is how we can understand the numerous examples of pollution discourse used to describe the relationships of clerics in major orders with women, both in conciliar legislation and in decretals. Such language, which had a long history of associations with clerical marriage in the West, was redeployed in the eleventh and twelfth centuries by both proponents and opponents of celibacy in order to describe, analyse, and understand clerical marriage.[107] Even those who wished to relax the rules of celibacy expressed a negative view of clerical sexuality and its concomitant impurity. Yet not everyone was equally keen to emphasise pollution discourse. Master Honorius and the author of the *Summa Lipsiensis* upheld the rules of clerical celibacy but abstained from using expressions emphasising the impurity brought about by clerical sex. Instead they laid greater emphasis on the lack of contagion: the priest might be polluted, but the sacrament is safe. Unlike the Gregorian reformers who were eager to enforce the law, the two decretists were more interested in its historical development as well as its more practical implications for the property of the Church or the family of the priest.

The Byzantine canonical commentators, on the other hand, dealt with clerical marriage in a more incidental way. They commented on it as they came across it, but did not produce separate treatises on this topic, as in the case of nocturnal emissions. Even in the comments they do make, we do not find a particularly high level of introspection: the reasons behind episcopal celibacy given by the canonists do not go much further than a repetition of what was already said at the Council in Trullo (691/2). Similarly, they make little reference to the practice of clerical celibacy in the Western Church.[108] Instead, a stable compromise had been reached and there was no great need to question the *status quo*, despite the occasional neglect of the laws.[109]

The second question we can ask is how dealing with legal transgressions fitted more generally within contemporary societal hierarchies and the policing of boundaries between lay and clerical. Paul Beaudette explained the use of impurity language in the fourth and eleventh centuries as a result of boundary anxiety about the place of the Western Church 'in the world'. In the fourth century, the closer ties between lay and religious had come as a result of the gradual toleration shown to Christians through measures such as the Edict of Milan (313); in the eleventh they had been formed by the involvement of Church officials and ecclesiastical institutions in the economic and political affairs of secular government and society.[110] As a reaction against these ties, there emerged a drive to firmly separate clerics from laymen. In the eleventh century, Cardinal Humbert expressed the principle eloquently: 'Just as within the walls of the basilicas clerics ought to be separated and differentiated from the laity through their place and duties, so also outside those walls [they ought to be separated and differentiated] through their activities.'[111]

Enforcing clerical celibacy was one way of increasing this separation between clergy and laity: thanks to their abstinence clerics were meant to be purer than and thus superior to laymen. As Christopher Brooke put it, there was a growing sense that 'the priesthood and all who stood by the altar at the mass were a race apart.'[112] They were meant to form a separate group altogether, one that was already distinguished in the West through the clergy's Latinity and superior education as well as their liturgical duties, their ecclesiastical dress, and, in the twelfth century, their clerical exemptions. Henrietta Leyser has called this a 're-ordered world' that turned out to be 'made up not, as had once been thought, of three groups, of clerks, monks and laymen, but only of two: the clerical and the lay'.[113]

In the twelfth century this process had been long in the making and had created certain expectations that needed to be policed and maintained. This further increased the feeling of discrepancy between law and practice in the case of clerical celibacy. When transgressions occurred, it was not one isolated rule that was not maintained, but the whole status of the priest as a man of the Church rather than a man of the world was at stake.

In Byzantium, on the other hand, there was less of a drive to divide clerics firmly from laymen and as such less of an imperative to present clerics as more pure. That is not to say, of course, that Byzantine clerics and laymen were not clearly distinct and distinguishable. Clerics were visually different from the laity, and even on the topic of clerical marriage itself they were legally differentiated in terms, for example, of what kind of women they could marry and whether they were allowed to contract second marriages. But the difference more generally does not seem to have been as great as in the West, nor was there any ambition to make it so.

In twelfth-century Byzantium there were developments in both directions, some separating clerics from laymen and others bringing the two groups closer together. Inside the church, we can see the beginnings of a drive for greater division between clergy and laity through the progressive addition of curtains and eventually the iconostasis, a wall of icons that obstructed the view of the laity inside the sanctuary, as well as the introduction of intinction specifically for the laity – that is, the reception of the two elements of the Eucharist together on a spoon.[114] Yet, Balsamon can still complain that the faithful of the church of Christ in Chalke and those of the church of the Hodegetria followed a peculiar custom which allowed the laity to enter the sanctuary.[115] What is more, some among the laity claimed for themselves the status of preacher (*didaskalos*), interpreting and teaching divine doctrines, a role that was canonically reserved for bishops and for those authorised by them as a gift of the Holy Spirit.[116] This was facilitated by the fact that education could not be used in Byzantium to firmly divide ecclesiastics from laymen. Similar confusion between lay and clerical could be witnessed in judicial affairs, as Balsamon again laments that ecclesiastics would resort to civil courts, abandoning ecclesiastical ones, if they thought it to their best advantage.[117]

Such intrusions of the lay into the clerical and defections of clergy from the clerical to the lay sphere led to some attempts to separate the two, with the notable example of readers, whose position between laity and clergy was debated in the twelfth century and ultimately claimed in favour of the Church through legislation by Patriarch Michael Anchialos.[118] On other occasions, however, Byzantine ecclesiastics were eager to emphasise the commonality between clerics and laymen. When it came to entertainment, for example, both Zonaras and Balsamon sought to minimise any distinctions between laity and clergy found in the original canons, even suggesting that going to the hippodrome could be an acceptable pastime for those clerics who could not abstain from all earthly pleasures.[119] Similarly, as we have seen, in the case of nocturnal emissions the distinction between clerics and laymen was not especially emphasised. It was accepted that clerics were human too and as such prone to weakness.

It is within this context that we can understand the twelfth-century Byzantine comments on the rules of temporary abstinence. As we have seen, they were not linked to fears of pollution; instead, the canonists emphasised the purity of marriage and marital sex. In the case of subdeacons, the commentaries offered no clear answer as to the reasons why they were expected to abstain. The canonists simply repeated the formulas they found in the original canons. It was probably more of a question of respecting the law as it had been established in Late Antiquity. Similarly in the case of bishops, celibacy was not justified on grounds of ritual purity; rather, the need to maintain a good reputation and lead by example was emphatically put forward both by the canonists and by the emperor in the twelfth century. What is more, transgression of the rules by both bishops and priests did not induce fears of pollution: although those who did transgress were sinners, they were not described using the language of moral pollution. Such language could have been used to define firmer boundaries between bishops and the laity or bishops and the rest of the clergy. But that was not the case here. The imperative provided by the Gregorian reforms in the West, to create a separate and superior caste for the clergy, was lacking in Byzantium.

Overall, we have seen that impurity language was never used in relation to clerical marriage in the twelfth-century Byzantine canonical commentaries, as it was in the West. On one hand, there is an obvious reason for this; in the twelfth century clerical marriage became not only illicit but also invalid in the West, while it was still perfectly lawful in Byzantium. Yet this does not account for a more deeply entrenched tendency on the Byzantine side to see sexual intercourse, both lay and clerical, as a source of distraction and to deny its potential impurity. On the other hand, the language of pollution had long been used in the West to talk about clerical marriage. Therefore, to some extent the difference in language had deep roots that lie in Late Antiquity and beyond the scope of this book. But such language can also be explained within the context of the eleventh and twelfth centuries, by going beyond the simple difference in legislation and looking at something the two societies shared: both needed to deal with transgressions of their own rules of clerical continence. First, it is worth emphasising that both Western and Eastern canon lawyers, perhaps unsurprisingly, highlighted the importance of the laws as they found them: clerical celibacy and clerical marriage were good because they were law. Nonetheless, when it came to their transgression, reactions were very different. This was partly because in Byzantium these transgressions created less of a discrepancy between law and practice than in the West: (1) Byzantine clerics had more opportunities to 'play by the rules' and combine their ecclesiastical careers with a family; (2) when they ignored the rules this was more difficult to prove; (3) and in a sense it was perhaps also more acceptable, because of the more positive image of the clerical wife in society and the smaller distance between what was expected of clerics and what was expected of all Christians.

Notes

1 Cunningham, 'Clergy, Monks, and Laity', 529. Cf. 'Marital relations themselves came to be considered polluting. Such attitudes entered into legislation at the Council of Trullo in 692 with the requirement of continence on the part of clergy the day before they were to celebrate the liturgy'; in D. Casey, 'The Spiritual Valency of Gender in Byzantine Society', in *Questions of Gender in Byzantine Society*, eds. B. Neil and L. Garland (London, 2013), 167–81, at 178.

2 *Syntagma* 3.302: 'πάντες οἱ τὰ ἱερὰ ψηλαφῶντες'.

3 *Syntagma* 2.334: 'τοὺς ὑποδιακόνους, τοὺς τὰ ἱερὰ μυστήρια ψηλαφῶντας'.

4 *Syntagma* 3.370: 'τοὺς ὑποδιακόνους τοὺς τὰ ἱερὰ μυστήρια ψηλαφῶντας'.
5 *Syntagma* 3.372: 'Οἱ τὰ ἱερὰ χειριζόμενοι καὶ ἀπὸ τῶν συμβίων κατὰ τοὺς ἰδίους ὅρους ἐγκρατευέσθωσαν. Χρὴ τοὺς τῷ θυσιαστηρίῳ προσεδρεύοντας ἐν τῷ καιρῷ τῆς τῶν ἁγίων μεταχειρίσεως καὶ ἀπὸ τῶν ἰδίων γυναικῶν ἐγκρατεύεσθαι, ὅπως δυνηθῶσιν ὃ παρὰ τοῦ Θεοῦ αἰτοῦσιν ἁπλῶς ἐπιτυχεῖν.'
6 *Syntagma* 3.301.
7 *Syntagma* 3.371. For canon 21 of Laodicea, see *Syntagma* 3.190. For more on the *diakonikon*, see Marinis, *Architecture and Ritual*, 35.
8 *Syntagma* 3.371: 'Σημείωσαι οὖν ὅτι καὶ οἱ ὑποδιάκονοι τὰ ἅγια μεταχειρίζονται· καὶ μὴ εἴπῃς ἐναντιοῦσθαι τὸν παρόντα κανόνα τῷ κα κανόνι τῆς ἐν Λαοδικείᾳ συνόδου, διοριζομένῳ τοὺς ὑποδιακόνους μὴ ἔχειν χώραν ἐν τῷ διακονικῷ, μηδὲ ἅπτεσθαι τῶν ἱερῶν, ἀλλ' εἰπέ, ὅτι ἕτερόν ἐστι τὸ ψηλαφᾶν, καὶ ἕτερον τὸ ἅπτεσθαι· τὸ μὲν γὰρ ψηλαφᾶν, ἤγουν τὸ μετακινεῖν ἀπὸ τόπου εἰς τόπον, ὑπηρεσία ἐστί, καὶ οὐδὲ ὁ ὑποδιάκονος τοῦτο ποιεῖν ἐμποδισθήσεται· τὸ δὲ ἅπτεσθαι, μόνοις ἐνεδόθη τοῖς ἱερεῦσι καὶ τοῖς ὑπουργοῦσιν ἐν τῇ θυσίᾳ, ἤγουν τοῖς διακόνοις. Ὀφείλουσι δὲ κατὰ τὸν παρόντα κανόνα οὐ μόνον οἱ ἁπτόμενοι τῶν ἱερῶν ἀλλὰ καὶ οἱ ψηλαφῶντες αὐτὰ ἐγκρατεύεσθαι κατὰ τὸν καιρὸν τῆς τούτων ἐφημερίας.'
9 *Syntagma* 3.483: 'Τοὺς δὲ λοιποὺς κληρικοὺς ταῦτα οὐκ ἀπαιτοῦσιν, ὡς μὴ ψηλαφῶντας τὰ ἅγια'. The canon itself had not mentioned subdeacons this time. See also *Syntagma* 3.302.
10 Troianos, 'Le célibat épiscopal', 190–1.
11 *Syntagma* 2.330: 'Καὶ τοῦτο δὲ εἰς γνῶσιν ἡμετέραν ἦλθεν, ὡς ἔν τε τῇ Ἀφρικῇ καὶ Λιβύῃ, καὶ ἑτέροις τόποις, οἱ τῶν ἐκεῖσε θεοφιλέστατοι πρόεδροι, συνοικεῖν ταῖς ἰδίαις γαμεταῖς, καὶ μετὰ τὴν ἐπ' αὐτοῖς προελθοῦσαν χειροτονίαν, οὐ παραιτοῦνται, πρόσκομμα τοῖς λαοῖς τιθέντες, καὶ σκάνδαλον. Πολλῆς οὖν ἡμῖν σπουδῆς οὔσης, τοῦ πάντα πρὸς ὠφέλειαν τῶν ὑπὸ χεῖρα ποιμνίων διαπράττεσθαι, ἔδοξεν, ὥστε μηδαμῶς τὸ τοιοῦτον ἀπὸ τοῦ νῦν γίνεσθαι.' In the Late Antique West, on the other hand, married clerics were expected to continue to live with their wives, while observing absolute sexual continence. This proved difficult to enforce and, especially in the case of bishops, some Western canons insisted that the presence of other clerics in the episcopal house was necessary to supervise the couple's relations. See Hunter, 'Married Clergy in Eastern and Western Christianity', 133–4.
12 *Syntagma* 2.330–1: 'Τοῦτο δέ φαμεν οὐκ ἐπ' ἀθετήσει ἢ ἀνατροπῇ τῶν ἀποστολικῶς νενομοθετημένων, ἀλλὰ τῆς σωτηρίας καὶ τῆς ἐπὶ τὸ κρεῖττον προκοπῆς τῶν λαῶν προμηθούμενοι, καὶ τοῦ μὴ δοῦναι μῶμόν τινα κατὰ τῆς ἱερατικῆς καταστάσεως.'
13 In the Old Testament the word μῶμος expressed the presence of physical defect. For example, see Leviticus 3:1 in A. Rahlfs (ed.), *Septuaginta*, vol. I (Stuttgart, 1935, 9th edn.), 160: 'Ἐὰν δὲ θυσία σωτηρίου τὸ δῶρον αὐτοῦ τῷ κυρίῳ, ἐὰν μὲν ἐκ τῶν βοῶν αὐτοῦ προσαγάγῃ, ἐάν τε ἄρσεν ἐάν τε θῆλυ, ἄμωμον προσάξει αὐτὸ ἐναντίον κυρίου'. The canonists understood this obligation to be 'whole' as part of the Judaic rules of purity which were rejected with the coming of Jesus. This can be seen in Zonaras' commentary discussing canon 77 of the Apostles on physical defects in the case of clerics. Zonaras used the word μῶμος instead of the word λώβη found in the original canon, harking back to Leviticus 3:1. He wrote, 'The decree given by Moses to the Israelites ordered that only those who are whole in body, and not anyone who might have a blemish (μῶμον), are to become priests.' *Syntagma* 2.100: 'Ἡ μὲν διὰ Μωσέως δοθεῖσα τοῖς Ἰσραηλίταις διαταγή, ὁλοκλήρους τὸ σῶμα, καὶ μή τινα μῶμον ἔχοντας, τοὺς παρ' ἐκείνοις ἱερωμένους εἶναι ἀπήτει, καὶ οὐδεὶς λελωβημένος κατά τι μέρος τοῦ σώματος εἰς ἱερωσύνην προσίετο'. Although Zonaras went on to deny that any impurity existed any longer with regard to bodily defects, his vocabulary was suggestive: within the context of physical deformity, the word μῶμος had retained its old-testamentary connotations of impurity.
14 *Syntagma* 2.331–2: 'ὅτι οἱ μὲν θεῖοι Ἀπόστολοι, ἀρχὴν ἐχούσης τῆς πίστεως, καὶ τοῦ θείου κηρύγματος οὔπω πλατυνθέντος, συγκαταβατικώτερον διετίθεντο πρὸς

τοὺς τῇ πίστει προσερχομένους, καὶ οὐ πάντῃ ἀπῄτουν τὸ τέλειον, ἀλλ' ἐνεδίδουν τῇ ἀσθενείᾳ αὐτῶν, καὶ τοῖς ἔθεσι τοῖς ἐθνικοῖς καὶ ἰουδαϊκοῖς. Οἵ τε γὰρ τῶν Ἰουδαίων ἀρχιερεῖς γυναιξὶ συνοικεῖν συγκεχωρημένον εἶχον ἐκ τοῦ νόμου, καὶ τοῖς Ἑλλήνων ἀρχιερεῦσιν ὁ γάμος ἀκώλυτος ἦν. Ἄρτι δὲ τοῦ κηρύγματος πλατυνθέντος, καὶ εἰς κρείττονα κατάστασιν καὶ τάξιν τῶν πιστῶν ἐληλυθότων, καὶ τῆς εὐαγγελικῆς πολιτείας ἐπιδιδούσης, χρῆναί φασι καὶ τοὺς ἀρχιερεῖς τὸν οἰκεῖον βίον πρὸς ἀκριβῆ σωφροσύνην ἀπευθύνειν, ὡς μὴ μόνον ἀλλοτρίων ἀπέχεσθαι γυναικῶν, ἀλλὰ καὶ τῶν πρότερον αὐτοῖς συνευναζομένων· καὶ μὴ μόνον εὐνῆς αὐταῖς μὴ κοινωνεῖν, μηδὲ μίξεως, ἀλλὰ μηδὲ συνοικεῖν αὐταῖς καὶ ἐν τῇ αὐτῇ κατοικίᾳ συζῆν. Οἱ μὲν γὰρ ἴσως καὶ οὕτω σωφρόνως ζήσονται, ἄλλοις δὲ πρόσκομμα καὶ σκάνδαλον ἔσονται.'

15 Aristenos too emphasises the need for bishops to maintain high standards in order to be an example to the heterodox, quoting extensively from 1 Corinthians 10:32–3 and 11:1. See *Syntagma* 3.333.

16 *Syntagma* 2.370. On the 'barbarian' churches, see J. Herrin, '"Femina Byzantina": The Council in Trullo on Women', *DOP*, 46 (1992), 97–105, at 101; Pitsakis, 'Clergé marié et célibat', 285. Similarly, canon 18 of Nicaea II (787) prohibited both bishops and abbots from having female slaves or servants in the episcopal palace, the monastery, or their suburban estates during their visits there. See *Syntagma* 2.628–30.

17 *Syntagma* 5.321–3; *JGR* 1.435–6.

18 Angold, *Church and Society*, 124–5.

19 *Syntagma* 5.321: 'ὡς γὰρ ὄμφακες ὀδοῦσι καὶ καπνὸς ὄμμασι βλαβερὸν οὕτω καὶ παρανομία τοῖς χρωμένοις αὐτῇ'.

20 *Syntagma* 5.321. The same vocabulary is used to talk about the marriage of clerics in the prologue of the Nomokanon in *Syntagma* 1.6: 'ὧν ἓν καθέστηκε τὸ παρ' αὐτῶν διορισθέν, ὥστε τοὺς ὑπὲρ τοὺς ἀναγνώστας ἐν κλήρῳ καταλεγομένους ἐκ τρόπου παντὸς τῶν πρὸ τῆς τοιαύτης χειροτονίας συζευχθεισῶν αὐτοῖς ἀπέχεσθαι νομίμων γαμετῶν· οὐ γὰρ ἐξ ἐπιτάγματος ἀλλ' αὐθαιρέτῳ γνώμῃ τῶν τοιούτων προσώπων ἕκαστον ἢ τὴν ἀποχὴν διὰ φιλόθεον ἄσκησιν ἢ τὴν ἀμίαντον συνάφειαν διὰ τὸ τοῦ γάμου τίμιον ἐν ἡμῖν ἐπιτηδεύει, μῶμον οὐδένα δίκαιον ἐκ τοῦ γινομένου παντελῶς ὑφιστάμενον'.

21 *Syntagma* 5.322–3.

22 *Syntagma* 2.67: 'Εἴ τις ἐπίσκοπος ἢ πρεσβύτερος ἢ διάκονος, ἢ ὅλως τοῦ καταλόγου τοῦ ἱερατικοῦ, γάμου καὶ κρεῶν καὶ οἴνου οὐ δι' ἄσκησιν ἀλλὰ διὰ βδελυρίαν ἀπέχηται, ἐπιλαθόμενος ὅτι πάντα καλὰ λίαν, καὶ ὅτι ἄρσεν καὶ θῆλυ ἐποίησεν ὁ θεὸς τὸν ἄνθρωπον, ἀλλὰ βλασφημῶν διαβάλλῃ τὴν δημιουργίαν, ἢ διορθούσθω ἢ καθαιρείσθω καὶ τῆς ἐκκλησίας ἀποβαλλέσθω.'

23 *Syntagma* 2.67–8.

24 *Syntagma* 2.7: 'ἔοικε γὰρ εἰς διαβολὴν εἶναι τοῦτο τοῦ γάμου, ὡς ἀκαθαρσίαν τῆς μίξεως ἐμποιούσης· τὸν δὲ τίμιον ἡ γραφὴ λέγει, καὶ τὴν κοίτην ἀμίαντον.'

25 *Syntagma* 2.7: 'Μέμνηται δὲ ὁ κανὼν καὶ ἐπισκόπων ἐχόντων γυναῖκας, ὅτι τότε ἀκώλυτον εἶχον καὶ οἱ ἐπίσκοποι τὴν πρὸς γυναῖκας νόμιμον συζυγίαν· ἡ γὰρ ἐν τῷ Τρούλλῳ σύνοδος, ἡ λεγομένη ἕκτη, τοῦτο ἐκώλυσεν ἐν δωδεκάτῳ αὐτῆς κανόνι.'

26 See Zonaras' comment in *Syntagma* 2.7: 'Τὸ παλαιὸν ἐξῆν διαζεύγνυσθαι τοὺς συνοικοῦντας, καὶ χωρὶς αἰτίας, ὁπηνίκα ἐβούλοντο'. Balsamon finishes his commentary with a list of the acceptable reasons for divorce according to Justinian's legislation. He notes that during the time between Justinian and the Council in Trullo bishops too had to abide by this law. In his day, they were no longer allowed to keep their wife after their ordination. *Syntagma* 2.8.

27 Balsamon tells us that in the past (Nicaea II, 787) clerics in rural areas had been allowed to serve several churches at a time due to lack of personnel. In Balsamon's time this was no longer necessary, because tax exemptions had incited many clerics to move from the capital to the provinces. See *Syntagma* 2.620–1.

28 *Syntagma* 2.621.

29 *Syntagma* 3.484.

30 *Syntagma* 3.483: 'ἔδοξέ μοι καινὸν τὸ καθαιρεῖσθαί τινα ἐκ τούτων μὴ ἐγκρατευόμενον, διὰ τὸ ἄδηλον καὶ ἀναπόδεικτον· τίς γὰρ οἶδεν ὅτε καὶ ὅπως ἐγκρατεύεται, εἴτε καὶ μή, ὁ ἱερωμένος ἐκ τῆς ὁμοζύγου αὐτοῦ, ὥστε καθαιρεῖσθαι τὸν μὴ ἐγκρατευόμενον'.

31 *Syntagma* 3.484: ''Όπως γοῦν σήμερον οἱ πλείους τῶν ἱερέων καὶ τῶν διακόνων, ἑβδομαδικῶς μὴ ἱερουργοῦντες ἀλλὰ καθ' ἑκάστην ἢ ὡς σουπερεύοντες ἢ ὡς ἐν εὐκτηρίῳ δουλεύοντες, οὐ κολάζονται, ἀγνοῶ, καὶ ζητῶ τὴν διόρθωσιν.'

32 *Syntagma* 2.336: 'Οἱ γοῦν διόλου καὶ σχεδὸν καθ' ἑκάστην λειτουργοῦντες καὶ ψηλαφῶντες τὰ ἅγια, τί ἀπολογήσονται;'

33 This was an issue that was also discussed in the West, but it was of secondary importance compared to purity. For example, Thomas of Chobham put forward the link between continence and intercession: spouses should abstain 'so that what is desired may be more easily obtained', and later on he added, 'Just as a wise man says: he who wallows in lasciviousness venerates Lawrence on the grill in vain; he who practises the delights of the sexual embrace celebrates the feast of the hanging of Peter and Andrew on the cross in vain' ('ut facilius possit impetrari quod optatur'; 'Sicut dicit quidam sapiens: frustra ueneratur Laurentius in craticula qui uolutatur in lasciuia; frustra celebrat festum Petri et Andree pendentis in cruce qui delicias exercet in amplexu'). Broomfield, *Thomae de Chobham*, 364–5.

34 *Syntagma* 2.334: 'ὅπως δυνηθῶσιν ὃ παρὰ τοῦ Θεοῦ ἁπλῶς αἰτοῦσιν ἐπιτυχεῖν'.

35 *Syntagma* 3.301. For Aristenos, see *Syntagma* 2.337; 3.372; for Zonaras, see *Syntagma* 2.335; 3.301.

36 *Syntagma* 3.301–2: 'ὅπως, φησί, δυνηθῶσιν ἐπιτυχεῖν ἃ ἁπλῶς αἰτοῦσι παρὰ Θεοῦ, ἤγουν ἀδιστάκτως καὶ μὴ διακρινόμενοι. Οὗτοι γάρ εἰσι μεσῖται Θεοῦ καὶ ἀνθρώπων, ἐξιλεούμενοι τὸ θεῖον τοῖς ἄλλοις καὶ σωτηρίαν αἰτούμενοι τοῖς πιστοῖς καὶ εἰρήνην τῷ κόσμῳ. Εἰ οὖν πᾶσαν, φησί, μετέρχονται ἀρετὴν καὶ οὕτω παρρησιάζονται πρὸς Θεὸν, τυγχάνοιεν ἂν καὶ τῶν αἰτήσεων· ὡς εἴγε μὴ παρρησίαν ἔχοιεν, πῶς ἄν ὑπὲρ ἄλλων πρεσβεύσωνται;'

37 *Syntagma* 3.302: 'Ὁ κανὼν οὗτος, πάσης ἀρετῆς ἐργάτας εἶναι θέλει τοὺς τὰ ἅγια μυστήρια μεταχειριζομένους, [. . .], καὶ ἐγκρατεῖς εἶναι μὴ διὰ μόνης σωφροσύνης, ἀλλὰ καὶ διὰ παντὸς ἔργου καὶ πράγματος. Οὕτω γάρ, φησιν, εἰσακουσθήσονται παρὰ τοῦ Θεοῦ εὐχόμενοι ὑπὲρ τοῦ λαοῦ'.

38 See John Chrysostom's *Homilies on the Epistles of Paul to the Corinthians*, homily 19: ''Ινα σχολάζητε, ὡς ἀσχολίαν ἐμποιοῦντος τοῦ πράγματος, ἀλλ' οὐκ ἀκαθαρσίαν.' PG 61.153; M. Geerard, *Clavis Patrum Graecorum*, vol. II (Turnhout, 1974), 525.

39 Theophylact on Paul's 1 Corinthians in PG 124.640–1: 'Ὡς ἂν οὖν ἡ εὐχὴ σπουδαιοτέρα γένηται, ἀπέχεσθε, φησίν, ἀλλήλων, ὡς τῆς μίξεως ἀσχολίαν, οὐκ ἀκαθαρσίαν, ποιούσης.' See also his comment on Hebrews 13: 4 in PG 125.389–90: 'Τίμιος ὁ γάμος ἐν πᾶσι καὶ ἡ κοίτη ἀμίαντος'.

40 Euthymios was more famous for his *Panoplia dogmatike*, a refutation of heresies which he wrote at the invitation of Alexios I. On Euthymios as a biblical commentator, see Fr. M. Constas, 'The Reception of Saint Paul and Pauline Theology in the Byzantine Period', in *The New Testament in Byzantium*, eds. D. Krueger and R.S. Nelson (Washington, DC, 2016), 147–76.

41 N. Kalogeras (ed.), *Εὐθυμίου τοῦ Ζιγαβηνοῦ Ἑρμηνεία εἰς τὰς ΙΔ' Ἐπιστολὰς τοῦ Ἀποστόλου Παύλου καὶ εἰς τὰς Ζ' Καθολικάς* (Athens, 1887), 247: 'Εἰ γὰρ καὶ τίμιος ὁ γάμος, [. . .], οἷα θεόθεν ἐπιτετραμμένος καὶ ἔννομος, ἀλλ' οὐ μολύνει μέν, ἀσχολίαν δὲ ἐμποιεῖ τοῖς συνουσιάζουσι, τῆς ἐντεῦθεν ἡδονῆς διαχεούσης τὸν νοῦν καὶ χαυνούσης τὴν ψυχήν. Δεῖ δὲ ἡμᾶς ἐν τοῖς εἰρημένοις καιροῖς συντεταγμένους εἶναι καὶ προσέχοντας καὶ πάσης σωματικῆς ἀνέσεως ἀπεσχοινισμένους.'

42 *Syntagma* 2.7.

43 *Syntagma* 4.10: 'δεῖ γὰρ τοὺς νηστεύοντας ἡδυπαθείας πάσης ἀπέχεσθαι, ὅτι χαυνοῦν τὴν ψυχὴν καὶ συγχέειν τὸν λογισμὸν αἱ τῶν ἡδονῶν ἀπολαύσεις πεφύκασιν.'

44 According to Katsaros, Patriarch Mark of Alexandria addressed a set of questions to a Church council in Constantinople (1195). The initial answers were written by

Kastamonites and read aloud at the synod, but they were not deemed satisfactory and their rewriting was taken up by Balsamon. It was Balsamon's version that was sanctioned by the Church and given to Mark. Nonetheless, Kastamonites' answer gives us an insight into the attitudes towards marital sex of a twelfth-century bishop. See V. Grumel, 'Les réponses canoniques à Marc d'Alexandrie. Leur caractère officiel. Leur double rédaction', *Échos d'Orient*, 38 (1939), 321–33; Stevens, *De Theodoro Balsamone*, 112–9; V. Katsaros, *Ἰωάννης Κασταμονίτης. Συμβολὴ στὴ μελέτη τοῦ βίου, τοῦ ἔργου καὶ τῆς ἐποχῆς του* (Thessalonike, 1988), 349–400.

45 Katsaros, *Ἰωάννης Κασταμονίτης*, 366–7: 'Διδάσκει μὲν ὁ ἀπόστολος τὸ μὴ ἀποστερεῖν ἀλλήλους τῆς συνουσίας καὶ τὸ ἀποστεῖν, ἐκεῖνο διὰ τὸ τῆς κοινωνίας ἀμίαντον, τοῦτο διὰ τὸ σχολάσαι τῇ προσευχῇ'. We also have Balsamon's answer to the same question. He too emphasised the role of abstinence in gaining παρρησία for lay couples, asking, 'But if people do not observe continence during these days, how and when will they by common consent (as the great apostle has said) devote themselves to entreating God and praying?' See *Syntagma* 4.485: 'Οἱ γοῦν μὴ εἰς ταύτας τὰς ἡμέρας ἐγκρατευόμενοι, πῶς καὶ πότε κατὰ κοινὴν συμφωνίαν σχολάσουσιν (ὡς ὁ μέγας Ἀπόστολος εἴρηκε) τῇ πρὸς Θεὸν ἐντεύξει καὶ προσευχῇ;'

46 *Syntagma* 2.460–2; 3.466–7. It was also a common motif in Late Antique and Byzantine hagiography to see family members as a distraction, and saints are often found rejoicing at their children's deaths. For example, see the Life of Andronikos and Athanasia (c. sixth century) and the Life of Theodora (ninth century) in A.P. Alwis, *Celibate Marriage in Late Antique and Byzantine Hagiography* (London, 2011), 86–8. See also A.-M. Talbot (trans.), 'Life of St. Theodora of Thessalonike', in *Holy Women of Byzantium: Ten Saints' Lives in English Translation* (Washington, DC, 1996), 159–237, at 189.

47 On Glykas, see E.-S. Kiapidou, 'On the Epistolography of Michael Glykas', *Βυζαντινά Σύμμεικτα*, 21 (2011), 169–93, at 169–70; Magdalino, *Manuel*, 374–6.

48 Eustratiades, *Μιχαὴλ τοῦ Γλυκᾶ*, 2.178–9: 'Ἵνα καὶ γὰρ μὴ τῷ Θεῷ μάλιστα προσκρούσωμεν διὰ τῆς οὕτω ματαίας εὐχῆς ἡνίκα μᾶλλον αὐτὸν ἵλεων ἡμῖν ἀποκαταστῆσαι σπουδάζωμεν, κελεύει τηνικαῦτα κοίτης ἀπαλλάχθαι παντάπασιν ἔν γε τῷ τῆς προσευχῆς καὶ τῆς νηστείας καιρῷ. Τίνος ἕνεκεν; ὥστε μὴ τοὺς τῆς διανοίας ὀφθαλμοὺς διὰ τῆς πρὸς τὴν γυναῖκα συμπαθείας ἔνθεν κἀκεῖθεν ἀναρριπίζεσθαι, κἀντεῦθεν ἀπρόσδεκτον τὴν προσευχὴν ἀπεργάζεσθαι. Εἰ γὰρ θυμὸν ἀνθρώπου καταλλάξαι βουλόμενοι παντοίᾳ σπουδῇ καὶ συστολῇ πρὸς αὐτὸ τοῦτο κεχρήμεθα, τί ποιῆσαι λοιπὸν ὀφείλομεν, ἢ πῶς διακεισόμεθα τὸν Θεὸν αὐτὸν ἐπὶ ταῖς πλημμελείαις ἡμῶν καταλλάσσοντες;'

49 Eustratiades, *Μιχαὴλ τοῦ Γλυκᾶ*, 2.176: 'Ἔνθεν τοι καὶ ἡ ἐν Καρθαγένῃ συστᾶσα σύνοδος ἐν διαφόροις κανόσιν αὐτῆς διετάξατο τοὺς ἱερωμένους ἀπέχεσθαι τῶν ὁμοζύγων, καθ' ὃν ἄρα καιρὸν τὰ ἅγια μεταχειρίζονται μυστήρια. Ὡσαύτως ἡ δευτέρα καὶ οἰκουμενικὴ διωρίσατο σύνοδος ἀπέχεσθαι τῶν συμβίων καὶ αὐτοὺς τοὺς λαϊκοὺς ἔν τε Σάββασι καὶ Κυριακαῖς, διὰ τὸ πνευματικὰς θυσίας ἐν αὐτοῖς ἐπιτελεῖσθαι.'

50 There are also some examples, again pertaining to lay rather than clerical marriage, where quotations from the Old Testament (Samuel 21:4; Exodus 19:10–11 and 14–15) are employed which make use of such pollution discourse. *Syntagma* 4.456.

51 *Syntagma* 3.303: 'Τὸ ἀπέχεσθαι γυναικῶν, μὴ μόνον τοὺς ἱερωμένους, ἀλλὰ καὶ πάντας τοὺς πιστοὺς κατὰ τὸν καιρὸν τῆς ἁγίας μεταλήψεως, καὶ τῷ Ἀποστόλῳ νενομοθέτηται'. Tiftixoglu has argued that most such alternative interpretations were added later on by Balsamon himself. See Tiftixoglou, 'Zur Genese der Kommentare des Theodoros Balsamon', 486.

52 *Syntagma* 3.304: 'οἱ γὰρ μεμολυσμένοι ἀπὸ συνουσίας γυναικός, ἢ ἐξ ἄλλου τρόπου μυσαροῦ μὴ ὄντες ἅγιοι, τουτέστιν ἄξιοι, οὐκ ὀφείλουσι μεταλαμβάνειν.' The Patrologia Graeca has a slightly different version, in PG 138.36: 'Οἱ γὰρ μεμολυσμένοι ἀπὸ συνουσίας γυναικὸς ἢ ἄλλως οὐκ εἰσιν ἅγιοι· διὸ οὐδὲ ὀφείλουσι κοινωνεῖν.' 'For those who have been polluted from intercourse with a woman or in other ways are not holy. Therefore they should not receive communion.'

53 Although the text talks of sexual intercourse with 'women' and there is a certain ambiguity about whether these polluting women were indeed wives, it would be difficult to make sense of Balsamon's conclusion that *spouses* should abstain unless they were.

54 One of the greatest proponents of the need for clerical purity was Peter Damian (d. 1072 or 1073). In his *De celibatu sacerdotum* he explained that since Christ was born of a virgin, he preferred to be handled by virginal hands. See A.L. Barstow, *Married Priests and the Reforming Papacy: The Eleventh-century Debates* (New York, NY, 1982), 59. Cowdrey has also noted the great frequency with which Peter Damian and Cardinal Humbert used pollution language to talk about clerical marriage. See H.E.J. Cowdrey, 'Pope Gregory VII and the Chastity of the Clergy', in *Medieval Purity and Piety: Essays on Medieval Clerical Celibacy and Religious Reform*, ed. M. Frassetto (New York, NY, 1998), 279–89. See also Blumenthal, 'Pope Gregory VII and the Prohibition of Nicolaitism', 239–67.

55 H.E.J. Cowdrey (ed. and trans.), *The Epistolae Vagantes of Pope Gregory VII* (Oxford, 1972), 15, 21.

56 Cowdrey, *Epistolae Vagantes*, 44–5. Note, however, that Pope Gregory focused considerably less on the Anglo-Norman realm, addressing most of his letters to prelates of the German and Italian kingdoms of Henry IV (1056–1106). See Cowdrey, 'Pope Gregory VII and the Chastity of the Clergy', 272.

57 Cowdrey, *Epistolae Vagantes*, 44: 'nuptiis publice celebratis scortum potius quam sponsam ducere non erubuit'.

58 Fröhlich, *The Letters of Saint Anselm*, 2.244–5.

59 See also J.D. Thibodeaux, 'The Defence of Clerical Marriage: Religious Identity and Masculinity in the Writings of Anglo-Norman Clerics', in *Religious Men and Masculine Identity in the Middle Ages*, eds. P.H. Cullum and K.J. Lewis (Woodbridge, 2013), 46–63, at 54–5.

60 Greenway, *Henry, Archdeacon of Huntingdon: Historia Anglorum*, 451.

61 N. Partner, 'Henry of Huntingdon: Clerical Celibacy and the Writing of History', *Church History: Studies in Christianity and Culture*, 42 (1973), 467–75. On Henry's very long-running clerical dynasty, see also Diana Greenway's entry in D.E. Greenway, 'Henry (c. 1088 – c. 1157)', *Oxford Dictionary of National Biography*. www.oxforddnb.com/view/article/12970. Accessed 13/09/2014.

62 Melve, 'The Public Debate on Clerical Marriage', 698.

63 X.3.2.4: 'Vnde quum in Anglia prava a detestabili consuetudine et longo tempore sit obtentum, ut clerici fornicarias in suis domibus habeant, nos uolentes tam grave scandalum de populo remouere, et praedictos clericos ad honestatem ecclesiasticam reducere'.

64 1 Comp. 3.2.9: 'in spurcitia uitiorum manere'.

65 1 Comp. 3.2.11: 'indecens et rationi contrarium est, ut hii qui altario seruiunt feminarum complexiones maculentur aut per tabernas discurrant, cum eos sobrios et castos esse oporteat'.

66 Cheney, *Roger*, 170.

67 Cheney, *Roger*, 171.

68 We find such language, for example, being used in penitential literature composed by English ecclesiastics. See Morey, *Bartholomew of Exeter*, 239–40; *Gemma Ecclesiastica*, 132.

69 Baldwin has argued that Gerald of Wales and Thomas of Chobham along with Robert of Courson, Raoul Ardent, and Gilles de Corbeil were part of a campaign of resistance to clerical celibacy and advocated instead that the legislation should be modified or relaxed. See J.W. Baldwin, 'A Campaign to Reduce Clerical Celibacy at the Turn of the Twelfth and Thirteenth Centuries', in *Études d'histoire du droit canonique dédiées à Gabriel* (Paris, 1965), 2.1041–53, at 2.1044.

70 Broomfield, *Thomae de Chobham*, 379: 'quod animam suam occidit quamdiu celebrat pollutus'.

71 Broomfield, *Thomae de Chobham*, 380: 'Consilium tamen esset utile cuilibet qui est astrictus ut missas faciat celebrari querere mundum sacerdotem quem secure posset inuitare ad missam celebrandam.'
72 *Gemma Ecclesiastica*, 150; *Gir. Camb. opera* 2.195.
73 D.81 c.6: 'alieni efficiantur a ministerio, quod uiuendo illicite polluerunt'.
74 D.81 c.23: 'Sacerdotes mei contaminant sancta et reprobant legem' and 'offerentes ad altare meum panes pollutos'.
75 *Magistri Honorii* 1.229; 1.231.
76 *Summa Lipsiensis* 1.202, D.49 c.2 s.v. *Sacerdotes* usque *quantum ad se*: 'Hinc habetur quod sacramentum non polluitur quantum ad se ipsum, etsi reperiatur aliquando pollui. Hoc debet intelligi, ut hic dicitur, quantum ad illum qui pollute offert.'
77 *Summa Lipsiensis* 1.117, D.31 c.1 s.v. *et futura*: 'Hoc autem licite poterat statuere propter reuerentiam sacramentorum et munditiam ministrorum'.
78 M. Perisanidi, 'Anglo-Norman Canonical Views on Clerical Marriage and the Eastern Church', *Bulletin of Medieval Canon Law*, 34 (2017), 113–142.
79 Boelens has noted that already in 1031 at the synod of Bourges wives and concubines had been equally forbidden. In later canons, the word *uxor* is even dropped and the word *concubina* stands for both wives and concubines. The word 'concubine' comes to signify any woman with whom a cleric has sexual relations. See M. Boelens, *Die Klerikerehe in der Gesetzgebung der Kirche* (Paderborn, 1968), 117.
80 The canon did not specify if these sons had been born before or after their father's accession to sacred orders. See G.D. Mansi, *Sacrorum conciliorum nova et amplissima collectio* (repr. Paris, 1902) 20.498–9.
81 Canon 7 of Lateran II in Tanner, *Decrees of the Ecumenical Councils*, 198.
82 See also J. Gaudemet, 'Le célibat ecclésiastique. Le droit et la pratique du XIe au XIIIe siècles', *Zeitschrift der Savigny Stiftung für Rechtsgeschichte: Kanonistiches Abteilung*, 68 (1982), 1–31, at 8.
83 Gaudemet, 'Le célibat ecclésiastique', 21–3.
84 This chapter is not to be found in the first recension. See Winroth, *Making of Gratian's Decretum*, 222. Overall, Gratian's *Decretum* offers scattered material on the topic of clerical marriage. For example, the main sections dealing with this (distinctions 27 to 34) include many canons which state the rules we have seen for the Eastern Church and confusingly uphold clerical marriage. Gaudemet in his study of Gratian's treatment of the topic noted that, despite the wealth of information in the *Decretum*, the absence of an ordered arrangement of the canons on clerical marriage makes it hard to establish a precise doctrine. See J. Gaudemet, 'Gratien et le célibat ecclésiastique', *Studia Gratiana*, xiii (1967), 339–70, at 350.
85 Morey, *Bartholomew of Exeter*, 237.
86 Firth, *Robert of Flamborough*, 239–42.
87 See also J.A. Brundage, 'Adultery and Fornication: A Study in Legal Theology', in *Sexual Practices & the Medieval Church*, eds. V.L. Bullough and J.A. Brundage (Buffalo, NY, 1982), 129–32.
88 C.36 q.1 d.p.c.2: 'Fornicatio, licet uideatur esse genus cuiuslibet illiciti coitus, qui fit extra uxorem legitimam, tamen specialiter intelligitur in usu uiduarum, uel meretricum, uel concubinarum.'
89 C.32 q.7 d.a.c.11 and C.32 q.7 c. 11: 'Adulterii malum uincit fornicationem, uincitur autem ab incestu. [. . .] Sed omnium horum pessimum est quod contra naturam fit'. On the hierarchy of sex offences, see J.A. Brundage, 'Carnal Delight: Canonistic Theories of Sexuality', in *Proceedings of the Fifth International Congress of Medieval Canon Law, Salamanca, 21–25 September 1976*, eds. S. Kuttner and K. Pennington (Vatican City, 1980), 361–85. On simple fornication, see also Bartlett, *England under the Norman and Angevin Kings*, 566–7. The relative unimportance of simple fornication is reflected in Bartholomew of Exeter's penitential. Bartholomew noted that 'there are many who, considering the enormity of the aforementioned offences, that is to say of adultery, incest, and fornication against nature, think that every other

fornication, which they even call simple, is not a sin or is a minor sin.' Morey, *Bartholomew of Exeter*, 236–7. The text is reproduced by Robert of Flamborough in Firth, *Robert of Flamborough*, 231. Payer, in his study of the literature of confession between 1150 and 1300, observes that such views about the denial of sinfulness of simple fornication seem to have been widespread among the laity from the late twelfth century onwards. He compares this to the treatment of contraception among Catholics today. See P.J. Payer, *Sex and the New Medieval Literature of Confession, 1150–1300* (Toronto, 2009), 113–20.

90 Broomfield, *Thomae de Chobham*, 341: 'Est autem simplex fornicatio cum solutus solutam naturali usu cognoscit. Et intelligatur hic solutus a uinculo coniugii, a uinculo consanguinitatis, a uinculo affinitatis, a uinculo ordinis, a uinculo religionis, a uinculo etiam alicuius uoti, quia si aliquo istorum uinculorum fuerit ligatus, non committit simplicem fornicationem sed adulterium uel incestum.' See also Payer, *Sex and the New Medieval Literature of Confession*, 190.

91 Broomfield, *Thomae de Chobham*, 376–87: 'ARTICULUS SEPTIMUS, Que penitentia cui peccato sit iniungenda, Distinctio prima, De penitentiis, Questio XVIa. De incestu ordinatorum., cap. i. De continentia clericorum.' The identification of clerical marriage with incest can also be found early on among the decretists. For example, the author of the *Ordinaturus Magister Gratianus* writes, 'Large intellige, id est incestus: proprie enim dicitur incestus cum quis post uotum sollempne continentie uxori sue carnaliter comiscetur.' The *Ordinaturus* was a gloss of Gratian's Decretum made between 1180 and 1182 by an unknown canonist from the Bolognese school. See F. Liotta, *La continenza dei chierici nel pensiero canonistico classico. Da Graziano a Gregorio IX* (Milan, 1971), 110.

92 Broomfield, *Thomae de Chobham*, 378: 'Dicimus etiam quod ex quo occidentalis ecclesia adstrinxit se ad continentiam in Nicena Synodo, ubi orientalis ecclesia contradixit et noluit continere, tenentur successores eandem legem tenere.' In fact, the turning point for this was Lateran II (1139), but the same misconception can be found in contemporary commentaries on Gratian. See, for example, *Summa Parisiensis*, 30: '*Nicaena*. Haec synodus in orientali ecclesia est facta, nec tunc fuit castitas, scilicet postea fuit, licet non a Graecis'.

93 Broomfield, *Thomae de Chobham*, 378: 'quamuis quidam dicant: quomodo potuerunt illi patres qui fuerunt in Nicena Synodo dare nobis legem, qui neque interfuimus neque consensimus?'

94 Broomfield, *Thomae de Chobham*, 378: 'Preterea, quomodo potuit eorum institutio irritare matrimonium constitutum a deo et ab apostolis inter legitimas personas? Sed ita disputare friuolum est, quia oportet nos institutionibus sancte romane ecclesie obedire.'

95 See Morey, *Bartholomew of Exeter*, 231–4; Firth, *Robert of Flamborough*, 234–5. Similarly, Gerald of Wales' *Jewel of the Church* asserts that not only baptism and penance but also catechism and confirmation make a woman the spiritual daughter of the priest who performs them. See *Gemma Ecclesiastica*, 38.

96 Broomfield, *Thomae de Chobham*, 384. The same idea can be found in Rufinus' commentary on D.32 c.10. See *Magister Rufinus*, 74–5.

97 C. Brooke, *The Medieval Idea of Marriage* (Oxford, 1989), 248–57, at 250. See also D. D'Avray, *Medieval Marriage: Symbolism and Society* (Oxford, 2005), 65; M.M. Sheehan, 'Marriage Theory and Practice in the Conciliar Legislation and Diocesan Statutes of Medieval England', *Mediaeval Studies*, 40:1 (1978), 408–60; J.-B. Molin and P. Mutembe, *Le rituel du marriage en France du XIIe au XVIe siècle* (Paris, 1976), 34–7, 285–91; *Gemma Ecclesiastica*, 46.

98 Broomfield, *Thomae de Chobham*, 384: 'Credimus autem hunc canonem de filiis illorum sacerdotum esse intelligendum qui perniciose presumpserunt matrimonium contrahere in facie ecclesie, dicentes neminem posse prohibere quin sacerdotes contrahant matrimonium sicut alii homines.'

99 Broomfield, *Thomae de Chobham*, 377: 'credimus minus peccatum esse uti uxore quam fornicari cum alia, si ex toto continere noluerit'.

100 However, Antony the Great and John Cassian believed that it was possible to put an end to nocturnal emissions and treated them as a measure of the monk's progress in his efforts to co-ordinate his soul and body or a sign of the monastic community's perfection. See Brakke, 'The Problematisation of Nocturnal Emissions in Early Antiquity', 437, 447. Zonaras did not believe this to be possible. See *Syntagma* 4.609: 'Οὐδὲ τὸ μὴ γίνεσθαι σπέρματος ἐκροὴν κατωρθώθη, τῆς γὰρ φύσεως ἔργον τὸ διωθεῖσθαι τοῦτό ἐστιν, ὡς περίττωμα, ἀλλὰ τὸ μὴ ἐμπαθῶς γενέσθαι τὴν ἔκκρισιν ἐκ φαντασίας, ἣν συνίστησιν ἐπιθυμία κακὴ ἐξ ἧς ἡ διάνοια κέχρανται.' *Syntagma* 4.76: 'Οὐδὲ τὸ μὴ γενέσθαι τινὶ τοῦ σπέρματος ἔκκρισιν, κατόρθωσις λογισθήσεται· φυσικὸν γὰρ τοῦτο, διὸ καὶ γινόμενον, ἀνέγκλητον. Ἀλλ' οὐδέ τις, οἶμαι, τὴν φυσικὴν ῥεῦσιν διόλου ἐκφεύξεται, εἰ μή τις εἴη λίαν ἠλίθιος.'

101 Kottje has shown that the earliest evidence for daily celebration of the Eucharist in the West can be found in the oldest surviving texts we have asking for clerical continence in sacred orders. We cannot prove that daily celebration was the catalyst for such demands of clerical celibacy, but it added a new urgency and a new justification: clerics in major orders always had to be pure for their daily holy service. See Kottje, 'Das Aufkommen der täglichen Eucharistiefeier', 224–5, 228.

102 This idea is based on David D'Avray's explanation of the origins of the eleventh-century reform. See Introduction and D'Avray, 'The Origins and Aftermath of the Eleventh-Century Reform', 211–27. I want to thank Professor D'Avray for sending me this article and advising me on the present chapter.

103 J. Barrow, 'Ideas and Applications of Reform', in *The Cambridge History of Christianity. Vol. III: Early Medieval Christianities, c. 600–c. 1100*, eds. T. Noble and J. Smith (Cambridge, 2008), 345–62, at 347: 'Appeals to tradition, coupled with official reluctance to effect changes, remained more deeply entrenched in the Greek East than in the Latin West.' See also J. Herrin, *The Formation of Christendom* (Princeton, NJ, 1987), 286.

104 *Syntagma* 3.483.

105 Byzantine clerics could become bishops quite late in life. We know, for example, that Eustathios of Thessalonike was ordained to the episcopate probably in his sixties. See S. Schönauer, *Eustathios von Thessalonike: Reden auf die Große Quadragesima* (Frankfurt, 2006), 3*–4*.

106 *Syntagma* 5.321–3; *JGR* 1.435–6; *Les regestes de 715 à 1206*, 585 n. 1171.

107 See, for example, Pope Siricius' (384–399) letter to the bishops of Gaul in PL 13.1185–1186.

108 There are only two brief references to the Western Church and clerical celibacy, largely rephrasing what the canons had already said: *Syntagma* 2.333–6, or curtly observing that the Westerners 'are wrong about this, as they are about other things', in *Syntagma* 3.303: 'σφάλλονται δὲ κἂν τούτῳ, ὥσπερ καὶ ἐν ἑτέροις'.

109 The most recent time this had been seriously challenged was probably the 1054 schism.

110 Beaudette, 'Clerical Celibacy as a Symbol of the Medieval Church', 23–46.

111 'Adversus simoniacos' 3.9 in PL 143.1153: 'Sicut clerici a laicis etiam intra parietes basilicarum locis et officiis sic et extra separari et cognosci debent negotiis.' See also H.E.J. Cowdrey, *Pope Gregory VII: 1073–1085* (Oxford, 1998), 495–583.

112 Brooke, 'Gregorian Reform in Action', 72.

113 H. Leyser, 'Clerical Purity and the Re-ordered World', in *The Cambridge History of Christianity: Christianity in Western Europe c. 1100–c. 1500*, eds. M. Rubin and W. Simons (Cambridge, 2009), 11–21, at 16.

114 Hiding the altar from the laity was a monastic custom unheard of before the eleventh century and did not take its full form until after the Fourth Crusade (1204). See R.F. Taft, 'The Decline of Communion in Byzantium and the Distancing of the Congregation From the Liturgical Action: Cause, Effect, or Neither?', in *Threshold of the*

Sacred, ed. S.E.J. Gerstel (Washington, DC, 2006), 27–50. We learn from Balsamon that in the late twelfth century some churches had begun to offer the Eucharist to the laity via a spoon, while others continued the old custom of placing the Eucharist in the hands of the faithful. *Syntagma* 2.548–9. The introduction of communion by spoon can be linked to increased fears of pollution of the sacred: it was no longer acceptable for laymen to kiss the Eucharist or use it to cover their eyes before ingesting it. Instead they were expected to consume it orally within the sacred space of the church, thus avoiding any contamination of the Eucharistic host through physical contact. See R.F. Taft, 'Byzantine Communion Spoons: A Review of the Evidence', *DOP*, 50 (1996), 209–38, at 228.

115 *Syntagma* 2.466–7. Balsamon does not give the reasons behind this custom. He simply states that the laity thought it to be an old tradition and claimed it as a right. Specifically in the case of the Hodegon monastery, however, it has been argued that the Hodegetria icon of the Virgin Mary was located in the *prothesis* inside the sanctuary and that laymen and laywomen were allowed entrance so as to gain access to it. See Pitsakes, 'Ἡ ἔκταση τῆς ἐξουσίας ἑνὸς ὑπερόριου πατριάρχη', 121 n. 75. The sanctuary was a space reserved for clerics in major orders and exceptionally for the emperor, whose status, however, cannot be described simply as 'lay'. See also Angold, *Church and Society*, 153. For the peculiar status of the emperor, see G. Dagron, *Emperor and Priest: The Imperial Office in Byzantium*, trans. J. Birrell (Cambridge, 2003); G. Dagron, 'Le caractère sacerdotal de la royauté d'après les commentaires canoniques du XIIe siècle', in *Byzantium in the 12th Century: Canon Law, State and Society*, ed. N. Oikonomides (Athens, 1991), 165–78. Insufficient reverence towards the altar was one of the Byzantine grievances against the Latins. This reflected to a large extent internal debates about visual and physical access to the sanctuary. See Kolbaba, *The Byzantine Lists*, 58–61.

116 *Syntagma* 2.455–6.

117 *Syntagma* 3.333–40.

118 Angold, *Church and Society*, 152.

119 M. Perisanidi, 'Entertainment in the Twelfth-Century Canonical Commentaries: Were Standards the Same for Byzantine Clerics and Laymen?', *Byzantine and Modern Greek Studies*, 38:2 (2014), 185–200.

8 Conclusion

In this study, I have used legal sources and in particular conciliar canons, decretals, and canonical commentaries in order to explain why clerical marriage was condemned in the post-Gregorian West, while it maintained a sanctifying nature in the East. These sources to a large extent took a prescriptive approach which was not always aligned with what was happening on the ground. But they can also be seen as reactions to contemporary needs, especially when they confirmed existing customs or tried to abolish them. My primary aim has been to show how clerical marriage was conceptualised by educated twelfth-century clerics, but where possible I have combined the prescriptions with evidence of real practice to show what impact they had among other societal groups.

My investigation focused on three main factors which led Western ecclesiastics to condemn clerical marriage: married clerics could alienate ecclesiastical property for the sake of their wives and children; they could secure positions in the Church for their sons, restricting ecclesiastical positions and lands to specific families; and they could pollute the sacred by officiating after having sex with their wives. To be sure, attitudes towards clerical marriage cannot be reduced solely to attitudes towards sex, property, and dynastic interests. However, these topics do recur in both Western and Eastern canon law, with significant differences in their precise connection to clerical marriage, and limits of space led me to confine my research to them.

I concluded that many of the offending risk factors were missing in Byzantium: clerics below the episcopate did not have enough access to ecclesiastical resources to put the Church at financial risk; clerical dynasties were understood within a wider framework of desirable friendship allegiances; and sex within clerical marriage was considered not impure but simply distracting. In what follows, I will summarise my findings and provide some suggestions for further research.

Property

In Chapters 3 and 4 I examined fears of alienation of Church property, focusing in turn on bishops and clerics below the episcopate. In the case of bishops, a number of similarities between England and Byzantium emerged. In both societies, bishops could have considerable control over ecclesiastical finances and were encouraged to limit their personal and familial spending. This great access to ecclesiastical resources, as well as the legal limitations that came with it, was to a large extent connected to the bishop's familial status. Already in Late Antiquity, Justinian's laws had required bishops to be not only celibate but also without descendants, stating explicitly the incompatibility of the bishop's role as an administrator with his role as a father and provider for the family. But this extreme requirement did not survive in the twelfth century in either East or West. In both cases, clerics had only to put their wife away to be eligible for episcopal ordination, and children did not constitute an impediment. These wives and children could be provided for financially either through the bishop's personal property or through the Church if they were thought to be poor. However, one difference which emerges from the sources involves the possible beneficiaries imagined in cases of misappropriation: in England, children are singled out in a way not paralleled in Byzantium.

A greater difference can be seen in the case of clerics below the episcopate. In England, the fear that ecclesiastical property would be misappropriated for the sake of the clerical family extended to clergy of all grades, from priests to acolytes. Clerics in minor orders were discouraged from forming families, which would at that stage have been canonically allowed but would later become a financial burden to the Church if the cleric decided to accede to major orders. Their ecclesiastical income was linked to their marital status. In Byzantium, financial concerns arose only in the case of a few categories of clerics who held administrative positions, especially the *oikonomoi*. Unlike for bishops, no marital restrictions existed for these administrators, who in practice could even be laymen. Other clerics below the episcopate were allowed to have private property and to spend it as they saw fit. No mention was made of their family status. I have argued that this difference was connected to how clerics were remunerated and how much they earned. Most Byzantine priests, deacons, and subdeacons did not earn enough for their spending to represent a threat to the Church, and what they earned was distributed to them in an annual salary, which was more difficult to alienate than the more lucrative prebends and benefices of their English counterparts. Fear of misuse of Church property was one of the factors which contributed to the different attitudes towards clerical marriage in twelfth-century England and Byzantium.

Clerical dynasties

In Chapter 5, I turned to another important difference between East and West: the fact that Byzantine canonists, unlike their Western counterparts, did not associate clerical marriage with the issue of hereditary succession to churches and lands. Clerical dynasties as a whole were not prohibited in either society, but certain restrictions did exist. In Byzantium, bishops were forbidden from appointing their successors; but like clerics below the episcopate, any bishop could be succeeded by his son if he was a suitable candidate. Hereditary succession could become problematic if it meant creating a priestly caste, something the Byzantines associated with Judaism, or if it led to churches and lands falling into the hands of laymen, as could be the case with some of the *klerikoparoikoi* who passed down their *klerikato* to unordained heirs. The latter practice, which was not prevalent in the twelfth century, could cause problems if no sons were available to take up their father's liturgical and agricultural duties but the family nonetheless continued to treat the land as their own private property. Even then, however, the financial benefits for *klerikoparoikoi* were hardly comparable to those of Western benefice-holders. Although these rules applied in the case of legitimate children, illegitimate sons would not have been treated substantially differently: civil law limited their ability to inherit their father's property, but canon law did not restrict their right to join the clergy.

In England, on the other hand, hereditary possession of churches and benefices was open to criticism because it was intimately tied to clerical marriage. Laws about father-to-son succession and even ordination of illegitimate clerical sons were made progressively harsher in the twelfth century. But in this general climate of hostility towards clerical families, legitimate sons could also suffer: the burden was upon them to prove their legitimacy and they too could be prohibited from direct hereditary succession. Illegitimate sons were further discouraged from joining the secular clergy, but were allowed to join a regular or monastic community. This meant both a vow of celibacy and a renunciation of private property. Such attitudes were driven by both religious and financial motives: (1) the rules of celibacy were to a great extent implemented through the self-serving attitude of certain celibate clerics who were eager to denounce and replace their irregular colleagues; (2) the requirement for illegitimate sons of clerics to join a monastic or regular community, and so abandon their personal property, was meant to set a limit on the financial impact of hereditary succession; (3) through dispensations the whole process of ordination and appointment came under the control of the Church; (4) all these restrictions acted as a deterrent to future clerics who might have wished to form a family. Nonetheless, clerical dynasties continued, with the father-to-son pattern being replaced by a pattern of uncle-to-nephew succession.

If we take these three chapters together two common themes emerge. First, the different systems of ecclesiastical remuneration that we find in East and West had a role to play in determining attitudes towards clerical marriage. In the case of bishops, their control of landed property and lay offerings determined their marital status from an early date. In the case of other clerics, the greater their access to resources, the more likely they were to be affected by legislation regulating both their spending and their family status. This difference had an impact on attitudes towards both property and hereditary succession to churches. Second, ideas about who constituted a possible beneficiary of misappropriations were strikingly different. In Byzantium, after Justinian, clerical sons were never singled out; whenever they were mentioned, they were accompanied by other family members, such as parents and brothers, but also by friends. In England, the focus was firmly on clerical sons and wives, and secondly on nephews; more distant relatives and friends were not mentioned.

Purity

In the next two chapters I focused on the question of impurity, first establishing whether the two societies had comparable ideas about pollution, and then examining why the language of ritual impurity was used in the context of clerical marriage in England but not in Byzantium. In Chapter 6, I discussed the potential impurity of nocturnal emissions and found that Western and Byzantine canon law exhibited many similarities. Sources from both areas assumed three possible reasons for such emissions: a superfluity of nature, excessive eating and drinking, or sexual thoughts. In all cases, however, there was a consensus that it was at most a question of moral and not physical impurity: the secretion itself was not polluting. In both areas, in cases of emergency, practical considerations prevailed: even if polluted by nocturnal emissions, priests were to perform the Eucharist for the benefit of their parishioners, and the priest's impurity did not invalidate the sacrament. However, in England the law put more emphasis on the responsibility of *clerics* to remain pure from nocturnal pollution before they approached the sacred. In Byzantium, discussions of the issue hardly differentiated between its significance for clerics and laymen. However, they did highlight the similarity between nocturnal emissions and marital sex: neither was to be condemned simply because it involved a natural secretion or pleasure, but both could act as a distraction which would not allow one to communicate effectively with God.

Having established that both Byzantine and Anglo-Norman canon lawyers used pollution discourse to describe physical and moral impurity in the case of nocturnal emissions, in Chapter 7 I turned to clerical marriage in order to examine whether it, too, could be considered polluting. Focusing on the reasons for abstinence put forward in conciliar legislation and canonical commentaries, I found that marital sex was not described using such language in the case of Byzantine clerics. Instead the canonists emphasised the undefiled nature of the marital bed. Even bishops, who, like their English counterparts, were expected to observe absolute abstinence, were not asked to do so on grounds of purity; rather, emphasis was placed on their respecting the laws that had been established and maintaining a good reputation. What is more, transgression of the rules by both bishops and priests did not induce fears of pollution. In fact, these transgressive instances, which went relatively unnoticed, highlight a contrast between East and West which goes beyond the simple fact that marriage was allowed in one society but prohibited in the other. They create a parallelism where we might expect illicit clerical affairs to be condemned using the same language in both societies. What we find instead, however, is that in Byzantium an emphasis is laid on sexual intercourse as a distracting activity: temporary abstinence was necessary because sexual intercourse could sway the cleric's mind away from prayer and communion with God.

In England, on the other hand, both proponents and opponents of clerical celibacy used the language of impurity to refer to clerical marriage, emphasising both the physical aspects of sex (stains on body and hands) and the moral failing that it signified. This emphasis is not surprising given the reformist efforts of the eleventh and twelfth centuries to finally enforce the rules of clerical celibacy.

But is it simply that the West was more prone to reform than Byzantium? When it came to clerical marriage, the discrepancy between law and practice was simply greater in the West. In the case of Byzantine clerics below the episcopate who were expected to abstain temporarily, it would have been difficult to check whether the rules were being followed. As such, transgressions could more easily go unnoticed. In the case of Byzantine bishops, who, like their Western counterparts, were meant to observe complete abstinence, the presence of a woman or, even worse, a new child in the house would have been a sure sign that they had contravened the laws. But such breaches might have been neither too common nor too offensive in a society which did not make men choose early between an ecclesiastical career and fatherhood, was used to clerical wives, and did not place much emphasis on cast-iron distinctions between lay and clerical.

Avenues for further research

From celibacy to authority

This study has focused primarily on sex and property as driving factors behind attitudes towards clerical marriage. Two other factors were briefly mentioned: the need to communicate with God effectively in the case of both clerics and laymen, and the need to enhance one's reputation in the case of bishops in particular. Both deserve further exploration. With regard to bishops' reputations, the relevance of several of the differences we find between East and West may spring to mind. Importantly, bishops in Byzantium were much more numerous than bishops in England and, although many had significant control of ecclesiastical lands and wealth, their position could also be more precarious, owing, for example, to Turkish raids. Such material aspects could be exacerbated by religious challenges. Byzantium was a multicultural empire and bishops faced competition not only from Latins but also from Jews, Muslims, and heretics. As we have mentioned, a recent heresy in the twelfth century was that of the Bogomils, which condemned marriage as an obstacle to holiness and saw sexual intercourse as a capitulation to human weakness. Such challenges must have increased the pressure placed on bishops as leaders of the flock to maintain high standards. A comparative study of the numerous eleventh- and twelfth-century Byzantine episcopal and patriarchal encomia with Western hagiographies and *gesta pontificum* could reveal how bishops dealt with these challenges and what these differences meant for the creation of the portrait of the ideal bishop in East and West.[1]

The Byzantine emphasis on the need for effective communication with God could also provide an interesting point of comparison, especially in the case of the laity. Several factors of difference again suggest some tantalising hypotheses. One could argue that the presence of icons and their accepted power of intercession lessened the need for priestly intervention and encouraged a more direct form of communication between laymen and God. Confession could even be made to an icon, a function preserved in the West only for those ordained into the priesthood.[2]

Such differences had an impact on the relationship between priests and their flocks. This becomes more evident when we consider another major difference between East and West on the issue of confession and penance: in Byzantium, laymen often confessed to, and were absolved by, unordained monks. A comparative study of lay and clerical interactions with a focus on intercession could help us to assess the divide between clerics and laymen in Byzantium, re-evaluating the place of both.

The clerical family

In Chapter 5 I considered the effect that the laws of clerical celibacy had on clerical sons in England, both illegitimate and legitimate, while in Chapter 4 I discussed the financial implications for both children and wives. Many more avenues could be explored regarding the impact that contemporary rules and rhetoric on marriage and sexuality had on the clerical family. First, they affected the clerical father's perception of his own gender identity. Indeed, it has been argued that the Gregorian reforms marked a period of unease about clerical masculinity in the West. The reformers' stress on celibacy and chastity meant that clergy were excluded from a definition of gender based on marriage and procreation. Western medievalists have asked the question of how these clerics could remain men 'without deploying the most obvious biological attributes of manhood'.[3] Keeping this Western framework in mind, we could ask the same question of the Byzantine material, making a clear distinction between the celibate episcopate and the married priesthood. Secondly, the rules of clerical abstinence affected the clerical spouse. In the West, clerical wives turned into mere concubines and were sometimes deliberately erased from history.[4] Attitudes towards such 'transgressive' women could be compared to those faced by Byzantine women who had committed adultery. Similar language of impurity was used to describe both groups. On the other hand, a fruitful comparison of clerical wives in East and West would prove more difficult; Byzantine wives occupied a place of prominence within the community which would have set them too far apart from their Western counterparts, at least in the twelfth century.[5]

Society at large

Some of the conclusions that we have reached in this study with regard to the Church could be extended into a discussion of Byzantine society more generally. For one, we have seen that the Byzantine canon lawyers understood familial love more broadly than the Anglo-Norman decretists. The focus was not only on sons but also on parents and brothers, as well as more distant relatives and friends. Examining such statements within the wider context of the concept of friendship in East and West could help us agree or disagree with Mullett's statement that 'friendship fulfilled a functional role in eastern society for which there was no place in the west with its formal feudal ties.'[6] Similarly, our canonical sources allow us to evaluate attitudes towards familial networks occurring outside the

Church. A close parallel can be found in the views of Zonaras, who, talking of Alexios I, lamented that the emperor 'gave away public money in cartloads to his relatives and certain of his servants'.[7] Indeed, parallels are illuminating in more than one way when we think of Church and state as two structures which controlled resources that were in one way or another public. In the same speech, Zonaras complains that Alexios treated the public resources as his private property: 'he considered himself to be not their steward (*oikonomos*) but their master (*oikodespotes*).' The nod towards the ecclesiastical office of *oikonomos* calls for further investigation of Byzantine views on property, ecclesiastical and imperial, private and public.

Clerical marriage in different periods

Finally, comparative explorations of the history of clerical marriage also allow us to see modern debates from a different perspective. As mentioned in the introduction, the question of clerical celibacy is still of importance today, dividing Catholics from Protestants and Orthodox Christians. In current historical discussions of this division, emphasis is often placed on whether the origins of the institution of celibacy are apostolic. But this focus on origins is itself only the current phase in a long historical development of the discourse about clerical celibacy. We have seen in this study that the debate was structured very differently in twelfth-century canon law: both 'sides' acknowledged that their celibacy requirements were in some ways an innovation, contrasting with apostolic traditions, while defending them and attacking prohibited clerical marriages with alternative lines of argument. If we were to turn to a different period a comparative study of East and West could produce different results yet again. Going forward into the fourteenth century, we could examine how views on sexuality evolved and what impact they had on clerical sexuality. A starting point could be the following comment by Blastares: 'thus not even infants are free of Adam's sin, since their conception occurs in iniquity; for intercourse and the conception which follows are born of pleasure.'[8] The striking difference between this statement and the views which Balsamon and Zonaras expressed on the same topic suggests the importance of such an investigation. Similarly, going back into the eleventh century, we could examine the fight against the imposition of clerical celibacy in Western polemical literature, noting the similarities between Byzantine and Western understandings of the usefulness of marriage.[9] This is, in fact, the phase of clerical marriage which I plan to study in the immediate future, within the wider context of the clergy's authority and masculinity.

Notes

1 For examples of Byzantine encomia, see R. Maisano, *Niceforo Basilace: gli encomi per l'imperatore e per il patriarca* (Napoli, 1977); R. Anastasi, *Michele Psello: Encomio per Giovanni, piissimo metropolita di Euchaita e Protosincello* (Padova, 1968). For Western examples, see M. Winterbottom and R.M. Thomson (eds.), *Gesta Pontificum Anglorum:*

The History of the English Bishops (Oxford, 2007); R.E. Pepin (trans.), *Anselm & Becket Two Canterbury Saints' Lives by John of Salisbury* (Toronto, 2009).

2 Wortley, *Spiritually Beneficial Tales*, 101–2.

3 J.A. McNamara, 'The Herrenfrage: The Restructuring of the Gender System, 1050–1150', in *Medieval Masculinities: Regarding Men in the Middle Ages*, ed. C.A. Lees (Minneapolis, MN, 1994), 3–29, at 5. On this topic, see also R.N. Swanson, 'Angels Incarnate: Clergy and Masculinity From Gregorian Reform to Reformation', in *Masculinity in Medieval Europe*, ed. D.M. Hadley (London, 1999), 160–77; M.C. Miller, 'Masculinity, Reform, and Clerical Culture: Narratives of Episcopal Holiness in the Gregorian Era', *Church History*, 72 (2003), 25–52; J. Murray, 'Masculinizing Religious Life: Sexual Prowess, the Battle for Chastity and Monastic Identity', in *Holiness and Masculinity in the Middle Ages*, eds. P.H. Cullum and K.J. Lewis (Cardiff, 2004), 24–42.

4 'The Priest's Wife: Female Erasure and the Gregorian Reform' in Elliott, *Fallen Bodies*, 81–106.

5 Nonetheless, the status of their clerical husband came with limitations that affected the sexual life of both. As I have argued elsewhere, clerical wives, as opposed to lay spouses, were given less of a voice by the canons when it came to deciding when to engage in sexual intercourse and when to abstain. See M. Perisanidi, 'Should We Abstain? Spousal Equality in Twelfth-century Byzantine Canon Law', *Gender & History*, 28:2 (2016), 422–37.

6 Mullett, 'Byzantium: A Friendly Society?', 24. See also M. Mullett, 'Friendship in Byzantium: Genre, Topos and Network', in *Friendship in Medieval Europe*, ed. J. Haseldine (Stroud, 1999), 166–84.

7 Magdalino, 'Byzantine *Kaiserkritik*', 330.

8 *Syntagma* 6.117: 'οὐδὲ τὰ νήπια τῆς τοῦ Ἀδὰμ ἄρα ἁμαρτίας ἐλεύθερα, ὡς τῆς συλλήψεως αὐτῶν ἐν ἀνομίαις γινομένης· ἐξ ἡδονῆς γὰρ ἡ συνάφεια καὶ ἡ ἑπομένη σύλληψις'.

9 See, for example, B. Meijns, 'Opposition to Clerical Continence and the Gregorian Celibacy Legislation in the Diocese of Thérouanne: Tractatus Pro Clericorum Conubio (c. 1077–1078)', *Sacris Erudiri*, XLVII (2008), 223–90.

Bibliography

Primary sources

Byzantium

Anastasi, R., *Michele Psello: Encomio per Giovanni, piissimo metropolita di Euchaita e Protosincello* (Padova, 1968).

Antonin, Arch. (ed.), *O drevnikh khristianskikh nadpisakh v Athinakh* (St. Petersburg, 1874).

Bekker, I. (ed.), *Theophanes Continuatus* (Bonn, 1838).

Bekker, I. (ed.), *George Cedrenus, Historiarum Compendium*, 2 vols. (Bonn, 1838–9).

Darrouzès, J., *Notitiae Episcopatuum Ecclesiae Constantinopolitanae. Texte critique, introduction et notes* (Paris, 1981).

Darrouzès, J., 'L'éloge de Nicolas III par Nicolas Mouzalon', *REB*, 46 (1988), 5–53.

Declerck, J.H. (ed.), *Maximi Confessoris quaestiones et dubia* (Turnhout, 1982).

Eustratiades, S. (ed.), *Μιχαὴλ τοῦ Γλυκᾶ. Εἰς τὰς ἀπορίας τῆς Θείας Γραφῆς*, vol. II (Alexandria, 1912).

Festugière, A.J. (ed.), *Vie de Théodore de Sykéon*, vol. I (Brussels, 1970).

Gautier, P., 'Le chartophylax Nicéphore. Œuvre canonique et notice bibliographique', *REB*, 27 (1969), 159–95.

Gautier, P. (ed.), *Michel Italikos, Lettres et Discours* (Paris, 1972).

Gautier, P., 'L'édit d'Alexis Ier Comnène sur la réforme du clergé', *REB*, 31 (1973), 165–201.

Gautier, P., 'Le typikon du Christ Sauveur Pantocrator', *REB*, 32 (1974), 1–145.

Gautier, P. (ed. and trans.), *Théophylacte d'Achrida, I, Discours, traités, poésies* (Thessalonike, 1980).

Gedeon, M., 'Λύσεων Κανονικῶν Διάφοροι Γραφαί', *Ἐκκλησιαστικὴ ἀλήθεια*, 24 (1915), 185–9.

Geerard, M., *Clavis Patrum Graecorum*, vol. II (Turnhout, 1974).

Gregoriades, I., *Ιωάννης Τζέτζης, ΕΠΙΣΤΟΛΑΙ: Εισαγωγή-Μετάφραση-Σχόλια* (Athens, 2001).

Grumel, V. and Darrouzès, J. (eds.), *Les regestes des actes du patriarcat de Constantinople, I: Les actes des patriarches, fasc.ii et iii: Les regestes de 715 à 1206* (Paris, 1947).

Hesseling, D.C. and Pernot, H., *Poèmes prodromiques en grec vulgaire* (Amsterdam, 1910).

Joannou, P.-P., *Discipline générale antique: Vol. 2. Les canons des pères grecs* (Rome, 1963).

Jordan, R. (trans.), 'Kecharitomene: Typikon of Empress Irene Doukaina Komnene for the Convent of the Mother of God Kecharitomene in Constantinople', in *Byzantine Monastic Foundation Documents*, eds. J. Thomas and A. Constantinides Hero (Washington, DC, 2000), 649–724.

Kalogeras, N. (ed.), *Εὐθυμίου τοῦ Ζιγαβηνοῦ Ἑρμηνεία εἰς τὰς ΙΔ' Ἐπιστολὰς τοῦ Ἀποστόλου Παύλου καὶ εἰς τὰς Ζ' Καθολικάς* (Athens, 1887).

Karpozilos, D.A. (ed. and trans.), *The Letters of Ioannes Mauropous, Metropolitan of Euchaita: Greek Text, Translation, and Commentary* (Thessalonike, 1990).

Kolovou, F. (ed.), *Michaelis Choniatae Epistulae* (Berlin, 2001).

Kroll, W. and Schöll, R. (eds.), *Corpus iuris civilis*, vol. III (Berlin, 1895; repr. 1968).

Lampros, S. (ed.), *Μιχαὴλ Ἀκομινάτου τοῦ Χωνιάτου τὰ σωζόμενα*, vol. II (Athens, 1880).

Laurent, V., 'Réponses canoniques inédites du patriarcat byzantin', *Échos d'Orient*, 33 (1934), 298–315.

Magoulias, H.J. (trans.), *O City of Byzantium: Annals of Niketas Choniates* (Detroit, MI, 1984).

Maisano, R., *Niceforo Basilace: gli encomi per l'imperatore e per il patriarca* (Napoli, 1977).

Makarios of Corinth and Hagiorites, N. (eds.), *Εὐεργετινὸς ἤτοι Συναγωγὴ τῶν θεοφθόγγων ῥημάτων καὶ διδασκαλιῶν τῶν θεοφόρων καὶ ἁγίων πατέρων*, 4 vols. (Venice, 1783; 6th ed., repr. Athens 1996–7).

Melville-Jones, J.R. (trans.), *Eustathios of Thessaloniki: The Capture of Thessaloniki* (Canberra, 1988).

Migne, J.-P. (ed.), *Patrologiae cursus completus. Series graeco-latina*, 166 vols. (Paris, 1857–66).

Noailles, P. and Dain, A. (eds.), *Les novelles de Léon VI le Sage* (Paris, 1944).

Orlandos, A.K. and Branouses, L. (eds.), *Τα χαράγματα του Παρθενώνος* (Athens, 1973).

Pitra, J.-B. (ed.), *Iuris ecclesiastici graecorum historia et monumenta*, vol. II (1868; repr. Rome: Bardi, 1963).

Prinzing, G. (ed.), *Demetrii Chomateni Ponemata diaphora* (Berlin, 2002).

Rhalles, G.A. and Potles, M. (eds.), *Σύνταγμα τῶν θείων καὶ ἱερῶν κανόνων*, 6 vols. (Athens, 1852–9).

Roskovány, A. *Coelibatus et breviarium: duo gravissima clericorum officia e monumentis omnium seculorum demonstrata, accessit completa literatura*, vol. IV (Pestini, 1861).

Roueché, C., *Kekaumenos, Consilia et Narrationes*. www.ancientwisdoms.ac.uk/folioscope/greekLit%3Atlg3017.Syno298.sawsEng01%3Adiv3&viewOffsets=-4442. Accessed 18/06/2014.

Schaff, P. (trans.), *The Seven Ecumenical Councils of the Undivided Church* (Grand Rapids, MI, 1979).

Scheltema, H.J., van der Wal, N., and Holwerda, D. (eds.), *Basilicorum libri LX, Text*, 8 vols. (Groningen, 1953–88).

Stade, C. (trans.), *The Explanation by Blessed Theophylact of The Holy Gospel According to St. Matthew* (House Springs, MO, 1994).

Talbot, A.-M. (trans.), 'Life of St. Theodora of Thessalonike', in *Holy Women of Byzantium: Ten Saints' Lives in English Translation* (Washington, DC, 1996), 159–237.

Thomas, J. and Constantinides Hero, A. (eds.), *Byzantine Monastic Foundation Documents* (Washington, DC, 2000).

Uspenskij, Th., 'Mnemija i postanovlenija Konstantinopol'skikh pomestnykh soborov', *Izvestija russkago arkheologicheskago instituta v Konstantinopole*, 5 (1900), 1–48.

Vranouse, E., 'Τὸ ἀρχαιότερο σωζόμενο ἔγγραφο γιὰ τὴ θεσσαλικὴν ἐπισκοπὴ Σταγῶν', *Σύμμεικτα*, 7 (1987), 19–32.

Will, C., *Acta et scripta quae de controversiis ecclesiae Graecae et Latinae saeculo undecimo composita extant* (Leipzig, 1861).
Wortley, J., *John Skylitzes: A Synopsis of Byzantine History, 811–1057: Translation and Notes* (Cambridge, 2010).
Zepos, I. and Zepos, P. (eds.), *Ius graecoromanum*, 6 vols. (Athens, 1931; repr. Aalen, 1962).

England

Barlow, F. (ed.), *The Letters of Arnulf of Lisieux* (London, 1939).
Berry, V.G. (ed. and trans.), *Odo of Deuil: The Journey of Louis VII to the East* (New York, NY, 1965).
Brasington, B., *Ivo's Decretum*. http://imaging.mrc-cbu.cam.ac.uk/ivo/. Accessed 21/08/2017.
Brewer, J.S., Dimock, J.F., and Warner, G.F. (eds.), *Giraldi Cambrensis Opera*, 8 vols., RS, 21 (London, 1861–91).
Broomfield, F. (ed.), *Thomae de Chobham summa confessorum* (Paris, 1968).
Cheney, C.R. and Jones, B.E.A. (eds.), *English Episcopal Acta, II: Canterbury, 1162–1190* (London, 1986).
Colgrave, B. and Mynors, R.A.B. (eds. and trans.), *Ecclesiastical History of the English People* (Oxford, 1991).
Cowdrey, H.E.J. (ed. and trans.), *The Epistolae Vagantes of Pope Gregory VII* (Oxford, 1972).
Douie, D.L. and Farmer, H. (eds.), *The Life of St. Hugh of Lincoln*, vol. I (London, 1961).
Fairweather, J. (trans.), *Liber Eliensis: A History of the Isle of Ely From the Seventh Century to the Twelfth* (Woodbridge, 2005).
Firth, J.J.F. (ed.), *Robert of Flamborough, Liber Poenitentialis* (Toronto, 1971).
Foreville, R., *Latran I, II, III et Latran IV* (Paris, 1965).
Friedberg, E. (ed.), *Decretum Magistri Gratiani* (Leipzig, 1879).
Friedberg, E. (ed.), *Corpus Iuris Canonici, Pars secunda: Decretalium Collectiones* (Leipzig, 1881; repr. Graz, 1959).
Friedberg, E. (ed.), *Quinque Compilationes Antiquae* (Leipzig, 1882).
Fröhlich, W. (ed. and trans.), *The Letters of Saint Anselm of Canterbury*, 3 vols. (Kalamazoo, MI, 1990).
Giles, J.A. (trans.), *Roger of Wendover's Flowers of History*, vol. II (London, 1849).
Greenway, D.E. (ed. and trans.), *Henry, Archdeacon of Huntingdon: Historia Anglorum* (Oxford, 1996).
Greenway, D.E. (I–VII and X), Barrow, J.S. (VIII), Pearson, M. (IX), Brooke, C., Denton, J., and Greenway, D. (XI) (eds.), *Fasti Ecclesiae Anglicanae 1066–1300* (London, 1968–2011).
Grimm, B. (ed.), *Die Ehelehre des Magister Honorius: ein Beitrag zur Ehelehre der anglonormannischen Schule* (Rome, 1989).
Hagen, J.J. (trans.), *The Jewel of the Church: A Translation of Gemma Ecclesiastica by Giraldus Cambrensis* (Leiden, 1979).
Hoskin, P.M. (ed.), *English Episcopal Acta XXIX: Durham, 1241–1283* (Oxford, 2005).
Johnson, D.P. (ed.), *English Episcopal Acta, XXVI: London, 1189–1228* (Oxford, 2003).
Karn, N. (ed.), *English Episcopal Acta, XXXI: Ely, 1109–1197* (Oxford, 2005).
Kelly, S.E. (ed.), *Charters of St Paul's, London* (Oxford, 2004).
Kemp, B.R. (ed.), *English Episcopal Acta, XVIII: Salisbury, 1078–1217* (Oxford, 1999).
Landau, P. et al. (eds.), *Summa 'omnis qui iuste iudicat' Sive Lipsiensis*, 3 vols. (Vatican City, 2007, 2012, 2014).

Lefèvre, Y. and Huygens, R.B.C. (eds.) and Dawson, B. (trans.), *Speculum Duorum, or A Mirror of Two Men* (Cardiff, 1974).
Lovatt, M. (ed.), *English Episcopal Acta, XXVII: York, 1189–1212* (Oxford, 2004).
Mansi, G.D. (ed.), *Sacrorum conciliorum nova et amplissima collectio*, 54 vols. in 59 (repr. Graz 1960–1 from Paris 1901 edition).
McLaughlin, T. (ed.), *The "Summa Parisiensis" on the "Decretum Gratiani"* (Toronto, 1952).
Migne, J.-P. (ed.), *Patrologiae Latinae Cursus Completus*, 221 vols. (Paris, 1844–64).
Moravcsik, G.Y. (ed.) and Jenkins, R.J.H. (trans.), *Constantine Porphyrogenitus De administrando imperio* (Washington, DC, 1967).
Morey, A. (ed.), *Bartholomew of Exeter: Bishop and Canonist. A Study in the Twelfth Century* (Cambridge, 1937).
Morey, A. and Brooke, C.N.L. (eds.), *The Letters and Charters of Gilbert Foliot* (Cambridge, 1967).
Ordnance Survey, *Map of Monastic Britain: South Sheet* (Chessington, 1950).
Pepin, R.E. (trans.), *Anselm & Becket Two Canterbury Saints' Lives by John of Salisbury* (Toronto, 2009).
Rahlfs, A. (ed.), *Septuaginta*, vol. I (Stuttgart, 9th edn., 1935).
Raine, J. (ed.), *Liber Vitae ecclesiae Dunelmensis* (London, 1841).
Revell, E. (ed.), *The Later Letters of Peter of Blois* (Oxford, 1993).
Richter, M., 'A New Edition of the so-called vita Dauidis secundi', *Bulletin of the Board of Celtic Studies*, 22 (1966–68), 245–9.
Rollason, D. (ed. and trans.), *Symeon of Durham, Libellus de Exordio atque Procursu istius hoc est Dunhelmensis Ecclesie* (Oxford, 2000).
Schulte, J.F.v. (ed.), *Die Summa des Stephanus Tornacensis über das Decretum Gratiani* (Giessen, 1891).
Searle, E. (ed. and trans.), *The Chronicle of Battle Abbey* (Oxford, 1980).
Singer, H. (ed.), *Die Summa decretorum der Magister Rufinus* (Padeborn, 1902).
Smith, D.M. (ed.), *English Episcopal Acta, I: Lincoln, 1067–1185* (London, 1980).
Tanner, N.P. (ed. and trans.), *Decrees of the Ecumenical Councils: Volume One Nicaea I to Lateran V* (London, 1990).
Thompson, A. (trans.), Gordley, J. (trans.) and Christensen, K., *The Treatise on Laws (Decretum DD. 1–20) With the Ordinary Gloss* (Washington, DC, 1993).
Thorpe, B. (ed.), *Ancient Laws and Institutes of England*, vol. II (London, 1840).
Weigand, R., Landau, P., and Kozur, W. (eds.), *Magistri Honorii Summa "De iure canonico tractaturus"*, 3 vols. (Vatican City, 2004, 2010).
Whitelock, D., Brett, M., and Brooke, C.N.L., *Councils & Synods: With Other Documents Relating to the English Church, Vol. I: 871–1066, Vol. II: 1066–1204* (Oxford, 1981).
Winterbottom, M. and Thomson, R.M. (eds.), *Gesta Pontificum Anglorum: The History of the English Bishops* (Oxford, 2007).

Secondary sources

Byzantium

Adam, W., *Legal Flexibility and the Mission of the Church: Dispensation and Economy in Ecclesiastical Law* (London, 2011).
Ahrweiler, H., 'Recherches sur la société byzantine', *Travaux et mémoires*, 6 (Paris, 1976), 103–23.

Allen, P. and Neil, B., *Crisis Management in Late Antiquity (410–590 CE)* (Leiden, 2013).

Alwis, A.P., *Celibate Marriage in Late Antique and Byzantine Hagiography* (London, 2011).

Angelidi, C., 'Αισθήσεις, σεξουαλικότητα και οπτασίες', in *Ανοχή και καταστολή στους μέσους χρόνους*, ed. K. Nikolaou (Athens, 2002), 221–9.

Angelov, D., 'Ursprung und Wesen des Bogomilentums', in his *Les Balkans au Moyen Age: la Bulgarie des Bogomils aux Turcs* (London, 1978), VI 144–56.

Angold, M., 'The Imperial Administration and the Patriarchal Clergy in the Twelfth Century', *Byzantinische Forschungen*, 19 (1993), 17–24.

Angold, M., *Church and Society in Byzantium Under the Comneni, 1081–1261* (Cambridge, 1995).

Angold, M., *The Fourth Crusade: Event and Context* (Harlow, NY, 2003).

Angold, M. and Whitby, M., 'III.11.1 Church Structures and Administration', in *The Oxford Handbook of Byzantine Studies*, eds. E. Jeffreys, J. Haldon, and R. Cormack (Oxford, 2008), 571–82.

Banchich, T.M., 'Introduction: The Epitome of Histories', in *The History of Zonaras. From Alexander Severus to the Death of Theodosius the Great*, ed. and trans. T.M. Banchich and trans. E.N. Lane (London, 2009), 1–19.

Beck, H.-G., 'Zur byzantinischen Mönchschronik', in *Speculum historiale: Geschichte im Spiegel von Geschichtsschreibung und Gesichtsdeutung, Festschrift K. Adler*, eds. A. Bauer, L. Boehm, and M. Müller (Freiburg and Munich, 1965), 188–97.

Binns, J., *An Introduction to the Christian Orthodox Churches* (Cambridge, 2002).

Boelens, M., *Die Klerikerehe in der Gesetzgebung der Kirche* (Paderborn, 1968).

Booth, P., 'Gregory and the Greek East', in *A Companion to Gregory the Great*, eds. B. Neil and M. Dal Santo (Leiden, 2013), 109–31.

Brakke, D., 'The Problematisation of Nocturnal Emissions in Early Antiquity', *Journal of Early Christian Studies*, 3:4 (1995), 419–60.

Browning, R., 'An Unpublished Address of Nicephoros Chrysoberges to Patriarch John X Kamateros of 1202', *Byzantine Studies*, 5 (1978), 37–68.

Browning, R., 'Theodore Balsamon's Commentary on the Canons of the Council in Trullo as a Source on Everyday Life in Twelfth-Century Byzantium', in *Η καθημερινή ζωή στο Βυζάντιο*, ed. C. Angelide (Athens, 1989), 421–7.

Callam, D., 'Clerical Continence in the Fourth Century: Three Papal Decretals', *Theological Studies*, 41 (1980): 3–50.

Caseau, B., 'Too Young to be Accountable: Is 15 Years Old a Threshold in Byzantium?', in *Coming of Age in Byzantium Adolescence and Society*, ed. D. Ariantzi (Berlin, 2018), 19–28.

Casey, D., 'The Spiritual Valency of Gender in Byzantine Society', in *Questions of Gender in Byzantine Society*, eds. B. Neil and L. Garland (London, 2013), 167–81.

Chadwick, H., *East and West: The Making of a Rift in the Church: From Apostolic Times Until the Council of Florence* (Oxford, 2003).

Charanis, P., 'The Monastic Properties and the State in the Byzantine Empire', *DOP*, 4 (1948), 53–118.

Cholij, R., *Clerical Celibacy in East and West* (Leominster, 1988).

Ciggaar, K.N., 'England and Byzantium on the Eve of the Norman Conquest', in *Anglo-Norman Studies V: Proceedings of the Battle Conference 1982*, ed. R.A. Brown (Woodbridge, 1983), 78–96.

Ciggaar, K.N., *Western Travellers to Constantinople: The West and Byzantium, 962–1204, Cultural and Political Relations* (Leiden, 1996).

Cochini, C., *Apostolic Origins of Priestly Celibacy*, trans. N. Marans (San Francisco, CA, 1990).

Constantelos, D.J., 'Marriage and Celibacy of the Clergy in the Orthodox Church', *Concilium: Theology in the Age of Renewal*, 8 (1972), 30–8.

Constantelos, D.J., 'Clerics and Secular Professions in the Byzantine Church', *Byzantina*, 13:1 (1985), 375–400.

Constas, M., 'The Reception of Saint Paul and Pauline Theology in the Byzantine Period', in *The New Testament in Byzantium*, eds. D. Krueger and R.S. Nelson (Washington, DC, 2016), 147–76.

Crostini, B., 'Byzantine World (to 1453)', in *The Oxford Guide to the Historical Reception of Augustine*, vol. II (Oxford, 2013), 726–34.

Cunningham, M.B., '"Shutting the Gates of the Soul": Spiritual Treatises on Resisting the Passions', in *Desire and Denial in Byzantium Papers From the 31st Spring Symposium of Byzantine Studies, Brighton, March 1997*, ed. L. James (Farnham, 1999), 23–32.

Cunningham, M.B., 'Clergy, Monks, and Laity', in *The Oxford Handbook of Byzantine Studies*, eds. R. Cormack, J.F. Haldon, and E. Jeffreys (Oxford, 2008), 527–35.

Dagron, G., 'Le caractère sacerdotal de la royauté d'après les commentaires canoniques de XIIe siècle', in *Byzantium in the 12th Century: Canon Law, State and Society*, ed. N. Oikonomides (Athens, 1991), 165–78.

Dagron, G., 'Remarques sur le statut des clercs', *Jahrbuch der Österreichischen Byzantinistik*, 44 (1994), 33–48.

Dagron, G., *Emperor and Priest: The Imperial Office in Byzantium*, trans. J. Birrell (Cambridge, 2003).

Darrouzès, J., *Recherches sur les offikia de l'Église byzantine* (Paris, 1970).

Demacopoulos, G.E., and Papanikolaou, A., 'Augustine and the Orthodox: "The West" in the East', in *Orthodox Readings of Augustine*, ed. A. Papanikolaou (New York, NY, 2008), 11–40.

Douglas, M., *Purity and Danger: An Analysis of Concepts of Pollution and Taboo* (London, 1966; 2nd ed., repr. 2002).

Dvornik, F., *Byzantium and the Roman Primacy* (New York, NY, 1966).

Eastmond, A. and James, L., 'Eat, Drink . . . and Pay the Price', in *Eat, Drink and Be Merry (Luke 12:19): Food and Wine in Byzantium*, eds. L. Brubaker and K. Linardou (Aldershot, 2007), 175–89.

Efthymiadis, S., 'Michael Choniates' Inaugural Address at Athens: Enkomion of a City and a Two-Fold Spiritual Ascent', in *Villes de toute beauté, l'ekphrasis des cités dans les littératures byzantine et byzantino-slaves*, eds. P. Odorico and C. Messis (Paris, 2012), 63–80.

Evans-Grubbs, J., 'Illegitimacy and Inheritance Disputes in the Late Roman World', in *Inheritance, Law and Religions in the Ancient and Mediaeval Worlds*, eds. B. Caseau and S. Huebner (Paris, 2014), 1–25.

Fine, V.A.J., *The Early Medieval Balkans: A Critical Survey From the Sixth to the Late Twelfth Century* (Ann Arbor, MI, 1991, 2nd edn.).

Fögen, M.T., 'Unto the Pure all Things Are Pure: The Byzantine Canonist Zonaras on Nocturnal Pollution', in *Obscenity: Social Control and Artistic Creation in the European Middle Ages*, ed. J. Ziolkowski (Leiden, 1998), 260–78.

Foss, C., *Byzantine and Turkish Sardis* (London, 1976).

Frevel, C. and Nihan, C., 'Introduction', in their *Purity and the Forming of Religious Traditions in the Ancient Mediterranean World and Ancient Judaism* (Leiden, 2013), 1–46.

Gallagher, C., 'Gratian and Theodore Balsamon: Two Twelfth-Century Canonistic Methods Compared', in *Byzantium in the 12th Century: Canon Law, State and Society*, ed. N. Oikonomides (Athens, 1991), 61–89.

Gallagher, C., *Church Law and Church Order in Rome and Byzantium* (Aldershot, 2002).

Gallagher, C., 'Marriage in Eastern and Western Canon Law', *Law & Justice*, 157 (2006), 7–16.

Gallagher, C., 'The Episcopal Councils in the East', in *The Oxford Handbook of Byzantine Studies*, eds. R. Cormack, J.F. Haldon, and E. Jeffreys (Oxford, 2008), 583–91.

Gallagher, C., 'The Two Churches', in *The Oxford Handbook of Byzantine Studies*, eds. R. Cormack, J.F. Haldon, and E. Jeffreys (Oxford, 2008), 592–8.

Galone, A., *Georgios Bardanes: A Contribution on the Study About His Life, His Work and His Time* (Thessalonike, 2008).

Gress-Wright, D., 'Bogomilism in Constantinople', *Byzantion*, 47 (1977), 163–85.

Grumel, V., 'Les réponses canoniques à Marc d'Alexandrie. Leur caractère officiel. Leur double rédaction', *Échos d'Orient*, 38 (1939), 321–33.

Gryson, R., *Les origines du célibat ecclésiastique du premier au septième siècle* (Gembloux, 1970).

Gryson, R., 'Dix ans de recherches sur les origines du célibat ecclésiastique', *Revue theologique de Louvain*, 11 (1980), 157–85.

Guilland, R., 'Vénalité et favoritisme à Byzance', *REB*, 10 (1952), 35–46.

Guilland, R., 'Études sur l'histoire administrative de l'empire byzantin: L'Orphanotrophe', *REB*, 23 (1965), 205–21.

Guilland, R., *Recherches sur les institutions byzantines*, vol. II (Berlin, 1967).

Hajjar, J., *Le synode permanent (σύνοδος ἐνδημοῦσα) dans l'Église byzantine des origines au XIe siècle* (Rome, 1962).

Harris, J. (ed.), *Palgrave Advances in Byzantine History* (New York, NY, 2005).

Heid, S., *Celibacy in the Early Church: The Beginnings of a Discipline of Obligatory Continence for Clerics in East and West* (San Francisco, CA, 2000).

Hendy, M.F., *Studies in the Byzantine Monetary Economy c. 300–1450* (Cambridge, 1985).

Herman, E., 'Les bénéfices dans l'église orientale', in *Dictionnaire de droit canonique*, ed. R. Naz, vol. II (Paris, 1937), 706–35.

Herman, E., 'Das bischöfliche Abgabenwesen im Patriarchat von Konstantinopel von XI. bis zur Mitte des XIX. Jahrhunderts', *OCP*, 5 (1939), 434–513.

Herman, E., 'Ricerche sulle istituzioni monastiche bizantine. Typika kletorika, caristicari e monasteri liberi', *OCP*, 6 (1940), 361–72.

Herman, E., 'Die kirchlichen Einkünfte des byzantinischen Niederklerus', *OCP*, 8 (1942), 378–442.

Herman, E., 'Le professioni vietate al clero bizantino', *OCP*, 10 (1944), 23–44.

Herman, E., 'The Secular Church', in *The Cambridge Medieval History, Vol. IV: The Byzantine Empire, Part II*, ed. J.M. Hussey (Cambridge, 1967), 104–33.

Herrin, J., 'Realities of Byzantine Provincial Government: Hellas and Peloponnesos, 1180–1205', *DOP*, 29 (1975), 253–84.

Herrin, J., *The Formation of Christendom* (Princeton, NJ, 1987).

Herrin, J., '"Femina Byzantina": The Council in Trullo on Women', *DOP*, 46 (1992), 97–105.

Herrin, J., 'Public and Private Forms of Religious Commitment Among Byzantine Women', in *Women in Ancient Societies*, eds. L.J. Archer, S. Fischler, and M. Wyke (London, 1994), 181–203.

Herrin, J., 'The Quinisext Council (692) as a Continuation of Chalcedon', in *Chalcedon in Context. Church Councils 400–700*, eds. R. Price and M. Whitby (Farnham, 2009), 148–68.

Hussey, J., *The Orthodox Church in the Byzantine Empire* (Oxford, 1986).

Kaldellis, A., *The Christian Parthenon: Classicism and Pilgrimage in Byzantine Athens* (Cambridge, 2009).

Kampianaki, T., *John Zonaras' Epitome of Histories: A Compendium of Jewish-Roman History and Its Readers* (DPhil, Oxford, 2018).

Kaplan, M., *Les hommes et la terre à Byzance du VIe au XIe siècle* (Paris, 1992).

Kaplan, M., 'The Producing Population', in *A Social History of Byzantium*, ed. J. Haldon (Oxford, 2009), 143–67.

Karpozilos, A., *Συμβολή στη μελέτη του βίου και του έργου του Ιωάννη Μαυρόποδος* (Ioannina, 1982).

Karras, V., 'Female Deacons in the Byzantine Church', *Church History*, 73:2 (2004), 272–316.

Katsaros, V., *Ἰωάννης Κασταμονίτης. Συμβολὴ στὴ μελέτη τοῦ βίου, τοῦ ἔργου καὶ τῆς ἐποχῆς του* (Thessalonike, 1988).

Kazhdan, A.P., 'Chrysoberges', *The Oxford Dictionary of Byzantium*. www.oxfordreference.com/view/10.1093/acref/9780195046526.001.0001/acref-9780195046526-e-1087#. Accessed 5/01/2018.

Kazhdan, A.P. and S. Franklin, 'Nicephorus Chrysoberges and Nicholas Mesarites: A Comparative Study', in their *Studies on Byzantine Literature of the Eleventh and Twelfth Centuries* (Cambridge, 1984), 224–36.

Kiapidou, E.-S., 'On the Epistolography of Michael Glykas', *Βυζαντινά Σύμμεικτα*, 21 (2011), 169–93.

Klawans, J., *Impurity and Sin in Ancient Judaism* (Oxford, 2000).

Koder, J. (trans.), *Syméon le Nouveau Théologien: Hymnes 41–58, Texte critique et index*, vol. III (Paris, 1973).

Kolbaba, T., *The Byzantine Lists: Errors of the Latins* (Chicago, IL, 2000).

Kotsis, K., 'The Greek Orthodox Church', in *Handbook of Medieval Culture: Fundamental Aspects and Conditions of the European Middle Ages*, ed. A. Classen (Berlin, 2015), 628–52.

Kottje, R., 'Das Aufkommen der täglichen Eucharistiefeier in der Westkirche und die Zölibatsforderung', *Zeitschrift für Kirchengeschichte*, 82 (1971), 218–28.

Laiou, A.E., 'God and Mammon: Credit, Trade, Profit and the Canonists', in *Byzantium in the 12th Century: Canon Law, State and Society*, ed. N. Oikonomides (Athens, 1991), 261–300.

Laiou, A.E., 'Priests and Bishops in the Byzantine Countryside, Thirteenth to Fourteenth Centuries', in *Church and Society in Late Byzantium*, ed. D.G. Angelov (Kalamazoo, MI, 2009), 45–57.

Laiou-Thomadakis, A., *Peasant Society in the Late Byzantine Empire* (Princeton, NJ, 1977).

Lampsides, O., 'Πῶς εἰσάγουν εἰς τὰ κείμενά των οἱ ἐξηγηταὶ τῶν κανόνων τὰς εἰδήσεις διὰ τὸν σύγχρονόν των κόσμον', in *Byzantium in the 12th Century: Canon Law, State and Society*, ed. N.Oikonomides (Athens, 1991), 211–27.

Laurent, V., 'Etienne Chrysobergès, archevêque de Corinthe', *REB*, 20 (1962), 214–8.

Lázaro Sánchez, M.J., 'L'état actuel de la recherche sur le concile d'Elvire', *Revue des sciences religieuses*, 82:4 (2008), 517–46.

Lefort, J., 'The Rural Economy, Seventh-Twelfth Centuries', in *The Economic History of Byzantium: From the Seventh Through the Fifteenth Century*, ed. A.E. Laiou (Washington, DC, 2002), 231–315.

Lemerle, P., 'Le testament d'Eustathios Boïlas (avril 1059)', in his *Cinq études sur le XIe siècle byzantin* (Paris, 1977), 15–63.

Leontaritou, B.A., *Εκκλησιαστικά αξιώματα και υπηρεσίες στην πρώιμη και μέση βυζαντινή περίοδο* (Athens, 1996).

L'Huillier, P., 'Episcopal Celibacy in the Orthodox Tradition', *St. Vladimir's Theological Quarterly*, 35 (1991), 271–300.

L'Huillier, P., 'The First Millenium: Marriage, Sexuality, and Priesthood', in *Vested in Grace: Priesthood and Marriage in the Christian East*, ed. J.J. Allen (Brookline, MA, 2001), 23–65.

Lössl, J., 'Augustine in Byzantium', *Journal of Ecclesiastical History*, 51:2 (2000), 267–95.

Louth, A., *Greek East and Latin West: The Church AD 681–1071* (Crestwood, NY, 2007).

Louth, A., 'Gregory the Great in the Byzantine Tradition', in *A Companion to Gregory the Great*, eds. B. Neil and M. Dal Santo (Leiden, 2013), 343–58.

Macrides, R.J., 'Killing, Asylum, and the Law in Byzantium', *Speculum*, 63 (1988), 509–38.

Macrides, R.J., 'Nomos and Kanon on Paper and in Court', in *Church and People in Byzantium*, ed. R. Morris (London, 1990), 61–85.

Macrides, R.J., 'Perception of the Past in the Twelfth-century Canonists', in *Byzantium in the 12th Century: Canon Law, State and Society*, ed. N. Oikonomides (Athens, 1991), 589–99.

Madariaga, E., 'Η βυζαντινή οικογένεια των Αγιοθεοδωριτών (I): Νικόλαος Αγιοθεοδωρίτης, Πανιερώτατος Μητροπολίτης Αθηνών και Υπέρτιμος', *Βυζαντινά Σύμμεικτα*, 19 (2009), 147–81.

Magdalino, P., 'Enlightenment and Repression in Twelfth-Century Byzantium. The Evidence of the Canonists', in *Byzantium in the 12th Century: Canon Law, State and Society*, ed. N. Oikonomides (Athens, 1991), 357–74.

Magdalino, P., *The Empire of Manuel I Komnenos, 1143–1180* (Cambridge, 1994).

Magdalino, P., 'The Reform Edict of 1107', in *Alexios I Komnenos, I: Papers*, eds. M. Mullett and D. Smythe (Belfast, 1996), 199–218.

Magdalino, P., 'Court Society and Aristocracy', in *A Social History of Byzantium*, ed. J. Haldon (Chichester, 2009), 212–32.

Mango, C., 'Twelfth-Century Notices From cod. Christ Church Gr. 53', *Jahrbuch der Österreichischen Byzantinistik*, 42 (1992), 221–8.

Marinis, V., *Architecture and Ritual in the Churches of Constantinople Ninth to Fifteenth Centuries* (Cambridge, 2004).

Meigne, M., 'Concile ou collection d' Elvire?', *Revue d'histoire ecclésiastique*, 70 (1975), 361–87.

Mercati, S.G., 'Poesie giambiche di Niceforo Chrysoberges, metropolitano di Sardi', in *Collectanea Byzantina*, vol. I (Bari, 1970), 574–94.

Merianos, G., 'More than a Shepherd to His Flock: Eustathios and the Management of Ecclesiastical Property', in *Reading Eustathios of Thessalonike*, eds. F. Pontani, V. Katsaros, and V. Sarris (Berlin, 2017), 309–30.

Messis, C., 'Public hautement affiché et public réellement visé dans certaines créations littéraires byzantines: le cas de l'*Apologie de l'eunuchisme* de Théophylacte d'Achrida', in *La face cachée de la littérature byzantine*, ed. P. Odorico (Paris, 2012), 41–85.

Messis, C., 'Fluid Dreams, Solid Consciences: Erotic Dreams in Byzantium', in *Dreaming in Byzantium and Beyond*, eds. C. Angelidi and G.T. Calofonos (Farnham, 2014), 187–205.

Millet, G., 'Inscriptions byzantines de Mistra (Pl. XIV–XXIII)', *Bulletin de correspondance hellénique*, 23:1 (1899), 97–156.

Moran, N.K., *Singers in Late Byzantine and Slavonic Painting* (Leiden, 1986).

Moran, N.K., 'Byzantine Castrati', *Plainsong and Medieval Music*, 11:2 (2002), 99–112.

Morrisson, C. and Cheynet, J.-C., 'Prices and Wages in the Byzantine World', in *Economic History of Byzantium: From the Seventh Through the Fifteenth Century*, ed. A.E. Laiou (Washington, DC, 2002), 815–78.

Moulet, B., 'Le goût des autres. Correspondances gourmandes et culture du goût à Byzance', in *L'échange: Journées de maison des Sciences de l'homme Ange-Guépin*, ed. J. Tolan (Paris, 2009), 163–77.

Moulet, B., *Évêques, pouvoir et société à Byzance (VIIIe–XIe siècle)* (Paris, 2011).

Mullett, M.E., 'Byzantium: A Friendly Society?', *Past and Present*, 118 (1988), 3–24.

Mullett, M.E., 'Patronage in Action', in *Church and People in Byzantium*, ed. R. Morris (Birmingham, 1990), 125–50.

Mullett, M.E., *Theophylact of Ochrid: Reading the Letters of a Byzantine Archbishop* (Farnham, 1997).

Mullett, M.E., 'Friendship in Byzantium: Genre, Topos and Network', in *Friendship in Medieval Europe*, ed. J. Haseldine (Stroud, 1999), 166–84.

Munier, C., *Les sources patristiques du droit de l'Église du VIIIe au XIIIe siècle* (Strasbourg, 1954).

Nichols, A., 'The Reception of St. Augustine and his Work in the Byzantine – Slav Tradition', *Angelicum*, 64 (1987), 437–52.

Ohme, H., 'Greek Canon Law to 691/2', in *The History of Byzantine and Eastern Canon Law to 1500*, eds. W. Hartmann and K. Pennington (Washington, DC, 2012), 24–114.

Oikonomides, N., 'Quelques Boutiques de Constantinople Au Xe S.: Prix, Loyers, Imposition (Cod. Patmiacus 171)', *DOP*, 26 (1972), 345–56.

Oikonomides, N., 'L'évolution de l'organisation administrative de l'empire byzantin au XIe siècle (1025–1118)', *Travaux et mémoires*, 6 (1976), 125–52.

Oikonomides, N., 'Title and Income at the Byzantine Court', in *Byzantine Court Culture from 829 to 1204*, ed. H. Maguire (Washington, DC, 1995), 199–215.

Papachryssanthou, D., 'Un évêché byzantin: Hierissos en Chalcidique', *Travaux et mémoires*, 8 (1981), 373–96.

Papadoyannakis, Y., 'Instruction by Question and Answer: The Case of Late Antique and Byzantine Erotapokriseis', in *Greek Literature in Late Antiquity: Dynamism, Didacticism, Classicism*, ed. S.E. Johnson (Aldershot, 2006), 91–105.

Papagianni, E. 'Επιτρεπόμενες και απαγορευμένες κοσμικές ενασχολήσεις του βυζαντινού κλήρου', in *Δ' Πανελλήνιο Ἱστορικό Συνέδριο. Πρακτικά* (Thessalonike, 1983), 143–66.

Papagianni, E., *Τὰ οἰκονομικά τοῦ ἔγγαμου κλήρου στό Βυζάντιο* (Athens, 1986).

Papagianni, E., 'Legal Institutions and Practice in Matters of Ecclesiastical Property', in *The Economic History of Byzantium: From the Seventh Through the Fifteenth Century*, ed. A.E. Laiou (Washington, DC, 2002), 1059–69.

Payaslian, S., *The History of Armenia: From the Origins to the Present* (New York, NY, 2007).

Perentidis, S., 'Un canon peut-il être périmé? Mentalités et autorité du texte canonique au XIIe siècle', in *Byzantium in the 12th Century: Canon Law, State and Society*, ed. N. Oikonomides (Athens, 1991), 141–7.

Perisanidi, M., 'Entertainment in the Twelfth-Century Canonical Commentaries: Were Standards the Same for Byzantine Clerics and Laymen?', *Byzantine and Modern Greek Studies*, 38:2 (2014), 185–200.

Perisanidi, M., 'Should We Abstain? Spousal Equality in Twelfth-century Byzantine Canon Law', *Gender & History*, 28:2 (2016), 422–437.

Perisanidi, M., 'Was there a Marital Debt in Byzantium?', *Journal of Ecclesiastical History*, 68:3 (2017), 1–19.

Peters, E., 'History, Historians, and Clerical Celibacy', in *Medieval Purity and Piety: Essays on Medieval Clerical Celibacy and Religious Reform*, ed. M. Frassetto (London, 1998), 3–21.

Petzold, H., 'Das Verhältnis des Subdiakonats zum Weihesakrament in der alten Kirche und seine Stellung im klassisch-orthodoxen Kirchenrecht', *Österreichisches Archiv für Kirchenrecht*, 18 (1967), 394–455.

Pieler, P., 'Zonaras als Kanonist', in *Byzantium in the 12th Century: Canon Law, State and Society*, ed. N. Oikonomides (Athens, 1991), 601–20.

Pitsakes, C., 'Ἡ ἔκταση τῆς ἐξουσίας ἑνὸς ὑπερόριου πατριάρχη: ὁ πατριάρχης Ἀντιοχείας στὴν Κωνσταντινούπολη τὸν 12ο αἰώνα', in *Byzantium in the 12th Century: Canon Law, State and Society*, ed. N. Oikonomides (Athens, 1991), 91–139.

Pitsakis, C., 'Clergé marié et célibat dans la législation du Concile in Trullo: le point de vue oriental', in *The Council in Trullo Revisited*, eds. G. Nedungatt and M. Featherstone (Rome, 1995), 263–306.

Prinzig, G., 'Observations on the Legal Status of Children and the Stages of Childhood in Byzantium', in *Becoming Byzantine: Children and Childhood in Byzantium*, eds. A. Papaconstantinou and A.-M. Talbot (Washington, DC, 2009), 15–34.

Rapp, C., *Holy Bishops in Late Antiquity: The Nature of Christian Leadership in an Age of Transition* (Berkeley, CA, 2005).

Rey, A.-L., 'Les erotapokriseis dans le monde byzantin: tradition manuscrite des textes anciens et production de nouveaux textes', in *Erotapokriseis, Early Christian Question-and-Answer Literature in Context*, eds. A. Volgers and C. Zamagni (Leuven, 2004), 165–80.

Richard, J., 'The Eastern Churches', in *The New Cambridge Medieval History IV, c. 1024–c. 1198, Part I*, eds. D. Luscombe and J. Riley-Smith (Cambridge, 2004), 564–98.

Rigo, A., 'Il processo del bogomilo Basilio (1099 ca.). Una riconsiderazione', *OCP*, 58 (1992), 185–211.

Rigotti, G., 'Gregorio il Dialogo nel mondo Bizantino', *L'eredità spirituale di Gregorio Magno tra Occidente e Oriente*, ed. G.I. Gargano (Verona, 2005), 271–92.

Roueché, C., 'The Literary Background of Kekaumenos', in *Literacy, Education and Manuscript Transmission in Byzantium and Beyond*, eds. C. Holmes and J. Waring (Leiden, 2002), 111–38.

Runciman, S., *A History of the Crusades*, vol. I (Cambridge, 1951).

Ryder, J.R., 'Changing Perspectives on 1054', *Byzantine and Modern Greek Studies*, 35:1 (2011), 20–37.

Schminck, A., 'Zur Entwicklung des Eherechts in der Komnenenepoche', in *Byzantium in the 12th Century: Canon Law, State and Society*, ed. N. Oikonomides (Athens, 1991), 555–87.

Schönauer, S., *Eustathios von Thessalonike: Reden auf die Große Quadragesima* (Frankfurt, 2006).

Shepard, J., 'The English and Byzantium: A Study of their Role in the Byzantine Army in the Later Eleventh Century', *Traditio*, 29 (1973), 53–92.

Stevens, G.P., *De Theodoro Balsamone: analysis operum ac mentis iuridicae* (Rome, 1969).

Stickler, A.M., *The Case for Clerical Celibacy: Its Historical Development and Theological Foundations* (San Francisco, CA, 1995).

Stolte, B.H., 'Balsamon and the Basilica', *Subseciva Groningana*, 3 (1989), 115–25.

Stolte, B.H., 'Civil Law in Canon Law: A Note on the Method of Interpreting the Canons in the Twelfth Century', in *Byzantium in the 12th Century: Canon Law, State and Society*, ed. N. Oikonomides (Athens, 1991), 543–54.

Taft, R.F., 'Byzantine Communion Spoons: A Review of the Evidence', *DOP*, 50 (1996), 209–38.

Taft, R.F., 'The Decline of Communion in Byzantium and the Distancing of the Congregation From the Liturgical Action: Cause, Effect, or Neither?', in *Threshold of the Sacred*, ed. S.E.J. Gerstel (Washington, DC, 2006), 27–50.

Talbot, A., 'A Monastic World', in *The Social History of Byzantium*, ed. J. Haldon (Chichester, 2009), 257–78.

Thetford, G., 'The Christological Councils of 1166 and 1170 in Constantinople', *St. Vladimir's Theological Quarterly*, 31:2 (1987), 143–61.

Thomas, J.P., 'The Rise of the Independent and Self-governing Monasteries as Reflected in the Monastic Typika', *Greek Orthodox Theological Review*, 30 (1985), 21–30.

Thomas, J.P., *Private Religious Foundations in the Byzantine Empire* (Washington, DC, 1987).

Tiftixoglu, V., 'Gruppenbildungen innerhalb des konstantinopolitanischen Klerus während der Komnenenzeit', *Byzantinische Zeitschrift*, 62 (1969), 25–72.

Tiftixoglou, V., 'Zur Genese der Kommentare des Theodoros Balsamon. Mit einem Exkurs über die unbekannten Kommentare des Sinaiticus gr. 1117', in *Byzantium in the 12th Century: Canon Law, State and Society*, ed. N. Oikonomides (Athens, 1991), 483–532.

Troianos, S.N., 'Ein Synodalakt des Sisinios zu den bischöflichen Einküften', *Fontes Minores*, 3 (1979), 211–20.

Troianos, S.N., 'Ιατρική επιστήμη και γιατροί στο ερμηνευτικό έργο των κανονολόγων του 12ου αιώνα', in *Byzantium in the 12th Century: Canon Law, State and Society*, ed. N. Oikonomides (Athens, 1991), 477–81.

Troianos, S.N., 'Ράλλης και Ποτλής', in *Byzantium in the 12th Century: Canon Law, State and Society*, ed. N. Oikonomides (Athens, 1991), 17–24.

Troianos, S.N., 'Zölibat und Kirchenvermögen in der früh- und mittelbyzantinischen kanonischen Gesetzgebung', in *Eherecht und Familiengut in Antike und Mittelalter*, ed. D. Simon (Munich, 1992), 133–46.

Troianos, S.N., 'Le célibat épiscopal dans la "civitas augescens"', in *Roman Law as Formative of Modern Legal Systems: Studies in Honour of Wieslaw Litewski*, eds. J. Reszczyński, P. Ściślicki, and J. Sondel, vol. II (Cracow, 2003), 185–95.

Troianos, S.N., 'Byzantine Canon Law From the Twelfth to the Fifteenth Centuries', in *History of Byzantine and Eastern Canon Law to 1500*, eds. W. Hartmann and K. Pennington (Washington, DC, 2012), 170–214.

Troianos, S.N., 'Byzantine Canon Law to 1100', in *History of Byzantine and Eastern Canon Law to 1500*, eds. W. Hartmann and K. Pennington (Washington, DC, 2012), 115–69.

Troianos, S.N., 'Η νεαρά Κωνσταντίνου του Μονομάχου ἐπὶ τῇ ἀναδείξει καὶ προβολῇ τοῦ διδασκάλου τῶν νόμων', *Βυζαντινά Σύμμεικτα*, 22 (2012), 243–63.

Van de Wiel, C., 'Les différentes formes de cohabitation hors justes noces et les dénominations diverses des enfants qui en sont nés dans le droit romain, canonique, civil et byzantin jusqu'au treizième siècle', *Revue internationale des droits de l'antiquité*, 3rd ser. 39 (1992), 327–58.

Viscuso, P., 'Christian Participation in Warfare: A Byzantine View', in *Peace and War in Byzantium: Essay in Honor of George T. Dennis, S.J.*, eds. T.S. Miller and J. Nesbitt (Washington, DC, 1995), 33–41.

Viscuso, P., 'The Prohibition of Second Marriage for Women Married to Priests', *OCP*, 66 (2000), 441–8.

Vryonis, S., 'The Will of a Provincial Magnate, Eustathius Boilas (1059)', *DOP*, 11 (1957), 267–70.

Wagschal, D., *Law and Legality in the Greek East: The Byzantine Canonical Tradition, 381–883* (Oxford, 2014).

Weiss, G., 'Die "Synopsis Legum" des Michael Psellos', *Fontes Minores*, 2 (1977), 147–214.

Whalen, B.E., 'Rethinking the Schism of 1054: Authority, Heresy, and the Latin Rite', *Traditio*, 62 (2007), 1–24.

Wortley, J., 'The Genre and Sources of the Synagoge', in *The Theotokos Evergetis and Eleventh-Century Monasticism*, eds. M. Mullett and A. Kirby (Belfast, 1994), 306–24.

England

Addleshaw, G.W.O., *Rectors, Vicars and Patrons in the Twelfth and the Early Thirteenth-century Canon Law* (London, 1956).

Aird, W.M., *St Cuthbert and the Normans: The Church of Durham, 1071–1153* (Woodbridge, 1998).

Airlie, S., 'Patrick Wormald the Teacher', in *Early Medieval Studies in Memory of Patrick Wormald*, ed. S.D. Baxter (Farnham, 2009), 29–35.

Austin, G., *Shaping Church Law Around the Year 1000: The Decretum of Burchard of Worms* (Farnham, 2009).

Baldwin, J.W., 'A Campaign to Reduce Clerical Celibacy at the Turn of the Twelfth and Thirteenth Centuries', in *Études d'histoire du droit canonique dédiées à Gabriel, II* (Paris, 1965), 1041–53.

Baldwin, J.W., *Masters, Princes, and Merchants: The Social Views of Peter the Chanter & His Circle*, vol. I (Princeton, NJ, 1970).

Baldwin, J.W., 'Masters at Paris From 1179 to 1215: A Social Perspective', in *Renaissance and Renewal in the Twelfth Century*, eds. R.L. Benson and G. Constable with C.D. Lanham (Toronto, 1991), 138–72.

Barlow, F., 'John of Salisbury and His Brothers', *Journal of Ecclesiastical History*, 46 (1995), 95–109.

Barraclough, G., *Papal Provisions: Aspects of Church History, Constitutional, Legal and Administrative in the Later Middle Ages* (Westport, CT, 1971).

Barrow, G.W.S., 'Puiset, Hugh du, Earl of Northumberland (c. 1125–1195)', *Oxford Dictionary of National Biography*. https://doi.org/10.1093/ref:odnb/22871. Accessed 2/12/2017.

Barrow, J.S., 'Gerald of Wales' Great-Nephews', *Cambridge Medieval Celtic Studies*, 8 (1984), 101–6.

Barrow, J.S., 'Cathedrals, Provosts and Prebends: A Comparison of Twelfth-Century German and English Practice', *The Journal of Ecclesiastical History*, 37:4 (1986), 536–64.

Barrow, J.S., 'Hereford Bishops and Married Clergy c. 1130–1240', *Historical Research*, 60 (1987), 1–8.

Barrow, J.S., 'Education and the Recruitment of Cathedral Canons in England and Germany 1100–1225', *Viator*, 20 (1989), 117–37.

Barrow, J.S., 'Churches, Education and Literacy in Towns 600–1300', in *The Cambridge Urban History of Britain*, ed. D.M. Palliser (Cambridge, 2000), 127–52.

Barrow, J.S., 'Clergy in the Diocese of Hereford in the Eleventh and Twelfth Centuries', in *Anglo-Norman Studies XXVI: Proceedings of the Battle Conference 2003*, ed. J. Gillingham (Woodbridge, 2004), 37–53.

Barrow, J.S., 'Grades of Ordination and Clerical Careers, c. 900–c. 1200', in *Anglo-Norman Studies XXX: Proceedings of the Battle Conference 2007*, ed. C.P. Lewis (Woodbridge, 2008), 41–61.

Barrow, J.S., 'Ideas and Applications of Reform', in *The Cambridge History of Christianity. Vol. III: Early Medieval Christianities, c. 600–c. 1100*, eds. T. Noble and J. Smith (Cambridge, 2008), 345–62.

Barrow, J.S., 'Way-Stations on English Episcopal Itineraries, 700–1300', *English Historical Review*, CXXVII (2012), 549–65.

Barrow, J.S., *The Clergy in the Medieval World: Secular Clerics, Their Families and Careers in North-Western Europe c. 800–c. 1200* (Cambridge, 2015).

Barstow, A.L., *Married Priests and the Reforming Papacy: The Eleventh-century Debates* (New York, NY, 1982).

Bartlett, R., *Gerald of Wales, 1146–1223* (Oxford, 1982).

Bartlett, R., *England Under the Norman and Angevin Kings 1075–1225* (Oxford, 2000).

Bartlett, R., 'Gerald of Wales', *Oxford Dictionary of National Biography*. https://doi.org/10.1093/ref:odnb/10769. Accessed 19/12/2017.

Beaudette, P., '"In the World but Not of It": Clerical Celibacy as a Symbol of The Medieval Church', in *Medieval Purity and Piety: Essays on Medieval Clerical Celibacy and Religious Reform*, ed. M. Frassetto (London, 1998), 23–46.

Belich, J., Darwin, J., and Wickham, C., 'Introduction', in *The Prospect of Global History*, eds. J. Belich, J. Darwin, M. Frenz, and C. Wickham (Oxford, 2016), 3–22.

Biddle, M. (ed.), *Winchester in the Early Middle Ages: An Edition and Discussion of the Winton Domesday* (Oxford, 1974).

Blake, D., 'The Development of the Chapter of the Diocese of Exeter 1050–1161', *Journal of Medieval History*, 8:1 (1982), 1–11.

Blumenthal, U.R., *The Investiture Controversy: Church and Monarchy From the Ninth to the Twelfth Century* (Philadelphia, PA, 1988).

Blumenthal, U.R., 'Pope Gregory VII and the Prohibition of Nicolaitism', in *Medieval Purity and Piety: Essays on Medieval Clerical Celibacy and Religious Reform*, ed. M. Frassetto (New York, NY, 1998), 239–67.

Boureau, A., 'Hypothèses sur l'émergence lexicale et théorique de la catégorie de séculier au XIIe siècle', in *Le clerc séculier au Moyen Âge*, ed. F. Rapp (Paris, 1993), 35–43.

Brett, M., *The English Church Under Henry I* (Oxford, 1975).

Brett, M., 'The Church at Rochester, 604–1185', in *Faith and Fabric: A History of Rochester Cathedral, 604–1994*, ed. N. Yates (Woodbridge, 1996), 1–27.

Brett, M., 'The Bishop's Charter and the Law in Twelfth-Century England', in *Proceedings of the Thirteenth International Congress of Medieval Canon Law; Esztergom, 3–8 August 2008*, eds. P. Erdő and Sz.A. Szuromi (Vatican, 2010), 3–16.

Brodman, J., *Charity and Religion in Medieval Europe* (Baltimore, MD, 2009).

Brooke, C.N.L., '1. The Composition of the Chapter of St Paul's, 1086–1163', *Cambridge Historical Journal*, 10:2 (1951), 111–32.

Brooke, C.N.L., '1. The Gregorian Reform in Action: Clerical Marriage in England, 1050–1200', *Cambridge Historical Journal*, 12 (1956), 1–21.

Brooke, C.N.L., '2. Married Men Among the English Higher Clergy, 1066–1200', *Cambridge Historical Journal*, 12 (1956), 187–8.

Brooke, C.N.L., 'The Archdeacon and the Norman Conquest', in *Tradition and Change: Essays in Honour of Marjorie Chibnall*, eds. D. Greenway, C. Holdsworth, and J. Sayers (Cambridge, 1985), 1–19.

Brooke, C.N.L., 'The Central Middle Ages: 800–1270', in *City of London From Prehistoric Times to c. 1520*, ed. M.D. Lobel (Oxford, 1989), 30–41.

Brooke, C.N.L., *The Medieval Idea of Marriage* (Oxford, 1989).

Brundage, J.A., 'Carnal Delight: Canonistic Theories of Sexuality', in *Proceedings of the Fifth International Congress of Medieval Canon Law, Salamanca, 21–25 September 1976*, eds. S. Kuttner and K. Pennington (Vatican City, 1980), 361–85.

Brundage, J.A., 'Adultery and Fornication: A Study in Legal Theology', in *Sexual Practices & the Medieval Church*, eds. V.L. Bullough and J.A. Brundage (Buffalo, NY, 1982), 129–34.

Brundage, J.A., *Law, Sex, and Christian Society in Medieval Europe* (London, 1987).

Brundage, J.A., 'The Teaching and Study of Canon Law in the Law Schools', in *The History of Medieval Canon Law in the Classical Period, 1140–1234: From Gratian to the Decretals of Pope Gregory IX*, eds. W. Hartmann and K. Pennington (Washington, DC, 2008), 98–120.

Burger, M., *Bishops, Clerks, and Diocesan Governance in Thirteenth-Century England* (Cambridge, 2012).

Burton, J., 'Les chanoines réguliers en Grande-Bretagne', in *Les Chanoines réguliers: Émergence et expansion (XIe–XIIIe siècles)*, ed. M. Parisse (Saint-Étienne, 2009), 477–98.

Burton, J., 'Thurstan (c. 1070–1140)', *Oxford Dictionary of National Biography*. www.oxforddnb.com/view/article/27411. Accessed 8/12/2017.

Cheney, C.R., *From Becket to Langton: English Church Government 1170–1213* (Manchester, 1956).

Cheney, C.R., *Pope Innocent III and England* (Stuttgart, 1976).

Cheney, C.R. and Cheney, M., *Letters of Pope Innocent III (1198–1216) Concerning England and Wales* (Oxford, 1967).

Cheney, M.G., *Roger, Bishop of Worcester 1164–1179* (Oxford, 1980).

Clarke, P.D. and Duggan, A.J. (eds.), *Church, Faith and Culture in the Medieval West: Pope Alexander III (1159–81): The Art of Survival* (Farnham, 2012).

Corbet, P., *Autour de Burchard de Worms* (Frankfurt am Main, 2001).

Cowdrey, H.E.J., *Pope Gregory VII: 1073–1085* (Oxford, 1998).

Cowdrey, H.E.J., 'Pope Gregory VII and the Chastity of the Clergy', in *Medieval Purity and Piety: Essays on Medieval Clerical Celibacy and Religious Reform*, ed. M. Frassetto (New York, NY, 1998), 279–89.

Crosby, E.U., *Bishop and Chapter in Twelfth-Century England: A Study of the Mensa Episcopalis* (Cambridge, 2008).

Crosby, E.U., *The King's Bishops: The Politics of Propaganda in England and Normandy 1066–1216* (New York, NY, 2013).

Crouch, D. and de Trafford, C., 'The Forgotten Family in Twelfth-Century England', *Haskins Society Journal*, 13 (2004), 41–63.

Cubitt, C., 'Images of St Peter: The Clergy and the Religious Life in Anglo-Saxon England', in *The Christian Tradition in Anglo-Saxon England: Approaches to Current Scholarship and Teaching*, ed. P. Cavill (Cambridge, 2004), 41–54.

Darlington, R.R., 'Ecclesiastical Reform in the Late Old English Period', *The English Historical Review*, 51:203 (1936), 385–428.

D'Avray, D., *Medieval Marriage: Symbolism and Society* (Oxford, 2005).

D'Avray, D., 'The Origins and Aftermath of the Eleventh-Century Reform in the Light of Niklas Luhmann's Systems Theory', in *"Vicarius Petri", "Vicarius Christi" La titolatura del Papa nell'XI secolo Dibattiti e prospettive*, eds. F. Amerini and R. Saccenti (Pisa, 2017), 211–27.

De Jong, M., *In Samuel's Image: Child Oblation in the Early Medieval West* (Leiden, 1996).

Deutinger, R., 'The Decretist Rufinus – A Well-known Person?', *Bulletin of Medieval Canon Law, New Series*, 23 (1999), 10–15.

Dickinson, J.C., *The Origins of the Austin Canons and their Introduction into England* (London, 1950).

Duggan, A.J. 'Conciliar Law 1123–1215: The Legislation of the Four Lateran Councils', in *The History of Medieval Canon Law in the Classical Period, 1140–1234: From Gratian to the Decretals of Pope Gregory IX*, eds. W. Hartmann and K. Pennington (Washington, DC, 2008), 341–66.

Duggan, A.J., 'Making Law or Not? The Function of Papal Decretals in the Twelfth Century', in *Proceedings of the Thirteenth International Congress of Medieval Canon Law*, eds. P. Erdő and Sz.A. Szuromi (Vatican City, 2010), 41–65.

Duggan, A.J., 'Master of the Decretals: A Reassessment of Alexander III's Contribution to Canon Law', in *Pope Alexander III (1159–1181): The Art of Survival*, eds. P.D. Clarke and A.J. Duggan (Burlington, VT, 2012), 365–417.

Duggan, C., *Twelfth-Century Decretal Collections and their Importance in English History* (London, 1963).

Duggan, C., 'The Reception of Canon Law in England in the Later-Twelfth Century', in *Proceedings of the Second International Congress of Medieval Canon Law, Boston College, 12–16 August 1963*, eds. S. Kuttner and J.J. Ryan (Vatican City, 1965), 359–90.

Duggan, C., 'Equity and Compassion in Papal Marriage Decretals to England', in his *Decretals and the Creation of the 'New Law' in the Twelfth Century: Judges, Judgements, Equity and the Law* (Aldershot, 1998), 59–87.

Duggan, C., 'Honorius, canonist', *Oxford Dictionary of National Biography*. www.oxforddnb.com/view/article/50350. Accessed 17/01/2017.

Egger, C., 'The Canon Regular: Saint-Ruf in Context', in *Adrian IV The English Pope (1154–1159)*, eds. B. Bolton and A.J. Duggan (Aldershot, 2003), 15–28.

Elliott, D., *Fallen Bodies: Pollution, and Demonology in the Middle Ages* (Philadelphia, PA, 1999).

Evans, J.W., 'Transition and Survival: St David and St Davids Cathedral', in *St David of Wales: Cult, Church and Nation*, eds. J.W. Evans and J.M. Wooding (Woodbridge, 2007), 20–40.

Fornasari, G., *Celibato Sacerdotale e "Autoconoscienza" Ecclesiale: Per la storia della "Nicolaitica Haeresis" Nell'Occidente Medievale* (Udine, 1981).

Fournée, J., 'Notes sur un évêque d'Avranches au XII siècle: Richard de Beaufou (1134–1143)', *Revue de l'Avranchin*, xxxiii (1946), 359–64.

Frazee, C.A., 'Late Roman and Byzantine Legislation on the Monastic Life From the Fourth to the Eighth Centuries', *Church History*, 51:3 (1982), 263–79.

Galbraith, V.H., 'Notes on the Career of Samson, Bishop of Worcester (1096–1112)', *English Historical Research*, 82 (1967), 86–101.

Ganz, D., 'The Ideology of Sharing: Apostolic Community and Ecclesiastical Property in the Early Middle Ages', in *Property and Power in the Early Middle Ages*, eds. W. Davies and P. Fouracre (Cambridge, 1995), 17–30.

Gaudemet, J., 'Gratien et le célibat ecclésiastique', *Studia Gratiani*, xiii (1967), 339–70.

Gaudemet, J., 'Le célibat ecclésiastique. Le droit et la practique du XIe au XIIIe siècles', *Zeitschrift der Savigny Stiftung für Rechtsgeschichte: Kanonistische Abteilung*, 68 (1982), 1–31.

Génestal, R., *Histoire de la légitimation des enfants naturels en droit canonique* (Paris, 1905).

Giandrea, M.F., *Episcopal Culture in Late Anglo-Saxon England* (Woodbridge, 2007).

Gibaut, J.St.H., *The Cursus Honorum: A Study of the Origins and Evolution of Sequential Ordination* (New York, NY, 2000).

Godden, M.R., 'Were It Not That I Have Bad Dreams: Gregory the Great and the Anglo-Saxons on the Dangers of Dreaming', in *Rome and the North: The Early Reception of Gregory the Great in Germanic Europe*, eds. R.H. Bremmer Jr, K. Dekker, and D.F. Johnson (Paris, 2001), 93–113.

Goering, J., 'The Internal Forum and the Literature of Penance', in *The History of Medieval Canon Law in the Classical Period, 1140–1234: From Gratian to the Decretals of Pope Gregory IX*, eds. W. Hartmann and K. Pennington (Washington, DC, 2008), 379–428.

Goering, J., 'Chobham, Thomas of (d. 1233x6)', *Oxford Dictionary of National Biography*. www.oxforddnb.com/view/article/5007. Accessed 09/06/2014.

Goody, J., *The Development of the Family and Marriage in Europe* (Cambridge, 1983).

Greenway, D.E., 'Henry (c. 1088–c. 1157)', *Oxford Dictionary of National Biography*: www.oxforddnb.com/view/article/12970. Accessed 13/09/2014.

Harper-Bill, C., 'The Struggle for Benefices in Twelfth-Century East Anglia', in *Anglo-Norman Studies XI: Proceedings of the Battle Conference 1988*, ed. R.A. Brown (Woodbridge, 1989), 113–32.

Harper-Bill, C., 'The Anglo-Norman Church', in *A Companion to the Anglo-Norman World*, eds. C. Harper-Bill and E. van Houts (Woodbridge, 2003), 165–90.

Harvey, P.D.A., 'English Cathedral Estates in the Twelfth Century', in *The Medieval English Cathedral: Papers in Honour of Pamela Tudor-Craig*, ed. J. Backhouse (Donington, 2003), 1–14.

Harvey, S.P.J., 'The Extent and Profitability of Demesne Agriculture in England in the Later Eleventh Century', in *Social Relations and Ideas: Essays in Honour of R.H. Hilton*, eds. T.H. Aston et al. (Cambridge, 1983), 45–72.

Hoeflich, M.H. and Grabher, J.M., 'The Establishment of Normative Legal Texts: The Beginnings of the Ius commune', in *The History of Medieval Canon Law in the Classical Period, 1140–1234: From Gratian to the Decretals of Pope Gregory IX*, eds. W. Hartmann and K. Pennington (Washington, DC, 2008), 1–21.

Hoskin, P., 'Robert Grosseteste and the Simple Benefice: A Novel Solution to the Complexities of Lay Presentation', *Journal of Medieval History*, 40:1 (2014), 1–20.

Hoskin, P., 'Poor [Poore], Richard', *Oxford Dictionary of National Biography*. https://doi.org/10.1093/ref:odnb/22525. Accessed 2/12/2017.

Howell, M., *Regalian Right in Medieval England* (London, 1962).

Hunter, D.G., 'Clerical Celibacy and the Veiling of Virgins: New Boundaries in Late Ancient Christianity', in *The Limits of Ancient Christianity: Essays on Late Antique Thought and Culture in Honor of R.A. Markus*, eds. W.E. Klingshirn and M. Vessey (Ann Arbor, MI, 1999), 139–52.

Hunter, D.G., 'Married Clergy in Eastern and Western Christianity', in *A Companion to Priesthood and Holy Orders in the Middle Ages*, eds. G. Peters and C. Colt Anderson (Leiden, 2016), 96–139.

Kealey, E.J., *Roger of Salisbury, Viceroy of England* (Berkeley, CA, 1972).

Kemp, B.R., 'Hereditary Benefices in the Medieval English Church: A Herefordshire Example', *Bulletin of the Institute of Historical Research*, 43 (1970), 1–15.

Kéry, L., *Canonical Collections of the Early Middle Ages (c. 400–1140): A Bibliographical Guide to the Manuscripts and Literature* (Washington, DC, 1999).

Knowles, D., *The Monastic Order in England* (Cambridge, 2nd ed., 1963).

Kuttner, S., 'The Father of the Science of Canon Law', *The Jurist*, 1 (1941), 2–19.

Kuttner, S. and Rathbone, E., 'Anglo-Norman Canonists of the Twelfth Century', *Traditio*, 7 (1949–51), 279–358.

Landau, P., 'Vorgratianische Kanonessammlungen bei den Dekretisten und die frühen Dekretalensammlungen', in *Proceedings of the Eighth International Congress of Medieval Canon Law, San Diego, University of California at La Jolla, 21–27 August 1988*, ed. S. Chodorow (Vatican, 1992), 93–116.

Landau, P., 'Das Weihehindernis der Illegitimität in der Geschichte des kanonischen Rechts', in *Illegitimität im Spätmittelalter*, ed. L. Schmugge (Munich, 1994), 41–53.

Landau, P., 'Überlieferung und Bedeutung der Kanones des Trullanischen Konzils im westlichen kanonischen Recht', in *The Council in Trullo Revisited*, eds. G. Nedungatt and M. Featherstone (Rome, 1995), 215–27.

Landau, P., 'X. Rodoicus Modicipassus – Verfasser der Summa Lipsiensis?', *Zeitschrift der Savigny-Stiftung für Rechtsgeschichte: Kanonistische Abteilung*, 92:1 (2006), 340–54.

Landau, P., 'Gratian and the Decretum Gratiani', in *The History of Medieval Canon Law in the Classical Period, 1140–1234: From Gratian to the Decretals of Pope Gregory IX*, eds. W. Hartmann and K. Pennington (Washington, DC, 2008), 22–54.

Larrainzar, C., 'El borrador del la "Concordia" de Graziano: Sankt Gallen, Stiftsbibliothek MS 673 (=Sg)', *Ius ecclesiae: Rivista internazionale di diritto canonico*, 9 (1999), 593–666.

Laudage, J., *Priesterbild und Reformpapsttum im 11. Jahrhundert* (Cologne, 1984).

Lesne, E., 'Les origines de la prébende', *Revue historique de droit français et étranger*, Ser. 4, 8 (1929), 242–90.

Lesne, E., 'Praebenda: Le sens primitive du terme prébende', in *Mélanges Paul Fournier* (Paris, 1929), 443–53.

Leyser, C., 'Masculinity in Flux: Nocturnal Emission and the Limits of Celibacy in the Early Middle Ages', in *Masculinity in Medieval Europe*, ed. D.M. Hadley (London, 1999), 103–20.

Leyser, H., 'Clerical Purity and the Re-ordered World', in *The Cambridge History of Christianity: Christianity in Western Europe c. 1100–c. 1500*, eds. M. Rubin and W. Simons (Cambridge, 2009), 11–21.

Liotta, F., *La continenza dei chierici nel pensiero canonistico classico. Da Graziano a Gregorio IX* (Milan, 1971).

Lynch, J. E., 'Marriage and Celibacy of the Clergy: The Discipline of the Western Church: An Historico-canonical Synopsis', *The Jurist*, 32 (1972), 189–212.

Macy, G., *The Hidden History of Women's Ordination* (New York, NY, 2007).

Marritt, S., 'Secular Cathedrals and the Anglo-Norman Aristocracy', in *Cathedrals, Communities and Conflict in the Anglo-Norman World*, eds. P. Dalton, C. Insley, and L.J. Wilkinson (Woodbridge, 2011), 151–67.

Mayr-Harting, H., *Religion, Politics and Society in Britain, 1066–1272* (Harlow, 2011).

McDougall, S., *Royal Bastards: The Birth of Illegitimacy, 800–1230* (Oxford, 2017).

McNamara, J.A., 'The Herrenfrage: The Restructuring of the Gender System, 1050–1150', in *Medieval Masculinities: Regarding Men in the Middle Ages*, ed. C.A. Lees (Minneapolis, MN, 1994), 3–29.

Meijns, B., 'Opposition to Clerical Continence and the Gregorian Celibacy Legislation in the Diocese of Thérouanne: Tractatus Pro Clericorum Conubio (c. 1077–1078)', *Sacris Erudiri*, XLVII (2008): 223–90.

Melve, L., 'The Public Debate on Clerical Marriage in the Late Eleventh Century', *Journal of Ecclesiastical History*, 61 (2010), 688–706.

Miller, M.C., 'Clerical Identity and Reform: Notarial Descriptions of the Secular Clergy in the Po Valley, 750–1200', in *Medieval Purity and Piety: Essays on Medieval Clerical Celibacy and Religious Reform*, ed. M. Frassetto (New York, NY, 1998), 305–35.

Miller, M.C., 'Masculinity, Reform, and Clerical Culture: Narratives of Episcopal Holiness in the Gregorian Era', *Church History*, 72 (2003), 25–52.

Molin, J.-B. and Mutembe, P., *Le rituel du marriage en France du XIIe au XVIe siècle* (Paris, 1976).

Moore, R.I., 'Family, Community and Cult on the Eve of the Gregorian Reform', *Transactions of the Royal Historical Society*, 30 (1980), 49–69.

Morris, C.J., *Marriage and Murder in Eleventh-Century Northumbria: A Study of the 'De Obsessione Dunelmi'* (York, 1992).

Morrison, K.F., 'The Gregorian Reform', in *Christian Spirituality: Origins to the Twelfth Century*, eds. B. McGinn and J. Meyendorff (New York, NY, 1985), 177–92.

Murray, J., 'Men's Bodies, Men's Minds: Seminal Emissions and Sexual Anxiety in the Middle Ages', *Annual Review of Sex Research*, 8 (1997), 1–26.

Murray, J., 'Masculinizing Religious Life: Sexual Prowess, the Battle for Chastity and Monastic Identity', in *Holiness and Masculinity in the Middle Ages*, eds. P.H. Cullum and K.J. Lewis (Cardiff, 2004), 24–42.

Muschiol, G., *Famula Dei: Zur Liturgie in merowingischen Frauenklöstern* (Münster, 1994).

Noonan, J.T., 'Gratian Slept Here: The Changing Identity of the Father of the Systematic Study of Canon Law', *Traditio*, 35 (1979), 145–72.

Oakley, A., 'Rochester Priory, 1185–1540', in *Faith and Fabric: A History of Rochester Cathedral, 604–1994*, ed. N. Yates (Woodbridge, 1996), 29–55.

Oggins, V.D. and Oggins, R.S., 'Richard of Ilchester's Inheritance: An Extended Family in Twelfth-Century England', *Medieval Prosopography*, 12 (1991), 57–128.

Parish, H., *Clerical Celibacy in the West: c. 1100–1700* (Farnham, 2010).

Partner, N., 'Henry of Huntingdon: Clerical Celibacy and the Writing of History', *Church History: Studies in Christianity and Culture*, 42 (1973), 467–75.

Payer, P.J., *Sex and the New Medieval Literature of Confession, 1150–1300* (Toronto, 2009).

Pelteret, D.A.E., *Slavery in Early Mediaeval England: From the Reign of Alfred Until the Twelfth Century* (Woodbridge, 1995).

Peltzer, J., *Canon Law, Careers and Conquest: Episcopal Elections in Normandy and Greater Anjou c. 1140–c. 1230* (Cambridge, 2008).

Pennington, K., '"Pro Peccatis Patrum Puniri": A Moral and Legal Problem of the Inquisition', *Church History*, 47 (1978), 137–54.

Pennington, K. and Müller, W.P., 'The Decretists: The Italian School', in *The History of Medieval Canon Law in the Classical Period, 1140–1234: From Gratian to the Decretals of Pope Gregory IX*, eds. W. Hartmann and K. Pennington (Washington, DC, 2008), 121–73.

Perisanidi, M., 'Anglo-Norman Canonical Views on Clerical Marriage and the Eastern Church', *Bulletin of Medieval Canon Law*, 34 (2017), 113–142.

Powicke, F.M., 'Gerald of Wales', *Bulletin of the John Rylands Library*, 12 (1928), 389–410.

Radding, C.M. and Ciaralli, A., *The Corpus Iuris Civilis in the Middle Ages* (Leiden, 2007).

Ramsey, N., Sparks, M., and Tatton-Brown, T. (eds.), *St Dunstan: His Life, Times and Cult* (Woodbridge, 1992).

Rasche, U., 'The Early Phase of Appropriation of Parish Churches in Medieval England', *Journal of Medieval History*, 26:3 (2012), 213–37.

Reynolds, R.E., 'The De officiis vii graduum: Its Origins and Development', in his *Clerical Orders in the Early Middle Ages: Duties and Ordination* (Aldershot, 1999), 113–151.

Reynolds, R.E., 'The Subdiaconate as a Sacred and Superior Order', in his *Clerics in the Early Middle Ages* (Aldershot, 1999), IV 1–39.

Reynolds, R.E. 'The Influence of the Eastern Patristic Fathers on the Canonical Collections of South Italy in the Eleventh and Early Twelfth Centuries', in *Proceedings of the Thirteenth International Congress of Medieval Canon Law,* eds. P. Erdő and Sz.A. Szuromi (Vatican City, 2010), 645–50.

Robinson, I.S., 'Reform and the Church, 1073–1122', in *The New Cambridge Medieval History VI*, eds. D. Luscombe and J. Riley-Smith (Cambridge, 2004), 268–334.

Rolker, C., *Canon Law and the Letters of Ivo of Chartres* (Cambridge, 2009).

Schimmelpfennig, B., 'Ex fornicatione nati. Studies on the Position of Priests' Sons from the Twelfth to the Fourteenth Century', *Studies in Medieval and Renaissance History*, 2 (1980), 3–50.

Schmugge, L., *Kirche, Kinder, Karrieren: Päpstliche Dispense von der unehelichen Geburt im Spätmittelalter* (Zürich, 1995).

Schulte, J.F.v., 'Die Summa Decreti Lipsiensis des Codex 986 der Leipziger Universitatsbibliothek', *Sitzungsberichte Vienna*, 68 (1871), 37–54.

Scragg, D.G. (ed.), *Edgar, King of the English, 959–975: New Interpretations* (Woodbridge, 2008).

Sheehan, M.M., 'Marriage Theory and Practice in the Conciliar Legislation and Diocesan Statutes of Medieval England', *Mediaeval Studies*, 40:1 (1978), 408–60.

Smalley, B., *The Becket Conflict and the Schools* (Oxford, 1976).

Somerville, R., *The Councils of Urban II*, vol. I (Amsterdam, 1972).

Somerville, R., *Pope Alexander III and the Council of Tours (1163)* (London, 1977).

Somerville, R. and Kuttner, S., *Pope Urban II, the Collectio Britannica, and the Council of Melfi (1089)* (Oxford, 1996).

Southern, R.W., *Saint Anselm and His Biographer* (Cambridge, 1963).

Southern, R.W., *Robert Grosseteste: The Growth of an English Mind in Medieval Europe* (Oxford, 1986).

Spear, D., *The Personnel of the Norman Cathedrals During the Ducal Period, 911–1204* (London, 2006).

Stone, R., 'Spiritual Heirs and Families: Episcopal Relatives in Early Medieval Francia', in *Celibate and Childless Men in Power: Ruling Eunuchs and Bishops in the Pre-Modern World*, eds. A. Hofert, M.M. Mesley, and S. Tolino (London, 2018), 129–48.

Summerson, H., 'Medieval Carlisle: Cathedral and City From Foundation to Dissolution', in *Carlisle and Cumbria: Roman and Medieval Architecture, Art and Archaeology*, eds. M. McCarthy and D. Weston (Leeds, 2004), 29–38.

Swanson, R.N., 'Titles to Orders in Medieval English Episcopal Registers', in *Studies in Medieval History Presented to R.H.C. Davis*, eds. H. Mayr-Harting and R.I. Moore (London, 1985), 233–45.

Swanson, R.N., 'Angels Incarnate: Clergy and Masculinity From Gregorian Reform to Reformation', in *Masculinity in Medieval Europe*, ed. D.M. Hadley (London, 1999), 160–77.

Taglia, K.A., '"On Account of Scandal . . .": Priests, Their Children, and the Ecclesiastical Demand for Celibacy', *Florilegium*, 14 (1995–96), 57–70.

Taliadoros, J., 'Bartholomew of Exeter's Penitential: Some Observations on His Personal Dicta', in *Proceedings of the Thirteenth International Congress of Medieval Canon Law*, eds. P. Erdő and Sz.A. Szuromi (Vatican City, 2010), 457–73.

Taliadoros, J., 'Law, Theology, and Morality: Conceptions of the Rights to Relief of the Poor in the Twelfth and Thirteenth Centuries', *Journal of Religious History*, 37:4 (2013), 474–93.

Tanner, N., 'Eastern Influences Upon the West: Canonical Evidence From Ecumenical and General Councils, and Some Other Sources, During the Middle Ages', in *Proceedings of the Thirteenth International Congress of Medieval Canon Law*, eds. P. Erdő and Sz.A. Szuromi (Vatican, 2010), 661–8.

Tellenbach, G., *The Church in Western Europe From the Tenth to the Early Twelfth Century*, trans. T. Reuter (Cambridge, 1993).

Thibodeaux, J.D., 'Man of the Church, or Man of the Village? Gender and the Parish Clergy in Medieval Normandy', *Gender & History*, 18 (2006), 380–99.

Thibodeaux, J.D., 'The Defence of Clerical Marriage: Religious Identity and Masculinity in the Writings of Anglo-Norman Clerics', in *Religious Men and Masculine Identity in the Middle Ages*, eds. P.H. Cullum and K.J. Lewis (Woodbridge, 2013), 46–63.

Thibodeaux, J.D., *The Manly Priest: Clerical Celibacy, Masculinity, and Reform in England and Normandy 1066–1300* (Philadelphia, PA, 2015).

Thomas, H.M., *The Secular Clergy in England, 1066–1216* (Oxford, 2014).

Thomson, R.M., *Catalogue of the Manuscripts of Lincoln Cathedral Chapter Library* (Woodbridge, 1989).

Tierney, B., *Medieval Poor Law: A Sketch of Canonical Theory and Its Application in England* (Berkeley, CA, 1959).

Tinti, F., *Sustaining Belief: The Church of Worcester From c. 870 to c. 1100* (Farnham, 2010).

Townley, S. 'Unbeneficed Clergy in the Thirteenth Century: Two English Dioceses', in *Studies in Clergy and Ministry in Medieval England*, ed. D.M. Smith (York, 1991), 38–64.

Turner, R.V., 'The Miles Literatus in Twelfth- and Thirteenth-Century England: How Rare a Phenomenon?', *The American Historical Review*, 83:4 (1978), 928–45.

Turner, R.V., *The English Judiciary in the Age of Glanvill and Bracton, c. 1176–1239* (Cambridge, 1985).

Van Houts, E., 'The Fate of Priests' Sons in Normandy', *The Haskins Society Journal*, 25 (2013), 57–105.

Van Houts, E., 'Orderic and His Father, Odelerius', in *Orderic Vitalis: Life, Works, and Interpretations*, eds. C.C. Rozier, D. Roach, G.E.M. Gasper, and E. van Houts (Woodbridge, 2016), 17–36.

Violante, C., *La pataria milanese e la riforma ecclesiastica* (Rome, 1955).

Weigand, R., 'Bemerkungen über die Schriften und Lehren des Magister Honorius', in *Proceedings of the Fifth International Congress of Medieval Canon Law, Salamanca, 21–25 September 1976*, eds. S. Kuttner and K. Pennington (Vatican, 1980), 195–212.

Weigand, R., 'The Transmontane Decretists', in *The History of Medieval Canon Law in the Classical Period, 1140–1234: From Gratian to the Decretals of Pope Gregory IX*, eds. W. Hartmann and K. Pennington (Washington, DC, 2008), 174–210.

Werckmeister, J., 'The Reception of the Church Fathers in Canon Law', in *The Reception of the Church Fathers in the West: From the Carolingians to the Maurists*, ed. I. Backus, vol. I (Leiden, 1997), 51–81.

Werckmeister, J., *Décret de Gratien – Causes 27 à 36: Le Mariage* (Paris, 2011).

Wertheimer, L., 'Illegitimate Birth and the English Clergy, 1198–1348', *Journal of Medieval History*, 31 (2005), 211–29.

Wertheimer, L., 'Children of Disorder: Clerical Parentage, Illegitimacy, and Reform in the Middle Ages', *Journal of the History of Sexuality*, 15:3 (2006), 382–407.

Wickham, C., 'Problems in Doing Comparative History', in *Challenging the Boundaries of Medieval History: The Legacy of Timothy Reuter*, ed. P. Skinner (Turnhout, 2009), 5–28.

Winroth, A., *The Making of Gratian's Decretum* (Cambridge, 2004).

Winroth, A., 'Roman Law in Gratian and the Panormia', in *Bishops, Texts and the Use of Canon Law Around 1100: Essays in Honour of Martin Brett*, eds. B.C. Brasington and K.G. Cushing (Aldershot, 2008), 183–90.

Winroth, A., 'Where Gratian Slept: The Life and Death of the Father of Canon Law', *Zeitschrift der Savigny Stiftung für Rechtsgeschichte: Kanonistische Abteilung*, 99 (2013), 105–28.

Witte, J., *The Sins of the Fathers: The Law and Theology of Illegitimacy Reconsidered* (Cambridge, 2009).

Wood, S., *The Proprietary Church in the Medieval West* (Oxford, 2006).

Wormald, P., 'Æthelwold and His Continental Counterparts: Contact, Comparison, Contrast', in *Bishop Aethelwold: His Career and Influence*, ed. B. Yorke (Woodbridge, 1988), 13–42.

Wormald, P., *The Making of English Law: King Alfred to the Twelfth Century* (Oxford, 1999).

Yorke, B. (ed.), *Bishop Æthelwold: His Career and Influence* (Suffolk, 1988).

Index